Research Methods in Education: An Introduction

Fourth Edition

William Wiersma
University of Toledo

Allyn and Bacon, Inc.
Boston   London   Sydney   Toronto

To
JOAN and SUSAN and LISA

Copyright © 1986, 1985, 1980, 1975, and 1969 by Allyn and Bacon, Inc. 7 Wells Avenue, Newton, Massachusetts 02159

Series Editor: Jeffery Johnston
Production Coordinator: Susan Freese
Editorial Services: Total Concept Associates
Cover Coordinator: Linda K. Dickinson
Cover Designer: Susan Hamant

Library of Congress Cataloging-in-Publication Data

Wiersma, William.
    Research methods in education.

    Includes bibliographies and indexes.
    1. Education—Research. I. Title

LB1028.W517   1986   370′.1′8   85-28709
ISBN 0-205-08747-7

Printed in the United States of America

10 9 8 7 6   90

Contents

Preface

Purpose

Some work in research methods is required in almost all graduate programs in education, in the United States and in other countries. The professional literature of education is expanding every year, and much of that literature deals with research results. It is increasingly important for educational professionals to be knowledgable about research—how it is done and how results are interpreted.

To that end, the purpose of this book is to present the language, principles, reasoning, and methodology of conducting educational research in such a way that the reader or student will be able to:

- understand the logic of conducting educational research.
- read the research literature with understanding.
- distinguish between different types of research and how they apply.
- understand how research studies are designed and conducted.
- design and conduct the research required in a graduate program.

Audience

This book is written primarily for graduate students in education, because the graduate level is usually the point in education at which the student first encounters formal training in research methods. However, because it is an introductory book, it is appropriate for undergraduates in programs that teach research methods at that level. Because education draws on several disciplines for its research methods, students in other areas, especially the behavioral sciences, should find the text useful, as well. Of course, the book can also be used independently as a professional reference tool.

Approach

The approach of this text is to provide the rationale for research procedures discussed here and to provide illustrations by means of numerous examples. Exercises, provided at the ends of all chapters, can be used by students to check their mastery of content; an appendix provides the solutions. The discussion is comprehensive in that it attempts to bring the reader from the beginning of a research study to successful completion of the report. The procedures discussed have wide applicability, and the ideas presented are general enough that they apply in many specific research situations.

Organization

The chapter organization of the text follows approximately the sequence in which a research study is conducted. The introductory chapter describes the nature of educational research and introduces the steps in the research process. The next three chapters deal with the early activities of a research project. Because adequate identification of a research problem is so important, an entire chapter is devoted to this topic (Chapter 2). Chapter 3 describes how to review the literature, including the identification of information sources. Chapter 4 discusses research design.

Chapters 5 through 9 deal with different types of research; a chapter is devoted to each type. Chapter 6 is new to this edition, expanding the discussion of quasi-experimental research and including single-subject designs. Chapter 9—also a new chapter—covers ethnographic research, a type of research that is receiving increasing attention in education.

Because many studies involve samples, Chapter 10 is devoted to sampling designs. This is followed by a chapter on measurement and data collection; Chapter 11 provides an overview of several approaches to measuring variables and also discusses the preparation of data sets for computer analysis.

After data are collected, they must be analyzed. Chapter 12 describes statistical procedures commonly used for analysis. It should be emphasized, however, that this is not a statistics text. Therefore, the emphasis in Chapter 12 is on the underlying reasoning of the various statistical procedures and the conditions under which they apply. There is no intention of developing computational mastery; in fact, little computation appears. (Appendix 2 describes selected advanced analysis procedures. With the general availability of computers, more sophisticated analyses are becoming increasingly common, so Appendix 2 provides a brief overview of some of the more widely used procedures for the interested reader.) Since most research data are analyzed by computer, the general procedures for using computer facilities are also described in Chapter 12.

Preparing a research report is usually the culminating activity of a research project, and Chapter 13, the final chapter, describes writing about research. Chapter 13 also discusses the preparation of a research proposal, which is actually an early activity in the entire research process. However, because there are numerous similarities between writing a research proposal and writing a research report, in the interest of continuity on the writing topic, proposals and reports are discussed in the same chapter.

Appendix 1 provides a sample research proposal for illustration. And as discussed above, Appendix 2 contains additional statistical procedures for data analysis. Appendix 3 contains the answers to the end-of-chapter exercises, and Appendix 4 contains five statistical tables for handy reference. Finally, a glossary of research methods terms is provided for the reader's convenience.

The Fourth Edition

Any new edition of a text contains the usual updating of examples, references, and the like. It is not necessary to list these changes here, in detail. However, it is appropriate to mention new content and highlight the pedagogical features of this fourth edition.

- The new chapter on quasi-experimental research, Chapter 6, describes the use of intact groups and single subjects in research studies. It provides an emphasis on research that can be conducted in natural educational settings.
- The new chapter on ethnographic research, Chapter 9, reflects the increasing interest in qualitative research. This chapter also emphasizes research that can be conducted in natural educational settings.
- A description of advanced analysis procedures has been added as an appendix for interested readers (Appendix 2).
- The appendix of tables (Appendix 4) has been expanded to include those commonly used for statistical analysis. Thus, for readers who wish to use those tables, it is not necessary to consult a separate statistics text.
- More than 100 figures and tables are included. Research designs of all types are diagrammed to illustrate their structures and the underlying concepts.
- The use of examples is extensive. Examples are taken from a wide variety of types and settings of educational research.
  The number of exercises has been increased over previous editions; answers for selected items are provided in Appendix 3.
- Important terms and concepts are summarized and set off (in boxes) throughout the book.
- Key concepts are listed at the end of each chapter and a glossary containing research terms is provided at the end of the book.

Acknowledgments

Special acknowledgment goes to Dr. George Bowdouris for his permission to reproduce material from his doctoral dissertation and to Dr. Homer Coker for his permission to reproduce the classroom observation inventory he developed. I would also like to acknowledge Professors Glen Nicholson (University of Arizona), Pietro

J. Pascale (Youngstown State University), and Nona Tollefson (University of Kansas) for their reviews of the manuscript.

Finally, I am grateful to the Literary Executor of the late Sir Ronald A. Fisher, F.R.S., to Dr. Frank Yates, F.R.S., and to Longman Group Ltd., London, for permission to reprint Tables III, IV, and VII (abridged) from their book *Statistical Tables for Biological, Agricultural and Medical Research* (6th edition, 1974).

W.W.

1

Educational Research: Its Nature and Characteristics

Introduction

Research is conducted in a host of situations by a variety of individuals. Scholars and practitioners of various levels of sophistication in the academic disciplines and professions engage in it. Research may be conducted in libraries, laboratories, and classrooms, in the ruins of ancient civilizations, and on the streets of modern cities, to mention just a few possible settings. Industries and businesses pour vast sums of money into research activities to which advances in many fields of endeavor have been attributed.

Graduate students may find it difficult to identify with any of these situations. Their financial resources are usually limited, so the approach of industry is not an option. Their experiences and knowledge are not those of sophisticated scholars, yet to pursue the degree, it is usually necessary to produce some original research. Although they may realize that research is necessary, having heard the term repeatedly, this familiarity provides little direction regarding how to go about doing research.

When it comes to matters of research, the situation of the average elementary or high school teacher, counselor, or administrator is not much different from that of the graduate student. In fact, a considerable portion of the graduate student population is often made up of school personnel pursuing graduate programs on a part-time basis. A professional educator may not be called upon to produce an original piece of research, but to ignore research entirely is an injustice both to the profession and to the educator. Change, innovation, and experimentation are occurring in education. Some research is prompted by federal and state programs, but much of it is initiated from within the profession itself, and to keep up with these changes, the professional educator should know about and be able to understand research results. Decision making at the local level is often based on a combination of experience, expert opinion, and research results, and some of those results are obtained at the local level.

Much educational research is reported in such a way that a knowledge of the methodology is invaluable, and in almost all cases, such knowledge is essential for a meaningful implementation of research results. Although graduate students may have a short-term or immediate need to conduct research for a thesis or dissertation, a long-term result of the research experience should be that they become better professional educators and that they use research results increasingly in decision making.

Educational research is to some extent complex and demanding. However, the broad spectrum of research activities uses various research methods, ranging from relatively simple, single operations to complex combinations of procedures, both qualitative and quantitative. Although educational research is a demanding task, it is not an impossible one. With organized and concentrated study, the aspiring educational researcher should be able to master necessary research methods. Basically, the only way to acquire competence in research is by doing it, but before research can be put into practice, some skills must be acquired. Knowing what to do in specific situations is important. How is the research problem identified? What procedures apply in pursuing the solution of the specific problem? How are the data to be collected and interpreted? How can a satisfactory, lucid report be produced? In the context of a specific research effort, all these questions call for certain skills.

The approach of this text is essentially one of emphasizing the application of procedures. To a large extent, what is done in educational research is based on common sense. We try to structure things so that we can tell what is going on, so that we can understand the information contained in the data. This text discusses general procedures and methods, but the potential researcher must project them into the specific situation. To some extent, the idea of a "typical" research project is a misconception. There is no typical project; each has unique problems and conditions. Although there may be considerable similarity among various types of projects, doing a research project is not like baking a cake from a recipe.

The educational researcher should always aim for a respectable, competently done product. However, a researcher should not become discouraged if the results are less than perfect—it is not likely that there has ever been a perfect study. Therefore, any finished product will not be totally exempt from criticism. In doing research, there are potential pitfalls, and errors are likely to occur. Any researcher should be willing to accept the suggestions of peers. Criticism of research should be offered and accepted in a strictly constructive sense for the purpose of improving a particular project or improving future research in the area. A receptive attitude should be maintained toward the research and toward the suggestions of others.

The Nature of Research

Research is essentially an activity, or process, and certain characteristics help define its nature. Since educational research also has these characteristics, they are described and illustrated here using educational examples. The few general characteristics are as follows:

1. Research can take a variety of forms.
2. Research should be valid.
3. Research should be reliable.
4. Research should be systematic.

These characteristics are related in that, as a composite, they describe the nature of research. They are somewhat separated in this discussion to focus on their individual meanings.

By just listening to others, it quickly becomes clear that research takes a variety of forms. Sometimes we hear an individual say, "I have researched this problem," which means that the individual has considered various solutions to a problem. An elementary school student may say, "I am supposed to do some research on Brazil." This means that the student has been assigned a report that will involve reading resource materials about Brazil. A graduate student in chemistry may say, "My research experiment will run for another two days," indicating that some laboratory activity will continue for that period.

Research can take any number of specific forms, depending on the unique characteristics of the subject or topic under investigation. In a general sense, however, all research is oriented toward one or both of two ends: the extension of knowledge and the solution of a problem. These two ends are not mutually exclusive, especially in education, and the orientation is one of emphasis. Is the research being done to solve an immediate, defined problem, or is it being conducted primarily for the purpose of extending the knowledge base, regardless of the immediate usefulness of the results?

Consider two contrasting examples from education. The mathematics supervisor of a large city school system is grappling with the problem of poor mathematics achievement by a segment of the student population in grades 5–8. The supervisor has the option of implementing any one of three teaching approaches (materials and methods) that may improve achievement. A decision must be made about which approach to use. If an experiment can be conducted using the approaches with samples of the population, useful information would undoubtedly be generated. If an experiment is not an option, the supervisor will have to rely on the data of others to make a decision. In any event, research is needed to solve an immediate problem.

Suppose that an educational psychologist is doing research in the area of learning—specifically, the mastery of abstract concepts—by conducting experiments in a learning laboratory that test young adults' ability to deal with unfamiliar concepts. Various contrasts in the type of materials, amount of information, and so forth, may be included in the experiment, the results of which may not be directed at any specific problem. Although this experiment may not be directly useful for devel-

> In a general sense, all research in education is directed to one or both of two ends: (1) the extension of knowledge and (2) the solution of a problem.

oping curriculum materials at any particular school level, it adds to knowledge about learning and may be useful in extending or developing a theory of learning.

The Validity of Educational Research

Regardless of the form research takes or the ends to which it is directed, we want research to be valid—that is, to possess validity. What is validity of research? Validity involves two concepts simultaneously: the extent to which the results can be accurately interpreted and the extent to which the results can be generalized to populations and conditions. The former concept is called *internal validity,* and the latter is called *external validity.* Consider two examples illustrating the concepts of validity.

Internal Validity.   Suppose that a researcher is interested in the differing effects of three types of materials upon performance in eighth-grade science. Three teachers are recruited for participation in the study. The teachers teach in different schools; two have four classes each of eighth-grade science, and the third has three classes. In one school, classes are assigned on the basis of ability grouping. It so happens that the participating teacher in this school has high-ability classes.

Each teacher uses one type of material for a period of nine weeks. The teachers use different materials, and no teacher uses more than one type of material. At the end of nine weeks, the students are tested on science achievement, each teacher using his or her own test. The overall scheme of the research study is presented in Figure 1.1.

The researcher computes average science achievement scores for the students taught using each of the three materials. What conclusions can be drawn about the

Figure 1.1
General Scheme of a Hypothetical Research Study That Lacks Internal Validity

Science Achievement Tested

School I Teacher A Materials 1	4 Classes Heterogeneous Ability	Test constructed by Teacher A
School II Teacher B Materials 2	3 Classes Heterogeneous Ability	Test constructed by Teacher B
School III Teacher C Materials 3	4 Classes High Ability	Test constructed by Teacher C

◄———— 9 Weeks Instruction ————►

relative effectiveness of the three types of materials? Essentially none. Suppose that the students in School III have the highest average score. Is it because they are high-ability students or because Teacher C is a superior teacher? Or is the test used by Teacher C easier than those used by other teachers? Or are Materials 3 more effective than the other materials? There is no way these results can be validly interpreted, regardless of the pattern of results. Too many plausible and competing explanations of the results cannot be discounted to be able to conclude that Materials 3 are the most effective. Thus, this research study lacks internal validity, because the results cannot be interpreted.

External Validity.   If results cannot be interpreted, it is not likely that they can be generalized. Thus, to a large extent, internal validity is a prerequisite for external validity. However, internal validity does not ensure external validity. Consider another example.

A study is conducted on the effect of length of visual exposure on the recall of nonsense symbols. (A nonsense symbol might be five letters randomly sequenced.) The researcher obtains ten volunteers from a graduate student population in educational psychology. There are five different lengths of exposure, so two volunteers are used in each. A volunteer participates in the study by being exposed to 20 nonsense symbols individually; after each exposure, the volunteer is to reproduce the symbol. A total performance score is then generated from the number of symbols correctly reproduced. The overall scheme of this study is shown in Figure 1.2.

Suppose that the results show that the performance scores generally increase with increased length of exposure. But to what populations and conditions can this result be generalized? Can it be generalized to elementary or secondary students

Figure 1.2
General Scheme of a Hypothetical Research Study That Lacks External Validity

	Total Performance Score Generated
Exposure time: .1 sec.	Volunteer 1 / Volunteer 2
Exposure time: .2 sec.	Volunteer 3 / Volunteer 4
Exposure time: .3 sec.	Volunteer 5 / Volunteer 6
Exposure time: .4 sec.	Volunteer 7 / Volunteer 8
Exposure time: .5 sec.	Volunteer 9 / Volunteer 10

◄────── 20 symbols exposed ──────►

learning meaningful materials? Can it be generalized to young adults working on meaningful tasks in a highly structured situation? Not likely. The results (for recalling nonsense symbols) may not even be generalizable to the graduate student population, since the participants in the study were volunteers. In summary, the results may be generalizable only to the ten volunteers who recalled the nonsense symbols. The study thus lacks external validity.

The foregoing example is somewhat extreme, and it should not be inferred that to have external validity, results must generalize to many and varied populations and conditions. For example, if a study involving only gifted students were conducted, the intent of the study could be to generalize to a gifted student population, not to all students. If a school system were doing a needs assessment, the results might generalize only to that system. When research is conducted at the local level, focusing on the solution of a specific problem, the matter of broad generalizability is not germane.

Validity of research is always a matter of degree. It is practically impossible to attain perfect internal and external validity in a study. As will be shown in later chapters, attempts in research design to enhance internal validity may decrease external validity and vice versa. The researcher attempts to attain a balance, so that results can be interpreted with reasonable certainty and still have some useful generalizability.

Validity in research deals with the accurate interpretability of the results (internal validity) and the generalizability of the results (external validity). Both types of validity are matters of degree.

The Reliability of Educational Research

When discussing validity, it is appropriate to consider a related concept—reliability of research. Reliability refers to the consistency of the research and the extent to which studies can be replicated. We sometimes distinguish between internal and external reliability. *Internal reliability* refers to the extent that data collection, analysis, and interpretation are consistent given the same conditions. For example, if multiple data collectors are used, a question of internal reliability is, "Do the data collectors agree?" Suppose that a study of teacher performance is being conducted, using a classroom observation inventory for data collection. The question of internal reliability would be, "Do the two or more observers agree when coding the same performance?" This may be called the extent of *observer agreement*. If internal reliability is lacking, the data become a function of who collects them, rather than what actually happened.

External reliability deals with the issue of whether or not independent researchers can replicate studies in the same or similar settings. Will researchers be able to replicate studies, and, if so, will the results be consistent? If research is reliable, a researcher using the same methods, conditions, and so forth, should obtain the same results as those found in a prior study. To be replicable, a research study must include adequate definitions of the procedures and conditions of the research; the amount of definition necessary may vary across studies.

> *Reliability* of research concerns the replicability and consistency of the methods, conditions, and results.

Reliability is a necessary characteristic for validity; that is, a study cannot be valid and lack reliability. If a study is unreliable, we can hardly interpret the results with confidence or generalize them to other populations and conditions. Essentially, reliability and validity establish the credibility of research. Reliability focuses on replicability, and validity focuses on accuracy and generalizability of the findings.

The Systematic Process of Research

What can be done to enhance the validity and reliability of research? Since research is a process, we can make it a systematic process. Indeed, many writers describe research as a systematic process. McMillan and Schumacher (1984) define research as "a systematic process of collecting and analyzing information (data) for some purpose" (p. 4), and Kerlinger (1973) defines scientific research as "systematic, controlled, empirical and critical investigation of hypothetical propositions about the presumed relations among natural phenomena" (p. 11).

Certainly, we would like to believe that educational research is systematic and scientific, but what characterizes research so that it has these attributes? In systematic research, the elements of the general system are (1) identifying the problem, (2) reviewing information, (3) collecting data, (4) analyzing data, and (5) drawing conclusions. First, for a research study to be systematic, the nature of the problem to be studied must be defined, even if only in broad terms. Related knowledge is identified, and, in essence, a framework is established in which to conduct the research. Closely related to establishing the framework or foundation for the research is the identification of any necessary assumptions or conditions related to the research problem.

The second step is gathering information about how others have approached or dealt with similar problems. Certainly, one can and should profit from the work of others—it is not necessary to "reinvent the wheel" each time a research problem is attacked. The research literature is the source of such information.

Collecting data relevant to the problem is the third step in systematic research. However, data cannot be collected in any available, haphazard, or ad hoc manner. The process of data collection requires proper organization and control, so that the data will enable valid decisions to be made about the research problem at hand. The fourth step is analyzing data in a manner appropriate to the problem. The fifth step is the process of drawing conclusions or making generalizations after the analysis has been made. The conclusions are based on the data and the analysis within the framework of the research study.

The five steps that characterize the systematic nature of the research process can be illustrated as follows:

This is a systematic and ordered approach, although it should not be inferred that research is necessarily a lock-step process. In an actual research project, there may be some overlapping and integration among the steps.

The Scientific Method

The systematic approach to research provides the context for the scientific method— a set of procedures for implementing research. The scientific method is usually described as a series of steps, beginning with the identification of some problem and proceeding to the final step of drawing conclusions. The terminology used for the various steps of the scientific method, as well as the number of steps, differ somewhat from writer to writer. However, the scientific method is a general formulation of steps and should not be viewed as a single correct method (for example, experimentation or survey) for attacking all problems. The initial step of the scientific method is observing some phenomenon indicative of a problem or obstacle or observing the presence of some unexplained situation or condition. This step does not involve systematic or detailed data collection. It is more like being aware that something requires attention, feeling the need to resolve the problem or situation, and preparing to do something about this need. The second step involves a more precise identification of the problem, including the formulation of tentative hypotheses based on the initially observed phenomenon. At this step, factors involved in the problem may be more closely identified and their relationships clarified.

The next steps—developing and applying a design and systematically observing the phenomena—may be somewhat concurrent. However, it is almost always necessary to develop some type of preliminary design before observations are conducted. After the observations are made, theories or hypotheses may be tested and retained, modified, or discarded. Continued testing and refinement of hypotheses and theories is the ongoing application of the design for solving the problem. Additional observation may also be necessary as results from initial tests are subjected to further analysis.

The final step of the scientific method is drawing conclusions based on the data and integrating these conclusions into the existing body of knowledge or applying them to the solution of the problem. Drawing conclusions is, to a large extent, synonymous with explaining results. Considering the observed facts and the procedures conducted in the research, the individual arrives at what appears to be the best solution to the problem or the most reasonable explanation of the situation.

The correspondence between the systematic process described earlier and the scientific method is shown in Figure 1.3. As the steps of the scientific method are usually presented (that is, 1, 2, . . .), it may seem that the steps follow a definite order and time sequence. The scientific method is not rigid, however, and research rarely follows the pattern in such an orderly fashion. Individual steps are not isolated. The researcher may be involved with two or more steps simultaneously, or there

Figure 1.3
The Correspondence Between the Systematic Process of Research and the Scientific Method

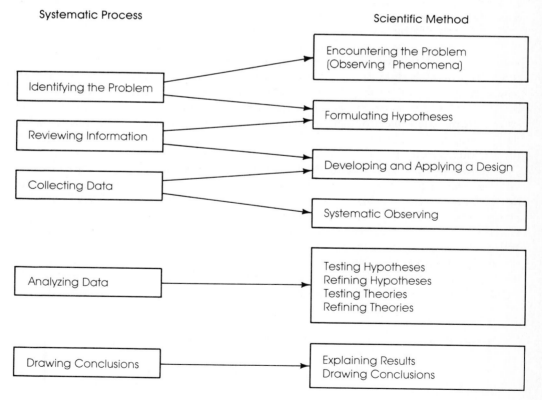

Systematic Process | Scientific Method

Identifying the Problem → Encountering the Problem (Observing Phenomena)

Reviewing Information → Formulating Hypotheses

Collecting Data → Developing and Applying a Design

Systematic Observing

Analyzing Data → Testing Hypotheses / Refining Hypotheses / Testing Theories / Refining Theories

Drawing Conclusions → Explaining Results / Drawing Conclusions may be some fluctuation back and forth among the steps. The steps of the scientific method are not an end in themselves but a means to an end—the systematic solution of a research problem.

> The primary characteristics of educational research are that it is systematic and that it follows the scientific method. A research process so implemented should enhance the validity and reliability of research.

The Activities in the Research Process

The systematic process of research and the scientific method lead into the general activities involved in conducting a research study. The activities, which are similar to the steps described earlier, are elaborated upon in this section. These activities are not limited to a specific type of research, such as ethnographic or experimental research, but apply generally. (Activities may receive varying emphasis, however, depending on the type of research.)

In summarizing the general activities involved in conducting a research study, we may appear to be emphasizing the sequential nature of the research process. To a certain extent this is fine, but we do not want to leave the impression that the research process is rigid or completely structured. Activities overlap to some degree, and at times two or more activities can be in process simultaneously. For example, in ethnographic research, hypothesis formulation often takes place throughout the study, from data collection on. In many studies, preliminary analysis begins while data collection is still in process. Nevertheless, it is helpful to impose some order on the various activities.

Figure 1.4 presents a sequential pattern of activities in flowchart form to provide an overview of the various research activities. The top row of boxes represents the general activities. More specific activities could be listed within each of these boxes. The lower boxes and the corresponding arrows reflect the relationships between the activities and existing knowledge, related theory, and expanded, revised, and new theory. Related theory is considered to be a part, but not necessarily all, of the body of knowledge relative to the research problem. Expanded, revised, and new theory, if forthcoming from the research project, then becomes part of the existing body of knowledge, as does new information not considered to be theory.

> The research process may be viewed as a sequence of activities, with the possibility of some overlap and fluctuation among the activities.

Figure 1.4
The Sequential Pattern of General Activities in Conducting a Research Study and the Relationship of Such Activities to Existing Knowledge

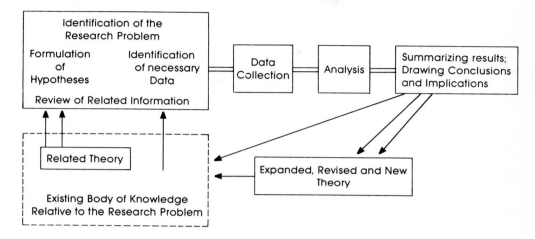

Obviously, all general activities draw on existing knowledge, but for the purpose of this figure, we associate the major impact of the body of knowledge with the research problem.

At this point, each of the activities will be described in more detail. However, this discussion is introductory and is designed only to provide an overview. In the following chapters, activities will be described in detail and illustrated with examples.

Identification of the Research Problem

This is the beginning activity of the research process (at least, it should be), and it is often the most difficult. The problem must be identified with adequate specificity. It is at this point that *hypotheses*—tentative guesses or conjectures about whatever is being studied—are generated. The variables must be identified and defined adequately for their use in the context of the study before the necessary data can be identified. This is done in the context of information. The literature is reviewed for information related to the research problem and to the possible methodology for conducting the research, basically to determine what others have done and have discovered that might be useful. The review of literature is a substantial task, and an entire chapter of this book (Chapter 3) is devoted to it.

Data Collection

Before data are collected, the measuring instruments must be identified and perhaps developed, as determined by the hypotheses and variables of the study. If an experiment is being conducted, the experimental treatments are administered or manipulated just before or during the data collection process. In essence, the experiment is being conducted at this point; the measures are taken. In the case of a survey, measuring instruments, such as achievement tests or questionnaires, are administered. If instruments are developed, they must be tried before the major data collection for the study is undertaken. Then the data must be assembled, coded, and prepared for analysis.

Analysis

Results of the study are generated when analysis is done. If statistical analyses are being done, they are completed at this point. The data are summarized, manipulated, and in essence reduced so that they provide the information necessary for testing the hypotheses. Computers or calculators are commonly used for analysis.

Summarizing Results and Drawing Conclusions

After the data have been analyzed and the results generated, the researcher must decide what information they provide. Results must be summarized and tied together, analyses must be interpreted, and conclusions must be drawn as they relate to the hypotheses and the research problem. The research report is prepared—a task that often requires rewriting. The conclusions are related to the existing body of knowledge, consistencies and inconsistencies with the results of other research studies are identified (and explained), and possible explanations of the results are provided.

The naive researcher may attempt to begin the research study by breaking into the sequence at a point such as data collection (a data collector in search of a research problem). Sometimes researchers formulate hypotheses on the basis of some data and then attempt to extract a problem from the hypotheses. Breaking the sequence in this manner tends to result in confusion and inefficiency. Adherence to the sequence tends to enhance the efficiency of the research process.

Conducting a research study involves a number of activities that are pieced together to bring the study to a conclusion. As indicated in Figure 1.3, developing and applying a design are also included. The specific research design—for example, an experimental design for an experiment—is developed early in the sequence, before data collection. The design is the specification of how the research activities will be conducted. To a large extent, however, the entire process concerns the application of the design. Thus, the issue of research design runs through the entire process.

Classification of Educational Research

There are many ways to classify educational research studies. Classification systems of various degrees of complexity have been developed. Two systems are described in this text, one based on the goal or purpose of the research and the other on the way the research is conducted. These classification systems are described here to provide the reader with additional background on the scope and nature of educational research.

Basic and Applied Research

Basic and applied research are differentiated by their goals or purposes. The purpose of *applied research* is to solve an immediate, practical problem. Such research is oriented to a specific problem. *Basic research* has a more general orientation—adding to the existing body of knowledge in the discipline. Basic research does not necessarily provide results of immediate, practical use, although such a possibility is not ruled out. If this result does occur, however, it is supplemental, not the primary purpose. On the other hand, in producing a solution to a specific problem, applied research may contribute to the general knowledge of the field. Both basic and applied research are important; they should not be differentiated by a hierarchy of value judgments.

An example of basic research would be conducting an experiment concerning learning in a laboratory setting. The purpose of such an experiment would be to contribute to the knowledge about how learning takes place. The experiment might be focused on one or a very limited number of factors associated with learning, such as the differences that result when learning materials are presented in a figural or a verbal manner.

An example of applied research would be conducting a survey of the elementary school teachers in a school system to determine their preferences and opinions about several available reading programs. The survey would be conducted by a curriculum committee or by the school system's administration, who are concerned with the problem of selecting the reading program or materials to be purchased. The results of the survey would provide information necessary for decisions about this purchase.

Unfortunately, misconceptions have developed with the use of the terms *basic* and *applied research*. One such misconception is that basic research is complex and applied research is simple in its methodology. A related misconception is that applied research is carried on by unsophisticated practitioners, whereas basic research is performed by abstract, impractical thinkers. Another misconception is that applied research is often sloppy and haphazard but of great practical value, whereas basic research is precise and exacting but of little or no value in a real situation. As indicated earlier, however, basic and applied research are differentiated not by their complexity or value, but by their goals or purposes.

Basic and applied research are differentiated by their purposes. The primary purpose of *basic research* is the extension of knowledge; the purpose of *applied research* is the solution of an immediate, practical problem.

One type of applied research is *action research*—research conducted by a teacher or administrator to aid in decision making in the local school. Action research focuses on the solution of day-to-day problems at the local level. There is little concern about generalizing the results of action research to other educational settings. Often, only a small, accessible population is used, such as the biology classes in a single high school.

Suppose that the science teachers in a junior high school are considering whether to use additional group work in conducting experiments or an individual, programmed workbook that simulates experiments. They conduct action research with the students enrolled in the science classes at their school to determine the relative effectiveness and efficiency of the two methods. The teachers are concerned about their own situation; they are not concerned about generalizing to other schools.

Action research usually is less rigorous in terms of design and methodology than other educational research. Often, intact groups are used; in some cases, only a single group is involved in the study. Nevertheless, action research, combined with what is known from the research literature, provides a useful and viable approach to making educational decisions at the local level.

Action research is usually conducted by teachers and administrators for solving a specific problem or for providing information for decision making at the local level.

General Methodology Classification

Another classification scheme based on general methodology is considered here. Although some writers use different methodological classifications, the one used here includes generally recognized major categories.

Experimental Research.   Educational research that is labeled "experimental" involves situations in which at least one variable,[1] the *experimental variable,* is deliberately manipulated or varied by the researcher to determine the effects of that variation. This implies that the researcher has the option of determining what the experimental variable will be and the extent to which it is varied. It is possible to have more than one experimental variable in a single experiment.

Suppose that a researcher in health education is interested in the effects of three different exercise periods (periods of varying length) on resting heart rate. Sixty young adults are randomly assigned, 20 to each period. The 60 participants exercise as specified each day, 20 for one-half hour, 20 for 45 minutes, and 20 for one hour. The exercise for each period is specified. The exercise program is in effect for 2 months. The participants are measured on resting heart rate before and after the program so that a measure of change can be taken.

The experimental variable here is the period of exercise. This variable—that is, the three levels of exercise—was constructed by the researcher and then administered to the participants, 20 for each level. If different periods of exercise have an effect on heart rate, this effect should be manifested by differences in the (average) heart rates of the three groups.

Ex Post Facto Research.

Kerlinger's (1973) definition will be used for the definition of ex post facto research: "systematic, empirical inquiry in which the scientist does not have direct control of *independent variables* because their manifestations have already occurred or because they are inherently not manipulable" (p. 379). Thus, the researcher does not manipulate any variables. The variables occur in the setting—usually a natural setting—and the researcher attempts to determine the relationships and effects occurring between the variables.

An example of ex post facto research would be a study of the relationship between attitude toward school and achievement of upper elementary school students in various cognitive and skill areas (mathematics, verbal skills, etc.). The researcher would administer to the students included in the study an appropriate attitude inventory and achievement measures for the cognitive and skills areas. No variables are manipulated; that is, the researcher does not administer any treatments to students to change or influence attitude scores or performance scores. The data are collected, and the researcher attempts to identify any effects that may exist and tries to explain how the effects are operating. For example, one question that would undoubtedly be considered is, "Are certain attitude patterns consistently associated with specific achievement scores, and, if so, are the attitudes influencing the achievement scores?"

Survey Research.

A variety of research studies can come under the heading of survey research. Generally, survey research deals with the incidence, distribution, and relationships of educational, psychological, and sociological variables. Thus, the distinction between ex post facto and survey research may not be very clear. Some surveys are limited to determining the status quo. But whatever the case, survey research deals more with questions of what is, rather than why it is so.

A researcher conducting a study of the professional practices of college-level counselors in the private colleges of Ohio would be engaged in survey research. One way to go about the study would be to construct an appropriate instrument, most likely a questionnaire, that could be completed either by a selected group of counselors or by the entire population of counselors. The responses of the counselors would provide a picture of the professional practices. From this information, the researcher could describe such characteristics as the relative importance (as perceived by the counselors) and the frequency of the practices. The study would emphasize the characteristics of the practices, not why they exist or what the rationales are behind them.

Historical Research.   In the context of education, historical research consists of "the study of a problem in the past that requires collecting information from the past, which serves as the data to be interpreted in the study" (Moore, 1983, p. 181). It consists of describing what was, rather than what is or what effects certain variables may have on others. Since events that have occurred in the past cannot be relived, they are described as accurately as possible through a process of critical inquiry.

An example of historical research might be a study of federal assistance programs for secondary education during the period 1945–1960. The researcher would inquire about the programs through various sources, such as legislative documents and historical summaries. Then the researcher would describe the programs and consider their possible effects, both good and bad. Specific factors might be considered in tracing the history of these programs, such as their economic impact. But whatever would be considered, it would be done in the context of events of some past period.

Ethnographic Research.   Ethnographic research is commonly associated with anthropology, but it is finding increasing use in education. An *ethnography* is an indepth, analytical description of a specific cultural situation, in the broad meaning of *culture*. Put into the context of education, we can define ethnographic research as the process of providing scientific descriptions of educational systems, processes, and phenomena within their specific contexts.

Ethnographic research relies heavily on observation, description, and qualitative judgments or interpretations of whatever phenomena are being studied. It takes place in the natural setting and focuses on processes in an attempt to obtain a holistic picture. Often, ethnographic research does not have a strong theoretical base and few hypotheses are specified before the research is conducted. Theory and hypotheses are generated as the research proceeds.

Suppose that a study of the nature of science instruction in a junior high school is being conducted. The research question is, "What is science instruction like in this school?" Observation is conducted in the science classrooms over the period of the school year. The observers take extensive field notes and interview students and teachers. On the basis of these results, they attempt to provide an accurate description and interpretation of science instruction in the school.

The foregoing examples are brief and superficial descriptions of different types of research using the general methodology classification, but they illustrate the definitions involved. Of course, any specific study would require a more detailed statement of the research problem and hypotheses, as appropriate. More detailed examples will be provided in the chapters that deal with these types of research. However, for the purposes here, the definitions do provide some contrasts between the various types. The classification of research by methodology is summarized in Table 1.1.

The Role of Theory

The term *theory* is used often in educational research; for example, we talk about *curriculum theory* or *learning theory*. Kerlinger (1973) has defined theory as "a set of interrelated constructs (concepts), definitions and propositions that presents a systematic view of phenomena by specifying relations among variables with the purpose of explaining and predicting the phenomena" (p. 9).

Brodbeck (1963) has included many of the same ideas in her discussion of theory, adding that a theory is a deductively corrected set of laws and that all statements in a theory, both explained and explaining, are generalizations. The laws doing the explaining are the *axioms;* those generalizations explained are the *theorems*. Theories can range from a single, simple generalization to a complex formulation of laws.

A *theory* is a generalization or series of generalizations by which we attempt to explain some phenomena in a systematic manner.

The use of theory is more commonly associated with basic research than with applied research. Sometimes the term *theory-testing research* is used as a part of basic

Table 1.1
Classification of Research by General Methodology

Type	Characteristics	Question Asked
Experimental	At least one variable is manipulated to determine the effect of the manipulation.	What is the effect of the experimental variable?
Ex post facto	Variables are studied as they occur in a natural setting, because they have already occurred or are not manipulable.	What are the relationships and possible effects among the variables?
Survey	The incidence, relationships, and distributions of variables are studied.	What are the characteristics of the variables?
Historical	A description of past events or facts is developed.	What was or what happened?
Ethnographic	A holistic description of present phenomena is developed.	What is the nature of the phenomena?

research. Consider an example. An educational psychologist is doing research on the relationship between frequency of encountering instructional materials (for example, word lists or mathematics problem solutions) and retention of the concepts included in the materials. A hypothesis is formulated that increased use enhances retention. Along with this hypothesis are hypotheses about several conditions relating to such factors as the complexity of the materials and the level at which continued use would no longer affect retention. Some relationships among factors may be hypothesized as well. Theory-testing research would enable us to test the theory with its primary and related hypotheses and, presumably, would either confirm or refute the theory, thus providing needed information for revising or extending the theory if necessary.

What is the role and purpose of theory in research? Basically, theory helps provide a framework by serving as the point of departure for the pursuit of a research problem. The theory identifies the crucial factors. It provides a guide for systematizing and interrelating the various facets of the research. However, besides providing the systematic view of the factors under study, the theory also may very well identify gaps, weak points, and inconsistencies that indicate the need for additional research. Also, the development of the theory may light the way for continued research on the phenomena under study.

In educational research, theory serves a synthesizing function, combining ideas and individual bits of empirical information into a set of constructs that provides for deeper understanding, broader meaning, and wider applicability. In a sense, a theory attaches meaning to facts and places them in proper perspective. Through this process, the theory aids in defining the research problem; that is, it helps identify the proper questions to be asked in the context of the specific project.

As indicated in Kerlinger's (1973) definition, a theory also serves the purposes of explaining and predicting. It suggests an explanation of observed phenomena, and it can also predict as yet unobserved or undiscovered factors by indicating their presence. Operating under the assumption that the theory is consistent, the researcher is then tipped off in terms of what to look for.

Another function of theory is to provide one or more generalizations that can be tested and then used in practical applications and further research. This development of generalizations is based on the assumption that generalizations do exist in education (or in any area under study) and that individual observations are special cases of such generalizations.

Conditions under which research is conducted and data obtained within and across studies must be incorporated into a meaningful whole; standing alone, they are not likely to mean much. As the facts of the research study, the data derive significance from the theory or theories into which they fit. Conversely, the theories become acceptable to the extent that they enhance the meaning of the data. Through this process, more adequate theories and unobstructed facts are secured; theory stimulates research, and, conversely, research stimulates theory development and theory testing. The criterion by which we judge a theory is not its truth or falsity, but rather its usefulness. Theories sometimes decrease in usefulness in the light of new knowledge, and they are combined, replaced, and refined as more knowledge is made available.

A good theory is developed in such a way that the generalizations can be tested. The theory must be compatible with the observations made relative to it and with already existing knowledge. It must adequately explain the events or phenomena under study. The greater the generalizability of the theory, the more useful it will be because of its wider applicability.

Another characteristic of a good theory is reflected in the *law of parsimony,* which holds that theories should be stated in the simplest form that adequately explains the phenomena. This does not mean that all theories should be simple statements; rather, they should be stated succinctly and precisely, avoiding ambiguities and unnecessary complexity. Important factors must not be overlooked, and the comprehensiveness of the theory must be adequate for its purpose.

> A theory provides a framework for conducting research, and it can be used for synthesizing and explaining (through generalizations) research results.

SUMMARY

This chapter has provided an overview of the nature of educational research and has introduced numerous concepts. In subsequent chapters, concepts and procedures will be expanded and described in detail. The intent of this chapter was to introduce the reader to educational research, thus providing the big picture.

Two classification systems for educational research were described to give some notion of the breadth and variety in educational research. Educational research can be put into the context of scientific research, but the would-be researcher should be cautioned against viewing educational research as a rigid and invariable lock-step set of procedures. Research is conducted through a variety of procedures.

The general activities of the research process were identified, described, and, in Figure 1.4, interrelated. Educational research involves many activities, some of which are simple, others complex. In fact, an entire continuum is encompassed, from simple to complex. Research is done in many different areas—curriculum, learning, and educational administration, to mention just a few. Research takes place at many different levels, from the individual action research conducted at the local school level, to large-scale projects conducted at universities or other agencies. Therefore, the description of educational research must be broad and must include many components. Even broad concepts, when projected into reality, are made up of specifics, however, and it is the specifics of research methods (activities, procedures, underlying reasoning, and so on) that are of major consideration in this text.

The Function of Educational Research

At the conclusion of this first chapter, it is well to consider the general role of educational research. A question might be raised by an already overloaded teacher: Why bother with educational research at all? What type of a role or function does educational research have in the overall enterprise of education and in its specific facets? One measure of its importance is its widespread use. Federal and state agencies and various foundations have allotted considerable funds for the pursuit of educational research, and numerous universities have been more or less involved in it for years. Such research often involves individual professors (with their research assistants); with external funding, however, there has been a trend toward more extensive projects involving several individuals and in some cases, more than one university. School systems are becoming increasingly willing to utilize the results of research, and in some instances, local school teachers and administrators conduct research themselves, especially as it relates to educational development.

It might be said that the overall function of educational research is to improve the educational process through the refinement and extension of knowledge. The refinement of existing knowledge or the acquisition of new knowledge is essentially an intermediate step toward the improvement of the educational process. This step is extremely important and may occupy a considerable proportion of the time allotted to the research endeavor. The refinement of existing knowledge should not be taken lightly, since in many situations the initial ideas and procedures of a research study may be relatively crude and may remain adequate for only a short time.

Within the broad framework of educational improvement, the specific roles of educational research are viewed differently by the people associated with various aspects of education. Two examples illustrate this point. A researcher concerned with a learning experiment may be attempting to reinforce or refute a theory of how learning takes place. The function of research here is to aid in making a decision concerning the refinement or extension of knowledge in this particular area. The classroom teacher, on the other hand, grappling with the problem of coming up with a more effective technique for teaching slow learners how to read, looks to research for tangible evidence that will help solve this immediate problem. Both are appropriate roles for educational research. That is, research should aid the theorist in making a decision about the theory, and it should provide the teacher with information that will lead to the solution of the nontheoretical classroom problem. The long-range goal of both theorist and teacher is to improve the educational process— the teacher in a much more immediate situation and the theorist on the assumption that knowing more about learning will increase the effectiveness of the learning process.

The demands of contemporary culture on today's educational systems are many and intense. The problems associated with the development, operation, and improvement of educational systems must be met with extensive and systematic applications of knowledge. As the various areas of education are exposed to objective examination, educational research provides the impetus, background, and means by which systematic examination, development, and improvement can take place.

The teacher, the administrator, the specialist of any kind in the schools, the college professor—all of these are taking part; all concerned should be consumers of research findings. At some stage or another, almost everyone should be an active participant in research studies. The practitioner, such as the teacher, will use research primarily to shed light on some immediate problem. Research involvement may make that individual a better educator. For the educator, some involvement with research, if only as a consumer of research results, should be a part of professional activity and growth. To be sure, there will be different types of research and different amounts of involvement, but all educators should view educational research as a helpful mechanism that all can use, in one way or another, for the improvement of the educational process.

KEY CONCEPTS

Systematic research   *Applied research*
Scientific method   *Role of theory*
Internal validity   *Law of parsimony*
External validity   *Experimental research*
Reliability of research   *Ex post facto research*
Basic research   *Survey research*
Historical research   *Ethnographic research*

EXERCISES

1.1 Identify the primary difference between basic research and applied research.

1.2 Define internal and external validity of a research study.

1.3 Why is it true that if a research study is completely lacking in internal validity, it also lacks external validity?

1.4 For each of the following, identify which type of validity (internal or external) is most likely lacking:

    a. An experimenter finds that there are four equally plausible interpretations of the results.

    b. The possible effects of different materials cannot be separated from the effects of the teachers who used them.

    c. A sixth-grade teacher finds that the results of a learning experiment do not apply to sixth-graders.

d. A superintendent attempts to determine voter feelings from the responses of a 12% return of a mailed questionnaire.

e. A researcher studies the effects of three different teaching methods on science achievement; each method was applied to a different class, and the classes differ substantially with respect to ability level.

f. Performance on a task involving recall of sets of random numbers is uncorrelated with achievement (in school subjects) test scores.

1.5 Define reliability of research. Describe how reliability might be threatened in (1) an experiment involving four experimenters administering the experimental treatment at different times; and (2) a study of teacher performance using ten different observers.

1.6 What distinguishes an experiment from nonexperimental types of research?

1.7 Describe how the focus of historical research differs from that of ethnographic research.

1.8 Develop an argument against the position: "Theory is useless in educational research."

NOTE

1. A *variable* is a characteristic that takes on different values (or conditions) for different individuals. Variables are described in greater detail in Chapter 2.

REFERENCES

Bogdan, R. C., & Biklen, S. K. (1982). *Qualitative research for education: An introduction to theory and methods.* Boston: Allyn and Bacon.

Borg, W. R. (1981). *Applying educational research: A practical guide for teachers.* New York: Longman.

Borg, W. R., & Gall, M. D. (1983). *Educational research: An introduction* (4th ed.). New York: Longman.

Brodbeck, M. (1963). Logic and scientific method in research on teaching. In N. L. Gage (Ed.), *Handbook of research on teaching* (pp. 44–93). Chicago: Rand McNally.

Kerlinger, F. N. (1973). *Foundations of behavioral research: Educational and psychological inquiry* (2nd ed.). New York: Holt, Rinehart & Winston.

McMillan, J. H., & Schumacher, S. (1984). *Research in education: A conceptual introduction.* Boston: Little, Brown.

Moore, G. W. (1983). *Developing and evaluating educational research.* Boston: Little, Brown.

Vockell, E. L. (1983). *Educational research.* New York: Macmillan.

2

Identification of a Research Problem

A good part of the research process deals with obtaining good answers—that is, solutions to research problems. However, the research process initially involves asking good questions or adequately identifying the problem, which may be one of the most difficult steps in a research study. Adequate identification is necessary to get the research process underway. The extent of detail in problem identification may vary somewhat with the type of research. For example, experimental studies usually have very specific research problems with accompanying hypotheses, whereas ethnographic research has more general problem statements, and hypotheses may be generated throughout the study.

The identification of a research problem involves more than simply providing an ad hoc statement or question about the area of interest. The first step in the identification involves selecting a research topic. Then a specific statement of the problem is generated from the topic. Usually one or more hypotheses are then identified, but the statements of the problem and the hypotheses involve the use of specific terminology about variables and conditions. This terminology must have meaning in the context of the problem, so before we can discuss the various components of problem identification, it is necessary to define the terminology that will be used.

Constants, Variables, and Measurement Scales

A *constant* is a characteristic or condition that is the same for all individuals in a study. A *variable,* on the other hand, is a characteristic that takes on different values or conditions for different individuals. If a researcher is interested in the effects of two different teaching methods on the science achievement of fifth-grade students, the grade level is a constant, since all individuals involved are fifth-graders. This characteristic is the same for everyone; it is a constant condition of the study.

After the different teaching methods have been implemented, the fifth-graders involved would be measured with a science achievement test. It is very unlikely that all of the fifth-graders would receive the same score on this test, so the score on the science achievement test becomes a variable, since different individuals will have different scores; at least, not all individuals will have the same score. We would say that science achievement is a variable, but we would mean, specifically, that the score on the science achievement test is a variable.

There is another variable in this example—the teaching method. In contrast to the science achievement test score, which would undoubtedly be measured on a scale with many possible values, teaching method is a categorical variable consisting of only two categories, the two methods. Teaching method is a *conditions variable;* that is, it determines certain conditions of the research. The fifth-graders would be assigned to one or the other teaching method, so all fifth-graders would be classified as having participated in one or the other teaching method.

A *constant* is a characteristic or condition that is the same for all individuals in a study. A *variable* is a characteristic that takes on different values or conditions for different individuals.

Types of Variables

The foregoing contrast between science achievement and teaching method implies that there are different types of variables. Actually, there are numerous ways in which variables are described. These descriptions are used to enhance the meanings of the variables in a study. The classification of variables follows the roles they play in a research study.

Independent and Dependent Variables.

The terminology of *independent* and *dependent variable* comes from mathematics. In a general sense, it is said that the values of the dependent variable depend on the independent variables. Pursuing such relationships and effects is often the purpose of conducting the research, but the researcher must not be misled into thinking that assigning labels generates causal relationships.

In many research studies, an independent variable is simply a classifying variable; it classifies the individuals of the study. In the science achievement example, teaching method would be an independent variable. A fifth-grader in the study would be taught by one of the two methods, which would comprise the two classifications, or levels, of this variable. (Two is the minimum number of levels for a variable.) The score on the science achievement test—the dependent variable—presumably will somehow be affected by the teaching method. In fact, the purpose of the study would be to determine whether or not there is an effect of teaching method. The researcher would attempt to explain the dependent variable in light of the independent variable.

The following example further illustrates the use of variables and constants. In a study conducted to determine the effect of three different teaching methods on achievement in elementary algebra, each of three ninth-grade algebra sections in the same school, taught by the same teacher, is taught using one of the methods. Both boys and girls are included in the study. The constants in the study are grade level, school, and teacher. (This assumes that, except for method, the teacher can hold teaching effectiveness constant.) The independent variables in the study are teaching method and sex of the student. Teaching method has three levels, which can arbitrarily be designated methods A, B, and C; sex of the student, of course, has two levels. Achievement in algebra, as measured at the end of the instructional period, is the dependent variable.

Other Possible Types of Variables.   In any research study, a number of influencing factors may be present, appearing in the form of variables. For convenience, these variables are given descriptive names, and they are often called by these names in the literature.

An *organismic variable* is a preexisting characteristic of the individuals under study. It is not a variable that can be randomly assigned to individuals. The sex and intelligence of the individuals are examples of organismic variables.

An *intervening variable* is one whose existence is inferred; but it cannot be manipulated or measured. If it has an effect, it must be inferred from a prior knowledge of what that effect might be in the context of the independent and dependent variables of the study. In the algebra example, learning style of students is an intervening variable. Intervening variables may go by other names, such as nuisance variables, mediator variables, or confounded variables. They are variables whose presence may confuse the interpretation of other variable effects.

A *control variable* is a variable other than the independent variables of primary interest whose effects are determined by the researcher. In the algebra example, if the difference between boys and girls on the dependent variable were determined, sex of the individual would be a control variable as well as an organismic variable.

Other names used for variables overlap with the foregoing terms above. An example is a *moderator variable*. Suppose that a study is done on the effects of three reading programs on fourth-grade reading achievement. There may be considerable difference between students on prior reading achievement, and one program may be more effective than the other two for students who have high prior reading achievement. In this case, prior reading achievement is a moderator variable, since program effects may be different for different levels of this variable; that is, program effects are moderated by prior reading achievement. If a moderator variable is uncontrolled, it is essentially an intervening variable. If it is controlled—that is, its effects have been determined—it becomes a control variable. In the reading achievement example, if there is no way to determine the effects of prior reading achievement, it becomes an intervening variable; if the effects of prior reading achievement can be identified, it becomes a control variable.

It can be seen from the foregoing examples that the descriptions of variables are not mutually exclusive. For example, organismic variables may also be control variables. These kinds of variables often take on the form of independent variables in a study, although they usually are not the independent variables of primary interest. If the algebra example were extended to include two or more schools, and if the differences between schools were determined, school would become a control variable. (However, school could not be an organismic variable.)

Any given study is not limited to a single independent, organismic, control, intervening, or dependent variable. Suppose that the fifth-grade science achievement example were extended to include five schools, that the students were grouped, on the basis of previous performance, as high, average, and low, and that both boys and girls were included and their differences determined. Another independent variable—type of material, with two kinds of materials—is introduced. It is decided to do a more comprehensive achievement study to observe the same group on both reading achievement and spelling achievement. These achievement scores would also be dependent variables—not because there are two or more measures of achievement, but because scores vary for any one type of achievement and may be affected by the independent variables. Possible intervening variables would now become the students' learning styles and the teaching styles of the teachers. This is a relatively complex example; the variables are summarized in Figure 2.1.

It should not be inferred that organismic variables are necessarily control variables. They are control variables only if their effects are determined—that is, controlled. The learning style of the students might be an organismic variable, and it would probably appear as an intervening variable.

Figure 2.1
Different Types of Variables Operating in a Fifth-Grade Achievement Study

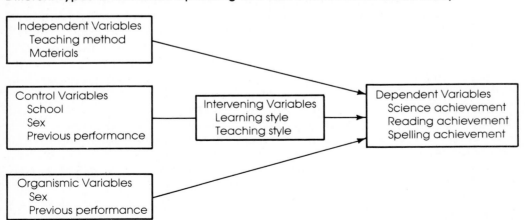

Measurement Scales

When all of the possible variables in education are considered, it soon becomes apparent that all measurement is not the same. In the science achievement example, the variable teaching method is simply a categorical variable; we know that the methods are different and can be given different names. On the other hand, if the dependent variable of the score on a science achievement test is considered, the measurement is not simply categorical; there is some kind of ordering and quantifying of the scores.

Essentially, there is a hierarchy of measurement scales—with four general categories, based on the amount of information contained in a score. The lowest type of scale is the *nominal scale,* which simply categorizes without order. Sex of the individual is a variable that is measured on a nominal scale.

Consider a variable such as attitude toward school. If one individual indicates a highly favorable attitude toward school and another individual indicates a neutral attitude, we not only know that they are different, but we can also order the individuals on the degree of favorableness in their attitudes toward school. Thus, besides having a difference, we also have order. A variable so measured is on an *ordinal scale.*

Suppose that we measure a variable such as IQ or performance on an achievement test in reading or mathematics. If three individuals have scores of 105, 110, and 115, respectively, the difference of five points between the first two individuals is considered equivalent to the difference of five points between the second two individuals. This gives not only difference and order but also a unit of equal differences established in the measurement. This level of measurement is called *equal-unit* or *interval scale.*[1]

A variable such as the weight of different quantities of apples is an example of a fourth level of measurement. If we have two bags of apples, a 25-pound bag and a 50-pound bag, we say that the 50-pound bag weighs twice as much as the 25-pound bag. We can say "twice" because having no apples is zero point in quantity of apples. Thus, we have not only difference, order, and an equal unit, but also a comparison in terms of the ratio of one observation to another. Hence, this level of measurement is called *ratio scale.* One can say that a 50-pound bag of apples weighs twice as much as one of 25 pounds, but not that an individual with an IQ of 140 has twice the intelligence (or whatever IQ measures) of an individual with an IQ of 70. If an individual scored no points on an IQ test, one would not say that the individual is completely lacking in intelligence. To establish a ratio, the scale must have a true zero point.

Ratio scale variables, except for physical measurements, seldom occur in educational research. For most practical purposes, however, ratio scale measurement is equivalent to interval scale in regard to statistical procedures. Therefore, whether measurement is interval or ratio scale is usually not an important distinction in educational research.

The four levels of measurement, which are hierarchical in terms of the amount of information contained in a score, can also be viewed as the number of conditions needed to attain the scale. The ratio scale is the highest level in the hierarchy. The measurement scales are summarized in Table 2.1.

Variables whose measurement scales are ordinal level or higher may be divided into those that are numerically scaled and those that are not. For example, observations for variables such as weight in pounds are on numerical scales. However, if more general categories are used, such as light weight, medium weight, and heavy weight, the variable weight would still be ordered, but it would no longer be numerically scaled. A variable measured as poor, fair, good, or excellent is another example of one that is ordered but not numerically scaled.

Measurement of the variables is almost always of some concern in a research study. The amount of effort required by the measurement depends on the specific variables of the study. (Measurement is more fully discussed in Chapter 11.) The scales were introduced here to expand more fully the concept of the variable as it is needed for identifying the research problem.

The Operational Definition

In any research study, the variables and conditions of the study must be defined operationally. Educators often deal with variables that do not readily manifest themselves. If a school nurse were interested in the weights of first-grade pupils, they could be measured using a common weight scale. Similarly, if we want to measure and quantify ability to learn or reading comprehension, we must have some tool to do so. Perhaps we could set up a chain of definition for ability to learn and thus reach a consensus. But to achieve measurement, we must include the processes or operations that are going to be used to measure the phenomenon or variable under study. Such a definition is called an *operational definition*.

The following examples illustrate this point. In studying ability to learn, a researcher might operationally determine this ability as the individual's score on an IQ inventory—specifically, the score attained on the LM form of the Stanford-Binet

Table 2.1
Measurement Scales and Their Conditions

Scale	Conditions	Example
Nominal	Measures without order; simply indicates that two or more classifications are different	Types of secondary schools: comprehensive, vocational, private college prep, etc.
Ordinal	Measures with order; indicates that the measurement classifications are different and can be ranked	The letter grading system
Interval (or equal unit)	Measures with order and establishes numerically equal distances on the scale	Performance on a standardized achievement test in science
Ratio	Contains an absolute or true zero point in addition to an equal unit	Height

Intelligence Scale. In the earlier science achievement example, the dependent variable might have been operationally defined as the score on the science subtest of the Iowa Test of Basic Skills.

Conditions of a research study also require operational definition. For example, if high school seniors are to be surveyed, who is a high school senior? A possible operational definition of a *senior* is a student who is presently enrolled in a recognized high school, has not yet graduated, but has earned 12 or more high school course credits. In this case, a senior is defined in terms of certain observable or identifiable characteristics or properties.

An *operational definition* is stipulative in that it specifies the operations or characteristics necessary to identify the variable or condition being defined.

Selection of a Research Problem

The selection of an appropriate research problem is a matter of asking good questions—that is, questions that are relevant and important in the educational context. Educators put a great deal of emphasis on obtaining good answers—that is, doing the research correctly—and rightly so, but it is also important to obtain a workable research problem. Without such a problem, the most carefully designed procedures for securing answers will be to no avail. Although no standardized set of procedures can be prescribed for selecting a research problem, consideration of certain factors will aid in the selection process.

The research problem should be of interest not only to the individual researcher but to at least some recognized segment of the educational community. Its place in the context of education should be assured. Originality should also be considered, especially if the research topic is being selected for a thesis, but a completely original research idea is rare. It is more likely that the research will be an extension of some already completed project. The extent of duplication or replication that is desirable in such studies depends on the specific area and the conditions of the research.

Another factor is the significance of the research problem for education from either a practical or a theoretical viewpoint. Trivial problems—for example, the proportions of elementary students who wear canvas or leather shoes and the relationship of this choice of footwear to achievement—can be procedurally researched. But such a problem has no theoretical framework and no significance, regardless of what the resulting proportions happen to be. A research problem should add to the existing knowledge or contribute to education in a meaningful way.

Not all problems in education are researchable. Some are philosophical in nature and can be discussed but not researched. An example is a question such as: "Should the history requirement in the senior high school be one or two courses?"

Chances are that if the requirement is two courses, the students will learn more history, but the question remains whether it is important that they have two courses. Answers to such questions are for the most part based on value judgments. If additional conditions are not stipulated, the questions are not researchable.

Even if problems are researchable, doing the research may not be feasible. The necessary data for the study may be excessive or may be too difficult to obtain. Ethical considerations may be involved; for example, the testing required to obtain the necessary data may be an invasion of the individual's privacy. Necessary resources, such as laboratory facilities and funds, may not be available. Many of these kinds of conditions can make it impractical to research a specific problem.

Research problems are selected in the context of information or experience. The researcher should be familiar with the area to be researched, including relevant theories. A premium is put on original and creative thinking, but the possibility of such thinking is remote if the researcher has no knowledge on which to base it.

A study of related research and a familiarization with practical or theoretical considerations in the area will aid the researcher in formulating appropriate questions that will help focus on the research problem. If an individual is interested in doing research related to learning—specifically, transfer of learning—the identical-elements theory of transfer, which assumes that elements present in the original learning are also present in the new learning, could be considered. This would provide a basis for considering transfer, but it would be necessary to decide (operationally define) what actually comprises identical elements. If it were desirable to test the theory relative to a unique learning task and the visual stimuli involved in that task, the following questions could be formulated.

> Would an identical element of color be adequate for transfer?
>
> Would shapes or sizes by themselves be adequate?
>
> Are certain combinations of the elements conducive to transfer?
>
> What implications would the results have for a practical learning situation?
>
> How could results be used for testing the theory in a practical learning situation?

In any research study, it is not adequate simply to accumulate empirical results. Questions such as those just listed, along with relevant theory and the statement of the research problem, provide the context for doing the research. They will also provide meaning to the results derived from the study.

Statement of the Research Problem

Selection of a research problem does not necessarily mean that it is adequately stated. Usually, a problem requires some reworking to get it into a suitable form for the study to proceed effectively. The statement of the problem must be specific enough that it is clear what is actually under investigation. A problem may be stated broadly and then systematically restricted through a review of the literature in the initial stages of the research effort. It is better to work in this direction than to begin with a problem that is too narrow and then attach pieces to expand it.

Research problems may be stated in a declarative or descriptive manner or in question form. Many researchers, possibly the majority, prefer the question form, but either form is acceptable. The question form may aid in focusing the problem, and it is especially effective when subproblems are included within the larger research problem. The most important characteristic of the problem statement is that it must provide adequate focus and direction for the research.

At this point, it might be useful to illustrate some unsatisfactory and satisfactory problem statements. A statement such as "the elementary school curriculum" is far too broad to serve as a problem statement; in fact, it really contains no problem. A satisfactory statement might be: "A study of the effects of elementary school curriculum practices on the reading achievement of fourth-grade students in City A." Or, in question form, we might have: "What are the effects of elementary school curriculum practices on fourth-grade reading achievement in City A?" The following are several examples of original statements and their subsequent restatements into more manageable statements of the problem, including the question form:

Original Creativity of elementary school students.

Restatement A study of the relationship between divergent thinking scores and selected characteristics of fifth-, sixth-, and seventh-grade students.

Question form What are the relationships between scores of fifth-, sixth-, and seventh-grade students on a divergent thinking test and scores on (1) a general IQ measure, (2) a reading achievement test, and (3) a measure of physical dexterity?

Original Achievement and teaching techniques.

Restatement A study of the effects of three teaching techniques on science achievement of junior high school students.

Question form Do three different teaching techniques have differing effects on science achievement scores of junior high school students?

Original Bilingual education.

Restatement A study of the nature and characteristics of bilingual education in the elementary schools of City A.

Question form What are the nature and characteristics of bilingual education as it is implemented in the elementary schools of City A?

Original A history of College A.

Restatement A study of the impact of federal aid to higher education on the expansion of the science and mathematics curriculums in College A during the period 1955–1972.

Question form What was the impact of federal aid on the expansion of the science and mathematics curriculums in College A during 1955–1972?

Original The role of the guidance counselor in the high school.

Restatement A survey of the practices of the guidance counselors in the high schools of City B.

Question form Four questions are given to illustrate the identification of subproblems:

> What proportion of guidance counselors' working day is taken up with nonguidance activities?
>
> What are the major strengths of guidance counselors' practices as perceived by the students?
>
> What are the major weaknesses of guidance counselors' practices as perceived by the students?
>
> What practices are perceived by guidance counselors as most effective in advising students about college selection?

A good statement of the problem should provide the researcher with direction in pursuing the project. The statement should identify key factors in the research project. For example, in the first of the foregoing restatements, the word *relationship* implies certain procedures, the three grade levels limit and define the population under study, and the term *divergent thinking scores* is certainly more specific than the word *creativity,* which was used in the original statement. Divergent thinking requires an operational definition, such as the score on a specific divergent thinking test.

It should be noted that in the restatements of the problems, considerable definition of terms would be necessary. The selected factors in the first example would require identification and definition, and the three teaching techniques of the second example would require definition for the specific situation. Such definitions should accompany the statement of the problem, but they are usually not included in the statement because they would make it excessively long, cumbersome, and awkward. Assuming that adequate definition accompanies the statement of the problem, there should be no ambiguity about what is to be investigated.

Whether or not research problems are stated in question form depends, to a large extent, on the preference of the researcher. If the question form appears to be helpful, it should be used. Actually, the form for stating the problem is relatively unimportant; what is important is that the statement be precise and definitive, so that there is no confusion about what is under study.

It often helps in understanding the nature of the statement of the research problem to consider examples. The following is a list of problem statements developed by students in a research methods course:

1. A survey of reading program components and practices in selected school systems of Ohio.
2. What are the effects of cerebral, hemispheric overload on auditory and motor performance in young children?

3. How does a pass/fail grading system affect the achievement of college juniors in major area coursework?

4. The design of a conceptual model for the implementation of minimum competency testing in Ohio.

5. What are the effects of different types of praise on attitude toward school of students in an integrated elementary school?

6. The effects of two different mathematics programs on the mathematics achievement of sixth-grade students in School A.

7. A survey of the scholastic achievement of students from nine elementary schools entering Junior High School A.

8. A survey of teacher attitudes toward collective bargaining in the schools of City A.

9. What are the effects of age, type of material, and amount of available information on performance on a concept attainment task?

10. What are teacher and administrator perceptions of the professional growth credits program in the City A public schools?

11. What are the extent and nature of the educational backgrounds and professional qualifications of the chief personnel officers in private, four-year colleges of the United States?

12. A study of the effects on achievement of different teaching materials in high school history courses.

> The statement of the research problem should be concise and should identify the key factors (variables) of the research study.

Hypotheses and Statement of the Problem

By itself, the statement of the research problem usually provides only a general direction for the research study; it does not include all the specific information. Including all this information would make the statement cumbersome and unmanageable. To obtain more specificity and direction, we develop *hypotheses*. Hypotheses may be derived directly from the statement of the problem, they may be based on the research literature, or in some cases, such as in ethnographic research, they may (at least in part) be generated from data collection and analysis. Although there are different forms or types of hypotheses, as discussed here in a broad sense, a hypothesis is a conjecture or a guess at the solution to the problem or the status of the situation. Hypotheses are more operational than statements of the problem; as such, they lend more specific structure to the study.

In a general sense, hypotheses take on some of the characteristics of a theory, which is usually considered a larger set of generalizations about a certain phenomena.

Thus, a theory might include several hypotheses. Logically, the approach is to proceed so that a decision can be made about whether or not the hypotheses are tenable. This is called *testing the hypothesis;* the results of such a test either sustain or refute the hypothesis.

Borg and Gall (1983) identify four criteria that hypotheses should satisfy:

1. The hypothesis should state an expected relationship between two or more variables.

2. The researcher should have definite reasons based on either theory or evidence for considering the hypothesis worthy of testing.

3. A hypothesis should be testable.

4. The hypothesis should be as brief as possible consistent with clarity. (pp. 91–93)

A weakness of many hypotheses is that they are too broad to pinpoint the specific problem under study—as, for example, in the following hypothesis: "Bright students have good attitudes toward school." The terms *bright* and *good* and *attitudes* represent types of broad, undefined generalities. Some type of vague relationship between brightness and good attitude is implied, but little direction for research is provided. To convert the statement into an acceptable hypothesis, it might be changed to read:

> *Students aged 9 through 11 who score in the upper 25% of their class on the (standardized) IQ test have a higher mean score on the "X-Y-Z Attitude Toward School Inventory" than students who score in the lower 75% of the class on the IQ test.*

Note that this statement has specificity and that it states an expected relationship (the upper 25% on the IQ test have higher mean attitude scores than the lower 75% on the IQ test). Assuming that the measurement can be made, the hypothesis is testable.

Another version could be:

> *A positive relationship exists between the scores on the (specific) IQ test and the (specific) attitude inventory for students aged 9 through 11.*

This statement of the hypothesis is shorter than the initial statement. It includes an expected relationship and it is testable.

In both instances, the hypothesis contains the operational definitions of the variables involved—academic aptitude (brightness) and attitude toward school. These variables are defined by scores on a specific test and a specific inventory. If the operational definitions make the statement of the hypothesis too cumbersome, they can be presented in a separate statement or section. However, the variables should be clearly identified so that the expected relationship is clearly defined—that is, that it will be positive or that the mean of a certain group will be higher than that of another group. The hypothesis is testable; that is, procedures exist for analyzing the data that will give results either supporting or refuting the hypothesis. (However, the two versions presented here would be tested in different ways.) The hypothesis declares the anticipated direction; supposedly, this is not just a wild guess. Overall, the hypothesis meets the criteria for a good statement, assuming that there are reasons that make the hypothesis worthy of testing.

> A *hypothesis* is a conjecture or proposition about the solution to a problem, the relationship of two or more variables, or the nature of some phenomenon.

Types and Forms of Hypotheses

Kerlinger (1973, p. 201) has indicated that, in a broad sense, researchers use two types of hypotheses—substantive and statistical. A *substantive hypothesis,* also called a *research hypothesis,* usually takes the form of a conjecture. For example we might hypothesize: "As punitive, disciplinary methods are increased in an elementary school, student achievement will decrease." In research in science education, a hypothesis might be: "Laboratory instruction enhances the student's understanding of scientific processes, over an instructional approach limited to lecture, discussion and theoretical problem solution."

A *statistical hypothesis* is given in statistical terms. Technically, in the context of inferential statistics, it is a statement about one or more parameters that are measures of the populations under study.[2] Statistical hypotheses are often given in quantitative terms—for example: "The mean reading achievement of the population of third-grade students taught by Method A equals the mean reading achievement of the population taught by Method B."

The foregoing statistical hypothesis is an example of a hypothesis stated in *null form;* that is, no difference in the means is hypothesized. The *null hypothesis* is sometimes described as the hypothesis of no difference or no relationship. Technically, when a statistical hypothesis is tested using inferential statistics, it is a null hypothesis that is being tested.

For any statistical hypothesis, there is an *alternative hypothesis,* which expresses the remaining possible outcomes. The alternative hypothesis for the reading achievement example would be: "The reading achievement means of the populations of third-graders taught by Method A and Method B are not equal." If we had initially hypothesized, "The mean reading achievement of the population of third-graders taught by Method A is greater than the mean of the population taught by Method B," the alternative hypothesis would be, "The mean of the population of third grades taught by Method A is less than or equal to the mean of the population taught by Method B." Note that the null hypothesis and its alternative cover all possible outcomes of the positioning of the two measures.

We can also distinguish between *directional* and *nondirectional hypotheses;* for the former, a direction of results is implied, whereas no direction is specified for the latter. Suppose that a teacher experimenting with a new technique for teaching third-grade spelling hypothesizes that the spelling achievement of third-grade pupils being taught with the new technique exceeds that of pupils being taught with traditional methods. Specifically, the hypothesis would be:

The mean score on the ABC Spelling Test of third-grade pupils taught by the new method will exceed the mean score of pupils taught by traditional methods.

This is a directional hypothesis in that a direction of results is implied—namely, the greater achievement (higher mean score) of pupils taught by the new method. Other examples of directional statements are as follows:

1. *The mathematics achievement of high-ability students exceeds that of average-ability students.*
2. *The reading level of first-grade girls is higher than that of first-grade boys.*
3. *There is a positive relationship between academic aptitude scores and scores on a social adjustment inventory.*
4. *As a teacher's salary increases, the teacher's opinion of school administrative personnel becomes more favorable.*

Nondirectional hypotheses do not specify a direction. Nondirectional hypotheses corresponding to the foregoing directional statements are as follows:

1. *The mathematics achievement of high-ability students equals that of average-ability students, or there is no difference between the mathematics achievement of average- and high-ability students.*
2. *The reading level of first-grade girls is the same as that of first-grade boys.*
3. *There is no relationship between academic aptitude scores and scores on a social adjustment inventory.*
4. *A teacher's opinion of school administrative personnel is independent of the teacher's salary.*

Should hypotheses be stated in directional or nondirectional form—or does it make any difference? The form used should be determined by the expected results. If the research literature in the area indicates that we can expect a difference or a direction of results, a directional hypothesis is called for; if the research literature does not present convincing evidence for a direction, or if an exploratory study is being done, a nondirectional hypothesis should be used. Because of the emphasis on null hypotheses in inferential statistics, educational research—and behavioral sciences research in general—has probably overused the nondirectional hypothesis and underused the directional hypothesis.

Statistical hypotheses are used in the analysis of data; *substantive hypotheses* indicate the direction of results. Hypotheses may be stated in *directional* or *nondirectional* form; the form used should be based on information from the research literature.

Examples of Hypotheses Related to Problem Statements. A statement of a research problem may have one or more (usually more) hypotheses associated with it. Hypotheses are formulated from the research problem statement and should follow directly from it. Each of the following examples provides a problem statement, several hypotheses, and operational definitions or comments on the operational definitions of the variables or conditions. To illustrate the different types of variables discussed earlier in the chapter, a listing of variables follows the operational definitions. In each example, the hypotheses, operational definitions, and variables are all tied together and are a direct result of the problem statement.

Example 2.1

Problem Statement

A survey of grading practices and patterns in academic areas of the senior high schools in Ohio.

Hypotheses

1. Average grades in the science areas of chemistry and physics are higher than those in biology and earth science.
2. Average grades in history and other social studies are higher than those in biological and physical sciences.
3. Average grades in advanced mathematics (second-year algebra and beyond) are higher than those in introductory algebra and consumer mathematics.
4. There is a positive relationship between grades received in English courses and those received in foreign language courses.
5. There is a positive relationship between grades received in Algebra II and those received in chemistry.
6. Grading patterns for courses in academic areas are higher as the size of the high school increases.

Operational Definitions

Academic areas: Sciences, mathematics, English, social studies, history, and foreign languages.

Senior high school: Grades 10, 11, and 12 of any accredited high school in Ohio.

Grades: The possible categories of the letter grading system A, B, C, and so forth, which may be converted to numerical scores.

Grading pattern: The proportions of grades in each category by course.

Size of high school: Total enrollment in grades 10–12; categories are: less than 200 students, 200–499, 500–799, 800–1,099, 1,100 and greater.

Independent Variables	*Dependent Variables*
Academic areas	Grades
Specific courses in certain areas	Grading patterns/proportions of grades by category
Size of high school	

Possible Intervening Variables	*Possible Control Variable*
Type of school	Size of school
Sex of the students (organismic)	
Location of school	

Example 2.2

Problem Statement

A study of the effects of two reading programs (A and B) on the reading achievement of third-grade students in School C.

Hypotheses

1. With students of heterogeneous reading achievement, there will be no difference in the mean gains in reading achievement for students taught by Program A and those taught by Program B.
2. For students scoring in the lower 30% on prior reading achievement, those taught by Program A will have a greater mean gain than those taught by Program B.
3. For students scoring in the upper 30% on prior reading achievement, those taught by Program B will have a greater mean gain than those taught by Program A.

4. For students scoring in the middle 40% on prior reading achievement, there will be no difference in mean gains for students taught by Program A and those taught by Program B.

Operational Definitions

Individuals included in the study: All third-graders of School C.

Program A: The set of reading materials purchased from Publisher Y and its suggested activities.

Program B: Materials purchased from Publisher X.

Independent Variable	*Dependent Variable*
Reading program—A and B	Gain score in reading achievement—for example, the difference between scores on two forms of a standardized reading test, one form given prior to the study, the second form given after the study
Possible Intervening Variables	*Possible Control Variables*
Teacher Teaching style (organismic) Learning style (organismic) Student scholastic ability (organismic)	Prior reading achievement (organismic) Sex (organismic)

Example 2.3

Problem Statement

A study of the effects of type of material, age, sex, and problem complexity on performance on a concept attainment task.

Hypotheses

1. There is no difference in the mean performance of individuals using figural materials and those using verbal materials.
2. There is no difference in the mean performance of individuals in the age range 20–25 years and of those in the age range of 26–30 years.
3. There is no difference in the mean performance of males and females.
4. Concept attainment problems containing two and three relevant dimensions are of equal difficulty.

Operational Definitions

Since a concept attainment task is very specific, it would have to be described as part of the procedures for doing the research.

Type of material: Figural: pictorial 3 by 3 cards in which the concepts are embedded; verbal: 3 by 3 cards with verbal statements corresponding to the pictorial cards.

Relevant dimension: A characteristic common to all cards that exemplify a concept. (A dimension might be a solid border.)

Performance: Time in minutes (to two decimal places) required to attain the concept.

Problem complexity: The number of relevant dimensions in the concept; the greater the number, the more complex the problem.

(Age and sex are operationally defined in the hypotheses.)

Independent Variables	*Dependent Variable*
Type of material	Time (in minutes) required to attain the concept
Age (organismic)	
Sex (organismic)	
Problem complexity	

Possible Intervening Variables	*Possible Control Variables*
General intelligence of the individual (organismic)	Age
Spatial relations skill of the individual (organismic)	Sex
Efficiency and accuracy of the experimenter administering the task	

Example 2.4

Problem Statement

A survey of teacher opinion of the school board policies in the City C Metropolitan Area.

Hypotheses

1. The proportion of teachers in agreement with the policy on compensation for in-service work exceeds .75.

2. At least .50 of the teachers are in agreement with the policy on teacher transfer.
3. There is no difference between the proportions of elementary and secondary teachers in agreement with the policy on sick leave.
4. There are differences among the proportions of elementary teachers in agreement with the policy on transfer for suburban systems and the city system.

Operational Definitions

School board policies: Statements of procedure and/or conditions of employment and activity as found in school board minutes or directives.

City C Metropolitan Area: City C and its suburbs, as defined in State Publication No. 1234.

Independent Variables

Type of teacher—elementary, secondary (organismic)

Location of teaching or school system—the city and various suburban systems

Dependent Variable

Proportions (or percentages) of teachers responding favorably to policy items

Possible Intervening Variables

Age of the teacher (organismic)

Sex of the teacher (organismic)

Marital status of the teacher (organismic)

Amount of graduate work completed by the teacher (organismic)

Size of the specific school

Possible Control Variable

Location of teaching

The preceding examples have not exhausted the number of possible hypotheses, which depends on the extent and conditions of the research study. In identifying the variables, possible intervening variables are listed; certainly, more may be operating in any specific situation. Note that sex is an independent variable in Example 2.3, a possible control variable in Example 2.2, and a possible intervening variable in Example 2.1. That is because in Examples 2.2 and 2.3, any differential performance between males and females would be determined, whereas in Example 2.1, if there is an effect of sex, it is not separated from the effects of other variables. In any event, sex is an organismic variable, as identified in parentheses.

The hypotheses of Example 2.1 are stated in directional form; those of Example 2.3 are stated in nondirectional or null form. In Examples 2.2. and 2.4, both types of hypotheses are used. Both forms can be used, although a single form is sometimes preferred for consistency.

Example 2.2 is one that would apply to action research, if it were conducted by the third-grade teachers in a single school to help them make a decision about which program to use in the school. Note that the dependent variable in this example is gain score in reading achievement, not simply reading achievement score. To determine gain scores, prior reading achievement scores must be known; therefore, prior reading achievement could be a control variable.

The various components for identifying a research problem are connected (see Figure 2.2). The statement of the problem is the springboard for developing the hypotheses. The process of generating hypotheses not only defines the problem more specifically, it also can effectively limit the research problem. Hypotheses are stated in the context of variables, operational definitions, and conditions. All this is done on a base of relevant theory and existing knowledge. Research problems are not identified and pursued in an informational vacuum. They have a place in the educational world—either theoretically or practically, or both.

Hypotheses are not ends in themselves; rather, they are aids in the research process. Although the overall consensus is in favor of stating hypotheses, occasionally a report of a research project may seem short on hypotheses. Possibly the researcher was working in an area with very little background information, or perhaps considerable theory development was necessary. In ethnographic research, for ex-

Figure 2.2
Connections Between the Components for Identifying a Research Problem

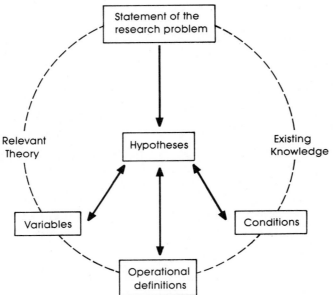

ample, initial hypotheses are often general and limited in number; as the research progresses, however, new hypotheses are generated and prior hypotheses may be revised, retained, or discarded. If at all feasible, hypotheses should be stated concisely and used as the framework for the research.

The Research Problem in the Research Proposal

The identification of a research problem is important, but it by no means comprises the entire research process. Adequately identifying the problem and related hypotheses gets the process off to a good start, but the research must still be conducted in a manner that permits valid conclusions to be drawn from the results. Doing the research usually involves a variety of activities that fit into the general steps of the research process. (Subsequent chapters of this text deal with these activities.)

Whether a researcher is a student preparing to do the research for a thesis or for some other reason or an experienced educator preparing to do a research project, a research proposal is almost always required. The proposal is a document that contains a statement of the research problem and a detailed description of how the research will be conducted. Proposals commonly contain sections covering the review of related literature and anticipated outcomes of the research.

The preparation of research proposals requires a variety of information—more information than is needed for identifying the problem. Thus, although it is premature to discuss proposal preparation in detail at this point (the topic is considered in Chapter 13), it is appropriate to comment on the place of the problem statement in the research proposal.

The statement of the problem typically comes very early in the research proposal. There are usually some introductory comments, possibly including a few references to the related literature, to provide a context for stating the research problem. Then the problem is explicitly identified. The introductory phrase may be one of the following:

> The problem of this proposed research is . . .
>
> The research question to be addressed is . . .
>
> The purpose of the research problem is . . .
>
> Specifically, the research problem is . . .

The related hypotheses and operational definitions then follow in the proposal, usually quite closely. Occasionally, the hypotheses statement may appear later in the proposal if the measurement and data descriptions might enhance the understanding of the hypotheses. However, unless somewhat unusual data are to be generated and uncommon analysis procedures are to be used, there is no point in separating the statement of the problem and the hypotheses.

Research proposals vary in length, depending on a variety of factors, including the magnitude of the proposed research and the complexity of the procedures necessary to conduct the research. However, the general format and sectioning of proposals are consistent; the statement of the problem appears early in the proposal, commonly in the first section.

Although proposals vary considerably in length, it might be helpful to consider the statement of the problem in a sample research proposal. The proposal in Appendix 1 was prepared by a student in an introductory research methods course. The first paragraph provides a brief introduction to the problem, and the statement of the problem appears early in the second paragraph. The major hypothesis of interest accompanies the statement of the problem. Since the proposed research is specific to special education, numerous terms are defined after the statement of the problem.

SUMMARY

This chapter has discussed the identification of the research problem, with its statement of the problem and related hypotheses. Concepts of variables, constants, measurement scales, and operational definition have been described. Different types of variables can enter into a research study, and the types of variables are, for the most part, identified by descriptive terms.

The concepts of variables, constants, and so forth are used not only in identifying the problem but throughout the research process. They are tied together conceptually to provide the context for the research problem. These concepts may be viewed as components for identifying a research problem and can be connected, as was shown in Figure 2.2.

The next chapter discusses the review of the literature. The position of this discussion in the book is somewhat arbitrary; it could have appeared before the discussion on identification of the problem, since some review of the literature often is done before the problem statement is refined and put into final form. However, the researcher must have some idea of what to look for, so the problem is usually identified before any extensive review of the literature is done.

KEY CONCEPTS

Constant
Variable
Independent variable
Dependent variable
Organismic variable
Intervening variable
Control variable
Moderator variable
Nominal scale

Ordinal scale
Interval scale
Ratio scale
Operational definition
Statistical hypothesis
Substantive hypothesis
Directional hypothesis
Nondirectional hypothesis
Research proposal

EXERCISES

2.1 A study is conducted to determine the effects of three sets of instructional materials on fourth-grade reading achievement. Three random samples of fourth-grade boys are selected within the same school. These three groups are then taught by three different teachers, each using one set of instructional materials. At the end of 10 weeks of instruction, the students are tested on reading achievement. Identify the constant(s), independent variable(s), and dependent variable(s) of this study. Identify possible intervening variables that might be operating in this situation.

2.2 Suppose that in the study described in Exercise 2.1, the instructional materials are used with six classes each of fourth- and fifth-graders. Both boys and girls are included. The study is conducted at two different schools, using three classes of each grade level in each school, each class being taught with a different set of materials. Identify the organismic variable(s) and the possible control variable(s) that are now included.

2.3 The problem statement of the study in Exercise 2.2 might be: "A study of the effects of different instructional materials on the reading achievement of fourth- and fifth-graders." Using the variables identified in the first two exercises, develop two or more related hypotheses. The hypotheses may be stated in directional or nondirectional form.

2.4 Two chemistry teachers in a high school are interested in determining whether varying amounts of lab work will affect performance on the theoretical portions of the chemistry exams. With flexible scheduling, students may spend 1, 2, or 3 hours per week in lab work. Develop a statement of the research problem and one or more related hypotheses. Identify the independent variable(s), dependent variable(s), control variables, and intervening variables.

2.5 Classify each of the following variables in terms of type of measurement scale (nominal, ordinal, interval, or ratio):

a. Type of residential dwelling: duplex, single-family residence, multiple apartments.

b. Amount of calcium deposits in the organs of rats that have been subjected to different experimental treatments (assume that organs are removed).

c. Performance on the essay section of an American history test.

d. Ratings assigned by supervisors to the performance of student teachers.

e. Strength of junior high boys on a physical task, as measured in pounds of force by an electronic device.

f. Ethnic background.

g. Socioeconomic level.

2.6 Suppose that a researcher is interested in doing a study on the effects of individualizing instruction on scholastic performance of elementary school students. What terms would require operational definitions? Provide examples of operational definitions for these terms.

2.7 What is the difference between hypotheses stated in a nondirectional or null form and those stated in a directional form?

2.8 From a professional journal, select an article that deals with a research study. Read the article and attempt to identify the statement of the problem and any hypotheses that may be tested in the study. Are the variables explicitly identified, and are operational definitions provided when needed?

NOTES

1. Some writers argue that some, possibly most, test scores are not quite interval scale level but approach such measurement, and that, for research purposes, they can be considered interval scale. In a given situation, the meaning attributed to the measurement should be clearly identified.

2. The use of statistical hypotheses, including the null hypothesis, is discussed in greater detail in Chapter 12.

REFERENCES

Borg, W. R., & Gall, M. D. (1983). *Educational research: An introduction* (4th ed.). New York: Longman.

Ennis, R. H. (1964). Operational definitions. *American Educational Research Journal, 1,* 183–201.

Kerlinger, F. N. (1973). *Foundations of behavioral research* (2nd ed.). New York: Holt, Rinehart & Winston.

Vockell, E. L. (1983). *Educational research.* New York: Macmillan.

3

The Review of the Literature

One of the early activities in the research process is the review of the research literature—the body of research information related to the research problem. After the problem has been identified, at least tentatively, information is needed about the problem so that it can be put in the proper context and the research can proceed effectively.

With the amount of information available from a variety of sources, the review of the literature is by no means a trivial task. It is a systematic process that requires careful and perceptive reading and attention to detail. In the review of the literature, the researcher attempts to determine what others have learned about similar research problems and to gather information relevant to the research problem at hand. This process centers on three questions:

1. Where is the information found?
2. What should be done with information after it has been found?
3. What is made of the information?

The first question deals with the specific sources of written reports or, possibly, reproductions such as microfiche. For most students, these sources can be found in or obtained through the library. Finding the information often involves using reference works such as indexes of periodical literature. Computer searches can also be used to sort through the literature and identify the potentially most useful sources.

The second question deals with how information is assembled and summarized. Assuming that the content of a report is relevant to the research problem under study, the information must be retained in a usable manner.

Dealing with the third question is somewhat more abstract than with the first two questions. To answer the first two questions, the researcher finds information and sets up a procedure for retaining it. Answering the third question requires making a judgment about the information in a research report. What parts of the reported results are relevant to the research problem? How well was the research conducted? Thus, answering the third question requires a somewhat critical analysis of the reports reviewed. Then information from the related reports can be put together.

What is the value of a review of the literature? Besides providing a context for the research study, the review may be useful in any or all of the following:

1. More specifically limiting and identifying the research problem and hypotheses.
2. Informing the researcher of what has already been done in the area.
3. Providing possible research design and methodological procedures that may be used in the research study.
4. Providing suggestions for possible modifications in the research to avoid unanticipated difficulties.
5. Identifying possible gaps in the research.
6. Providing a backdrop for interpreting the results of the research study.

> The review of related literature serves multiple purposes and is essential to a well-designed research study. It generally comes early in the research process, and it can contribute valuable information to any part of the research study.

The Activities of the Review of the Literature

As Figure 1.4 (in Chapter 1) indicated, the existing body of knowledge relative to the research problem provides information for identifying the problem. In that figure, the general activities of conducting a research study were ordered in their most likely sequence of occurrence. The review of the literature itself consists of several specific activities that, to a large extent, also take place in a sequence. These activities, shown in flowchart form in Figure 3.1, are initiated after the research problem has been identified, at least tentatively. The order of activities follows the flow of the arrows in the figure.

Like most activities or steps in a process, there are efficient and inefficient ways to review the literature. Rather than going to the library and haphazardly beginning to take notes, the researcher should follow a systematic process, as represented by the activities in the flowchart. Although even this process may involve some inefficiency in locating sources and reports, efficiency will be enhanced by following the process. Another important procedural point in conducting the activities is, for each activity, to do as complete and accurate an initial job as possible. For example, when a relevant report is located and an abstract is prepared, a complete bibliographic entry for the report should be included. This saves going back later just to complete the bibliography or reference. If a report is relevant enough to include in the review, sufficient information should be obtained from it so that there is no confusion later about what was done (conditions, procedures, individuals involved, etc.) or about the results. Doing the review of literature in the manner suggested not only reduces frustration but saves time.

Figure 3.1
Flowchart of Activities in the Review of the Literature

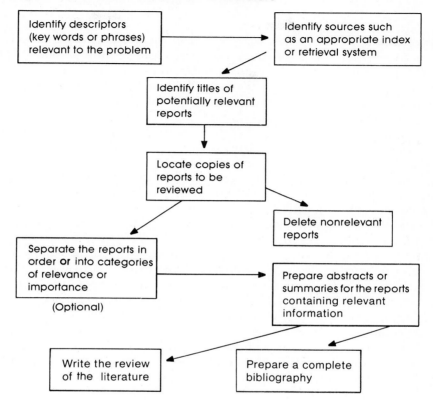

Sources of Information

The library is the most likely physical location for the research literature. There is no scarcity of reports of research studies related to education—published in books, periodicals, technical reports, and academic theses, available either in print or through a library's information retrieval system. This section deals with examples of sources commonly used in educational research.

Periodical Literature

Professional journals and periodicals regularly publish a large volume of research information, although some journals are more oriented to this type of material than others. The periodical indexes available in libraries provide concise and efficient guides to published contents. Of course, not all indexed content is research information, but the researcher may be interested in more that research results, such as discussion of theory. The following are some periodical indexes of particular interest to the educational researcher.

Education Index.   The *Education Index* is one of the most widely used periodical indexes. It covers more than 360 educational periodicals. Published since 1929, *Education Index* is a cumulative author-subject index to educational material in the English language. It is published monthly except July and August. Monthly issues are combined into quarterly issues, which in turn are combined in the annual volume for the year running from September through June. The entries include literature in periodicals, proceedings, yearbooks, bulletins, monographs, and governmental materials on education and education-related topics. The entries are arranged in alphabetical order in a combined author-keyword index. Under many primary keyword headings, such as "Health Education," are alphabetically ordered subheadings such as "Administration" and "curriculum." Under these subject headings are references to the related literature, including title, author, and complete bibliographic information. Author entries list all titles of the author's published works that have appeared since the previous volume of the *Education Index*.

Examples of entries from the *Education Index* are shown in Figure 3.2. The information contained in the entry, including abbreviations, is identified in the legends at the side. The *Education Index* provides only bibliographical information; it does not provide an abstract or summary. In the example in Figure 3.2, "Values" is a subject heading; if the researcher is interested in teaching values, the "Teaching" subheading could be consulted. From the title alone, it is sometimes difficult to judge the potential value of an entry's content to the research study at hand. However, even though all selected entries may not prove valuable when reviewed, the *Education Index* does provide a useful source for a manual search.

Educational Resources Information Center (ERIC).   ERIC is a national information system administered by the U.S. Department of Education. It has a central headquarters, located at the National Institute of Education in Washington, D.C., and currently 16 clearinghouses located throughout the country. The ERIC mandate is to screen, organize, and provide access to educational reports and documents by continual monitoring of the pertinent literature. Each clearinghouse is established for a single, broad topic; for example, the Clearinghouse for Tests, Measurement and Evaluation (TM) is located at Educational Testing Service in Princeton, N.J.

ERIC publishes two useful sources of information, *Resources In Education (RIE)* and *Current Index to Journals in Education (CIJE)*. ERIC tends to be more comprehensive in its coverage than some other abstracting and indexing services. For example, *RIE* includes abstracts of papers presented at conferences and annual meetings and reports of ongoing and completed research and development projects. These papers and reports do not usually appear in periodicals; if they do, it is often some time later. An advantage of *RIE* and *CIJE* over indexes such as the *Education Index* is that they include abstracts or short summaries of the articles or reports. *CIJE* covers approximately 780 major educational and education-related journals.

Figure 3.2
Sample Entries in *Education Index*

Author's Name ──────────────────────→ **Vallance, Elizabeth**
Curriculum as a field of practice. *Yearbook (Assoc Superv Curric Dev)* 1983:154-64 '83
Vallecorsa, Ada L.
Cross-categorical resource programs: an emerging trend in special education. bibl *Education* 104:131-6 Wint '83
Value education *See* Values—Teaching
Value judgments
Value clarification—a tool in developing value-judgment. L. Kremer. bibl *J Instr Psychol* 11:52-8 Mr '84

Subject Heading ──────────────────────→ **Values**
Counseling African children in the United States. K. N. Gbekobou. *Elem Sch Guid Couns* 18:225-30 F '84
Culture and constructs: communicating attitudes and values in the foreign language classroom. C. J. Kramsch. bibl *Foreign Lang Ann* 16:437-48 D '83
Indoctrination and stagnation. J. Colbeck. *Times Higher Educ Suppl* 587:14 F 3 '84
The ontology of mention. H. S. Broudy. *Educ Theory* 33:197-8 Summ/Fall '83
Values to live by. J. MacGregor. *J Environ Educ* 15:1-2 Wint '83-'84

Subheading ──────────────────────→ **Teaching**
Justice & peace education. See issues of Momentum (Washington, D.C.)

Illustrations ──────────────────────→ Should the public schools teach values? E. D. Davis. il *Phi Delta Kappan* 65:358-60 Ja '84
Training teachers to deal with values education: a critical look at social studies methods texts. W. B. Stanley. bibl *Soc Stud* 74:242-6 N/D '83
Values education in the public schools. I. B. Gluckman. *NASSP Bull* 68:98-104 Mr '84
Teaching methods
The effects of values clarification exercises on the value structure of junior high school students. H. E. A. Tinsley and others. bibl *Vocat Guid Q* 32:160-7 Mr '84
Evaluation
Value clarification—a tool in developing value-judgment. L. Kremer. bibl *J Instr Psychol* 11:52-8 Mr '84
Tests and scales
See also

Cross Reference ──────────────────────→ Rokeach value survey
Study of values (Test)
Work values inventory

Bibliography ──────────────────────→ The effects of values clarification exercises on the value structure of junior high school students. H. E. A. Tinsley and others. bibl *Vocat Guid Q* 32:160-7 Mr '84

Source: *Education Index*, 55 (June 1984), 509 (H. H. Wilson Co., Bronx, NY). (Taken from the paperback monthly edition.)

To illustrate the use of the ERIC system, we will use sample entries from *CIJE* and *RIE* relevant to the following research problem:

The effects of microcomputers used in mathematics instruction at the secondary level.

Thesaurus of ERIC Descriptors.   To gain entry to the ERIC system, it is necessary to use the subject headings of *CIJE* and *RIE*. These headings are listed in the *Thesaurus of ERIC Descriptors;* the 10th edition, published in 1984, contains 9,076 descriptors. The *Thesaurus* also contains an extensive description of the ERIC system.

One of the broad descriptors related to the sample problem is "microcomputers"; the entry for this descriptor in the *Thesaurus* is shown in Figure 3.3. Abbreviations and other information are indicated in the figure. The abbreviations in the left-hand column have the following meanings:

SN (Scope Note): A brief statement of the intended uses of the descriptor; for example, there may be restricted usage of a term.

UF (Used For): Terms following UF are *not* to be used in indexing. They represent terms that are synonymous or variant terms of the main descriptor or specific terms that, for purposes of storage and retrieval, are indexed under a more general term.

BT (Broader Term), RT (Related Term), and NT (Narrower Term): Indicate the hierarchical relationships between classes and subclasses of descriptors. (Note: There are no NTs listed for "Microcomputers.")

Figure 3.3
Sample Descriptors from the *Thesaurus of ERIC Descriptors*

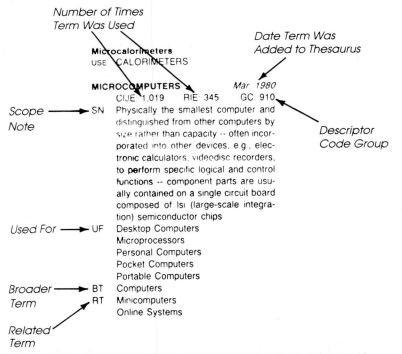

Source: Thesaurus of ERIC Descriptors (10th ed.). Phoenix: Oryx Press, 1984, p. 164.

The postings note at the top gives the numbers of times the descriptor was used in *CIJE* and *RIE*.

Other broad descriptors also apply to the sample research problem—for example, "Mathematics Education," "Secondary Education," and "mathematics curriculum." Because of their breadth, any of these descriptors would undoubtedly produce a large number of references. Therefore, the researcher would search on a combination of descriptors, such as "Microcomputer—Mathematics Instruction," so that the references located would simultaneously contain both descriptors. Three or more descriptors could be used; the researcher must make a judgment about the limits of the search. For example, a combination of three descriptors such as "Microcomputers—Mathematics Instruction—Secondary School Mathematics" could be used so that all three descriptors would have to appear in a reference before it would be identified. As the number of descriptors used simultaneously increases, the likelihood increases that the researcher will miss a reference that has peripheral relevance to the problem. For the purposes of the example, suppose that "Microcomputers—Mathematics Instruction" are used as simultaneous descriptors. The sample entries shown in Figures 3.4 and 3.5 would be identified using these descriptors.

Figure 3.4
Sample Entry from *CIJE*

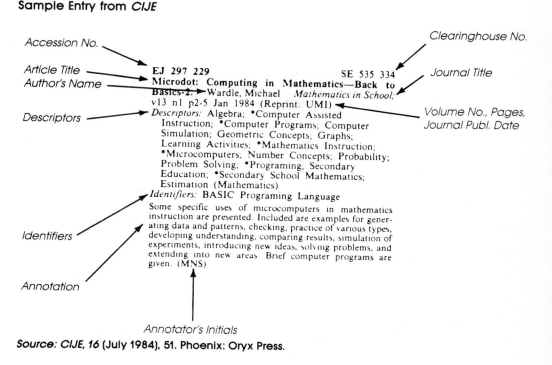

Source: *CIJE, 16* (July 1984), 51. Phoenix: Oryx Press.

Figure 3.5
Sample Entry from *RIE*

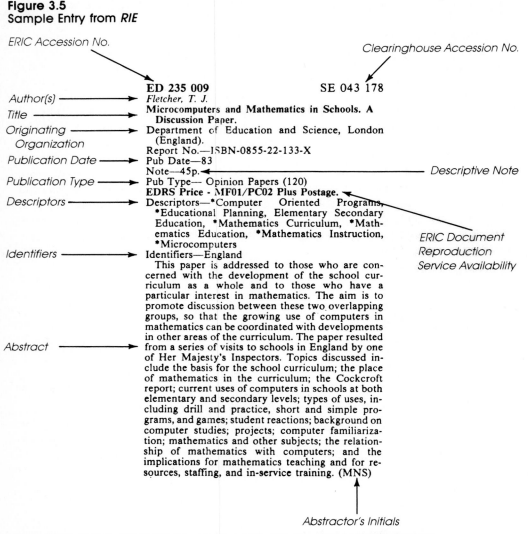

ERIC Accession No.

Clearinghouse Accession No.

Author(s)

Title

Originating
    Organization

Publication Date

Publication Type

Descriptors

Identifiers

Abstract

ED 235 009   SE 043 178
Fletcher, T. J.
**Microcomputers and Mathematics in Schools. A
    Discussion Paper.**
Department of Education and Science, London
    (England).
Report No.—ISBN-0855-22-133-X
Pub Date—83
Note—45p.
Pub Type— Opinion Papers (120)
EDRS Price - MF01/PC02 Plus Postage.
Descriptors—*Computer   Oriented   Programs,
    *Educational Planning, Elementary Secondary
    Education, *Mathematics Curriculum, *Math-
    ematics Education, *Mathematics Instruction,
    *Microcomputers
Identifiers—England
    This paper is addressed to those who are con-
cerned with the development of the school curriculum as a whole and to those who have a
particular interest in mathematics. The aim is to
promote discussion between these two overlapping
groups, so that the growing use of computers in
mathematics can be coordinated with developments
in other areas of the curriculum. The paper resulted
from a series of visits to schools in England by one
of Her Majesty's Inspectors. Topics discussed include the basis for the school curriculum; the place
of mathematics in the curriculum; the Cockcroft
report; current uses of computers in schools at both
elementary and secondary levels; types of uses, including drill and practice, short and simple programs, and games; student reactions; background on
computer studies; projects; computer familiarization; mathematics and other subjects; the relationship of mathematics with computers; and the
implications for mathematics teaching and for resources, staffing, and in-service training. (MNS)

Descriptive Note

ERIC Document
Reproduction
Service Availability

Abstractor's Initials

Source: RIE, 19 (Feb. 1984), 138. Washington, D.C.: U.S. Government Printing Office.

CIJE.   CIJE is an index to periodical literature that is published monthly, with semi-annual cumulations published every 6 months. It contains a subject index, a main entry index, and an author index. The researcher would go to the subject index using the descriptors, identify potential references, and then go to the main entry section, which contains the information necessary to make a decision about the relevance of the references identified. Figure 3.4 shows an entry from the main entry section that is relevant to the sample research problem. Most of the information is straightforward. The accession number is an identification number assigned by ERIC as documents are processed (EJ stands for educational journal). *Descriptors* are the terms used by ERIC; *identifiers* are additional terms that are not found in the *Thesaurus of ERIC Descriptors*. The *clearinghouse number* identifies the clearinghouse through which the document entered ERIC (SE designates Science, Mathematics and Environmental Education Clearinghouse). The *annotation* contains an abstract of the article; on the basis of the abstract, the researcher can decide whether or not to obtain a complete copy of the reference, either in hard copy (HC) or microfiche (MC).

The author index would be used if the researcher is interested in any other publications by a particular author. Entries in the author index contain the author's name, the article title, and the accession number.

RIE.   Like *CIJE, RIE* is published monthly, and it too has semiannual index volumes for previous years. In searching for information, descriptors from the *Thesaurus of ERIC Descriptors* are used in the subject index of *RIE*. The subject index contains the reference information and the accession numbers, or ED numbers (ED stands for education document). When a potentially relevant entry is found, the ED number can be used to locate the entry in the document resumes of the document section. A sample entry from the document resumes, shown in Figure 3.5, is relevant to the sample research problem.

The *descriptive note* in this entry gives only the number of pages, but it might also contain other information, such as the date and location of a paper presented at a conference. The MF and PC after EDRS Price indicate that the document is available in both microfiche and reproduced paper copy. Prices are not given, because they are subject to change; however, the latest price list can be obtained in the most recent issue of *RIE*. Of course, the abstract is of primary interest, since a decision about whether or not to pursue the reference would be based on the abstract's content.

If a researcher desires the complete document, it can be ordered through the ERIC Document Reproduction Service; the address of the service and the price list are given in the latest issue of *RIE*. A document needed quickly can be provided by computer systems available at most universities. The document can be ordered on microfiche (MC) or hard copy (HC). Microfiche is usually less costly and it is smaller, of course, but it requires a special microfiche reader, which is available at most universities. University libraries often have collections of ERIC microfiches, in which case documents may be available immediately.

ERIC has published *CIJE* since 1969 and *RIE* since 1966. Therefore, there is a limitation on how far back a researcher can go in searching these sources. The *Education Index* can be used as far back as the researcher desires.

Other Indexes and Abstracts.   Numerous other indexes and abstracts reference documents about educational research, in related disciplines or in particular areas of education. An example from a related discipline is *Psychological Abstracts (PA),* a bimonthly publication that contains abstracts of reports or articles in more than 950 journals, technical reports, monographs, and scientific documents. Many of the periodicals from which articles are abstracted for *PA* are educational journals. Biannual issues of *PA,* with author and subject indexes, are published for the 6-month periods January–June and July–December.

An example from an educational area is *Exceptional Child Education Resources (ECER),* published quarterly by the Council for Exceptional Children, which reviews more than 200 periodicals for information on exceptional children. The format for indexing in *ECER* is similar to that used in *CIJE.* Custom computer searches are also available; included in the computer search is an abstract of about 200 words.

Abstracts and indexes of other professions often contain educational information. For example, *Crime and Penology Abstracts* references current research into school violence, school vandalism, and school absence. The *Nursing Index* contains references to research into school health, diet, and nutrition, which have implications for education.

Indexes and abstracts are available in almost all university libraries, and the procedures for using them are very much the same. The introduction to an index usually contains detailed information about availability and costs of documents and addresses for obtaining information. Detailed information is also provided about codes used in the entries and about how to locate references.

Review of Educational Research (RER).   The *RER,* issued quarterly by the American Education Research Association, publishes critical integrative reviews of research literature bearing on education. From its inception in 1931 through 1969, each issue of the *RER* contained solicited papers organized around a single educational topic or subdivision, such as "Educational and Psychological Testing." Topics were reviewed in 3-year cycles; more active topics were reviewed every cycle, less active ones on alternate cycles.

Beginning with Volume 40 (June 1970), the *RER* has published unsolicited reviews of research on topics of the reviewer's own choosing. The papers in both the pre-1970 and post-1970 issues include excellent bibliographies that contain many references to the educational research literature. As an example of topics covered, the reviews that appeared in the Summer 1984 issue (Volume 54) were as follows:

"Perceived Problems of Beginning Teachers"

"Alternative Conceptions of Intelligence and Their Implications for Education"

"The Effects of Nonpromotion on Elementary and Junior High School Pupils: A Meta-Analysis"

"The Use of High-Inference Measures to Study Classroom Climates: A Review"

"Three Ideological Orientations in School Vandalism Research"

Issues of the *RER* are very useful to researchers who want to locate a quantity of research literature on a broad research topic without conducting an initial search. Reviews are helpful, but they do cover broad topics. As usual, the researcher must go through the content and retain information that is relevant to the research problem at hand. Other disciplines related to education also have their own reviews or review journals; an example is the *Annual Review of Psychology*.

Abstracts and Reports in Periodicals.

Numerous periodicals are devoted almost exclusively to abstracts or reviews. Some of them are in the academic disciplines, and others are in professional education. Any university library will have at least some of these periodicals on hand and in most cases, can provide access to all of them. Examples of such periodicals are as follows:

> *Sociological Abstracts,* published 1952–
>
> *Child Development Abstracts and Bibliography,* published 1927–
>
> *Biological Abstracts,* published 1926–
>
> *Educational Administration Abstracts,* published 1922–

These periodicals include, but are not limited to, abstracts of articles dealing with research.

There are also many periodicals in education-related disciplines and in professional education that contain research articles, some of them more so than others. It would be impractical to present a comprehensive listing of such periodicals, but a representative sampling is as follows:

> *American Education Research Journal* (Washington, DC: American Educational Research Association)
>
> *Anthropology and Education Quarterly* (Washington, DC: Council on Anthropology and Education)
>
> *British Journal of Educational Psychology* (London: British Psychological Society)
>
> *British Journal of Educational Studies* (London: Faber & Faber)
>
> *California Journal of Educational Research* (Burlingame, CA: California Teachers Association)
>
> *Canadian Education and Research Digest* (Toronto: Canadian Education Association)
>
> *Educational and Psychological Measurement* (Durham, NC: Copyright by Frederic Kuder)
>
> *Florida Journal of Educational Research* (Tallahassee: Florida Educational Association)
>
> *Journal of Educational Measurement* (Washington, DC: National Council on Measurement in Education)
>
> *Journal of Educational Psychology* (Washington, DC: American Psychological Association)
>
> *Journal of Educational Research* (Washington, DC: HELDREF Publications)

Journal of Educational Sociology (New York University; New York: Payne Educational Sociology Foundation)

Journal of Experimental Education (Washington, DC: HELDREF Publications)

Journal of Experimental Psychology (Washington, DC: American Psychological Association)

Journal of Research in Science Teaching (National Association for Research in Science Teaching and Association for the Education of Teachers in Science; New York: Wiley)

Louisiana Education Research Journal (Natchitoches: Louisiana Education Research Association)

Measurement and Evaluation in Guidance (Washington, DC: Association for Measurement and Evaluation in Guidance, a division of the American Personnel and Guidance Association)

NEA Research Bulletin (Washington, DC: National Education Association)

Psychological Bulletin (Washington, DC: American Psychological Association)

Psychological Review (Washington, DC: American Psychological Association)

School Science and Mathematics (Tempe, AZ: School Science and Mathematics Association)

The Research Quarterly (Washington, DC: American Association for Health, Physical Education, and Recreation)

Theses and Dissertations

Theses and dissertations prepared to meet the requirements for graduate degrees usually contain descriptions of completed research. The library of a university usually contains copies of theses completed at that university. To obtain information about dissertations completed at other universities, the most widely used comprehensive source is *Dissertation Abstracts* and its related services.

Dissertation Abstracts was renamed *Dissertation Abstracts International (DAI)* beginning with Volume 30, No. 1 (1969). *DAI* is a reference tool that provides a monthly compilation of abstracts of doctoral dissertations submitted to University Microfilms International (Ann Arbor, Michigan) by more than 450 universities and institutions in North America and Europe. There are two broad sections under which dissertations are abstracted: Humanities (A) and Sciences (B). There is also a third section, European Abstracts.

Beginning with Volume 30 and ending with Volume 33, each section was cumulated annually by keyword title index and author index. Starting with Volume 34, only author indexes are cumulated annually. From Volume 36 on, each section is divided into five main parts, as follows:

Humanities
  IA. Communications and the Arts
 IIA. Education
IIIA. Language, Literature, and Linguistics
 IVA. Philosophy, Religion, and Theology
  VA. Social Sciences

Sciences
  IB. Biological Sciences
 IIB. Earth Sciences
IIIB. Health and Environmental Sciences
 IVB. Physical Sciences
  VB. Psychology

Each main part is divided into numerous subject categories, the names of which are given at the beginning of each volume. Education has 38 subject categories, including, for example, "Early Childhood."

   If a researcher were doing research about writing at the college level, the keyword title index would be entered, using "Writing" as the keyword. Keywords are printed in alphabetical order, followed by the titles in which they occur. Of course, keywords may be used in combination. An example of three entries in the keyword title index is shown in Figure 3.6. Following up on the middle entry, the dissertation by Reavley, Figure 3.7 shows the entry (abstract) from the document resumes section.

Figure 3.6
Sample Entry from Keyword Title Index, *DAI*

Source: DAI, 45 (Aug. 1984), 147.

Figure 3.7
Sample Entry of an Abstract from Document Resumes Section, *DAI*

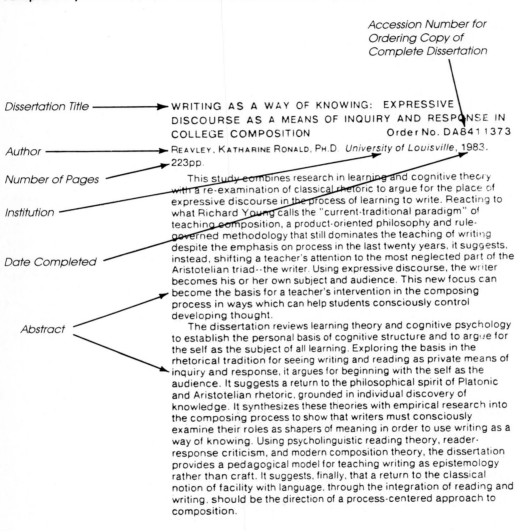

Source: DAI, 45 (Aug. 1984), 442-A.

If the search goes back to Volume 29 or earlier, the researcher can use the *DAI Retrospective Index,* which contains bibliographic references in nine subject volumes for *DAI* Volumes 1–29. The nine subject volumes are as follows:

Volume I: Mathematics and Physics

Volume II: Chemistry

Volume III: Earth/Life Sciences

Volume IV: Psychology/Sociology/Political Science

Volume V: Social Sciences

Volume VI: Engineering

Volume VII: Education

Volume VIII: Communication/Information/Business/Literature/Fine Arts

Volume IX: Author Index

The *DAI Retrospective Index* would be used for a broad area or subject of interest, such as Education, Volume VII. The table of contents of the volume enables the researcher to narrow the scope of search to specific subheadings—for example, "Health, Vol. VII, part 2, page 1391." Under the subheading of "Health Education," the principal words in the title are used as keywords, arranged in alphabetical order in columns. If the area of research involves evaluation of health attitudes, the keywords to search for are "Evaluation," "Health," and "Attitudes."

As an example of a search under the keyword "Attitudes," the following dissertation reference would appear:

Attitudes
   The Evaluation of Attitudes toward Selected Areas of School Health Education—Moore, Oscar A. BOSU 18/03/920

24782

The dissertation reference contains the complete dissertation title, followed by a dash before the author's name. The abbreviation following the author's name indicates the cooperating university or college at which the dissertation was completed (in this case, BOSU for Boston University). This is followed by a reference to the volume, issue, and page number of the abstract. The number in the far right column represents the publication or order number by which a xerographic or microfiche copy of the complete dissertation can be requested. Complete copies of dissertations may be obtained from University Microfilms International, Ann Arbor, Michigan.

Selected Books

The host of books dealing with research—both education and education-related research—can be located through various bibliographies, reviews, book indexes, and so on. It would be impossible, of course, to provide a comprehensive listing of books that partially or entirely deal with educational research; three publications are briefly described here because they are comprehensive and can be especially useful to the educational researcher.

The Encyclopedia of Educational Research (EER).   The publication of the *EER* is a project of the American Educational Research Association that represents a compendium of research covering five major issues in education. Five editions of the *EER* have been published, the most recent in 1982. The original edition appeared in 1941, with subsequent editions at approximately 10-year intervals.

The *EER* does not simply catalogue the research that has been done; each article provides critical evaluation, synthesis, and interpretation of much of the literature in educational research, as well as a relatively extensive bibliography. Each edition has more than 150 articles, written by noted educators who are familiar with the literature and research in their chosen topics. The most recent edition of the *EER* (the fifth) was edited by H. E. Mitzel and published by the Free Press, New York.

Handbook of Research on Teaching.   There are three *Handbooks of Research on Teaching;* the first two were published by Rand McNally and Company (Skokie, IL), and the third was published by Macmillan Publishing Company (New York, NY). The preparation of the handbooks has been a project of the American Educational Research Association. The original was edited by N. L. Gage and published in 1963; the second, edited by R. M. W. Travers, was published in 1973; and the third, edited by M. C. Wittrock, was published in 1985. Both the second and third handbooks are original volumes, not subsequent revisions of the first.

The handbooks contain comprehensive presentations of research on teaching, including higher education and the teaching of subject matter. A variety of topics are given in-depth coverage in all three volumes, which are large and comprehensive; the first contains 23 chapters, the second, 42 chapters, and the third, 35 chapters. Not only is the content valuable to educational researchers, but each chapter has an extensive bibliography of references (in some cases, over 200 entries). The bibliographies themselves represent extensive searches of the research literature.

Review of Research in Education.   This is a publication of the American Educational Research Association (AERA); some of the early issues were published in cooperation with F. E. Peacock Publishers, Itasca, Illinois. The purpose of the *Review of Research in Education* is to survey disciplined inquiry in education through critical and synthesizing essays. Each of the essays, written by an author selected for expertise in that area, represents an attempt to appraise, evaluate, and criticize the more recent important empirical studies in the area.

The first volume of the *Review* was published in 1973, and it has been published yearly since then. Varied topics from the field of education are covered, with more important topics reviewed more often than others. As an example, the topics considered in Volume 11 (1984) were as follows:

Section I. Education and Human Variance

Section II. Education and Ecology of Human Development

Section III. Methodological Issues and Trends in Knowledge Production and Transformation

To a large extent, the *Review* replaces the pre-1970 editions of the *Review of Educational Research,* which was described earlier in this chapter. Indeed, the *Review of Research in Education* was initiated by AERA to fill the void left by the *Review of Educational Research* when it adopted its new editorial policy of publishing unsolicited manuscripts on a variety of topics.

The *Review* is intended to be a source of information that highlights the strengths and weaknesses in educational research and provides direction for future research in the areas discussed. Although it is intended only secondarily to serve as a bibliographic reference source, it does contain a wealth of information and detailed reference lists with each article.

This section has presented several different sources of research information. Any difficulties encountered at this stage of a literature review are usually due not to lack of information, but to an inability to find the relevant references. Because there is such a large quantity of educational research information, it is important to conduct a systematic search, using the indexes, retrieval systems, reviews, and so forth, that are available.

Conducting A Computer Search

Computer-assisted searches of the literature are available through almost all university libraries, many public libraries and state departments of education, and some school systems. A number of databases are available that contain educational research information. Probably the most frequently used database for education is the ERIC database, which can be searched by computer back through 1966. There are also databases in selected areas of education, such as the Bilingual and Bicultural Education Database, and related databases are available, such as Psychological Abstracts and Social Science Citation Index. Many university libraries have more than 200 bibliographic databases across all academic and professional areas that can be computer-searched. Thus, computer searches make available the maximum reservoir of information on a topic.

There are numerous advantages to a computer search; two obvious ones are comprehensiveness and speed. Descriptors can be used in "and" and "or" combinations, which can pinpoint or broaden the search as desired. Multiple databases can be searched, and bibliographic citations and complete citations with abstracts can be obtained. Finally, although a computer-assisted search may cost up to $50 (a more typical charge is in the $15–$30 range, and some may be free-of-charge), it is highly cost-effective in terms of time and effort.

A computer search is conducted with the assistance of someone at the library who inputs the information through the computer terminal, monitors the search as necessary, and receives the printouts of the citations. However, a search does require planning so that it can be properly focused. An example research problem will be used here to illustrate the steps in the search.

Identifying the Research Problem and the Extent of Search

The research problem should be stated in specific terms so that the problem is focused and so that descriptors can be identified for the search. If a problem is too broad, an excessively large number of references may be identified, many of which will be irrelevant to the problem. If an exhaustive search is done, as would be the case for a dissertation, the problem would be narrowed. For the review of a journal article, the researcher might request only 15 or 20 most recent references. The researcher has some flexibility in the extent of the search. If too many references appear, the search can be narrowed; if too few appear, it can be broadened through the use of descriptors. For the example, the research problem will be stated as follows:

> *A study of measures of teacher effectiveness obtained through observation.*

Selecting a Database

As indicated earlier, many databases are available. More than one database may be used, but descriptors must be applicable for the specific database. Of course, there is overlap among the descriptors of databases, and it is also possible to use certain descriptors for one database and other descriptors for another database. Related literature for most educational research problems is found in the ERIC database, *CIJE* and *RIE*. The ERIC database is used for the example.

Selecting and Combining Descriptors

Descriptors are the search words used for telling the computer what to look for. Since the ERIC database is being used, descriptors are selected from the *Thesaurus of ERIC Descriptors*. Descriptors are used in combintions to broaden or narrow the search. The connecting words are "and" and "or." They can be used singly or in combination in the search.

Using the connector "and" between descriptors narrows the search, because all references must contain *all* terms so connected. The connector "or" broadens the search because references containing *any* of the descriptors will appear. For the example, we use "Teacher Effectiveness" and "Observation" as descriptors. If we connect them with "or," we would obtain all references that contain either one or both descriptors. This would give us a very large number of references, many of which would be irrelevant. If we connect the descriptors with "and," a reference must contain both descriptors. This would greatly reduce the number of references.

The relative volume of references using the two connectors is indicated by the shaded area in the two parts of Figure 3.8.

Before conducting the search using the "and" connector, as indicated in the lower part of Figure 3.8, we must consider that terms such as *teacher competence* and *teacher performance* are sometimes used instead of *teacher effectiveness*. *Teacher competence* and *teacher performance* are not descriptors in the ERIC system, but "Competence" and "Performance" are. Using these terms singly is not feasible, however, because the number of references would be overwhelming. We can instruct the computer to search for "Teacher" with "Competence" *adjacent* (ADJ) to it and do the same for "Teacher" and "Performance." For the search, these descriptors are combined with

Figure 3.8
Relative Volumes of References (shaded area) Using Connectors for Combining Descriptors

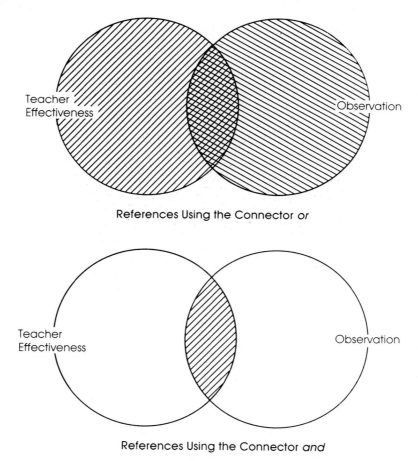

References Using the Connector *or*

References Using the Connector *and*

"Observation," using the connector "and." These combinations narrow the search considerably, as shown in Figure 3.9.

> Descriptors can be used in combinations with the connectors "or" and "and" to broaden or limit the search.

Searching the Database for Number of References

When the descriptors are input through the computer terminal, numbers of references appear to assist in deciding how to broaden or narrow the search. Figure 3.10 shows this numerical information, which is interpreted as follows.

1. "Teacher Effectiveness" yields 6,764 references.
2–4. "Teacher ADJ Competence," "Teacher ADJ Peer," and "Teacher ADJ Per-

Figure 3.9
The Combination of Descriptors for the Example

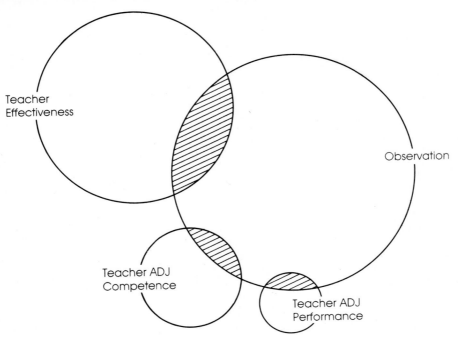

Figure 3.10
Computer Printout Indicating Numbers of References for Descriptors and Combinations of Descriptors

```
BRS - SEARCH MODE - ENTER QUERY
     1_:          TEACHER-EFFECTIVENESS
     RESULT          6764

     2_:          TEACHER ADJ COMPETENCE
     RESULT          151

     3_:          TEACHER ADJ PEER
     RESULT          55

     4_:          TEACHER ADJ PERFORMANCE
     RESULT          1718

     5_:          1 2 4
     RESULT          7953

     6_:          OBSERVATION
     RESULT          7856

     7_:          5 AND 6
     RESULT          581

     8_:          OBSERVATION.MJ.
     RESULT          607

     9_:          5 AND 8
     RESULT          17
```

formance" (ADJ means adjacent to) are inserted, yielding the numbers indicated. It is decided to delete "Teacher ADJ Peer" because of the small number of references.

5. The combination of Results 1, 2, and 4 of the computer printout gives 7,953 references. This is Result 5, references that contain "Teacher Effectiveness" *or* "Teacher ADJ Competence" *or* "Teacher ADJ Performance." Note that 7,953 is not a total of the numbers in Results 1, 2, and 4 because some references are contained in two or all three of these results.

6. "Observation" by itself yields 7,856 references.

7. Combining Result 5 and Result 6 gives 581 references (Result 7). These 581 references are based on descriptors combined as "Teacher Effectiveness" *or* "Teacher ADJ Competence" *or* "Teacher ADJ Performance" *and* "Observation."

8. To limit or narrow the search further, it is decided to include observation as a major descriptor (designated by MJ). This means that in the initial indexing of the article or document, it was classified under the term "Observation," rather

than simply having the word appear in the document. This reduces the number from 7,856 to 607.

9. Finally, combining Result 5 and Result 8, we have 17 references. The same descriptors are used as for 7, except "Observation" is included in its more restricted form.

Obtaining the Desired Abstracts

At this point, we could ask for a listing of the references or we could obtain abstracts of the 17 references. Figure 3.11 shows an abstract produced by the computer. References can be obtained in the usual manner, as desired—for example, on microfiche.

Broadening the Search, If Necessary

The example search was very narrow, producing only 17 references from 1966 to the time the search was done. (The ERIC system was computerized in 1966.) If a researcher decided that 17 references were not enough, the search could be broadened by reverting to "Observation" as a descriptor (rather than a major descriptor), as in Result 7. This would yield an additional 564 references (581 minus the 17 identified by the narrower search). But we do not want so many references. Suppose that we designate 30 references. We could keep the original 17 obtained from the narrower search and instruct the computer to add the 13 most recent references. This would give us a total of 30 references.

A computer search is generally an efficient approach to identifying relevant references. It is not necessary to know how to operate the terminal; assistance will

Figure 3.11
Sample Abstract from a Computer Search of the ERIC Database

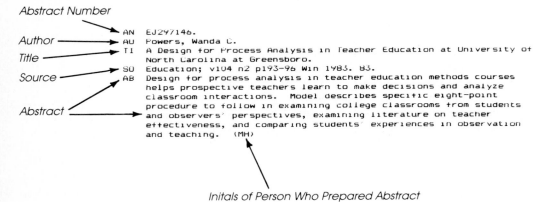

be provided by someone at the library. Various combinations of descriptors can be used to get some idea of the numbers of references available and whether or not they will be relevant. The available databases undoubtedly have something relevant to any educational research problem. There are limitations, however, to when indexes were computerized, and earlier references will have to be searched manually. Some indexes have been computerized for 20 years or more. When the printouts of abstracts become available, the researcher must still make a decision about the relevance of the reference and about whether or not to obtain a copy.

Assembling and Summarizing Information

After locating and reviewing the references from the literature search, the researcher must consider the question, "What should I do with the information?" The initial decision is to determine whether or not the content of the report (article, etc.) is relevant to the research problem under study. If it is not relevant, it can be deleted; if it is relevant, the information it contains must be summarized or somehow put into a usable form so that it is retrievable when the researcher needs it. In Figure 3.1, the separation of reports in order of importance was indicated as an optional activity. Sometimes it may be difficult to do this, because the distinctions between levels of importance may not be clear. Therefore, this activity may be omitted or it may be done after the abstracts or summaries have been prepared.

There are many formats or information recording procedures that can be used to assemble information from reported studies. Most researchers develop systems that seem to work well for them. For example, a straightforward note-taking procedure can be used. Regardless of the specific procedure used, it is best to use a systematic approach so that information is recorded consistently and important components are not omitted. Some formats and procedures are suggested here.

Bibliographic Entry

A complete and accurate bibliographic entry should be made for each relevant report reviewed. This entry is usually part of an abstract or summary; for quick reference, however, it may be best to place the bibliographic entry on a 3 × 5 card. If for no other purpose, such cards are useful for compiling a complete bibliography when the review of the literature is completed. The cards can be put in alphabetical order by the last names of the authors.

Bibliographic entries can be prepared as shown in Figure 3.12. Since it is not usually possible to carry a typewriter around in the library, most entries are handwritten, although they may be typed later if this is desired. If the entry is run together on consecutive lines, the title of an article should be in quotation marks.

A bibliographic entry contains the following information: the name(s) of the author(s), the title of the report (article, book, etc.), facts about publication, and, if an article is in a periodical, the inclusive page numbers. Facts about publication

Figure 3.12
Sample Bibliography Card

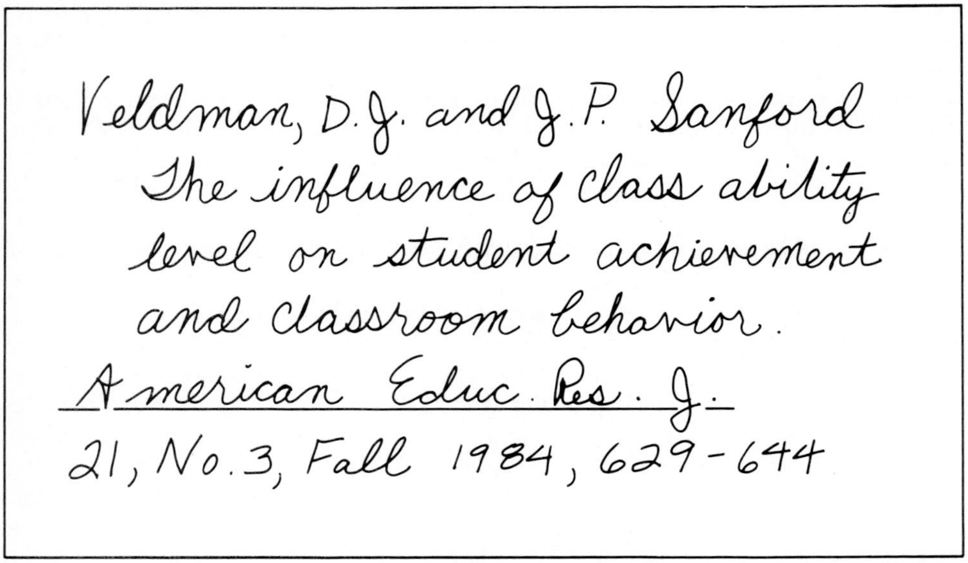

> Veldman, D. J. and J. P. Sanford
> The influence of class ability
> level on student achievement
> and classroom behavior.
> American Educ. Res. J.
> 21, No. 3, Fall 1984, 629-644

include the place, publisher, and date for a book, or the volume number and date of the periodical for an article. Titles of books, reports, and periodicals are underlined.

Whenever information from a report is to be used, a complete and accurate bibliographic entry should be made at the start. This saves time and possible confusion. It is frustrating to have to look up a report again just because the bibliographic entry is not complete.

Abstract or Summary

A researcher who is reviewing the literature is faced with extracting the information from relevant reports and summarizing this information in a usable form. To use research results effectively—that is, to fit them into the context of the research problem—considerable information must be obtained from the report. For example, it is usually necessary to know something about the conditions under which the results were obtained. The problem of the reported research should be known, so that it can be related to the research problem under study. Thus, as the report is being reviewed, judgments must be made about which information will be retained—that is, written down.

Rather than just taking notes on research reports, the researcher usually uses some form of abstracting. An *abstract* is a summary of a research report that contains certain kinds of information. The form of the information should be consistent across the reports reviewed. There are slight variations among the components of an abstract suggested by different authors, but generally some form of the following are included:

> *Bibliographic Entry:* An accurate and complete bibliographic entry heads the abstract.
>
> *Problem:* This is a statement of the research problem of the report being reviewed; it may include statements of hypotheses.
>
> *Subjects:* The individuals involved in research studies are often called "subjects" of the research; for example, "50 college sophomores enrolled in elementary education, 25 males and 25 females."
>
> *Procedures:* This section describes how the research was conducted. It includes such items as the measurements used and the analyses performed. This section may also be called "Methodology."
>
> *Results and Conclusions:* This section identifies the relevant results and conclusions of the study. A distinction may be made between results and conclusions—results being whatever occurred, such as certain statistics; conclusions being what the researcher has made of the results. In long reports with many results and conclusions, it is best to number them.

An *abstract* is a summary that contains the relevant information from a research report according to specified categories.

The length of an abstract must always be considered, because it is not efficient to retain the entire report. Many journals publish a very brief abstract at the beginning of each report. However, this abstract is limited in length and is usually not sufficient for the researcher's purpose. The abstract developed by the researcher should be somewhere between these two extremes.

When abstracting a report, the researcher attempts to condense the relevant information as briefly as possible while including all the necessary details. Although the abstract should be brief, the importance of having all necessary information must be emphasized. It is frustrating and inefficient to find that the information in an abstract is incomplete and that it is necessary to search out the report again. A number of factors affect the length of the abstract, including the length of the report, the complexity of the research, and the extensiveness of the findings. Some authors suggest limiting abstracts to a single page or to material that can be placed on a 5 × 8 card. There is some merit to these suggestions, since they facilitate manipulation of the reference information, but it may be difficult to stay within such strict space limitations. The content of the abstract should be as brief as possible, but including all necessary information will usually result in abstracts of varying length when several reports are abstracted.

The two sample abstracts in Figures 3.13 and 3.14 illustrate different abstract lengths. The first is an abstract of a 9-page article and the second is from a 16-page article. Although the length of the report does influence the length of the abstract, it is not the only determining factor. The number of conclusions drawn, the complexity of the research, and the extent of relevance to the research study at hand also affect the abstract's length.

Figure 3.13
Sample Abstract (Shorter Form)

Yager, R. E. and R. J. Bonnstetter, "Student Perceptions of Science Teachers, Classes and Course Content," *School Science and Mathematics,* 84, No. 5, May–June, 1984, 406–414.

Problem: To determine the perceptions of students of various ages and young adults toward factors of their science instruction.

Subjects: Approximately 700 (total) Iowa students and young adults at ages 9, 13, 17 and (24–35) years old. Data from a comparison, national sample of 2,500 from the National Assessment of Educational Progress (NAEP) study were also used.

Procedure: Subjects were surveyed in 1982 using an affective inventory including 13 items that were common to the inventory used in the 1977 NAEP study. Science consultants in Area Educational Agencies of Iowa were used for data collection. Responses to individual items were summarized using percentages, and compared to patterns of responses found in the 1977 NAEP study.

Results and Conclusions: Results of the 1982 survey in Iowa and those of the NAEP study were highly consistent. Almost one-half of elementary-level teachers admit to not knowing answers to student questions, yet as students get older, decreasing percentages of students indicate that teachers make science exciting (68, 56, 45, 34 percent of the four age groups in order). It appears that as teachers become more knowledgeable in science, they are less successful in making it exciting to their students. As students advance through the grades, there are substantial drops in the percentages that find science to be fun, interesting, or fulfilling. The lowest percentages (around 30%) were found among the young adults. Perceptions of the usefulness of course content, now and in the future, drop somewhat as students get older, but the big decline is between 17-year-olds and young adults.

Figure 3.14
Sample Abstract (Longer Form)

Veldman, D. J. and J. P. Sanford, "The influence of class ability level of student achievement and classroom behavior," *American Educational Research Journal,* 21, No. 9, Fall 1984, 629–644.

Problem: The research problem was posed in three questions:
    (1) Are the classroom behaviors and achievement levels of students systematically different among classes of higher and lower ability?
    (2) Within classes, are the behaviors of higher- and lower-ability students systematically different?
    (3) Does student ability level interact with the ability level of the class to affect systematically students' classroom behavior and achievement?

Subjects: Junior high school students (grades 7 and 8) from 58 mathematics and 78 English classes (located in Texas); approximately 500 in math and 650 in English.

Procedures: An ex post facto study; achievement measures in math and English were analyzed along with 25 high-inference ratings of students by observers and 25 low-inference measures of teacher and student behaviors; regression models (equations) were developed (math and English separately) to determine the contributions of grade, class mean ability, student ability, and class ability by student ability interaction; criterion variables were class mean or student, achievement or behavior measure.

Results: A. For student achievement
    (1) High-ability students performed better than low-ability students in both math and English (certainly expected).
    (2) Interaction effects (for class ability by student ability) for both math and English; in math, membership in a high-ability class has more impact on low-ability than high-ability students; in English, the same pattern only stronger.

  B. For classroom behaviors, observer ratings
    (1) For 25 observer ratings of students, 14 showed significant relationships with class and pupil-within-class ability levels in both math and English; these ratings reflected behaviors associated with work habits, motivation, persistence, self-confidence, dependability, academic leadership, and class participation, for which higher-ability classes and students had higher ratings, correspondingly higher-ability classes and students had lower ratings on student behavior problems, aggression, profane language, and academic dependence; no significant class or student effects for ratings on extroversion, interaction with the teacher, physical maturity, unhappiness, cooperation, and frequent talking to neighbors.
    (2) For interactions, math had 8 variables, English, 4, with only 3

common to both; generally class ability level has more impact on the behavior of low-ability students than on high-ability students, placing low-ability students with high-ability students tends to have a positive impact on behavior of low-ability students.

C. For classroom process variables
   (1) High-ability classes have fewer procedural contacts, less misbehavior, and fewer call outs.
   (2) High-ability students were given more response opportunities, gave more correct and fewer answers, had fewer adverse teacher contacts, and less misbehavior.
   (3) Four of the five interactions that were significant showed the same patterns in math and English; generally, low-ability students in low-ability classes tended to display more undesirable process behaviors than their counterparts in high-ability classes; in English but not in math, low-ability students showed less misbehavior in high-ability classes.

Each of the sample abstracts has a complete bibliographic entry. The second abstracted article (Figure 3.14) had the research problem stated in the form of three questions, which added to the length of the problem statement. Since the research problem was extensive, a considerable number of results were generated, and the results are separated more explicitly than the results of the first article. For the second article, the results are extensively synthesized. If the results were separated for the three questions, the abstract would be too long.

The abstracts shown in the figures are typed, but when a researcher reviews an article, the abstract is usually written in longhand. It is not necessary to type abstracts. Abstracts are a means to an end, not an end in themselves. They may be written on cards or on regular-sized paper, but the important thing is that they are useful and contain the necessary information. Although formats tend to be similar, there is enough flexibility for researchers to meet their individual needs.

Interpreting and Using Information

The interpretation of results and other information found in research reports begins when the report is being reviewed. It is a good idea first to skim a report to get an overview, without being too concerned with the specifics. From this overview, a decision can usually be made about the relevance of the report to the research problem being studied. Assuming that a report is relevant, the reviewer can then focus on the specifics and begin the abstracting process.

Critical Review

It is well known that there is considerable variability in the quality and comprehensiveness of reports in the educational research literature. Thus, as a researcher reads a report, it is necessary to take a somewhat critical perspective. But how does one read critically? There are certain elements of a report that a researcher can look for; if these elements are missing in any substantial numbers, the report may be suspect. Although a good bit of the burden of communication is on the report writer, the reader is also responsible for having at least some familiarity with the area (not necessarily with the research in the area) and some knowledge of research procedures. Indeed, one of the purposes of studying research methods is to better understand the research literature.

When evaluating a particular report, the researcher can consider many specifics, but as indicated earlier, there are certain elements that should be included in any report. Figure 3.15 is a checklist of 16 general elements, ordered as they would be

Figure 3.15
Checklist for the Elements of a Research Report

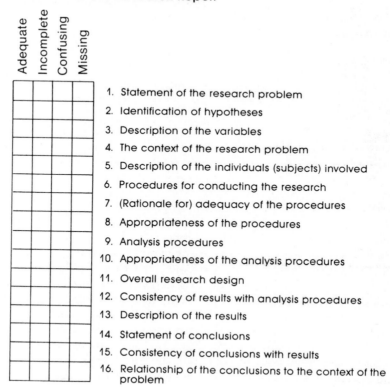

Adequate	Incomplete	Confusing	Missing	
				1. Statement of the research problem
				2. Identification of hypotheses
				3. Description of the variables
				4. The context of the research problem
				5. Description of the individuals (subjects) involved
				6. Procedures for conducting the research
				7. (Rationale for) adequacy of the procedures
				8. Appropriateness of the procedures
				9. Analysis procedures
				10. Appropriateness of the analysis procedures
				11. Overall research design
				12. Consistency of results with analysis procedures
				13. Description of the results
				14. Statement of conclusions
				15. Consistency of conclusions with results
				16. Relationship of the conclusions to the context of the problem

likely to appear in a report. At the left of the checklist, the reviewer can check his/her perception of how well each element is covered. The options "adequate, incomplete, confusing, and missing" are suggested, which essentially mean the following:

Adequate: The element is discussed in a clear, understandable way with nothing essential omitted.

Incomplete: The element is discussed; what there is is clearly stated, but one or more parts are missing.

Confusing: The element is discussed but in a way that is vague or not understandable, and it is difficult to tell whether or not the discussion is complete.

Missing: The element is not discussed

A researcher can use the checklist while reviewing the article. Then, if the report is abstracted, the completed checklist can be attached to the abstract. If there are too many checks in the last three categories, it may be wise to omit the report from the review. The reviewer must decide how many checks are too many. Most reviews can tolerate some checks in the last three columns; for example, the problem may not be stated well, but may become quite clear later in the report. Generally, if more than five or six checks appear in columns other than "adequate," the report becomes suspect. Also, if an entire section, such as procedures or analysis, is missing, the content very likely will not be usable to the researcher, because it will be difficult to fit into the problem under study.

> Reports can be reviewed by using a checklist of elements to consider. In the final analysis, however, the researcher must decide the adequacy, relevance, and usefulness of the information in the report.

Writing the Review

When the researcher has reviewed the reports to be used, or at least a substantial number of them, the information must be synthesized and put in the review of the literature. Now the researcher must decide what to make of the information. The abstracts can be organized according to several factors: the amount of information that bears directly on the research problem, the part of the problem to which the results are relevant (if the problem is complex), and possibly even the recency of publication if the review will follow a chronological order. If there are obvious gaps, it may be necessary to return to the literature and enlarge the search. It is at this point that the researcher uses the abstracts and pieces together the review puzzle.

The length of the review will vary according to the type of research report being prepared. In an article for a professional journal, the review is often limited, possibly to one page; essentially, it sets the context for the research problem and little more. In such situations, the review may contain only six or eight references, sometimes less. (In some articles, only a reference or two is used because of space limitations imposed by the publication.) This does not mean that the researcher has reviewed only two or three reports. Many more may have been reviewed, but only the most relevant ones have been referenced. When a review is being done for an extensive research study, such as a doctoral dissertation, many reports, possibly 50 or more, may be included. In this case, the review of the literature becomes a major task. The written review itself usually contains subheadings, and information from the abstracts is organized according to the subheadings. Such reviews may cover 40 or more typewritten pages.

Regardless of the length of the review, the researcher should, if at all possible, include recent information. This does not mean that older information is not relevant, but the review should be up to date. For example, any review of the research on teacher effectiveness that had no entries more recent than 10 years ago would certainly be suspect. Such a review would have a serious gap or deficiency.

Referencing

When information is reported from a source, it must be adequately referenced. A number of acceptable formats may be used, one of which is a footnote at the bottom of the page. In referencing information from the article abstracted in Figure 3.13, for example, a footnote might be used in the review narrative as follows:

> *Yager and Bonnstetter[1] found consistent results for the students in the 1982 Iowa survey and those surveyed in 1977 by NAEP.*

At the bottom of the page, the following footnote would appear:

> [1]*Yager, R. E. and R. J. Bonnstetter, "Student Perceptions of Science Teachers, Classes and Course Content,"* School Science and Mathematics, 84, No. 5 (1984), p. 409.

For the narrative, if there are three or more authors of an article, the last name of the first author may be listed, followed by *et al.* (which means "and others"), rather than writing the names of all authors. A modification of this procedure is to list all names the first time the reference is used, then use *et al.* if it is referenced again. This is done simply for brevity. The footnote would contain the names of all authors.

A shorter format for references that does not require the footnote at the bottom of the page can be used. It involves a reference list or bibliography at the end of the chapter or report. One format is the author-date format. Using the sample reference, the author-date format would be:

> *Yager and Bonnstetter (1984) found consistent . . .*

or, if the names of the authors are not to be emphasized in the narrative:

> *Other researchers (Yager and Bonnstetter, 1984) found consistent . . .*

This format requires an alphabetical listing of references, which should be included in any case. If Yager and Bonnstetter were referenced more than once in the bibliography and if this reference was the second 1984 entry for them, the reference would be Yager and Bonnstetter (1984b). If the writer wishes to include the page number in the reference, it can follow the year, preceded by a comma.

    The short method of referencing can also be used in an author-number format. In this case, the entries in the bibliography are numbered, and the reference number is used instead of the year of publication. The page numbers then follow the reference number if they are included. For example, if the Yager and Bonnstetter entry were number 30 in the bibliography, the reference would be:

> *Yager and Bonnstetter (30:409) found consistent . . .*

or

> *Other researchers (Yager and Bonnstetter, 30:409) found consistent . . .*

The author-date format is generally preferred to the author-number format because in the latter format, if a reference is added or deleted, all numbers of references following the addition or deletion have to be changed. If a reference is added after a good bit of the review is written, the necessary changes will be a bother and a potential source of error.

> *Referencing* can be done in a number of ways—the traditional footnote or shorter methods, using the author-date or author-number formats.

Preparing the Bibliography

Usually, the final step of the review is putting together the bibliography. Some journals distinguish between a reference list and a bibliography; a reference list is limited to references cited in the report, whereas a bibliography may also include references for background information or further reading. The American Psychological Association (1983), for example, makes this distinction. Although a bibliography may include entries not cited directly in the review, it is not wise to include a large number of uncited entries.

The entries in a bibliography are ordered alphabetically according to the last name of the primary author (the one listed first). If the entries have been put on bibliography cards, as shown in Figure 3.12, the cards can be arranged in alphabetical order and the entries taken from them. This simplifies the task of typing the bibliography, especially if not all of the original sources are used. Abstracts can also be used, although they may be a little cumbersome.

An entry in a bibliography begins with the last name of the primary author, then includes any other authors before giving the title of the publication. Titles of articles or chapters are put within quotation marks (but note the difference in APA, 1983), and titles of books, names of periodicals, and so forth, are underlined. Publication date and volume numbers are given for periodicals. The publisher's name and location and the publication date are given for books. Finally, page numbers are given, if necessary, as for articles in periodicals.

Several special situations can arise with respect to format and notation. For example, how are works with no author or an anonymous author referenced? How is a reference made to a statute in a state code? There are procedures for handling such situations, and they are discussed in manuals such as those referenced at the end of this chapter (see, for example, APA, 1983). Dealing with these situations is a matter of consistently following an accepted procedure.

SUMMARY

This chapter has described the process of reviewing the literature. A review serves a number of purposes: it puts the research problem in context; it provides information on what has been done; and it often provides information about how to conduct the research, including suggestions for instrumentation and research design.

The extent of a review of the literature depends on a number of factors, but it generally requires some time and attention to detail. Sometimes a researcher might comment, "There isn't anything in the literature on my research problem." What this means is that the researcher has not found a study exactly like the one being contemplated. A review of literature may include studies even indirectly related to the research problem, and it is the reviewer's responsibility to identify their relevance and synthesize the information from the several studies reviewed.

Figure 3.1 generally outlined the activities in a review of the research literature. Although a researcher may return to the literature at times for additional information and may rewrite parts of the review, the activities are generally done in order from top to bottom as in the flowchart in Figure 3.1. A review often occurs early in a research effort; if the study is conducted over an extended time period, additional entries may be necessary to bring the review up to date.

This chapter also provided several suggestions regarding where to find information, how to synthesize it, and what to do with it. Examples involving a manual search and a computer search were provided, and a checklist was suggested for evaluating research reports. Following consistent procedures enhances the review process by speeding the synthesis of information and reducing the likelihood of errors and repetition. In the final analysis, however, the researcher must write the review, organizing it and pulling things together in a way that will make sense to the reader. A well-organized review brings together the information on a single point or on similar ideas, provides some continuity among the results and conclusions of different research reports, and moves logically and smoothly from one point to another. Transition sentences, such as "Considering other factors that may affect teacher effectiveness, we move now to questioning behaviors," can be very helpful in leading the reader from topic to topic. After the review is written, it should be left alone for a week or two and then reread carefully. It will undoubtedly need some rewriting if it is an initial draft, but if it makes sense and there are no gaps or confusing sections, the researcher is well on the way to putting together a good review.

KEY CONCEPTS

Flowchart of activities	*Combinations of descriptors*
Periodical literature	*Bibliographic entry*
Periodical indexes	*Critical review*
Abstract	*Referencing*
Computer-assisted search	*Bibliography*
Descriptors	*Microfiche*

EXERCISES

3.1 Select a topic of interest and compile a list of possible references for this topic, using the *Education Index* as a source. If you are doing this in connection with a real project, follow up on the references.

3.2 Suppose that a teacher is interested in finding information about the content of mathematics programs for students aged 8–10 in Western European countries and the United States. If the teacher were using the ERIC system, what possible descriptors might be used? What descriptors would be used in combination, and for which publications would they be used?

3.3 Suppose that a researcher is reviewing the literature by using a computer search for a research problem stated as follows:

A study of the relationship between teacher classroom behavior and student achievement in science, grades 6–12.

Using the ERIC database, identify descriptors that could be used in the search. What descriptors would broaden the search? What descriptors would narrow the search? Specify combinations of descriptors and the connectors.

3.4 Using the research problem in Exercise 3.3, or a research problem of your own choosing, conduct the initial part of a computer search, identifying the numbers of references for the descriptors as they are used either singly or in combination. Use any relevant database if you are using your own problem.

3.5 Select a journal article dealing with research that does not exceed five pages, and prepare an abstract in the shorter form. Use the checklist in Figure 3.15 to evaluate the article.

3.6 Select a longer article than the one used in Exercise 3.5, and prepare an abstract in the longer form. Again, use the checklist in Figure 3.15 to evaluate the article.

REFERENCES

American Psychological Association. (1983). *Publication manual of the American Psychological Association* (3rd. ed.). Washington, DC: APA.

Campbell, W. G., Ballou, S. V., & Slade, C. (1982). *Form and style: Theses, reports, term papers* (6th ed.). Boston: Houghton Mifflin.

Dissertation Abstracts International. A: The Humanities and Social Sciences, 45(2). (1984, August). Ann Arbor, MI: University Microfilms International.

Dissertation Abstracts Retrospective Index (Vols. 1–29). (1970). Ann Arbor, MI: Xerox University Microfilms.

Glasman, N. S., & Pellegrino, J. W. (Eds.). (1984). *Review of Educational Research* (Vol. 54, No. 2). Washington, DC: American Educational Research Association.

Gordon, E. W. (Ed.) (1984). *Review of Research in Education* (Vol. 11). Washington, DC: American Educational Research Association.

Thesaurus of ERIC descriptors (10th ed.). (1984). Phoenix: Oryx Press.

4

Principles of Research Design

After a researcher has identified a research problem and has completed at least some review of the literature, it is time to develop a *research design*—a plan or strategy for conducting the research. Research designs tend to be quite specific to the types of research. The conditions that determine the specific design to be used are discussed in subsequent chapters, but some general principles of research design apply to all research, regardless of the type of research or the specific study. These principles are discussed in this chapter.

The Purposes of Research Design

To a large extent, the need for research design is implicit. How could we proceed otherwise? There must be a plan by which the specific activities of the research can be conducted and brought to successful closure. Kerlinger (1973, p. 300) has identified two basic purposes of research design: (1) to provide answers to research questions and (2) to control variance.

The first purpose is general and straightforward—to provide answers to the specific research questions. But going through the motions of conducting research or engaging in research activities alone will not necessarily yield answers. This relates to a point made in Chapter 1, regarding our concern about making educational research systematic and scientific. Research should be valid, which includes being able to interpret results and, through those results, answer the research questions or problems being posed. Good research design assists in understanding and interpreting the results of the study and ensures that a researcher obtains usable results.

The Concept of Controlling Variance

It has been said that all research is conducted for the purpose of explaining *variance*—the fact that not all individuals are the same or have the same score or measurement.

In a broad definitional sense, this may be true, but variance can be evident in a number of ways. For example, variance in elementary school students' achievement, motivation, attitude, age, and family background can be considered. Also when the variance of any one variable is considered, it may be influenced by any number of factors. Variance in achievement, for example, may be due to aptitude and motivation, to mention two possible factors.

How does variance manifest itself ? Consider an example. A high school chemistry teacher is studying the effects of three different methods of teaching on achievement in chemistry. The research problem could be stated as follows:

> *A study of the effects of teaching method on the performance of high school students enrolled in chemistry.*

The problem implies that an experiment will be conducted, since teaching method, the independent variable of primary interest, will be manipulated by the chemistry teacher. Teaching method has three different categories (also called levels), say M_1, M_2, and M_3. The dependent variable is performance on a chemistry achievement test administered after one semester of instruction. Ninety students, all juniors enrolled in the same school and taught by the same teacher, participate in the study. When the students are tested on chemistry achievement, there will be 90 scores, but they will not be identical. There will be a distribution of scores, and this distribution will have variance.

Why are the 90 scores not all identical? This may be due to a variety of causes. The teaching methods may have different effects, and since method is the independent variable, the researcher certainly wants to be able to determine whether or not they have different effects. Some students are undoubtedly more able than others, regardless of the instructional method. Possibly the time of day that instruction takes place has some effect. These are examples of variables that may be control variables or intervening variables, as discussed in Chapter 2. There undoubtedly is inherent variation in the way students respond to a chemistry test. Any number of factors might be operating to cause variance in the dependent variable scores.

It is unsatisfactory to allow factors to operate so that the variance they cause cannot be determined or restricted. To conduct research and not be able to explain the effects of variables means that results cannot be interpreted and that the study lacks internal validity. Consider the variance in the 90 chemistry test scores. As will be seen in Chapter 12, variance can be quantified; it is a real, positive number. Although variance does not come in circles, it can be represented as in Figures 4.1 and 4.2. If we let the entire circle represent all the variance in the 90 chemistry test scores, Figure 4.1 illustrates a situation in which too much of the variance is unexplained or unrestricted. The only variance identified, other than random variance, is due to method. This situation is lacking in control, not because only one variable is included but because too much of the variance is unexplained. In Figure 4.2, additional variables are included as control variables (using the terminology of Chapter 2) to explain parts of the variance, thus reducing the amount of random or unexplained variance.

Figure 4.1
Quantitative Representation of the Variance of the 90 Chemistry Test Scores—Lack of Control over Variance

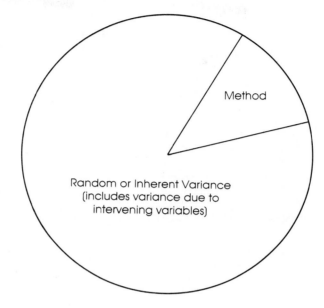

Figure 4.2
Quantitative Representation of the Variance of the 90 Chemistry Test Scores—Increased Control of Variance

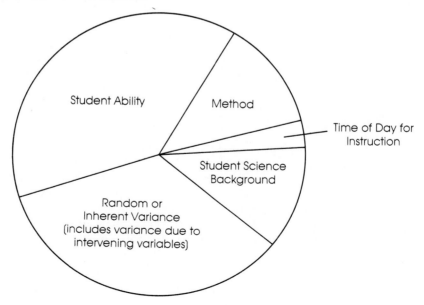

It is important to design research so that the effects variables or factors are having on the dependent variable can be determined. Possibly some variables can be eliminated. In the chemistry example, the same materials would likely be used, so materials is not a variable. Amount of class time should also be constant for the three methods. Structuring some variables in certain ways or possibly restricting how the research is conducted can control variance. Controlling variance means being able to explain what is causing it.

One of the purposes of research design is to control or explain variance. This is done by putting certain restrictions on the research conditions, such as including control variables.

Procedures for Controlling Variance

This section will continue the chemistry example and illustrate procedures by which control of variance can be enhanced. There are basically four ways by which this can be done:

1. Randomization.
2. Building conditions or factors into the design as independent variables.
3. Holding conditions or factors constant.
4. Statistical adjustments.

The first three procedures are directly involved in structuring the research design. The fourth includes computational manipulations in an attempt to obtain control, so it is done at the analysis stage of the research, although preparation for it must be done when the research is designed.

Randomization

Suppose in the chemistry example that the same teacher will teach the 90 students, having three classes of 30 students each, each class taught by a different method. Assume that the 90 students comprise a representative sample of some larger population but that they are a heterogeneous group with respect to ability level, which may well have some effect on performance on the chemistry test. Thirty students are randomly assigned to each of the three methods, as diagrammed in Figure 4.3. Thus, ability level is randomly distributed among the three methods, and one would expect its effect to be the same in each group of 30 students. In essence, the ability level effect has been spread evenly among the three groups, and the effect should be

Figure 4.3
Research Design Using Randomization to Control for Ability Level

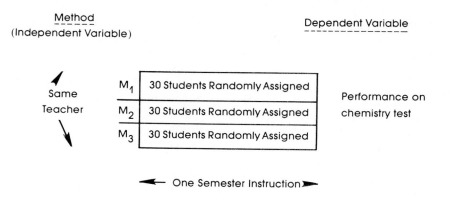

the same for all the groups. Although this procedure distributes the effect of ability level evenly, it does not allow the researcher to determine the differences caused by ability level.

It can also be noted that, in this example, randomization would also control other variables—primarily, organismic variables associated with the student. Motivational level, for example, would be randomly distributed among the three methods or groups. Mathematical knowledge or skill that might well be related to performance in chemistry would also be randomly distributed.

> Randomization spreads an effect of a variable evenly across the groups of the study. Often, organismic variables are so controlled.

Building in Factors as Independent Variables

In the design in Figure 4.3, the students are separated into three groups according to method. If an ability level measure were available—possibly a score on a recent IQ test—the students could also be grouped according to ability level. If the top 45 students on the ability level measure were designated as "higher" and the remaining 45 students as "lower" ability level, ability level would be an independent variable with two levels. Fifteen students of each of the two ability groupings would be randomly assigned to each method. (Any difference in ability levels *within* the groups would be randomly distributed.) This design is presented in Figure 4.4. Now it can be determined not only whether or not there is a difference among methods but also whether or not there is a difference between the higher and lower ability groups. The variance that might be caused by the ability level effect can be accounted for.

The division of the students into two rather than more ability level groups is arbitrary in this example. (Three groups could have been used, designated high, medium, and low.) It should be noted that the researcher arbitrarily formed the groups so that equal numbers were maintained. To do this, the IQ test publisher's definition of higher and lower ability level would not be used (if a definition were available), because a published definition would undoubtedly make for considerable inequality in the numbers of students in each ability level. Indeed, for chemistry, one would expect few, if any, students of low ability level.

Building in a variable does allow the researcher to determine the effect of that variable—that is, to determine any differences attributable to that variable, or the variance accounted for by the variable. Then why is this procedure not always used? For one thing, measures on which the individuals can be separated, in this case the chemistry students, are not always available. For example, motivational level may have an effect, but scores on this variable would be difficult if not impossible to come by. Therefore, motivational level remains an intervening variable, but it is randomly distributed if random assignment is used. Also, including increasing numbers of independent variables may make the design unnecessarily complicated. Therefore, factors so included are usually those that are expected to cause some variance in the dependent variable scores.

Figure 4.4
Research Design with Ability Level Built In as an Independent Variable

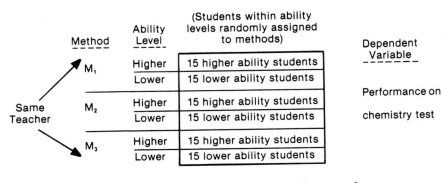

> Building factors into the research design as independent variables enables the researcher to determine the effects of those factors. Too many independent variables, however, can unnecessarily complicate the research design.

Holding Factors Constant

Holding a factor constant essentially consists of reducing a variable to a constant. In the chemistry example, the teacher could reduce ability level to a constant if only students with one defined ability level—say, those scoring between 98 and 108 on an IQ test—were included in the study. If ability level does tend to affect performance on the dependent variable, its effect would now be considerably diminished from what it would have been with the entire range of ability level included. Most of the variance in the chemistry test scores due to ability level would have been eliminated. The design would be essentially the same as that in Figure 4.3, except that only students within the designated IQ range would be randomly assigned to the methods. This number would likely be less than 30 per group if the teacher had started with the original 90 students.

Holding factors constant can have some disadvantages. One has already been indicated: the possible elimination of individuals from the study, causing logistical problems or reducing the amount of data available on the dependent variable. Also, such results generalize only to the restricted group. The chemistry example already has several constants built into the design, such as teacher and length of instruction.

> When a factor is held constant, a potential variable is reduced to a constant. This eliminates, or at least substantially reduces, any effect the factor may have on the dependent variable.

Statistical Control

Statistical control, when used, is attained through computational procedures applied when the data are analyzed, but the variable to be so controlled must still be planned for in conducting the research. For the variable of ability level in the chemistry example, assume that an ability measure consisting of performance on a recently administered IQ test is available for each of the 90 students. It is likely that a relationship exists between performance on the IQ test and performance on the chemistry test such that high scores on one tend to go with high scores on the other and, similarly, low scores on one go with low scores on the other.

If we could somehow adjust the chemistry test scores for this difference in ability level, we would be controlling the effect of student ability on the chemistry test scores. This can be done with a relatively sophisticated statistical procedure. Depending on the strength of the relationship between the chemistry test and IQ test scores, high chemistry test scores would be lowered (by statistical computation) if the students had high ability level scores, and students with low ability level scores would have their chemistry scores raised. These adjusted chemistry test scores, now independent of ability level, would then be analyzed. *Independent of ability level* means that the effect of ability level has been removed.

The process of statistical control can be conceptually diagrammed as in Figure 4.5. The specific statistical procedure most commonly used is the analysis of covariance. It is computationally complex, and when applied the analysis is typically done by computer.

Statistical control, in essence, consists of adjusting the dependent variable scores to remove the effect of the control variable.

If statistical control is simply a matter of putting an analysis through the computer, why is it not used more frequently? One reason is that it is often difficult to obtain adequate scores on a control variable. Scores must be available for all participants in the research. Preferably, the scores on the control variable should be obtained prior to conducting the research so that there is no possibility of the scores being affected by the independent variable—in the chemistry example, the teaching method. Then, too, control variables are effective only to the extent that they are related to the dependent variable and account for variance in the scores of that vari-

Figure 4.5
Conceptual Diagram of Statistical Control

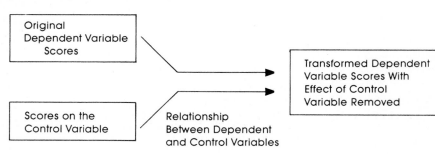

able. Furthermore, certain statistical assumptions must be met; if they are not tenable, the statistical procedure should not be used.

Using Procedures for Control in Combination

The four procedures for enhancing control can be used singly or in combination with each other. One procedure might be used for controlling one variable and another procedure for a second variable. Extending the chemistry example somewhat will illustrate this point.

Instead of using only 90 students, a large high school in which there are at least 180 chemistry students will be used. Teaching method, with the same three levels, is still the independent variable of primary interest. Two teachers (T_1 and T_2) will be used, since there will be six chemistry classes. It is known that the students come from various science and mathematics backgrounds in the elementary schools they attended and in courses they have taken thus far in high school. (For example, some students may have taken Algebra II, others not.) Scores on an IQ test given to all students when they were in eighth grade are available. There are two other high schools in this district, but there is considerable difference in the composition of the student bodies (for example, socioeconomic background) among the high schools. The four variables (in addition to the independent variable) and their methods of control are as follows:

Variable	Method of Control
1. Science background of the student	1. Randomization. The 180 students participating in the research are randomly assigned, 60 to each teaching method.
2. Teacher	2. Built in as an independent variable. Each teacher uses the three teaching methods.
3. School	3. Reduced to a constant. Students of only one school are included.
4. Ability level	4. Statistical control. The IQ test scores are used.

The research design is diagrammed in Figure 4.6. With the relatively high degree of control, if large enough differences occurred among the chemistry test scores of students taught by the three methods, the result would be an indication that the differences are in fact due to the methods. The research design has a high degree of internal validity; the results can be interpreted quite conclusively. However, it should be noted that the generalizability of results may be somewhat limited. Only one school and only two teachers in that school were used. The results generalize only to the extent that the student body and the teachers in this school are

Figure 4.6
Diagram of a Research Design in Which School, Science Background, Teacher, and Ability Level Are Controlled by Different Control Procedures

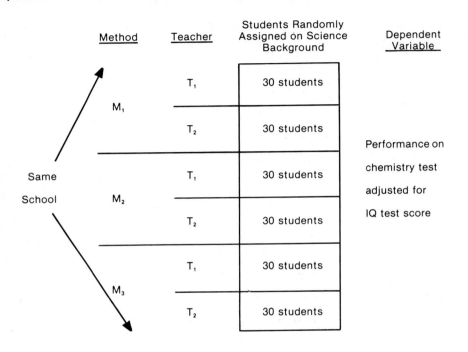

representative of some larger populations. It may be that the intent is to generalize only to students of this school.

The purpose of controlling variance is to enhance the interpretation of results so the researcher can tell what effects, if any, the variables are having. The time to think about control is when the research design is being developed. Carefully designing the research does much to enhance the validity of the research; failing to do so may well lead to uninterpretable or nongeneralizable results.

Characteristics of Good Research Design

What makes for a good research design? There are some general answers, such as that the design should be appropriate for the hypotheses or that it should be feasible within available resources. However, to be more specific, we will discuss four characteristics that enhance research design. A good research design must not only be appropriate and "doable" but must yield results from the research that can be interpreted with confidence.

Freedom from Bias

One characteristic of a good research design is that it will provide data that are free from bias. This means that the data and the statistics computed from them do not vary in any systematic way, but only as would be expected on the basis of random fluctuations. Any differences that appear, therefore, can be attributed to the independent variables under study. If some type of bias exists in the data and differences appear that cannot be attributed to random fluctuation, it is not possible to determine whether this difference is due to the bias or to the effect of the independent variable.

Bias can enter into the data in a number of ways, including biased assignment of the individuals to the experimental treatments. For instance, in the chemistry example, if the higher ability students were all assigned to one teaching method, a bias would have been introduced.

Bias in the data may be eliminated by random assignment of individuals or random sampling, but the bias can be introduced independently of the random procedure. In the chemistry example, random assignment to the methods would have eliminated the bias of putting the higher ability students in one method. (The possibility of a "wild assignment" does exist, but its probability would be very small.) It would still be possible to introduce bias if, for example, three teachers were used, each using only one method, and there was considerable difference in their effectiveness. In that case, possible bias would have been introduced after the random assignment of students to methods. This leads to the concept of confounding.

Freedom from Confounding

One way bias can enter the data is through confounding of variables. Two (or more) independent and/or other variables are confounded if their effects cannot be separated. A good research design eliminates confounding of variables or keeps it to a minimum so that effects can be separated and results can be interpreted without confusion. In the example with three teachers, each using only one method, teacher and method have been confounded. If the students of one method scored higher on the chemistry exam than those of the other two methods, we would not know whether the higher performance was due to the method or to the teacher. The effects

> Two or more variables are *confounded* if their effects cannot be separated.

of teacher and method cannot be separated, because each teacher uses only a single method.

Control of Extraneous Variables

Although extraneous variables are not the variables of primary interest in a research study, they may have an effect on the dependent variable. To control such variables is to be able to identify, balance, minimize, or eliminate their effects. The effects are manifested as they influence the variance in the dependent variable, so the control of extraneous variables is accomplished through the control of variance, as described earlier. In the chemistry example, the ability level of the students was considered an extraneous variable, and various approaches to its control were discussed. Figure 4.2 identifies other possible extraneous variables. A good research design controls such variables, rather than confound their effects with those of other variables or ignore their effects altogether.

Statistical Precision for Testing Hypotheses

Another characteristic of a good research design is that it will provide appropriate data with enough precision to test adequately those hypotheses that require statistical tests. In a statistical sense, precision is increased as random (or error) variance is decreased. (The term *error variance* is commonly used in a statistical context.) *Random or error variance* is the natural or inherent variance that is not attributable to any of the independent variables. This variance contains differences due to random assignment. The 30 chemistry students taught by the same teacher and method in the same school would not have identical scores on the chemistry test. This difference among the scores of students treated in the same way is an example of random or error variance.

To test at least some hypotheses adequately, it is necessary to obtain an estimate of random variance from the analysis. The more precise this estimate, the more likely it is that the statistical test of the hypothesis will reach statistical significance. (These analysis concepts are discussed in Chapter 12.) Extraneous variables inflate the estimate of random variance and tend to make the statistical tests insensitive to the real differences that exist.

The research design should provide data for testing all of the hypotheses of the study. Sometimes numerous and complex hypotheses are involved, so the researcher should check the design carefully and identify which part of the design will provide for testing each hypothesis.

Organizing the Research Activities

The research design is basically a plan or blueprint to be followed when conducting the research, and implementing a design consists of engaging in a number of activities. In Figure 1.4 (Chapter 1), the activities of a research study were diagrammed in a flowchart. The activities are to a large extent sequential, although specific procedures may be flexible, and for certain projects their order may be concurrent or even reversed. For example, in an exploratory study, some data collection might actually precede the final identification of the necessary data. Some review of the literature might be done before the problem is stated in final form and all variables and constants are identified.

The activities are presented here in outline form, with the more specific procedures listed as subtopics. The order in which they are presented is the one most generally used or most closely followed. For certain studies, one or more of the subtopics may not apply; for example, test revision would be unnecessary if a standardized test were used for a population or sample for which the test was intended— nor would a trial run be necessary. In a nonexperimental study, experimental treatments would not be applied. An outline of the activities for a research project is as follows:

I. Identification of the Problem
   1. Statement of the problem
   2. Review of the literature
   3. Formulation of hypotheses
   4. Identification of constants and variables
   5. Identification of necessary data
II. Data Collection
   1. Development or selection of the measuring instrument(s)
   2. Training for data collection procedures
   3. Pilot study[1] or trial run with the measuring instruments
   4. Reliability checks and any necessary revision
   5. Sample selection for the project
   6. Application of experimental treatments
   7. Data collection for the project
   8. Data assembly
III. Analysis
   1. Superimposing the analysis design on the data
   2. Completion of the actual analysis procedures
   3. Assembly of the results
IV. Conclusion of the Research
   1. Interpretation of the results
   2. Synthesis
   3. Preparation for writing

The climax of a research endeavor is usually the writing of a report or thesis or some other form of written communication. This is an important step, since research findings are of little value unless they are communicated to other people. Chapter 13 gives suggestions for writing about research.

The identification of the research problem, its variables and constants, and the review of literature have already been discussed in considerable detail, and other activities will be discussed in subsequent chapters. It is at the research design stage, however, that the various procedures are identified and the plans are made for dealing with them. For example, in the chemistry example discussed earlier, the following activities in the data collection component need to be operationally defined:

Procedure	*Operationally Defined*
1. Development of the measuring instrument	1. Construction of a teacher-made test covering the chemistry content
2. Validity checks and any necessary revision	2. Another chemistry teacher could review the test for quality and appropriateness of items
3. Sample selection for the project	3. Randomly assigning the students to the three methods
4. Application of experimental treatments	4. The three methods used for a one-semester period
5. Data collection for the project	5. Administering the chemistry test at the end of the semester
6. Assembling the data	6. Correcting the completed tests and placing each student's score with the appropriate method

Since the data collection consists of administering a teacher-constructed test, it is not likely that any training for administering the test is necessary. Also, a pilot study or trial run probably would not be necessary. A carefully constructed test by a competent chemistry teacher would be appropriate. It would be difficult to find a corresponding group for a trial run unless the test were used with chemistry students of another school. However, a reliability check should be run on the test data of the study, since this would help explain variability in the data.

The specific activities involved in conducting the research are identified and organized at the research design stage.

SUMMARY

This chapter has discussed the general principles of research design and the overall organization of research activities. Besides providing answers to research questions, one of the basic purposes of research design is controlling variance. Controlling variance means being able to explain what is causing it, at least to the point that results can be interpreted with confidence. Four ways of controlling variance were discussed, which may be used in combinations in specific research designs.

Four characteristics of a good research design were identified, and they are by no means independent of each other. For example, as we construct the design to avoid confounding, we may also be controlling extraneous variables. Although problems inevitably arise while conducting research, they can usually be circumvented or corrected with a well-planned design.

Of necessity, research designs are specific to the types of research. The chemistry example discussed in this chapter, for example, was an experiment—most likely consisting of action research. The specific design used depends on the purposes and conditions of the research. In the next several chapters, different types of research are discussed, and each type has its underlying, general design, with many possible variations. Chapter 5 discusses experimental research, which is sometimes more structured by the design than nonexperimental research. Nevertheless, all research activities should be organized according to a design.

Sometimes we talk about "selecting" a research design. Certainly designs are selected, but the variables, conditions, and so forth of a specific study flesh out the design. Thus, it is not correct to infer that selecting a design completes the task of obtaining an adequate research design. The selected design must be translated into the specifics of the study.

Regardless of the type of research, the process of conducting a research project is made up of separate but interrelated activities. Some activities can be more easily isolated than others, and although many follow a logical sequence, others may vary in order of occurrence or may overlap. The overall scope of the research project must be accurately identified. Getting the research completed, however, is a matter of doing it piece by piece. Various generalizations can be considered and applied, but for a single project, it is attention to the details of the specific activities that gets the job done.

KEY CONCEPTS

Variance
Controlling variance
Random variance
Randomization
Building in independent variables
Holding factors constant
Bias

Confounded variables
Extraneous variables
Control of extraneous variables
Statistical precision
Error variance
Statistical control

EXERCISES

4.1 A study is conducted in which the attitudes of high school students toward the school athletic program are surveyed. The researcher is interested in how attitudes might differ among the sophomore, junior, and senior classes. Random samples of students to be surveyed are drawn from each class. Describe one or more ways in which the variance due to the sex of the student, an organismic variable, might be controlled. What would probably be the most effective way to enhance control over this variable?

4.2 Suppose that the attitude survey in Exercise 4.1 was being conducted in the high schools of a relatively large school system. Although the class is the independent variable of primary interest, suggest other variables (in addition to the sex of the student) that would merit control. What procedures would you use for controlling these variables?

4.3 An educational psychologist is designing an experiment in which three different types of motivational techniques will make up the levels of the independent variable. The dependent variable is performance on a cognitive task that has been shown to be related to an ability level measure. The participants (subjects) will be 60 randomly selected college freshmen enrolled in an introductory psychology course. Discuss possible variables that might be controlled in this experiment, and suggest procedures for enhancing such control.

4.4 Two high school history teachers who each teach two classes of American history have available two different packets of instructional materials. They are interested in whether or not the materials have differing effects on achievement in history, as measured by the final exam for the course (a common exam for all classes). A specific class will use only one packet of materials, but the teachers have the option of randomly assigning students to classes. Besides the independent variable of primary interest (materials), it is desirable to control the variance due to (1) learning style of students, (2) sex of the student, (3) teacher, and (4) ability level of the student. The students are high school juniors, and there are no recent IQ test scores available, but the GPA for the first two years of high school is available. Develop a research design to control the variance due to the four variables. Use at least two of the four basic methods of controlling variance. Diagram the design.

4.5 Define what is meant by *confounding of variables,* and describe a research study in which confounding could occur.

4.6 Suppose that an experiment in instructional methods was designed in which the levels of the independent variable consisted of five different instructional methods. The methods were used in five different elementary schools with 10-year-old students, but only one method was used in each school. Discuss how confounding of variables would enter into this research design. Describe how the independent variable could have been manipulated to avoid confounding. Suggest additional variables that would merit controlling in the experiment.

4.7 A researcher is doing a study of two different approaches to remedial reading instruction, implemented with elementary-age students in grades 2–5 during a 6-week summer school period. A total of 182 students will be involved, and since the school district is relatively small, they all attend the same school. There will be two teachers for each grade level. The students will be pre- and posttested at the beginning and end of the 6-week period. The research problem of primary interest is whether the two methods have differing effects on the reading performance of the students. Consider the eight subtopics under data collection in the outline provided earlier in this chapter, and decide which of these procedures are necessary for this study. Describe how the procedures would be done.

4.8 In the study in Exercise 4.7, the use of eight teachers with two methods might cause some confounding problems. It would be difficult to have a single teacher use both methods, since a teacher would likely have only a single class. How might this confounding of teacher and method be dealt with, if not entirely controlled? What variables probably would be controlled by randomization or by being included as independent variables?

4.9 From a professional journal, select a research article and read it carefully. Attempt to identify the specific procedures (as described in the outline in this chapter) that apply to the article you have read. This may take some reading between the lines, since the procedures may not be explicitly defined in the article.

NOTE

1. A *pilot study* is a preliminary use of the instrument with (usually) a small number of individuals. The purpose of the pilot study is to refine the instrument, including the correction of deficiencies, and so forth. A pilot study is *not* the major data collection for the research.

REFERENCE

Kerlinger, F. N. (1973). *Foundations of behavioral research* (2nd ed.). New York: Holt, Rinehart & Winston.

5

Experimental Research

The word *experiment* has a vaguely familiar, broad meaning in contemporary usage—so broad that if someone tries a new approach or procedure to see what its effects will be, we may refer to this as an experiment or to the process as experimenting. In his attempts to develop a light bulb, Thomas Edison tried different filament materials to determine which would work. He was experimenting.

In educational research, rather specific descriptions are provided of how experiments are designed. However, a basic concept from the broad usage of *experiment* is retained; that is, something is tried—one or more independent variables are manipulated to determine the effects. An independent variable that is manipulated is called an *experimental variable*.

An *experiment* is a research situation in which at least one independent variable, called the *experimental variable,* is deliberately manipulated or varied by the researcher.

The Meaning of Experimental Design

In its broadest sense, an experimental design is a preconceived plan for conducting an experiment. More specifically, an experimental design is the structure by which variables are positioned, arranged, or built into the experiment. The design includes the independent variable(s), which must include the experimental variable(s) and possibly other variables, such as organismic variables. Since the measures (the data to be analyzed) are taken on the dependent variable(s), the points in the experiment where these measures are to be taken may also be indicated. Experimental designs are often diagrammed with symbols to indicate the arrangement of the variables, and so forth. Such diagrams and their arrangements and symbols have certain meanings, which will be explored in this chapter.

Consider an example. An educational psychologist uses three types of instructions—verbal, written, and combination verbal-written—to determine the effects of instruction on performance in solving abstract number problems. The participants in the experiment are college freshmen, 20 of whom are randomly assigned to each type of instruction. A participant comes to a learning laboratory, receives the instructions, and attempts to solve a series of number problems. The dependent variable is the score on the number of problems solved correctly in the series. Each participant goes through the experiment singly, and the entire activity takes about one hour. The experimental variable is type of instruction, and there are three levels (the different types) of this variable.[1]

The experiment is diagrammed in Figure 5.1. In the upper part of the figure, the entire design is written out. The experimental procedure consists of administering the appropriate instruction and solving the problems. The measures on the dependent variable are collected during the experiment and usually recorded when it is completed. Depending on the experiment, the data may be collected while the experiment is in process or shortly after it is concluded. In this example, the data are collected after the instructions have been given and the participants are solving the problems.

Below the dotted line in Figure 5.1, the experiment is diagrammed in symbol form.[2] The R indicates random assignment to the three groups, designated by the

Figure 5.1
Experimental Design for the Problem-Solving Experiment

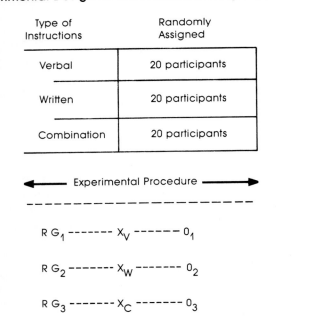

Type of Instructions	Randomly Assigned
Verbal	20 participants
Written	20 participants
Combination	20 participants

Dependent Variable

Number of

Correct Solutions

◄——— Experimental Procedure ———►

$R\ G_1$ ------- X_V ------ 0_1

$R\ G_2$ ------- X_W ------- 0_2

$R\ G_3$ ------- X_C ------- 0_3

Gs with subscripts. X is used as the symbol for the introduction or use of an experimental variable, and the subscript on the X simply indicates the level of that variable. In the diagram, the V, W, and C subscripts on the X indicate the type of instructions—verbal, written, and combination. The Os indicate data collection (in a general sense, observation taken), and, in this example, the subscripts on the Os correspond with the numbers of the groups. In this diagram, O_1 indicates the data from Group 1 (G_1), the group that had verbal instructions (X_V). The Os are scores on the dependent variable—in this case, number of correct solutions.

The experiment diagrammed in Figure 5.1 is relatively simple. It contains only one independent variable, the experimental variable. Data are collected only at the close of the experiment. The experimental procedures with the instructions and problem solving might be somewhat complicated, but the design does provide the researcher with considerable control. If, in analyzing the scores, the researcher found those of G_3 to be consistently and considerably higher (more correct solutions) than those of G_1 and G_2, it would be quite conclusive that the combination type of instruction is more effective than the other two types in enhancing this type of problem solution.

Why bother with experimental design? It enables the researcher to interpret and understand the data of an experiment. The purpose of experimental design is no different from the purpose of research design generally—to be able to make sense of the results—and experimental design enhances control. In the example, the researcher can draw conclusions about the effect of type of instructions on problem solving because the design structures the instructions so that their effects are separated and can manifest themselves. Patterns of results can be directly associated with certain effects of the independent variable.

> An *experimental design* is the structure by which variables are positioned or arranged in the experiment.

Experimental Variables

In Chapter 2, various types of variables were discussed. One type introduced was the independent variable, which may have an effect on the dependent variables. Independent variables can take different forms, such as an organismic variable or variables that indicate different treatments or procedures to be administered to the participants of the research. An experimental variable is an independent variable; but not all independent variables are experimental variables. In the foregoing example, had the participants been identified according to their sex, so that 10 boys and 10 girls were administered each type of instruction, the sex of the participant could have been designated an independent variable. However, it is an organismic variable, not an experimental variable. The type of instruction was the experimental variable.

There are any number of independent variables that can serve as experimental variables. Conceptually, an experimental variable can have any finite number of levels, but in educational research, experimental variables usually have relatively small numbers of levels—perhaps two to five, and rarely more than seven or eight. The levels of the experimental variable are sometimes called *experimental treatments.* The following are some examples of possible experimental variables in educational research:

Experimental Variable	*Possible Levels*
1. Type of instructional organization	1. a. team teaching b. self-contained classroom
2. Type of materials for concept attainment	2. a. verbal b. figural
3. Drug dosage for experimental animals	3. a. 5 grams b. 10 grams c. 15 grams
4. Length of time on task with no break	4. a. 5 minutes b. 10 minutes c. 20 minutes d. 30 minutes
5. Instructional process used in teaching history	5. a. lecture b. group discussion c. individualized instruction
6. Time of day for instruction	6. a. morning b. afternoon
7. Length of word lists used for spelling instruction	7. a. 10 words b. 25 words c. 40 words d. 60 words e. 100 words
8. Length of exercise period (per day)	8. a. 15 minutes b. 30 minutes c. 45 minutes d. 60 minutes
9. Type of therapy	9. a. medication alone b. exercise alone c. medication and exercise in combination

For each of the examples of experimental variables, the researcher can manipulate or control the levels or experimental treatments. In number 7, for example, the word lists can be prepared and used with five groups of students randomly assigned to the lists. The purpose of the experiment undoubtedly would be to determine the effects of word-list length on student performance on a spelling exercise.

Use of the Term *Subject*

In research generally, but especially in experiments, the term *subject* is used to mean someone who participates in an experiment. Subjects are the participants in the experiment, those who receive the experimental treatments. Thus, the subjects of the instructions example were college freshmen. If fifth-grade students are used in an experiment, they would be the subjects. The symbol *S* is used to designate a subject. The term *subject* and the symbol *S* are commonly used in the literature.

Criteria for a Well-Designed Experiment

Before specific experimental designs are introduced, some general criteria for a well-designed experiment will be considered. Essentially, the characteristics that make for a good research design also apply to the design of an experiment. The criteria are listed here with brief comments for each criterion to explain what it means:

1. *Adequate experimental control*—This means that there are enough restraints on the conditions of the experiment so that the researcher can interpret the results. The experimental design is so structured that if the experimental variable has an effect, it can be detected. This may also mean controlling other variables through randomization or by building them into the design as independent variables.
2. *Lack of artificiality*—This criterion is especially important in educational research if the results of the experiment are to be generalized to a nonexperimental setting—for example, a classroom. It means that the experiment is conducted in such a way that the results will apply to the real educational world. We do not want the artificial or atypical characteristic of an experiment to cause the experimental effects.
3. *Basis for comparison*—There must be some way to make a comparison to determine whether or not there is an experimental effect. In some experiments, a control group is used—a group that does not receive an experimental treatment. The control group in an instructional experiment usually consists of a group of students taught by a traditional method. In a drug experiment with animals, a control group would consist of the animals that receive no drug. Certainly, not all experiments require control groups. Comparisons can be made between two or more experimental treatments and, on occasion, with some external criterion.
4. *Adequate information from the data*—The data must be adequate for testing the hypotheses of the experiment. The data must be such that the necessary statistics can be generated with enough precision to make decisions about the hypotheses.

5. *Uncontaminated data*—The data should adequately reflect the experimental effects. They should not be affected by poor measurement or errors in the experimental procedure. The individuals from the various groups should not interact in such a way as to cancel experimental effects or to cause misrepresentation of the experimental effects.

6. *No confounding of relevant variables*—This criterion is closely related to adequate experimental control. There may be other variables operating that have an effect on the dependent variable. If so, these effects must not be misinterpreted as experimental effects. Their effects must be separated or controlled, usually through the experimental design.

7. *Representativeness*—The researcher usually wants to generalize the experimental results to some individuals, conditions, methods, and so forth. To obtain representativeness, the researcher commonly includes some aspect of randomness, either through the selection of the subjects for the experiment or through the assignment of the subjects to the experimental treatments (and control groups, if used).

8. *Parsimony*—The criterion of parsimony means that, with all other characteristics equal, a simpler design is preferred to a more complex one. Of course, a design must be complex enough for the purposes of the experiment, but complexity is not encouraged for its own sake. The simpler design is usually easier to implement and possibly easier to interpret.

Experiments, like any type of educational research, are susceptible to technical and procedural errors. The development of an appropriate experimental design and its adequate implementation require considerable and careful planning, but they provide the best safeguard against errors. Experimental design requires simultaneous attention to a variety of details. This planning is done prior to conducting the experiment.

Experimental Validity

The criteria of a well-designed experiment can be summarized as the characteristics that enhance experimental validity. In Chapter 1, the validity of educational research was discussed, and the concept of experimental validity is essentially the same. Experimental validity is used here as defined by Campbell and Stanley (1963) and is considered to be of two types, internal and external.

Internal validity is the basic minimum of control, measurement, analysis, and procedures necessary to make the results of the experiment interpretable. Internal validity deals with being able to understand the data and draw conclusions from them. It questions whether the experimental treatment really makes a difference in the dependent variable. To answer this question, the researcher must be confident that factors such as extraneous variables have been controlled and are not producing an effect that is being mistaken as an experimental treatment effect.

External validity of an experiment deals with the generalizability of the results of the experiment. To what populations, variables, situations, and so forth, do the results generalize? Generally, the more extensively the results can be generalized, the more useful the research, given that there is adequate internal validity.

Experimental validity is of two types, internal and external. *Internal validity* is the minimum control, and so forth, necessary to interpret the results. *External validity* deals with the extent of generalizability of the results.

Although the purpose of experimental design is to have experiments high in both types of validity, in some cases securing one type tends to jeopardize the other. As more rigorous controls are applied in the experiment, less carry-over can be anticipated between what occurred in the experiment and what would occur in a natural educational setting. For example, in research on instructional techniques, the control of the experiment may be so extensive that an essentially artificial situation is created and only the experimental variables are operating. This would greatly enhance internal validity, but the generalization might be so limited that the results could not be applied to a real classroom situation. This does not imply that it is never desirable to achieve maximum control; the objectives of the experiment dictate the extent of the validity requirements. Clearly, an experiment whose results are uninterpretable is useless even if wide generalizability would be possible. On the other hand, it is unsatisfactory to do an experiment and then discover that the results cannot be generalized as anticipated in the objectives of the experiment.

Internal validity involves securing adequate control over extraneous variables, selection procedures, measurement procedures, and the like. The experimental design should be so developed that the researcher can adequately check on the factors that might threaten the internal validity. To be sure, all possible factors are not operating in all experiments, but the researcher should have some knowledge about the variables and the possible difficulties that may arise in connection with internal validity. Then the experiment can be designed accordingly, so that the results can be interpreted adequately.

External validity certainly concerns the populations to which the researcher expects to generalize the results, but it also may include generalizing the findings to other related independent variables or modifications of the experimental variable. There may be factors such as size of class, type of school, and the like, across which the researcher hopes to generalize. For example, would the results of an experiment being conducted in a suburban school with fourth-grade pupils apply to an inner-city school? To eighth-graders? Most likely not, but again this would depend on the variables and the details of the experiment. The researcher may also desire to generalize to different measurement variations. For example, would the results of an experiment including pretesting be applicable to a classroom situation without pretesting? External validity is concerned with these types of questions.

Experimental designs in educational research are rarely, if ever, perfect. Through experimental design, the researcher attempts to attain adequate validity, both internal and external. Since enhancing one type of validity may tend to jeopardize the other, the researcher often must attempt an adequate balance, essentially by attaining sufficient control to make the results interpretable while maintaining enough realism so that the results will generalize adequately to the intended situations.

The following sections will describe a number of quite specific designs commonly used in educational research. The designs will be diagrammed in general and described, and an example will be provided for each design discussed.

Posttest-Only Control Group Design[3]

In discussing experimental designs, two terms, *pretest* and *posttest,* are often used in connection with the data collection. *Pretest* refers to a measure or test given to the subjects prior to the experimental treatment. A *posttest* is a measure taken after the experimental treatment has been applied. Not all designs involve pretesting, but posttesting is necessary to determine the effects of the experimental treatment.

Experimental designs commonly involve two or more groups, one for each of the experimental treatments and possibly a control group. The posttest-only control group design in its simplest form involves just two groups, the group that receives the experimental treatment and the control group. The subjects are randomly assigned to the two groups prior to the experiment, and the experimental group receives the experimental treatment. Upon the conclusion of the experimental period, the two groups are measured on the dependent variable under study. Preferably, this measurement is taken immediately after the conclusion of the experiment, especially if the dependent variable is likely to change with the passing of time.

The posttest-only control group design is an efficient design to administer. It does not require pretesting, which for many situations is not desirable or applicable. Pretesting and posttesting require that each individual subject be identified so that pre- and posttest scores can be paired. The posttest-only design requires the subjects to be identified only in terms of their group and, possibly, other independent variables if such variables are included in the design.

The two-group design can be diagrammed as follows:

$$R \ G_1 \quad X \quad O_1$$
$$R \ G_2 \quad — \quad O_2$$

In this diagram, G indicates group and R indicates that the members of the group are randomly selected or assigned to each group. An X indicates an experimental treatment, a dash, no experimental treatment. The Os indicate a measurement (test, task, or observation) on the dependent variable, and the vertical positioning of the

Os indicates when they take place. Since they are vertically aligned, they take place at the same point in the experiment. In this case, they are posttests, since they occur after the experimental treatment.

The posttest-only control group design may be extended to include more than two groups; that is, two or more experimental treatments may be used, increasing the number of groups to three or more. The subjects would be randomly assigned to the groups from the population, and the effects of the various experimental treatments could be investigated by comparing the performances of the groups. In the more general sense, the posttest-only control group can be diagrammed as follows:

$$
\begin{array}{lll}
R\ G_1 & X_1 & O_1 \\
R\ G_2 & X_2 & O_2 \\
\quad \bullet & \bullet & \bullet \\
\quad \bullet & \bullet & \bullet \\
\quad \bullet & \bullet & \bullet \\
R\ G_k & X_k & O_k \\
R\ G_{k+1} & — & O_{k+1}
\end{array}
$$

The subscripts on the Xs indicate the different experimental treatments. The number of these treatments in the specific experiment is k. Note that there is one group, the control group, which does not receive an experimental treatment. If no control group were needed, the design would be called a posttest-only randomized groups design.

Example 5.1

A fourth-grade teacher does an experiment on the effects of supplementary instructional materials on reading performance. Two kinds of supplementary instructional materials are to be used; along with the traditional materials, they make up the three levels of the independent (experimental) variable.

The research problem can be stated as follows:

A study of the effects of kinds of supplementary materials on the reading performance of fourth-grade students.

Fifteen students in fourth grade are randomly assigned to each level of the independent variable; thus, 45 students participate in the experiment. During daily reading instruction, the 15 students using each of the supplementary materials work with those materials for 20 minutes. The control group continues working with the traditional materials. After 8 weeks of instruction, the students are tested with a reading test. Performance on this test is the dependent variable. The experiment is diagrammed in Figure 5.2. The symbols for the experimental treatments are X_1 and X_2, with a dash for the control group. Referring to the general design, in this case the number of experimental treatments, k, would equal two.

Figure 5.2
Diagram of Example 5.1 Posttest-Only Control Group Design, Including Two Experimental Groups and a Control Group

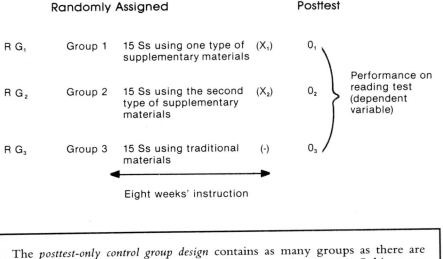

	Randomly Assigned			Posttest	
R G_1	Group 1	15 Ss using one type of supplementary materials	(X_1)	O_1	Performance on reading test (dependent variable)
R G_2	Group 2	15 Ss using the second type of supplementary materials	(X_2)	O_2	
R G_3	Group 3	15 Ss using traditional materials	(-)	O_3	

← Eight weeks' instruction →

> The *posttest-only control group design* contains as many groups as there are experimental treatments, plus a control or comparison group. Subjects are measured only after the experimental treatments have been applied.

Pretest-Posttest Control Group Design

The addition of a pretest given prior to administering the experimental treatments essentially extends the posttest-only control group design to the pretest-posttest control group design. The subjects are randomly assigned to the two or more groups and tested just prior to the experiment on a supposedly relevant antecedent variable, possibly a second form of the test that measures the dependent variable.

What is gained by pretesting? It may be that the pretest score can be used as a statistical control in the analysis. In some experiments, especially in instructional areas, it is desirable to analyze gain scores—the differences between posttest and pretest scores. However, some authors caution against the use of gain scores, especially in a simplistic manner. For example, Cronbach and Furby (1970) suggest quite complex mathematical models if gain scores are used at all. On the other hand, Zimmerman and Williams (1982) conclude that gain scores can be reliable and that there are many research situations in which gain scores are quite useful. Whenever gain scores are contemplated, their meaning and reliability in the specific situation should be considered carefully.

In its simplest form, the pretest-posttest control group design contains two groups—one receiving an experimental treatment, the other not. It is diagrammed as follows:

$$R \; G_1 \qquad O_1 \qquad X \qquad O_2$$
$$R \; G_2 \qquad O_3 \qquad - \qquad O_4$$

Now there are twice as many Os as in the posttest-only design, so the Os with odd-numbered subscripts indicate pretests and those with even-numbered subscripts indicate posttests.

The pretest-posttest control group design can be extended to include more than two groups. It can be diagrammed in general form as follows:

$$R \; G_1 \qquad O_1 \qquad X_1 \qquad O_2$$
$$R \; G_2 \qquad O_3 \qquad X_2 \qquad O_4$$
$$\cdot \qquad\qquad \cdot \qquad\quad \cdot \qquad\quad \cdot$$
$$\cdot \qquad\qquad \cdot \qquad\quad \cdot \qquad\quad \cdot$$
$$\cdot \qquad\qquad \cdot \qquad\quad \cdot \qquad\quad \cdot$$
$$R \; G_k \qquad O_{2k-1} \qquad X_k \qquad O_{2k}$$
$$R \; G_{k+1} \qquad O_{2k+1} \qquad - \qquad O_{2(k+1)}$$

The notation indicates k experimental treatments and a comparison group as a control group. If two or more experimental treatments are used and the experiment does not require a control group, the design would be called a pretest-posttest randomized groups design.

Example 5.2

A researcher is interested in the effects of length of intense instruction in geometric concepts on performance on a spatial relations test. The research problem can be stated as follows:

A study of the effects of different length of instruction in geometric concepts on spatial relations performance of high school juniors.

The problem statement clearly implies an experiment, since length of instruction is a variable manipulated by the researcher.

Two parallel forms of the spatial relations test are used—one as the pretest, the other as the posttest. The experiment is set up as follows. Forty high school juniors are randomly selected, with the condition that all have taken a geometry course. The 40 students are assigned to four groups of 10 each, and the experimental treatments are administered as follows:

G_1 will receive one 15-minute period of instruction in three-dimensional geometric concepts.

G_2 will receive two 15-minute periods of instruction in three-dimensional geometric concepts.

G_3 will receive three 15-minute periods of instruction in three-dimensional geo-metric concepts.

G_4 (control group) will receive no instruction in three-dimensional geometric concepts.

The members of G_1, G_2, and G_3 will receive the instruction individually in a tutorial situation. (Care must be taken that the instruction is consistent for the members of a group; across groups, the only thing that should vary is the length of instruction.) The entire instruction will be completed over the period of 1 week. Before anyone receives instruction, the students are pretested; shortly after instruction is completed, the students are posttested. The experiment is diagrammed in Figure 5.3.

The dependent variable in this experiment could be the gain scores between pre- and posttesting. Or the posttest scores could be the dependent variable, adjusted for pretest score. The adjusted scores would be generated through a statistical procedure. Using this design, the researcher can determine whether there are effects on spatial relations test performance from the different amounts of instruction in three-dimensional geometric concepts or, in comparison with the control group, whether instruction has any effects at all.

Figure 5.3
Diagram of Example 5.2 Pretest-Posttest Control Group Design, Including Three Experimental Groups and a Control Group

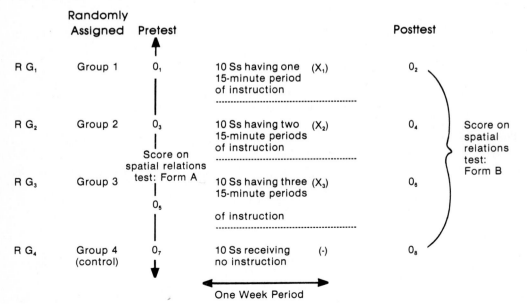

> The *pretest-posttest control group design* contains as many groups as there are experimental treatments, plus a control group. Subjects are measured before and after receiving the experimental treatments.

Solomon Four-Group Design

Combining the pretest–posttest control group design and the posttest–only control group design in their simplest forms produces a design described by Solomon (1949). This design, in its four-group form, includes two control and two experimental groups, but the experimental groups receive the same experimental treatment. Only one of each of the two types of groups is pretested, and all four groups are posttested at the conclusion of the experimental period. The assignment of subjects to all groups is random.

The diagram for the Solomon four-group design is as follows:

$$R \; G_1 \quad O_1 \quad X \quad O_2$$
$$R \; G_2 \quad O_3 \quad - \quad O_4$$
$$R \; G_3 \quad - \quad X \quad O_5$$
$$R \; G_4 \quad - \quad - \quad O_6$$

Since it is a four-group design, only four groups are included and only one experimental treatment is used, the effects of which are determined by comparison of the posttest scores of the experimental and control groups. Since there is only one experimental treatment, no subscript appears on the X. Groups 1 and 3 are experimental groups, Groups 2 and 4, control groups (indicated by the absence of X).

The advantage of the Solomon four-group design is that it enables the researcher to check on possible effects of pretesting, since some groups are pretested and others not. It is possible that pretesting affects the posttest score or that pretesting interacts with the experimental treatment. That is, the effect of the experimental treatment is not the same in pretested and nonpretested groups. Since pretesting is not the rule in actual classroom practice, this is often an important consideration for validity.

Example 5.3

An educational psychologist is experimenting with the effects of viewing a problem solutions film on performance on a logical reasoning test. The research problem can be stated as follows:

A study of the effects of viewing a problem solutions film on logical reasoning perfor-mance of young adults.

The experimental treatment is viewing the 30-minute film. The subjects for the experiment are college seniors enrolled in an educational psychology class. The psychologist wants to pre- and posttest so that at least some gain scores can be analyzed. However, there is concern that the pretesting may trigger a certain kind of reaction to the film, such that the subjects being pretested may be cued about what to learn from the film. This is the reason for using the Solomon four-group design rather than a posttest-only design or a pretest-posttest design.

Thirty-two students are used for the experiment, and 8 are randomly assigned to each of the four groups of the design. The design is diagrammed in Figure 5.4. The 16 students in G_1 and G_2 are pretested at a single time. The next day, the 16 students of the experimental groups view the film. Shortly thereafter, all 32 students are posttested. The pretest and posttest are parallel but different logical reasoning tests.

The psychologist can now check on possible effects of pretesting and the interaction of pretesting with the experimental treatment. Herein lies the advantage of the Solomon four-group design over the posttest-only and pretest-posttest control group designs. However, the Solomon four-group design has a disadvantage in that it requires more groups and consequently more subjects. The design can be extended

Figure 5.4
Diagram of Example 5.3 Solomon Four-Group Design

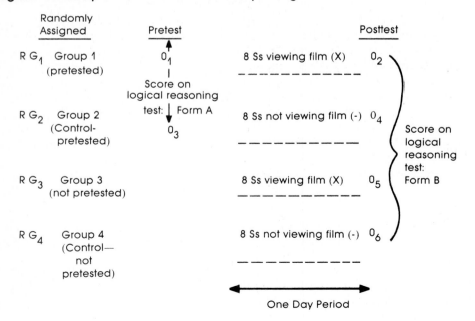

to include more experimental treatments, but for each additional treatment, two additional groups are required—one pretested and the other not. For example, if the experimental variable contained two treatments, six groups would be required; if it had three treatments, eight groups would be required.

The *Solomon four-group design* is a combination of the posttest-only control group design and the pretest–posttest control group design.

Factorial Designs

The factorial designs comprise a family of designs that are being used extensively in educational research. The basic construction of a factorial design is that all levels of each independent variable are taken in combination with the levels of the other independent variables (technically referred to as *complete factorial*). The design requires a minimum of two independent variables, with at least two levels of each variable. This minimum design is called a two by two (2 × 2) factorial. Theoretically, there could be any number of independent variables with any number of levels of each. Using the numerical designation for a design, such as 2 × 4, the number of digits indicates the number of independent variables, and the numerical values of the digits indicate the number of levels for the specific independent variables. These numbers need not be the same for the independent variables. A 2 × 3 × 5 factorial has three independent variables, with two, three, and five levels, respectively. An example that fits this factorial is two teaching methods, three ability levels, and five grades.

The number of different groups involved in a factorial design increases very rapidly with the increase of the number of independent variables and number of levels. The 2 × 2 factorial has four groups. Adding just one independent variable with two levels would increase this to a 2 × 2 × 2 (denoted by 2^3) factorial with eight groups. If one level is added to each of the independent variables of a 2 × 2 factorial, resulting in a 3 × 3 factorial, the number of groups is increased to nine. Since the levels must be taken in all combinations, the number of groups is the product of the digits that specify the factorial design.

At least one of the independent variables in an experiment is an experimental variable. The others may be organismic variables, built into the design for control purposes. Factorials can very rapidly become complex in terms of numbers of *cells*— the groups that receive the various combinations of the levels of the independent variables. To simplify the diagramming of factorials, variables can be indicated by letters and levels of variables by numbers. Then subscripts on letters designate the various cells. A 2 × 3 × 5 factorial that contains 30 groups is diagrammed in Figure 5.5. The independent variables are designated *A, B,* and *C*. The different levels of the independent variables are designated by 1, 2, and so forth to the required num-

Figure 5.5
Diagram of a 2 × 3 × 5 Factorial Design

		Variable A					
		1			**2**		
		Variable B			Variable B		
	1	$A_1B_1C_1$	$A_1B_2C_1$	$A_1B_3C_1$	$A_2B_1C_1$	$A_2B_2C_1$	$A_2B_3C_1$
	2	$A_1B_1C_2$	$A_1B_2C_2$	$A_1B_3C_2$	$A_2B_1C_2$	$A_2B_2C_2$	$A_2B_3C_2$
Variable C	3	$A_1B_1C_3$	$A_1B_2C_3$	$A_1B_3C_3$	$A_2B_1C_3$	$A_2B_2C_3$	$A_2B_3C_3$
	4	$A_1B_1C_4$	$A_1B_2C_4$	$A_1B_3C_4$	$A_2B_1C_4$	$A_2B_2C_4$	$A_2B_3C_4$
	5	$A_1B_1C_5$	$A_1B_2C_5$	$A_1B_3C_5$	$A_2B_1C_5$	$A_2B_2C_5$	$A_2B_3C_5$

Note: The 30 cells (groups) can all be designated by letters with subscripts, as they are in the body of the figure. Note that no cell designation is exactly like any other; any two cell designations differ in at least one subscript. These somewhat complicated subscripts must be used to represent a three-dimensional (three variables) design in a two-dimensional table.

bers. *A* contains two levels, *B,* three, and *C,* five. A control group may be built into a factorial design by considering "no experimental treatment" as one of the levels of the experimental variable. Also, although most factorial designs involve only post-testing, pretesting can be used if it serves the purposes of the research.

The advantages of factorial designs over simpler designs are generally twofold: factorial design provides the economy of a single design rather than separate designs for each of the independent variables, and it allows the researcher to investigate the interactions between the variables. For many research studies, a knowledge of interaction is of major importance, and investigating the existence of interaction is a primary objective of the study.

Interaction is an effect on the dependent variable such that the effect of one independent variable fails to remain constant over the levels of another. An interaction is present if the joint effect of two independent variables is not equal to their separate (additive) effects. This means that the effect of an independent variable by itself is not the same as when it is taken in combination with the levels of another independent variable. An example of interaction would be if students of different ability levels profited differently from different instructional content. Ability level and instructional content would be the independent variables.

The simplest type of interaction is that of two variables interacting. (This is sometimes called a *first-order interaction.*) More than two independent variables can be involved in an interaction. However, as more independent variables are involved in an interaction, it becomes increasingly complex, and interpretation becomes increasingly difficult.

> *Interaction* in an experiment is an effect on the dependent variable such that the effect of one independent variable changes over the levels of another independent variable.

The factorial design allows for the manipulation or control of more than one independent variable. For this reason, it is often used as a design for enhancing control by including relevant factors as independent variables. Theoretically, the factorial design may be extended to include any finite number of variables and levels. However, complex designs should be considered with caution, one reason being that such a design may not be economically feasible in terms of the available subjects. Also, the interpretation of complex interactions involving more than two independent variables may, for all practical purposes, be impossible. For example, an interaction involving four independent variables—ability level, sex of the subject, instructional method, and type of material—would be very difficult to interpret.

> *Factorial designs* involve two or more independent variables, called *factors,* in a single design. The cells of the design are determined by the levels of the independent variables taken in combination.

Example 5.4

A teacher is interested in the effectiveness of two different types of materials in learning American history—one highly graphic and pictorial, the other more abstract and more verbally detailed. The students available for the experiment are heterogeneous in ability, and academic aptitude test scores are provided for the students. Not only can academic aptitude serve as a control variable, but it is also possible that the types of materials are not consistently effective across ability levels. That is, type of material and ability may interact. The research problem can be stated as follows:

> *A study of the effects of graphic and verbal materials on American history achievement, when used with high-, average-, and low-ability high school students.*

The design is diagrammed in Figure 5.6.

The 120 students are categorized into three groups on ability, arbitrarily designated high, average, and low. The 40 students with the highest academic aptitude test scores are designated high, the next 40, average, and the remaining 40, low. Then 20 students from each of the ability levels are randomly assigned to each of the two

Figure 5.6
Diagram of Example 5.4 2 × 3 Factorial Design

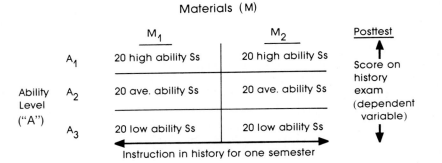

materials, and the instruction takes place over the period of one semester. The dependent variable is performance on a common history exam covering the content of the materials.

The scheme used to diagram the factorial designs is slightly different from the designs diagrammed earlier. The groups are designated in the various cells of the design, rather than only on the rows, and the designation of independent variables is arbitrary. In the example, the types of materials are the experimental treatments, but M (for materials) is used instead of X. It is understood that all six groups of the example are tested at the close of the semester's instruction. Os are not included in the diagram.

In the example, random assignment is used only for assigning students to methods. Obviously, students cannot be assigned ability level at random, since it is an organismic variable. Also, ability level is arbitrarily defined so that 40 students would be in each category. It is not a requirement that the cells of a factorial have equal numbers, but they usually do, since analysis of the data and, to some extent, interpretation of the results, are made less complicated if the cells have equal numbers.

Repeated Measures Designs

In some experiments, it is desirable to measure the same subjects more than once. In learning experiments, for example, a subject often performs a series of tasks, such as solving several problems in sequence, to demonstrate whether or not learning has taken place. Repeated measures designs can have the characteristics of designs discussed earlier. For example, pretesting could be done before any experimental treatments are administered. More commonly, the repeated measures are considered posttests only. As in a factorial design, other independent variables can be built into the design. In fact, most repeated measures designs are factorial, with the added characteristic of repeated measures.

The simplest form of a repeated measures design would consist of administering all the experimental treatments to all subjects. If there were k experimental treatments and n subjects, the design would be diagrammed as follows:

$$
\begin{array}{ll}
S_1 & X_1O—X_2O \ldots X_kO \\
S_2 & X_1O—X_2O \ldots X_kO \\
\cdot & \quad \cdot \quad \cdot \quad \cdot \\
\cdot & \quad \cdot \quad \cdot \quad \cdot \\
\cdot & \quad \cdot \quad \cdot \quad \cdot \\
S_n & X_1O—X_2O \ldots X_kO
\end{array}
$$

The S stands for the specific subject, and all subjects receive the same sequence of experimental treatments. The Os are placed in the diagram to indicate that measurement on the dependent variable takes place after each experimental treatment.

Example 5.5

The example presented here will be slightly more complex than the simplest design possible in that it contains two independent variables in addition to the experimental variable on the repeated measures. A learning experiment using college freshmen is being conducted in solving a series of four concept attainment problems. Subjects solve the problems individually in a learning laboratory setting. The problems can be solved using two types of materials, figural and verbal. This is one independent variable. The organismic variable, sex of the subject, is included as the other independent variable. The dependent variable is an efficiency of solution score, as defined by the experimenter. The research problem and related hypotheses can be stated as follows:

> A study of the effects of type of material and sex on performance in solving concept attainment problems.
>
> H_1: The mean performance of Ss using figural materials is greater than that of those using verbal materials.
>
> H_2: There is no difference in the mean performance of males and females.
>
> H_3: The mean performance of Ss increases across the four problem solutions.

The final hypothesis is that learning will take place in the experiment.

A total of 40 subjects, 20 females and 20 males, is included in the experiment. The design is diagrammed in Figure 5.7. The 20 males and 20 females are randomly assigned to the type of materials, with 10 of each to figural and 10 of each to verbal. The independent variables—sex of the subject and type of materials—are similar to a 2 × 2 factorial. Then there are four levels of the experimental variable problem, so that this could be called a 2 × 2 × 4 factorial with repeated measures on the experimental variable with four levels.

Figure 5.7
Diagram of Example 5.5 Repeated Measures Design

Problem (P)

Sex of S	Type of material	P_1	P_2	P_3	P_4	
Female	Figural	10 Ss randomly assigned				Dependent variable measured with each problem solution
	Verbal	10 Ss randomly assigned				
Male	Figural	10 Ss randomly assigned				
	Verbal	10 Ss randomly assigned				

One characteristic of repeated measures designs is that they generate consider-able data for the number of subjects involved. In the example, although there are 40 subjects, there will be 160 observations or scores, four for each subject. Repeated measures also have the characteristic that all observations are *not* independent; any two observations from different subjects are independent, but the observations from the same subject are not independent because they are from the same subject. This fact must be taken into consideration when the data are analyzed.

Repeated measures designs are designs in which the same subject is measured more than once on the dependent variable.

Counterbalanced Designs

When using repeated measures designs, it is often desirable to somehow balance the order of the experimental treatments rather than to have them administered in the same sequence to all subjects. In this way, if the order of receiving the experimental treatments has some effect, this effect can be balanced to some extent. Also, in a design such as the one in Figure 5.7, the problem is confounded with the position in which the problem occurs, because any given problem is always in the same position. If the scores for problem 4 were considerably better than those for the other problems, we could not determine whether this is due to problem 4 being an easier problem than the others or due to the learning taking place from solving the other problems. A counterbalanced design eliminates this confounding. With a coun-terbalanced design, all subjects enter into all experimental treatments. A counterbal-anced design is a special case of a repeated measures design in which the order of administering experimental treatments is varied according to some plan.

The plan or device by which this ordering of the experimental treatments is arranged is a Latin square, a $k \times k$ array in which the k letters or numbers appear once and only once in each row and column. The size of the square may vary from a 2×2 as a minimum to, at least theoretically, any finite number. The number of different possible squares increases greatly with an increase in k. For example, there are 12 different ways of arranging the letters of a 3×3 square and 161,280 ways for a 5×5 square. The size of the Latin square used in a specific experiment depends on the number of experimental treatments to be assigned by the use of the square.

Example 5.6

A researcher conducts an experiment involving subjects from three different grades solving a series of logical reasoning problems. Three groups of subjects are selected randomly—a group each of eighth-graders, tenth-graders, and twelfth-graders. Each subject is to solve three different problems—say, P_1, P_2, and P_3—in some sequence. The problems are administered under standardized conditions in a learning laboratory. The dependent variable is the time required to attain a correct solution to the problem; the lower the time, the more efficient the solution. The different positions in the sequence of problems make up different ordinal positions, which are actually the first, second, and third times in the solution sequence.

The research problem and related hypotheses can be stated as follows:

A study of the effects of grade level, problem, and sequence on performance in solving logical reasoning problems.

H_1: *The mean performance for grade levels eight, ten, and twelve is such that the higher the grade level, the more efficient the performance.*

H_2: *There is no difference between the mean performances for the three different problems.*

H_3: *There is no difference between the mean performances for the three different sequences in which the problems are solved.*

H_4: *There is a learning effect across ordinal position such that the mean for position 3 is less than that for position 2, which is less than the mean for position 1.*

Again, the concluding hypothesis is the hypothesis for learning in the experiment. H_3 would probably not be of major interest, but it is included for explanatory purposes.

The experiment requires a 3×3 Latin square. Suppose that the researcher has an equal number of six subjects in each of the three grade levels. In the diagram of the experimental design in Figure 5.8, the 18 subjects are numbered consecutively, with the first six subscripts assigned to the eighth grade, the second group of six to the tenth grade, and the final group of six to the twelfth grade. T_1, T_2, and T_3 represent the three times in the solution sequence—that is, the ordinal positions.

Figure 5.8
Diagram of Example 5.6 Counterbalanced Design, Using a 3 × 3 Latin Square and a Total of 18 Subjects

Grade Level	Subject	Time		
		T_1	T_2	T_3
	S_1	P_1	P_2	P_3
	S_2	P_3	P_1	P_2
8th grade	S_3	P_2	P_3	P_1
	S_4	P_1	P_2	P_3
	S_5	P_3	P_1	P_2
	S_6	P_2	P_3	P_1
	S_7	P_1	P_2	P_3
10th grade	.	.	.	.
	S_{12}	P_2	P_3	P_1
	S_{13}	P_1	P_2	P_3
12th grade	.	.	.	.
	S_{18}	P_2	P_3	P_1

Dependent variable measured with each problem solution

The specific Latin square used in this design is as follows:

$$\begin{array}{ccc} 1 & 2 & 3 \\ 3 & 1 & 2 \\ 2 & 3 & 1 \end{array}$$

The numbers of the Latin square make up the subscripts on the problems, as assigned to the first three subjects. After this, the Latin square repeats for each group of three subjects. It has only complete replications and is repeated the same number of times for each grade level. Thus, all sequences of problems, as designated by the rows of the Latin square, appear an equal number of times in each grade level. The problems appear the same number of times in the ordinal positions, designated by T_1, T_2, and T_3 in the diagram. In this respect, the design is balanced.

The Latin square defines three unique sequences of problems, but this does not exhaust the possible sequences. For example, the sequence P_3, P_2, P_1 does not appear. The specific Latin square used in a design is randomly determined.

The example has one dependent variable, time to solution. It is not uncommon to have more than one dependent variable when a counterbalanced design is used, but the design is applied in the same manner for all dependent variables. For example, another possible dependent variable for the example might be number of errors made before solving the problem.

Modification can be made in counterbalanced designs so that an entire group follows the same sequence but the different groups follow different sequences. This would apply if the group participated in the experiment as a unit. When several independent variables are included in a counterbalanced design, the structure and analysis tend to become complex. The lack of independence of the multiple observations on the same subject must be taken into consideration when the data are analyzed. This text provides only a general description of the designs; advanced texts such as Keppel (1982) provide more detail on the use of counterbalanced designs.

Threats to Experimental Validity

As mentioned early in the chapter, the purpose of experimental design is to assist the researcher in interpreting and generalizing the results of the experiment. Experimental design should enhance experimental validity, but experimental validity does not depend on experimental design alone. The specifics of the experiment have an influence, and a number of things can happen to threaten experimental validity, both internal and external. Essentially, these are factors that make it difficult to determine whether or not there has been an experimental effect. Threats to validity give rise to ambiguous explanations of the data.

Campbell and Stanley (1963), summarizing the threats to experimental validity, identified 12 threats, 8 to internal validity and 4 to external validity. Table 5.1 lists and describes these 12 threats and provides an example of how each could occur. All the examples assume that some experimental treatment has been administered.

With all the possible threats to validity, one might wonder whether results from experiments can be interpreted and generalized at all, but this is where the principles of good research design and the specifics of the experiment come in. Control can be enhanced in a number of ways already discussed. For example, random selection takes care of possible selection bias problems. Random assignment enhances the equivalency of groups prior to administering experimental treatments. Many times extraneous variables can be controlled as independent variables through a design such as factorial design.

Table 5.1
Threats to Experimental Validity

Threat	Example

Internal Validity:

1. History—unanticipated events occurring while the experiment is in progress that affect the dependent variable.

1. During a relatively short instructional experiment, one group of subjects misses some instruction because of a power failure at the school.

2. Maturation—processes operating within the subject as a function of time.

2. In a learning experiment, subject performance begins decreasing after about 50 minutes because of fatigue.

3. Testing—the effect of taking one test upon the scores of a subsequent test.

3. In an experiment in which performance on a logical reasoning test is the dependent variable, a pretest cues the subjects about the posttest.

4. Instrumentation—an effect due to inconsistent use of the measuring instruments.

4. Two examiners for an instructional experiment administered the posttest with different instructions and procedures.

5. Statistical regression—an effect caused by a tendency for subjects selected on the basis of extreme scores to regress toward an average performance on subsequent tests.

5. In an experiment involving reading instruction, subjects grouped because of poor pretest reading scores show considerably greater gains than the average and high readers.

6. Differential selection of subjects—an effect due to the groups of subjects not being randomly assigned or selected, but a selection factor is operating such that the groups are not equivalent.

6. The experimental group in an instructional experiment consists of a high-ability class, while the control group is an average-ability class.

7. Experimental mortality or differential loss of subjects—an effect due to subjects dropping out of the experiment on a nonrandom basis.

7. In a health experiment designed to determine the effects of various exercises, those subjects finding exercise most difficult stop participating.

8. Selection-maturation interaction—an effect of maturation not being consistent across the groups because of some selection factor.

8. In a problem-solving experiment, intact groups of junior high school students and senior high students are involved. The junior high students tire of the task sooner than the older students.

External Validity:

1. Interaction effect of testing—pretesting interacts with the experimental treatment and causes some effect such that the results will not generalize to an unpretested population.

1. In a physical performance experiment, the pretest clues the subjects to respond in a certain way to the experimental treatment that would not be the case if there were no pretest.

2. Interaction effects of selection biases and the experimental treatment—an effect of some selection factor of intact groups interacting with the experimental treatment that would not be the case if the groups had been randomly formed.

2. The results of an experiment in which teaching method is the experimental treatment, used with classes of low achievers, do not generalize to heterogeneous ability classes.

Table 5.1
(continued)

Threat	Example
3. Reactive effects of experimental arrangements—an effect that is due simply to the fact that subjects know that they are participating in an experiment and experiencing the novelty of it; also known as the Hawthorne effect.	3. An experiment in remedial reading instruction has an effect that does not occur when the remedial reading program (the experimental treatment) is implemented in the regular program.
4. Multiple-treatment interference—when the same subjects receive two or more treatments (as in a repeated measures design), there may be a carry-over effect between treatments such that the results cannot be generalized to single treatments.	4. In a drug experiment, the same animals are administered four different drug doses in some sequence. The effects of the second through fourth doses cannot be separated from possible (delayed) effects of preceding doses.

The shorter the duration of an experiment, the less likely history is to be a threat to validity. Careful specification and control over the measurement can do much to eliminate problems with instrumentation. If no subjects drop out of the experiment, experimental mortality is no problem. If only posttesting is used, after the experimental treatment is completed, there is no opportunity for an undesirable interaction between testing and the experimental treatment. Thus, it is through the planning and the careful conducting of the experiment that the threats to validity are countered. It may not be possible to eliminate all threats, but it is important to recognize and interpret the results accordingly, entertaining alternate explanations of the data if such explanations are plausible.

> Experimental validity must be considered in the context of each specific experiment. Attaining validity is not an all-or-nothing outcome. Possible threats to validity should be recognized and countered through the design and the way the experiment is conducted.

Designs Extended In Time

Sometimes, when working with educational variables and other variables in the behavioral sciences, it may be difficult to anticipate the time required for an effect to manifest itself. For some variables, the duration of an effect is unknown. Experimental designs can be extended to check on possible delayed effects or to check on the duration of an effect. This can be done by taking additional observations, extended in time. If we extended the posttest-only control group design in such a manner, a possible diagram of the design would be as follows:

$$R \ G_1 \quad X_1 \quad O_1—O_2—O_3$$
$$R \ G_2 \quad — \quad O_4—O_5—O_6$$

In this design, observations are taken on both groups after the experimental treatment has been administered to G_1. Then, at specified, regular intervals, subsequent observations are taken on both groups, although no additional experimental treatments are administered. The length of intervals between observations would depend on the variables under study.

Designs so extended are susceptible to an effect of multiple observation, since groups are measured more than once. Earlier observations may have an effect on subsequent ones. Whether or not there is a multiple observation effect depends on the variables involved. Also, as designs are extended in time, they become especially susceptible to history and maturation effects as threats to internal validity.

Designs can be extended by taking additional observations on the groups. Such observations provide information about possible delayed effects of the experimental variable and about the duration of an effect.

Example 5.7

A researcher is studying the effects of three different exercise programs (X_1, X_2, and X_3) on the resting heartrate, measured 1 minute after a brief, strenuous exercise. The research problem can be stated as follows:

A study of the effects, and duration of those effects, of three exercise programs on the resting heartrates of young male adults.

A random sample of 60 males, ages 18–22, is selected, and 20 are assigned to each of the three exercise programs. The subjects participate daily for 2 weeks in their respective programs; later, on the final day of the 2 weeks, they are measured on heartrate. When the heartrate data is being collected, a subject exercises strenuously for 5 minutes and rests for 1 minute; then the heartrate is measured. After the 2-week period, the subjects no longer participate in exercise programs and are instructed not to initiate exercise on their own. They are again measured on heartrate at 3-week intervals after the final day of the exercise program. The design is diagrammed in Figure 5.9.

Figure 5.9
Diagram of Example 5.7 Design Extended in Time

                    Randomly Assigned   Heartrate Measures
                     (20 Ss per group)   (dependent variable)

R G_1 Group 1 receives O_1 — — — — — — — O_2 — — — — — — — O_3
           Exercise Program A (X_1)

R G_2 Group 2 receives O_4 — — — — — — — O_5 — — — — — — — O_6
           Exercise Program B (X_2)

R G_3 Group 3 receives O_7 — — — — — — — O_8 — — — — — — — O_9
           Exercise Program C (X_3)

◄——————— Two Weeks ——————► ◄——— Three Weeks ———► ◄——— Three Weeks ———►

There is little likelihood of a multiple observation effect in this example. Simply having had heartrate measured 3 weeks earlier should have no effect on subsequent measures of heartrate. There may be a threat to internal validity if subjects continue to exercise on their own after the program has been completed. It would be desirable, almost necessary, to obtain the subjects' commitment prior to conducting the experiment that they will cooperate as instructed throughout the 8-week period of the experiment, including all observation.

Interpreting Results of Experiments

If an experiment is designed properly, the researcher should be able to draw some conclusions about the existence and nature of an experimental effect. There are any number of specific analyses that are used to analyze experimental data. (Analysis procedures are discussed in Chapter 12. The role of statistics, both descriptive and inferential, is one of providing analyses; therefore, statistics are very important to the entire research effort.) However, in interpreting results, we want to consider some patterns of the data (the Os in the designs) and what these patterns indicate about the experimental treatment.

The interpretation of results can be approached in two ways: (1) given a certain result (or pattern of Os), what does it mean? and (2) what comparison would be made to determine whether or not a certain kind of effect exists? Sample designs and interpretations will be considered shortly. The notation in the designs is the same as defined previously. Interpretation of results involves making comparisons between

Os. Although Os consist of observations, such as pretest or posttest scores, in the design, they also represent group data summarized by computing a mean or some group measure. The symbol = means that these group measures are close to being equal; ≠ means that they are substantially different. (A substantial difference would likely be identified through the use of inferential statistics.[4]) In the examples, the a, b, . . . sets of results are considered independently.

Interpretation Example 5.1

A four-group pretest-posttest control group design is used with three different experimental treatments, X_1, X_2, and X_3, and a control treatment. All groups are pretested and posttested. The design is diagrammed as follows:

$$
\begin{array}{ll}
R\ G_1 & O_1 - X_1 - O_2 \\
R\ G_2 & O_3 - X_2 - O_4 \\
R\ G_3 & O_5 - X_3 - O_6 \\
R\ G_4 & O_7 \rule{1cm}{0.4pt} O_8
\end{array}
$$

a. *Result:* $O_1 \neq O_2$, $O_3 \neq O_4$, $O_5 \neq O_6$, $O_2 = O_4$, but O_2, $O_4 \neq O_6$ and $O_1 = O_3 = O_5 = O_7 = O_8$.
   Interpretation: There are effects for all experimental treatments. The effects of X_1 and X_2 are the same, but they are different from that of X_3.
b. *Result:* $O_1 = O_3 = O_4 = O_5 = O_6 = O_7 = O_8$, but $O_1 \neq O_2$.
   Interpretation: There are no effects of X_2 and X_3, only an experimental effect for X_1.
c. *Result:* $O_1 = O_3 = O_5 = O_7$ and $O_2 = O_4 = O_6 = O_8$, but O_1, O_3, O_5, O_7 $\neq O_2$, O_4, O_6, O_8.
   Interpretation: There are no experimental treatment effects, but something, probably a maturation effect, is causing a change between pretest and posttest.
d. What comparison would be made to determine whether or not there is a change in subjects independent of the experimental treatment?
   Comparison: O_7 and O_8. If $O_7 = O_8$, there is no change; if $O_7 \neq O_8$, there is a change. (Comparisons could also be made between O_1, O_3, O_5, and O_8, since O_1, O_3, O_5, and O_7 are considered equivalent due to random assignment of subjects.)

It should be noted that there is no way to check on the effect of pretesting in this design, since *all* groups are pretested. There is no nonpretested comparison group. Also, when there are two or more experimental treatments (in this case, three), it is important to distinguish between them, because they may have differing effects. The sets of results for the example do not exhaust the possible patterns, but they illustrate possible outcomes.

Interpretation Example 5.2

A researcher uses a three-group design. There are two different experimental treat-ments, X_1 and X_2, and a control treatment. Groups are not pretested, but they are posttested twice, once shortly after the experimental treatments are completed and again later to determine whether there is a delayed effect of the treatments. The design is as follows:

$$R\ G_1 \qquad X_1{-}O_1{-\!\!-\!\!-\!\!-}O_2$$
$$R\ G_2 \qquad X_2{-}O_3{-\!\!-\!\!-\!\!-}O_4$$
$$R\ G_3 \qquad \quad {-}O_5{-\!\!-\!\!-\!\!-}O_6$$

a. *Result:* $O_1 = O_3$, but O_3 and $O_1 \neq O_5$, and $O_2 = O_4 = O_6$.
   Interpretation: There are immediate experimental effects, and they are the same for X_1 and X_2. There are no long-term experimental effects.

b. *Result:* $O_1 \neq O_3$, and O_1 and $O_3 \neq O_5$, and $O_2 \neq O_4$, and O_2 and $O_4 \neq O_6$, but $O_1 = O_2$, and $O_3 = O_4$, and $O_5 = O_6$.
   Interpretation: There are experimental effects in both the short and the long term, and they are different effects for X_1 and X_2. However, the effects are consistent over time; that is, the short-term and long-term effects are the same.

c. *Result:* $O_1 = O_3 = O_5 = O_6$, but O_2 and $O_4 \neq O_6$, and $O_2 \neq O_4$.
   Interpretation: There are no short-term experimental effects. There are different long-term experimental effects for X_1 and X_2.

d. *Result:* $O_1 = O_3$, but O_1, $O_3 \neq O_5$ and O_1, $O_3 \neq O_4$, but $O_2 = O_4$, and O_1 and $O_4 \neq O_6$.
   Interpretation: There are short-term experimental effects, and they are the same X_1 and X_2. There are long-term experimental effects, and they are the same for X_1 and X_2, but they are not the same as the short-term effects.

e. What comparison would be made to determine whether there are any long-term effects and whether they are the same for X_1 and X_2?
   Comparison: O_2 and O_4 with O_6. If O_2 and $O_4 \neq O_6$, then long-term experi-mental effects are indicated; then if $O_2 \neq O_4$, the effects of X_1 and X_2 are *not* the same.

f. What comparison would be made to check whether the passing of time affects the subjects on the dependent variable?
   Comparison: O_5 and O_6. These Os come from the control group, which receives no experimental treatment. If $O_5 \neq O_6$, there is some effect due to the passing of time; if $O_5 = O_6$, time has no effect.

g. Is there any way to check on the initial (preexperiment) equivalence of the three groups? Is this of concern? Why or why not?
   Answer: Since there were no pretests, there are no preexperimental Os to check equivalence, but this is of no concern, because the groups are considered equiv-alent due to the random assignment *(R)*.

Interpretation Example 5.3

This example is somewhat more complex since it involves six groups, three of which are pretested and three of which are posttested immediately after the experiment is completed. (It is a modification of the Solomon four-group design, extended in time.) All six groups are posttested some time after the experiment is completed. Only one experimental treatment (X) and a control treatment are used. The design is as follows:

$$
\begin{array}{lll}
R\ G_1 & O_1 - X - O_2 & \!\!\!\!\!\!-\!\!\!-\!\!\!- O_3 \\
R\ G_2 & O_4 - X & \!\!\!\!\!\!-\!\!\!-\!\!\!-\!\!\!-\!\!\!- O_5 \\
R\ G_3 & -\!\!\!- X - O_6 & \!\!\!\!\!\!-\!\!\!-\!\!\!- O_7 \\
R\ G_4 & -\!\!\!- X & \!\!\!\!\!\!-\!\!\!-\!\!\!-\!\!\!-\!\!\!- O_8 \\
R\ G_5 & O_9 \quad - \quad O_{10} & \!\!\!\!- O_{11} \\
R\ G_6 & \!\!\!\!\!\!-\!\!\!-\!\!\!-\!\!\!-\!\!\!-\!\!\!-\!\!\!-\!\!\!-\!\!\!- O_{12}
\end{array}
$$

a. *Result:* $O_3 \neq O_5$, and O_3 and $O_5 \neq O_{11}$.
   Interpretation: There is an experimental effect in pretested groups in the long term. (This result gives no information about nonpretested groups or about short–term effects.) However, the effect is not the same for a group previously posttested and a group not previously posttested.

b. *Result:* $O_2 = O_6$, and O_2, $O_6 \neq O_{10}$, but $O_3 = O_5 = O_7 = O_8 = O_{11} = O_{12}$.
   Interpretation: There is an experimental effect in the short term, and it is the same for pretested and nonpretested groups. There is no long-term experimental effect.

c. *Result:* $O_2 \neq O_6$, but $O_6 = O_{10}$, and $O_2 = O_3 = O_5$, and $O_6 = O_7 = O_8$, and $O_{11} = O_{12}$.
   Interpretation: There is an interaction effect of experimental treatment and pretesting, and this effect persists in the long term. Note that this is *not* simply a pretesting effect, because $O_2 \neq O_{10}$.

d. What comparison would be made to check whether there is a change in a *nonpretested* control group over the long term?
   Comparison: Compare O_9 and O_{12}. Since the groups are randomly assigned, had G_6 been pretested, it can be assumed that its pretest scores would have been similar to those of other groups. Pretesting occurs prior to the experimental treatment; therefore, O_4 and O_{12} or O_1 and O_{12} could also have been compared. If $O_9 \neq O_{12}$, there has been a change with the passing of time; if $O_9 = O_{12}$, there has been no change.

e. What comparison would be made to determine whether there is a long-term experimental effect in groups that are posttested only once
   Comparison: Compare O_5, O_8, and O_{12}. If $O_5 = O_8$, but O_5, $O_8 \neq O_{12}$, then there is an experimental effect that is not influenced by pretesting. If O_5, O_8, and O_{12} are all unequal, there appears to be an experimental effect, but there is

also an interaction of the experimental effect and pretesting. If $O_5 = O_8 = O_{12}$, there is no long-term experimental effect.

f. What three effects, other than interaction effects, can be checked by this six-way design?
Answer: (1) the experimental treatment effect, in both short term and long term; (2) effects of pretesting; and (3) effects of prior posttesting.

Other comparisons could be made in the foregoing designs, and, of course, there could be other patterns of results. An important characteristic of design and interpretation of results is that there must be a comparison group for a contrast to check on a possible effect. Therefore, in the first example, since all groups were pretested, an effect of pretesting cannot be checked. In the third example, a pretest effect can be checked, but only by comparing groups that have and have not been pretested. We cannot check on a pretest effect by considering only G_1, G_2, and G_5.

The interpretation of experimental results is a common-sense process. The design aids the researcher in structuring the desired comparisons or contrasts so that effects can be checked. In any specific experiment, a knowledge of the variables and possibly of the results of related studies is also helpful in interpreting and understanding the data.

Randomness and Representativeness

In the designs described in this chapter, some aspect of random selection or random assignment of the subjects was included. This characteristic makes for what Campbell and Stanley (1963) call "true" experimental designs. By randomly selecting a sample, the sample represents the population from which it was selected. If a number of subjects are randomly assigned to the experimental treatments (including the control treatment, if there is one), then prior to the experiment, the groups of subjects differ only on the basis of random sampling fluctuation. The experimental groups are equivalent because of the random assignment.

However, if there is a pool of available subjects and they are randomly assigned to experimental treatments, what population do these subjects represent? Suppose that a researcher uses the 120 students enrolled in a beginning education course as the subjects for an experiment. The students are randomly assigned to experimental treatments, but they have not been randomly selected from some larger population. It could not be argued that they randomly selected themselves into the education course, so what population do they represent? This is a question of external validity that can be answered only by the researcher through a knowledge of the subjects and the variables under study. Do the 120 students represent college students who have been enrolled in beginning education courses during the past several years? Do they represent college students in education generally? Or do they represent young adults generally? Probably not the latter, but cases could possibly be made for the others.

The point being made is that the matter of representativeness, and hence generalizability, must often be argued on a logical basis. It would be nice if there was always the option of random selection from the population under study, but this is not the case. In the example here, if the 120 students participated in a learning experiment, the results would likely have considerable generalizability. They might even generalize to other age groups, depending on the conditions of the experiment.

In some experiments in educational research, intact groups are used. The groups have not been randomly selected, nor have the members been randomly assigned to the groups. For example, this situation occurs when intact classes of students are used in an experiment. When such groups are used, we have what Campbell and Stanley (1963) call a "quasi-experimental" design. (Such designs are discussed in the next chapter.) When groups are initially not equivalent in a random sense, this condition not only influences the generalizability, but it may also affect the internal validity of the experiment, since there may have been some initial differences between the groups relative to the variables under study.

In summary, it is preferable to have some condition of randomness in designing an experiment, but this is not always possible. Even if random assignment is used, the subjects may not have been randomly selected from some larger population, and generalizability must be argued on a logical basis. (The difference between random selection and random assignment is discussed in the sampling chapter, Chapter 10.) Of course, the case for external validity of any experimental results must be made in the context of the specific variables and conditions of the experiment.

SUMMARY

This chapter has provided some of the more general designs used in experimental research. The distinguishing characteristic of experimental research is the manipulation of variables. The experimental design provides the structure for the experiment in which the variables are deliberately manipulated and controlled by the researcher. It might be mistakenly inferred that complexity of design is a desirable characteristic of a more sophisticated experimenter, but a truly sophisticated experimenter need only come up with an experimental design that will do the job—meet the objectives of the research and be adequate for testing the hypotheses. An experiment must have definitely stated hypotheses, and the design should test these hypotheses, providing for the meaningful interpretation of results, whatever the pattern of the data.

At this point, the reader should have an understanding of the underlying reasoning of experimental design and the logic of the various design structures. Characteristics of a good experimental design were discussed early in the chapter. A well-conceived design will not guarantee valid results, but an inappropriate and inadequate design is certain to lead to uninterpretable results and tenuous conclusions, if any can be drawn. The design must be conceived prior to the experimentation, and it should be carefully planned and applied. No postexperiment manipulations, statistical or otherwise, can take the place of a well-conceived experimental design.

KEY CONCEPTS

Experiment

Experimental design

Experimental variable

Experimental treatment

Subjects

Experimental control

Contamination

Parsimony

Internal validity

External validity

*Pretest-posttest control group
design*

Solomon four-group design

Factorial design

Repeated measures design

Counterbalanced design

Latin square

Threats to validity

Designs extended in time

Multiple observations

*Randomness and representa-
tiveness*

*Posttest-only control group
design*

EXERCISES

5.1 Define the concepts of internal and external validity of an experiment. Why do we say that for some experiments, an attempt at increasing one type of validity tends to jeopardize the other type?

5.2 Several teachers plan to do an experiment in the school setting concerning the effects of class size on achievement in chemistry. Class size is an independent variable and has four levels of size—10–14, 18–23, 26–31, and 34–38 students. Four high schools are involved in the study, each with eight chemistry classes, two of each class size. Students can be assigned at random to a class within a school, but students cannot be assigned randomly to a school. Two chemistry teachers are used in each school, each teaching four classes. The dependent variable is chemistry achievement, measured after an instructional period of one semester. Develop and describe one or more experimental designs that would apply to this research study. Consider possible uncontrolled variables and variables that might be controlled. Is there a possibility of confounding of variables? State one or more hypotheses that might be tested by this experiment.

5.3 Discuss in detail an example of an experiment for which the posttest-only control group design is appropriate. Consider such points as why you would not need pretests and the number of groups you would include. (You may want to extend the design to more than two groups.) Describe how you would enhance control in your proposed experiment. Also, identify the independent variable(s), dependent variable(s), and constants.

5.4 A researcher is doing an experiment on problem solutions. The experiment is done in a learning laboratory. The subjects for the experiment are college students enrolled in a sophomore-level education course. The problems, though similar, are of two types: geometric and algebraic. Type of problem is an independent variable. Other independent variables are sex of the student and group size. There are two group sizes: individual and pair. The dependent variable is number of errors to solution, and this is considered to be measured on an interval scale. There are 160 subjects (96 girls and 64 boys) available for the experiment. Each subject or pair of subjects is to solve only one problem. Present a factorial design that would be appropriate for this experiment. Discuss how you would assign the subjects and how many would be assigned to the various cells. (Use equal numbers of girls and boys for the experiment.) How would you build randomization into the assignment?

5.5 Discuss the possible gains in internal validity when going from a pretest-posttest control group design to a Solomon four-group design.

5.6 A teacher designs an experiment to determine the effects of programmed learning materials as supplementary aids in an advanced algebra course. The dependent variable is the amount of algebra learned during one semester of instruction. There are 83 students enrolled in four advanced algebra classes who are taught by this teacher, and these students were assigned randomly to the classes. The students make up the subjects for the experiment. One group of students has access to the programmed materials; the other group does not. Suggest an experimental design that would apply to this situation. Is it necessary for the teacher to use a pretest? How might the internal validity of the experiment be enhanced? Does this experiment have external validity, and if so, to what extent?

5.7 Discuss an experimental situation for which a counterbalanced design would be applicable. We say that multiple-treatment interference can be a threat to validity when using a counterbalanced design. What does this mean?

5.8 A five-group, posttest-only control group design is used. There are four experimental treatments and a control treatment. Using the notation introduced in the chapter, the design can be diagrammed as follows:

$$
\begin{array}{cccc}
R & G_1 & X_1 & O_1 \\
R & G_2 & X_2 & O_2 \\
R & G_3 & X_3 & O_3 \\
R & G_4 & X_4 & O_4 \\
R & G_5 & — & O_5
\end{array}
$$

   a. Is there any need to be concerned about the preexperiment equivalency of the groups? Why or why not?

b. Is there any way to check on whether or not groups change on the dependent variable from before the experiment to after the experiment, independent of any experimental treatment? Why or why not?

c. What would you conclude from the following results and comparisons? The equals sign means that the observations are about the same; the not-equals sign means that they are substantially different. (*Note:* Consider only the results given. Do not read into the comparison results not specified.) Consider each set of results independently.

(1) No pair of Os are equal.

(2) $O_1 = O_3$ and $O_2 = O_4$, but $O_1, O_3 \neq O_2, O_4$, and $O_1, O_2, O_3, O_4 \neq O_5$.

(3) $O_1 = O_2$ and $O_3 = O_4 = O_5$, but $O_1, O_2 \neq O_3, O_4, O_5$.

(4) $O_1 = O_2 = O_3 = O_5$, but $O_1, O_2, O_3, O_5 \neq O_4$.

5.9 A researcher uses the following experimental design. It involves six groups and is, in essence, a takeoff on the Solomon four-group design. Only one experimental treatment, X, is involved.

$$
\begin{array}{llll}
R\ G_1 & O_1 & X & O_2 \\
R\ G_2 & O_3 & - & O_4 \\
R\ G_3 & O_5 & X & \text{------}\ O_6 \\
R\ G_4 & O_7 & - & \text{------}\ O_8 \\
R\ G_5 & - & X & O_9 \\
R\ G_6 & \text{------------} & O_{10}
\end{array}
$$

a. What is gained (apparently) by including the middle two groups?

b. What comparisons could be made to determine whether or not there is an effect of pretesting?

c. What would you conclude from the following results and comparisons?

(1) $O_2 = O_9$ and $O_6 = O_8$, but $O_2, O_9 \neq O_6, O_8$.

(2) $O_2 = O_6 = O_9$, $O_4 = O_8 = O_{10}$, but $O_2, O_6, O_9 \neq O_4, O_8, O_{10}$.

(3) $O_1 = O_2 = O_3$, and $O_3 = O_4$.

(4) $O_2 = O_4 = O_9$, $O_6 \neq O_2$, and $O_6 \neq O_8$.

5.10 The following design is used, including three groups, all of which are pretested once and posttested twice. Two experimental treatments, X_1 and X_2, are used.

$$
\begin{array}{llll}
R\ G_1 & O_1 & X_1 & O_2\text{------}O_3 \\
R\ G_2 & O_4 & X_2 & O_5\text{------}O_6 \\
R\ G_3 & O_7 & - & O_8\text{------}O_9
\end{array}
$$

a. What is gained by including a pretest rather than only posttesting the subjects?

b. Is it possible to check on an effect of pretesting with this design? Why or why not?

c. What comparisons would be made to determine if there is an experimental effect in the long term?

d. Is it necessary to have the pretest to check on the preexperimental equivalence of the groups? Why or why not?

e. Suppose that $O_7 \neq O_8 \neq O_9$, the observations on the control group. What would you conclude from these results?

f. What would you conclude from the following results and comparisons?
   (1) $O_2 = O_5$, but O_2 and $O_5 \neq O_8$, and $O_3 = O_6 = O_9$.
   (2) $O_1 \neq O_2$, and $O_4 \neq O_5$, and $O_2 \neq O_5$, but $O_7 = O_8$.
   (3) $O_2 = O_5 = O_8$, but $O_3 \neq O_2$ and $O_5 \neq O_6$, and O_3 and $O_6 \neq O_9$.
   (4) $O_2 \neq O_5$, and O_2 and $O_5 \neq O_8$, $O_2 \neq O_3$, and $O_5 \neq O_6$, and $O_3 \neq O_6$, and O_3 and $O_6 \neq O_9$, but $O_7 = O_8 = O_9$.

5.11 Summarize the general characteristics of a well-designed experiment. Select one or more research articles that involve experimentation from such publications as the *American Educational Research Journal* or the *Journal of Educational Psychology*. Read the article carefully to determine the design used and the experimental procedure. Does the experiment seem to have high internal validity? Is there any indication of its external validity?

NOTES

1. The term *levels* is a holdover from the days when experimental variables were often such variables as drug dosages and fertilizer concentrations; that is, there were quantitative levels of the experimental variables. Now the term applies to qualitative and categorical variables as well as quantitative variables.

2. The symbolism used here and throughout this chapter is similar to that introduced by D. T. Campbell and J. C. Stanley, "Experimental and Quasi-Experimental Designs for Research on Teaching," in N. L. Gage (Ed.), *Handbook of Research on Teaching* (Chicago: Rand McNally, 1963), pp. 171–246.

3. The terminology and the diagramming format used here is very similar to that used by Campbell and Stanley in "Experimental and Quasi-Experimental Designs for Research on Teaching."

4. If inferential statistics are used in analyzing data from such designs, as they usually are, a substantial difference would be one that is statistically significant. Statistical concepts are discussed in Chapter 12.

REFERENCES

Campbell, D. T., & Stanley, J. C. (1963). Experimental and quasi-experimental designs for research on teaching. In N. L. Gage (Ed.), *Handbook of research on teaching* (pp. 171–246). Chicago: Rand McNally.

Cronbach, L. J., & Furby, L. (1970). How we should measure change—or should we? *Psychological Bulletin, 74,* 66–80.

Keppel, G. (1982). *Design and analysis: A researcher's handbook* (2nd ed.). Englewood Cliffs, NJ: Prentice-Hall.

Solomon, R. L. (1949). An extension of control-group design. *Psychological Bulletin, 46,* 137–150.

Zimmerman, D. W., & Williams, R. H. (1982). Gain scores in research can be highly reliable. *Journal of Educational Measurement, 19*(2), 149–154.

6

Quasi-Experimental Research

The designs described in Chapter 5 are what Campbell and Stanley (1963) call "true" experimental designs. This is because they have the characteristic of random assignment of subjects to the experimental treatments (groups). Thus, equivalence of the groups is achieved and is within the limits of random fluctuation due to the random assignment. When conducting educational research, it is not always possible to select or assign subjects at random. There are many naturally formed intact groups of subjects in the educational world, such as the students in a classroom. When intact groups of subjects are used in an experiment, we have what is called *quasi-experimental research*. Such research can make valuable contributions, but it is important that the researcher be especially cautious about interpreting and generalizing results.

> *Quasi-experimental research* involves the use of intact groups of subjects in an experiment, rather than assigning subjects at random to experimental treatments.

The Problems of Validity

Lack of random assignment potentially introduces problems with the validity of the experiment—both internal and external validity. In Chapter 5, it was noted that one of the threats to internal validity is differential selection of subjects. Suppose that two intact classes of fifth-grade students were used in an experiment for which the dependent variable was performance in science, operationally defined as the score on a science test. The classes had initially been formed on the basis of ability grouping, one class with high ability and the other with average ability. The classes receive different experimental treatments. If there were an effect favoring the high-ability lass, it would be difficult to argue that the effect was due to the experimental treatment. Ability level and experimental treatment are confounded, and there is no way to interpret an effect with confidence.

Any number of factors might be operating in the formation of intact groups, and it cannot be argued that such groups are random samples of some larger populations. Random selection or assignment is a process (described in Chapter 10), and it either has or has not been done. With quasi-experimental research, it has not been done, so there is the possibility that selection bias will jeopardize the generalizability of the results.

What is a researcher who uses intact groups to do? For the purposes of generalizability, representativeness must be argued on a logical basis. For internal validity, the researcher must attempt to establish the degree of equivalence between groups. This requires considering characteristics or variables that may be related to the variables under study. For example, if intact classrooms were involved in an instructional experiment in mathematics, the grade level probably would be included either as a constant or as another independent (control) variable. The researcher would also want evidence that the classes are of comparable ability level. If empirical data such as IQ test scores are available, they can be helpful in checking equivalence of groups. In fact, such data sometimes can be used for statistical control. Even with empirical data, checking and establishing equivalence always involves some subjective judgment on the basis of information about variables and conditions of the experiment. The lack of randomness must be given specific attention when interpreting the results, and the extent to which it can be countered determines the confidence in the internal validity of the experiment.

> When considering problems of validity of quasi-experimental research, limitations should be clearly identified, the equivalence of the groups should be discussed, and possible representativeness and generalizability should be argued on a logical basis.

Posttest-Only, Nonequivalent Control Group Design

Some of the quasi-experimental designs look very much like the experimental designs discussed in the preceding chapter, except that there is no random assignment of subjects to the groups. When the term *nonequivalent* is used, it means nonequivalent in a random sense. It does not mean that it will be impossible to make a case for the similarity of the groups on relevant variables or characteristics. Indeed, with quasi-experimental designs, the confidence that can be placed in the validity of results depends in large part on the case that can be made for the similarity of the groups.

Using the notation introduced in the preceding chapter, the posttest-only, non-equivalent control group design in its simplest form can be diagrammed as follows:

$$G_1 \qquad X{-}O_1$$
$$G_2 \qquad {-}O_2$$

The design indicates that one group receives the experimental treatment and another group, serving as a control group, does not receive the experimental treatment. Both groups are posttested at the same time, shortly after the experimental treatment is completed for G_1. The design can be extended to include any number of experimental treatments. For k treatments,

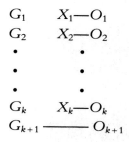

$$G_1 \qquad X_1{-}O_1$$
$$G_2 \qquad X_2{-}O_2$$
$$\vdots \qquad \vdots$$
$$G_k \qquad X_k{-}O_k$$
$$G_{k+1} \text{———} O_{k+1}$$

the design requires $k + 1$ groups. If two or more experimental treatments are used but no control group, the design would be called a posttest-only, nonequivalent multiple-group design.

> The *posttest-only, nonequivalent control group design* contains as many groups as there are experimental treatments, plus a control group. Intact groups are used, and subjects are measured only once, after the experimental treatments have been applied.

The validity of any experiment depends on the specific conditions of the experiment, but experiments using the posttest-only, nonequivalent control group design generally are weak in validity. The difficulty arises from the possibility of selection bias and the lack of pretests prior to the experimental treatments. The design should not be used unless some antecedent data are available that provide information about the extent of similarity between the groups. Such data will not eliminate selection bias if it exists, but they provide information that may avoid a misinterpretation of the results.

Example 6.1

A junior high school teacher who has four classes of eighth-grade science conducts a study using three different new approaches plus the traditional approach (control) to teaching the laboratory portion of the course. The teacher uses a different approach for teaching each of the four classes. The dependent variable is performance on an examination given at the end of the semester covering the laboratory content. The research problem can be stated as follows:

> *A study of the effects of instructional approach on the performance of eighth-graders on a science laboratory examination.*

The design is diagrammed in Figure 6.1.

No pretests were given, but to check on the similarity of the classes, other information was reviewed and the following data were discovered:

1. The proportions of boys and girls are about the same across the classes.
2. The previous seventh-grade science grades of the students were about the same for Classes 1, 2, and 4, but Class 3 students had somewhat higher grades. The same pattern was true for other areas of previous seventh-grade achievement, such as mathematics.
3. Although, for the most part, the school does not group students by ability, there is an honors program in English; because of scheduling restrictions, many of the students in Class 3 are also in the English honors program.

Figure 6.1
Diagram of Example 6.1 Posttest-Only, Nonequivalent Control Group Design, with Three Experimental Groups and a Control Group

	Intact Classes	Experimental Variable	Posttest	
G_1	Class 1	Approach 1 (X_1)	O_1	
G_2	Class 2	Approach 2 (X_2)	O_2	Dependent variable: score on science laboratory exam
G_3	Class 3	Approach 3 (X_3)	O_3	
G_4	Class 4	Traditional (−)	O_4	

One semester

The time of instruction and the teacher are constants in this study. Two classes, 1 and 4, meet in the morning; the other classes meet in the afternoon.

It appears that Classes 1, 2, and 4 are quite similar on variables that may affect performance on the examination. However, Class 3 seems to be a more able class, which will have to be considered when interpreting the results. There is a partial confounding between experimental treatment and ability level, since any one class receives only one treatment.

Example 6.1 Results and Interpretation. Suppose that the following pattern of results appears on the posttest: $O_1 = O_2$, but O_1 and O_2 are greater than O_4, and O_3 is greater than O_1 and O_2.

Interpretation: Approaches 1 and 2 are more effective than the traditional approach, and they appear to be equally effective. These approaches do not seem to be affected by the time of day, since one class meets in the morning and the other in the afternoon. No definite conclusion can be drawn about Approach 3; in fact, it may not be as effective as the traditional approach, and the higher posttest scores of G_3 may be due to the students' abilities.

This example illustrates the fact that there may be alternative explanations with quasi-experimental designs, depending on the pattern of results. It may be that Approach 3 is the most effective approach, explaining the high O_3, or it may be that the high O_3 is due to the higher ability of G_3. Suppose that O_3 had been less than O_1, O_2, and O_4. Then it would be quite conclusive that Approach 3 is not as effective as the others, at least not with higher ability students. The similarity of Classes 1, 2, and 4 allows us to be relatively confident about the conclusions for Approaches 1 and 2 and the traditional approach.

Pretest-Posttest, Nonequivalent Control Group Design

The pretest-posttest, nonequivalent control group design is similar to the posttest-only, nonequivalent control group design, except that the subjects are also pretested. In its general form, if there are k experimental treatments, it can be diagrammed as follows:

$$
\begin{array}{ll}
G_1 & O_1 \longrightarrow X_1 \longrightarrow O_2 \\
G_2 & O_3 \longrightarrow X_2 \longrightarrow O_4 \\
\quad \bullet & \qquad \qquad \bullet \\
\quad \bullet & \qquad \qquad \bullet \\
\quad \bullet & \qquad \qquad \bullet \\
G_k & O_{2k-1} \longrightarrow X_k \longrightarrow O_{2k} \\
G_{k+1} & O_{2k+1} \longrightarrow\longrightarrow O_{2k+2}
\end{array}
$$

Only two groups are required, an experimental group and a control group, for the design in its simplest form. If no control group is included, the design is called a pretest-posttest, nonequivalent multiple-group design.

The inclusion of the pretest greatly aids in checking the similarity of the groups, because the pretest scores are on variables that have a strong relationship with the dependent variable. The pretest is administered to all subjects, under consistent conditions, prior to conducting the experiment. Pretest scores also can be used for statistical control, and in some cases gain scores can be generated.

The *pretest-posttest, nonequivalent control group design* aids in checking the extent of group similarity, and the pretest scores may be used for statistical control or for generating gain scores.

Example 6.2

An instructional experiment involves the use of two new reading programs and their possible effects on reading achievement in the fourth grade. The new programs are the experimental treatments, and the traditional program is the control treatment. Thirty fourth-grade classrooms in the elementary schools of a single district are to participate, and there is no random assignment. Ten teachers have agreed to use each of the reading programs, the two new programs and the traditional program. Of course, each teacher uses only one program. The students are pretested on Form A of a reading achievement test; the programs are used for an 18-week period; and then the students are posttested on Form B of the test. The design is diagrammed in Figure 6.2.

The pretest score is helpful in checking on the similarity of the groups, but it is not the only variable that could be checked. Thirty teachers are involved, and no teacher uses more than one program. Are the groups of ten teachers similar on factors that may affect reading achievement? Although individual teachers may differ, groups of ten teachers may be quite similar when considering all the teachers. One factor to check might be the length of teaching experience of the teachers. If the most experienced teachers were all in one group, a systematic difference between the groups might exist.

If the schools in which the 30 classes are located differ on such factors as socioeconomic regions, this would have to be considered. It would not be satisfactory to have one program limited to schools at a certain socioeconomic level, because there would be confounding between the effect of school and the effect of the reading program. A desirable arrangement would be for each of three schools at a socioeconomic level to use one of the programs. It might be that some schools would have more than one program, although such an arrangement could lead to some contamination of the data due to interaction of students from different classes.

Figure 6.2
Diagram of Example 6.2 Pretest-Posttest, Nonequivalent Control Group Design, with Two Experimental Groups and a Control Group

	Intact Classes	Pretest	Experimental Variable	Posttest (dependent variable)
G_1	Class 1 ⋮ Class 10	O_1	New Program 1 (X_1)	O_2
G_2	Class 11 ⋮ Class 20	O_3	New Program 2 (X_2)	O_4
G_3	Class 21 ⋮ Class 30	O_5	Traditional Program $(-)$	O_6

←——————— Eighteen weeks' instruction ———————→

In Figure 6.2, although there are 30 classes, there are only three pretest Os and three posttest Os. When analyzing results, we initially check the group results, but in an extensive study such as this example, it is usually helpful—and even necessary—to break down or sort out results by making more detailed comparisons, such as the following:

1. Suppose that the pretest scores of classes in a program (group) are similar. Compare the ten posttest scores of the classes within a program. Are these scores close together or are they highly variable? If they are close together, the program appears to be having a consistent effect; if they are highly variable, the inherent variation is overiding any program effect, or the program effect is not consistent across classes within the program.
2. If classes vary on pretest scores, group the classes within a program into two or three categories (high, middle, low) on pretest score. Then check the posttest scores of these categories to determine whether the gains are consistent or different across categories within a program and across programs within a category. For example, suppose that for the classes scoring high on the pretest, the gains for New Program 1 are greater than those for New Program 2 and the traditional program. This is a comparison across programs within a category, and it appears that New Program 1 is the most effective for those students who were initially the most able readers.
3. If the pretest scores of classes are similar, compare the posttest scores of the classes within a program. If they are about the same, external factors such as

the teacher or school are having consistent effects; if they are different these external factors are having differing effects.

Example 6.2 Results and Interpretation. Suppose that the following pattern of results appears: $O_1 = O_3 = O_5$, but $O_2 \neq O_4$, and $O_2, O_4 \neq O_6$, but O_4 is greater than O_2 and O_2 is greater than O_6.

Interpretation: Based on pretest results, the groups appear to be quite similar initially. There are program effects: Both new programs are more effective than the traditional program, and New Program 1 is the most effective.

In many experiments involving nonequivalent groups, the design is extended to include control variables as independent variables. (If socioeconomic level could be included in this way, it would be an example of a control variable.) In essence, this extends the design to a factorial design. If some aspect of randomness could be included, the validity of the design would be enhanced. In the example, it would be helpful if the 30 classes could be randomly assigned to the programs. This still would not make for random assignment to the classes, but it would make the ten groups of teachers equivalent on a random basis. Such assignment would tend to equalize the differences among teachers over the experimental and control treatments. When using a quasi-experimental design, we attempt to build as much control as possible into the design. Then available information is used to check the equivalence of the groups. The results must be interpreted and generalized in the context of this information and the conditions of the experiment.

Time Series Designs

Time series designs comprise a group of quasi-experimental designs that involve repeated measurement of one or more intact groups. An experimental treatment is injected between two of the measurements for at least one of the groups. Time series designs are useful for situations in which there is periodic, naturally occurring measurement of the dependent variable over time, such as repeated testing in a class. Measurement should be consistent across the observations; with some dependent variables, it may be difficult to attain consistency.

Time series designs involve repeated measurement of one or more intact groups, with an experimental treatment inserted between two of the measurements of at least one group.

Single-Group Time Series Design

A single-group time series design can be diagrammed simply as follows:

$$G \qquad O_1 - O_2 - O_3 - X - O_4 - O_5$$

As indicated, there is no random assignment of subjects to the group. There can be any feasible number of observations or measurements, and the insertion of X should be done randomly. Observations may coincide with some routine measurement that takes place, such as a test every 4 weeks in a class.

One characteristic of time series designs is that there are numerous possible patterns of results. This introduces a problem with internal validity, especially with only one group in that there may be alternative explanations for the results other than the effect of the experimental treatment. Figure 6.3 shows three possible patterns of results. The Os on the horizontal axis represent the measurement occasions, and the vertical axis is the scale of the dependent variable.

For any particular experiment and dependent variable, there would be only one pattern. The interpretation of pattern A would be that the experimental treatment appears to have had an effect. The slope of the line returns to approximately the preexperimental treatment level, especially between the fifth and sixth measure-

Figure 6.3
Possible Results Patterns of a Single-Group Time Series Design

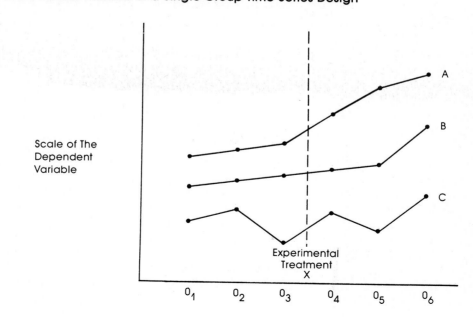

ments. On the surface, pattern B appears to include no experimental treatment effect. However, the marked increase between the final two measurements might be the result of a delayed effect. If no apparent external event could have produced this effect, an experimental effect is certainly plausible. For this reason, it is important to anticipate the time interval between the introduction of the experimental treatment and the appearance of its effect. For certain variables, the effect in pattern B is about as definite as it is in pattern A. It should be noted that as the time interval increases, the likelihood of an intervening extraneous event also increases.

The erratic pattern C almost excludes the possibility of drawing a conclusion about an experimental treatment effect. Since there is no control group, it is most difficult to infer the pattern without the experimental treatment. The fluctuation between observations may indicate that other factors are operating that override any experimental treatment effect. It is possible that the experiment would require an increase in control before there could be sensitivity to an experimental treatment effect. The conclusion of no experimental treatment effect cannot be drawn from pattern C, however.

The numerous observations of the time designs are useful, not only for locating a possible effect but also for avoiding inference of an effect when there likely is none. Consider pattern C. If O_3 and O_4 were the only measures taken, the researcher would conclude that there is an experimental effect, when the difference in the measurements may well be due to something else. In pattern B, the possible delayed effect would have been missed if only measures O_3 and O_4 (and even O_5) had been taken, so it is important to consider the entire pattern.

Example 6.3

A physical therapist is working with a group of 12 patients in an 8-week rehabilitation program. Members of the group receive therapy every day, and the group is tested at the end of each week on a physical performance test. A traditional type of therapy is used, except for the seventh week (determined on a random basis), during which an experimental therapy is administered. The design can be diagrammed as follows:

$$G \quad O_1—O_2—O_3—O_4—O_5—O_6—X—O_7—O_8$$

Suppose that the results of this experiment produce the pattern shown in Figure 6.4. How would these results be interpreted? There is strong evidence that the experimental therapy is more effective than the traditional therapy. The pattern of improvement is quite consistent for the first 6 weeks, but it shows a large increase during the seventh week. Improvement returns to the earlier level during the eighth week. Thus, unless there is some other reason why there would be increased performance during the seventh week, there is a good case for an experimental effect.

In this example, maintaining consistency of measurement poses no problem, because the same physical performance test is used throughout. Consider another

Figure 6.4
Pattern of Results for Example 6.3 Experiment, Using a Single-Group Time Series Design

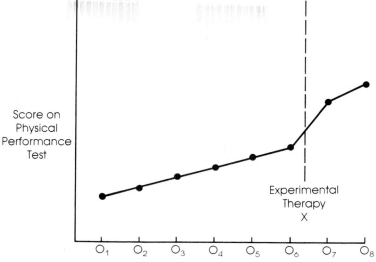

situation. An elementary school teacher uses a time series design to check the effects of individual versus group practice on performance in spelling. The class is used as the group. Each week the class is designated a certain amount of time for spelling practice (in addition to the instruction), and a test is given every Friday. The usual format for practice is on an individual basis, but during one week over a 6-week period, group practice is used as an experimental treatment.

One problem with this example is keeping the difficulty level of the spelling tests consistent. If the test after the group practice is easier than others and the class tends to perform better, the easier test is an alternative explanation for the results. Of course, the amount of practice time should be constant regardless of the practice format.

Multiple-Group Time Series Design

The single-group time series design can be extended to include two or more groups. A common design is to include a control group in the design, in which case an example design could be diagrammed as follows:

$$G_1 \quad O_1—O_2—X—O_3—O_4—O_5—O_6—O_7$$
$$G_2 \quad O_8—O_9\text{————}O_{10}—O_{11}—O_{12}—O_{13}—O_{14}$$

Again, any number of observations can be taken, and the experimental treatment is inserted randomly for one group. The groups are measured at the same times.

The *multiple-group time series design* includes two or more intact groups, one of which may be a control group, and an experimental treatment is inserted for at least one of the groups.

The inclusion of two or more groups strengthens the design because it provides for comparison, thus enhancing internal validity. For example, it provides a check for the possibility of an external event coinciding with the experimental treatment. Suppose that both groups in a control group design demonstrated an unusually large increase for the observations immediately following the administration of the experimental treatment to the experimental group. Since the increase occurred in both groups, it cannot be an experimental effect (since the control group had no experimental treatment), so it is likely due to some external factor that is affecting both groups.

The observations that occur prior to the experimental treatment can be used to check on the similarity of the groups. As with any multiple-group quasi-experimental design, the greater the similarity between the groups, the more confidence can be placed in the conclusions drawn from the results.

Example 6.4

A teacher who has three classes of first-year algebra decides to do a study for which the research problem can be stated as follows:

A study of the effects of different types of feedback on performance in algebra.

During the semester, the teacher gives five equally-spaced 1-hour exams. The exams are of about the same difficulty overall, because the teacher carefully constructs the exams using items of about equal difficulty levels, even though the tests cover different content as the instruction progresses. Between the second and third tests, the teacher provides positive feedback (X_1) to one class, negative feedback (X_2) to another class, and no feedback (control treatment) to the third class. The experiment is diagrammed in Figure 6.5.

This design enables the teacher to make comparisons, not only between experimental groups but also with a control group. Note that the experimental treatments are applied only between two observations. At this point, we can consider possible patterns of results and interpretations that might be made. Because of the numerous

Figure 6.5
Diagram of Example 6.4 Multiple-Group Time Series Design, with Two Experimental Groups and a Control Group

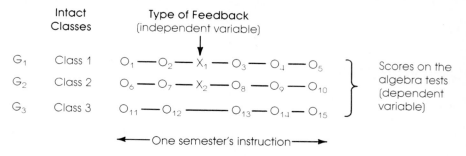

Os, interpreting results requires sorting through them. The following patterns are to be considered independently.

Example 6.4 Results Pattern 1. $O_1 = O_2 = O_5$, and $O_3 = O_4$, but O_3, O_4 are greater than O_1, O_2, O_5, and $O_6 = O_7 = O_9 = O_{10}$, but O_8 is less than O_7, and $O_{11} = O_{12} = O_{13} = O_{14} = O_{15}$, and $O_1 = O_6 = O_{11}$.

Interpretation: Positive feedback (X_1) increases performance, and its effect lasts through O_4; negative feedback (X_2) decreases performance, but it has only an immediate effect. Since performance in G_3 is highly consistent, it is unlikely that any external factors are causing changes in performance. Because the initial test scores of the classes were equal, the groups appear to be similar (on algebra test performance) prior to administration of the experimental treatments, even though there was no random assignment to the groups.

Example 6.4 Results Pattern 2. $O_1 = O_2$, and $O_3 = O_4 = O_5$, but O_3, O_4, O_5 are greater than O_1, O_2; $O_6 = O_7 = O_8$, and $O_9 = O_{10}$, but O_9, O_{10} are greater than O_6, O_7, O_8; $O_{11} = O_{12} = O_{13}$, and $O_{14} = O_{15}$, but O_{14}, O_{15} are greater than O_{11}, O_{12}, O_{13}; $O_1 = O_6 = O_{11}$, and $O_4 = O_9 = O_{14}$.

Interpretation: Negative feedback (X_2) has no effect, in that the patterns for G_2 and G_3 are the same. Positive feedback (X_1) increases performance; at least it appears to have an immediate effect. It is difficult to infer anything about long-range effects of X_1, in that all classes increased performance at the fourth testing. That consistent increase across classes is most likely due to an external factor. Whatever caused the increase had a persistent effect through the fifth testing. Since initial test scores of the classes were equal, the classes appear to be similar at the beginning of the experiment.

Of course, with numerous observations, such as in the example, a large number of different results patterns are possible. If patterns are erratic, it becomes difficult to draw conclusions; for example, the Os in classes keep fluctuating. Also, if test scores for classes prior to inserting the experimental treatments are different, there very likely is a selection bias.

Variations in Time Series Designs

The foregoing discussion focused on single-group and multiple-group time series designs—the basic configurations for time series designs. There are variations, however, that can be incorporated into these designs. The number of observations in the series depends on the variables under study, but there should be sufficient observations so that the pattern can become established. One variation is to increase the number of observations in the series, possibly even as high as 15 or 20, for long-term experiments or for experiments in which observations can be sequenced closely. Extending the number of observations does increase the likelihood of external factors having an effect if time is extended.

Another variation is to insert the experimental treatment more than once in the series. This variation is more possible if the series is lengthened. Multiple insertions provide a check on the consistency of an experimental effect if there is one. There are two ways to accomplish multiple insertion of the experimental treatment: (1) include it two or more times on a random basis, or (2) once it is inserted, persist with it for the remainder of the experiment. These two ways can be diagrammed as follows:

1. Multiple, random insertion of X:

$$G \quad O_1 — O_2 — X — O_3 — O_4 — O_5 — X — O_6 — O_7 — O_8$$

2. Persistent insertion of X:

$$G \quad O_1 — O_2 — O_3 — X — O_4 — X — O_5 — X — O_6 — X — O_7 — X — O_8$$

Either one of these approaches could have been used for the experimental treatments in the algebra classes example. The reinforcements, X_1 and X_2, could have been randomly inserted more than once in the series; or after their initial insertion, they could have been continued for the remainder of the semester.

Variations of multiple insertions can be included in time series designs.

Single-Subject Designs

Most experimentation in educational research involves groups of subjects; that is, we intend to generate results that apply to groups rather than to individuals. However, there are experimental situations in which it is desirable or necessary to use individual subjects—essentially, a sample size of one. In these single-subject situations, the basic experimental approach is to study the individual under both nonexperimental and experimental conditions.

Single-subject research can be useful for teachers who conduct research (probably action research) with individual students. Counselors who work with students on an individual basis may also have applications for single-subject designs. Researchers in such areas as rehabilitation and physical therapy encounter situations in which individual research is desirable. Generally, a subject is included in a study because of some condition or problem, and there is no random selection or assignment. Therefore, single-subject designs are usually considered quasi-experimental designs.

Single-subject designs commonly involve repeated measurement, sometimes several measurements of the dependent variable. Measurement is highly standardized and controlled, so that variations in measurement are not interpreted as an experimental effect. The conditions under which the study is conducted are described in detail, not only to enhance the interpretation of results but also to allow decisions about their generalizability.

Single-subject designs are characterized by what is sometimes called the *single-variable rule*. This means that only one variable, the treatment, is changed during the period in which the experimental treatment is applied. During the traditional or baseline treatment and the experimental treatment, all other conditions—such as length of time and number of measurements—are kept the same. This is necessary for interpreting the results so that some other effect is not misinterpreted as an experimental treatment effect.

The period during which the traditional treatment or normal condition is in effect is called the *baseline*. This period should be long enough that the dependent variable attains stability. If a dependent variable is fluctuating and the experimental treatment is applied, it is impossible to determine whether variation in the dependent variable is due to the experimental treatment.

Single-subject designs commonly involve repeated measurements, and they use the *single-variable rule*—changing only one variable at a time.

As with any quasi-experimental design, validity is a major concern in single-subject designs. Internal validity must be established to interpret the results. Alternative explanations of the results (other than an experimental effect) must be considered and, it is hoped, discounted. To deal with alternative explanations, it is necessary to maintain as much control as possible and to understand the nature of other variables that may be operating in the study. External validity depends on the similarities between the research study and other situations, and it must be argued on a logical basis.

A-B Design

Single-subjects designs are designated with a somewhat unique notation. The letters *A* and *B* are used to represent conditions; *A* indicates the baseline condition and *B* indicates the experimental treatment condition. Since individual subjects are used, there is no group notation.

The *A-B* design is the simplest of the single-subject designs. In general, it can be diagrammed as follows:

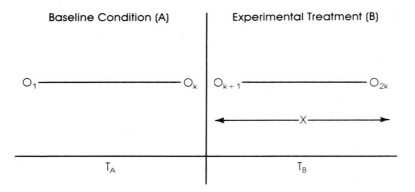

In this design, a single subject is observed under the baseline condition until the dependent variable stabilizes. Then the experimental treatment is introduced and the subject is again observed the same number of times. The T_A and T_B at the bottom of the design represent periods of time, and $T_A = T_B$.

The interpretation of results for the *A-B* design is based on the assumption that the observations would not have changed from those of the baseline condition if the experimental treatment had not been introduced. The design is susceptible to other variables, possibly those associated with history and maturation, causing an effect that may be interpreted as an experimental treatment effect; of course, such an effect would be a threat to internal validity. In a sense, the *A-B* design is the weakest of the single-subject designs with respect to internal validity, since the change between conditions is made only once.

Example 6.5

A beginning teacher is having difficulty with classroom management, and an experienced teacher is helping the beginning teacher deal with this problem. The experienced teacher observes the beginning teacher twice per week over a period of 4 weeks, using a teacher performance observation inventory such as the Classroom Observations Keyed for Effectiveness Research (COKER). This period is the baseline period *(A),* and the data from the eight observations comprise the baseline data. The classroom performance of the teacher is well stabilized during this 4–week period.

The experimental treatment *(B)* consists of half-hour consultations between the two teachers, in which the experienced teacher discusses the classroom performance of the beginning teacher and attempts to shift it to behaviors that will improve classroom management. There are nine of these consultations, one before the first observation in condition *B* and then one immediately following each observation. Like condition *A,* condition *B* is in effect for four weeks, and the eight observations of condition *B* are taken under corresponding conditions (same classes, same length of time, same time of day, etc.) as those of condition *A,* the only difference being the experimental treatment. The design for this study is diagrammed in Figure 6.6. The data consist of the observation data using the COKER inventory.

Example 6.5 Results Pattern 1.
Observations O_1 through O_8 are stable and show few teacher behaviors that are believed to enhance classroom management. Then, beginning with O_9 through O_{14}, the observations show increasing behavior that would improve classroom management, and O_{14} through O_{16} are stable. The results are plotted in Figure 6.6

Interpretation: With such a results pattern, there is quite conclusive evidence that the experimental treatment is having the desired effect. There has been an improvement in classroom management to a stability point. However, it is possible that the results are due to a natural maturation of the beginning teacher, although this is quite unlikely as an alternative explanation due to the relatively short time periods.

Example 6.5 Results Pattern 2.
There is considerable fluctuation among O_1 through O_5, but O_5 through O_8 are quite stable. O_9 through O_{16} had the same pattern of fluctuation as O_1 through O_5, except that the observations were slightly higher in behaviors that enhance classroom management.

Interpretation: It is practically impossible to make a conclusive interpretation of these results. The beginning teacher's performance is quite unstable, and although the experimental treatment does seem to improve performance slightly, it does not enhance stability of performance during the 4-week period. Apparently, there are other variables, such as conditions in the classroom or the feelings of the teacher, that have overriding effects.

Figure 6.6
Diagram of Example 6.5 *A-B*, Single-Subject Design, with Results Pattern 1

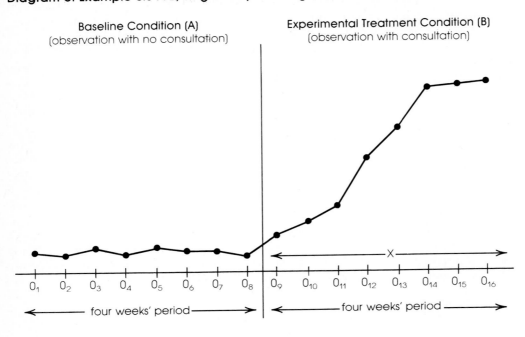

What about generalizability of results from this study? If Results Pattern 1 had appeared—the results for which we concluded an experimental effect—they would be generalizable to other beginning teachers who have characteristics similar to those of the teacher in this study and who teach under similar conditions. Generalizability would have to be established through detailed description, which makes the case for such similarities. Since the teachers were attempting to solve an immediate local problem, there may not be much concern with generalizability.

A-B-A Design

The *A-B-A* design extends the *A-B* design so that another period of the baseline condition is included following the period of experimental treatment. The design also may be called a *reversal* or *withdrawal* design,[1] since the experimental treatment is withdrawn. Except for the change from baseline to experimental treatment and back to baseline condition, other characteristics—such as duration and number of observations—are kept the same. The added period of baseline condition tends to enhance internal validity over the *A-B* design, since the pattern of results is extended. The general design can be diagrammed as follows:

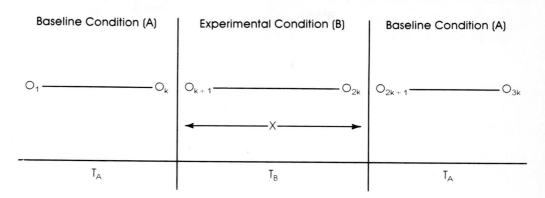

Note that in this design, there are the same number of observations for each duration of condition or treatment. Time would be constant, such that $T_A = T_B$.

Example 6.6

A teacher has one student whose classroom behavior is highly negative—character-ized by persistent, disruptive interruptions. The teacher keeps a weekly record of disruptive situations caused by this student. The behavior stabilizes over a 3-week period, designated the baseline condition. Then for 3 weeks the teacher requires two individual counseling sessions per week with the student. These sessions, which are considered the experimental treatment, are conducted for one-half hour each on Monday and Thursday. After 3 weeks, the counseling sessions are discontinued and the teacher continues to collect data on the dependent variable (number of disruptive situations during the week) for another 3 weeks. Discontinuing the counseling ses-sions is reverting back to the baseline conditions. No other apparent changes occur between the 3-week periods; the class, subjects taught, and so on, remain the same. The study is diagrammed in Figure 6.7.

Example 6.6 Results Pattern 1.   (Consistent with the symbolism introduced in Chapter 5, = means about the same.) $O_1 = O_2 = O_3 = O_7 = O_8 = O_9$, and $O_4 = O_5 = O_6$, but O_1, O_2, O_3, O_7, O_8, O_9 are greater than O_4, O_5, O_6. (Note that the dependent variable is the number of disruptive situations caused by the student in class, so a low score is preferred.)

Interpretation: The counseling sessions have the desired effect, but it is only an im-mediate effect. When the sessions are discontinued, the student reverts to the old behavior. It is not likely that an extraneous variable would have an effect that co-incided exactly with the experimental treatment.

Example 6.6 Results Pattern 2. $O_1 = O_2 = O_3$, and $O_4 = O_5 = O_6$, and $O_7 = O_8 = O_9$, but O_7, O_8, O_9 are less than O_4, O_5, O_6, which are less than O_1, O_2, O_3.

Figure 6.7
Diagram of Example 6.6 *A-B-A*, Single-Subject Design, with Results Pattern 1

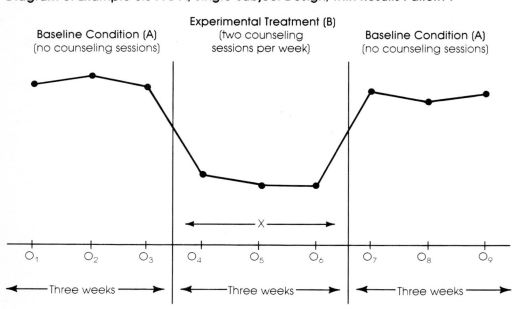

Interpretation: This pattern of results gives rise to alternative explanations; therefore, we cannot be conclusive about an experimental effect. There may be an experimental treatment effect; if there is, it is immediate, but it also has an accelerating long-range effect, which may be difficult to understand. There is a possibility that some other variable associated with maturation is operating. This explanation would be more likely if there was a constant decrease in O_4 through O_9, rather than the single decrease between O_6 and O_7.

There are any number of possible patterns of results. If O_4 through O_9 fluctuated considerably, it would be impossible to conclude anything about an experimental effect. The experimental treatment may be interacting with an extraneous variable, or the behavior may have become unstable and this may or may not have been caused by the experimental treatment.

A-B-A-B Design

If we extend the *A-B-A* design to include one more experimental treatment period, it becomes the *A-B-A-B* design. Because of the extended observation, and because the baseline condition and the experimental treatment go through two cycles, so to speak, internal validity tends to be increased over the *A-B* and *A-B-A* designs. If the patterns of results are consistent for the two cycles, conclusions about an experimental effect can be made with considerable confidence.

The general *A-B-A-B* design can be diagrammed as follows:

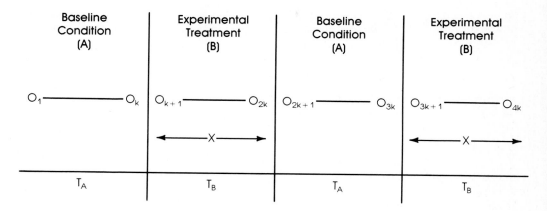

Baseline Condition (A)	Experimental Treatment (B)	Baseline Condition (A)	Experimental Treatment (B)

As with the preceding designs, characteristics are similar for the baseline condition and the experimental treatment, except for the introduction of the experimental treatment. The numbers of observations are the same, $T_A = T_B$, and so forth, so that the single-variable rule is observed.

Example 6.7

We will extend the example of the *A-B-A* design to the *A-B-A-B* design. The teacher decides to conduct counseling sessions with the disruptive student for a second 3-week period after the second baseline condition period is completed. The research study is diagrammed in Figure 6.8. Note that the design is simply an extension of the design in Figure 6.7. The major difference is that the research study is extended from 9 to 12 weeks, and an additional set of three observations is obtained for the experimental treatment.

Example 6.7 Results Pattern 1. $O_1 = O_2 = O_3$, and $O_4 = O_5 = O_6$, and $O_7 = O_8 = O_9$, and $O_{10} = O_{11} = O_{12}$; O_1, O_2, O_3 are greater than any other Os; O_{10}, O_{11}, O_{12} are less than any other Os; O_4, O_5, O_6 are less than O_7, O_8, O_9 but greater than O_{10}, O_{11}, O_{12}.

Interpretation: Since there are now 12 Os, it may be helpful to plot the dependent variable scores, as shown in Figure 6.9. In the figure, the scale of the dependent variable is the vertical axis, and the time periods are on the horizontal axis. The plot provides a pictorial representation of the data. We can conclude that the experimental treatment is having a positive effect. When the experimental treatment is discontin-

Figure 6.8
Diagram for Example 6.7 *A-B-A-B*, Single-Subject Design

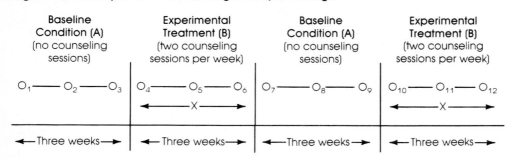

ued, the student reverts partially to the old behavior, but when the experimental treatment is initiated again, the positive effect is present. Behavior is stable within the conditions for the 3-week periods. It is unlikely that an effect of an extraneous variable would consistently coincide with the experimental treatment.

Example 6.7 Results Pattern 2. $O_1 = O_2 = O_3 = O_7 = O_8 = O_9$, and O_4, O_5, and O_6 are unequal to each other and not equal to O_1, and O_{10}, O_{11}, and O_{12} are unequal to each other and not equal to O_1 or O_4, O_5, and O_6.

Interpretation: Again we will plot the dependent variable scores for this pattern of results (Figure 6.10). The erratic pattern of the dependent variable during the exper-

Figure 6.9
Plot of Example 6.7 Results Pattern 1 for the *A-B-A-B*, Single-Subject Design

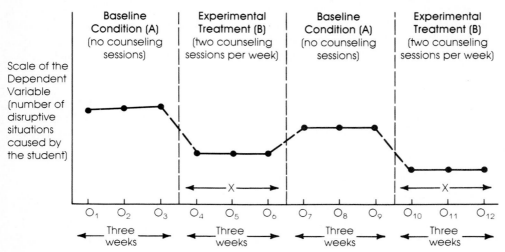

Figure 6.10
Plot of Example 6.7 Results Pattern 2 for the *A-B-A-B,* Single-Subject Design

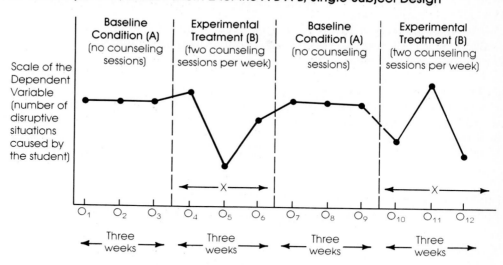

imental treatment periods almost precludes drawing any conclusions about either a positive or a negative effect of the counseling sessions. The patterns for the two experimental treatment periods differ, so if there is an effect of the counseling sessions, it is not consistent. About the only conclusion we can make is that the counseling sessions cause the student behavior to vary or become unstable. This could be due to an interaction of the experimental treatment with some extraneous variable. We can also note that the counseling sessions have no long-range effects, since the results for the two baseline periods are the same with stable behavior.

How generalizable are these results? The teacher could generalize to other students of similar age and disposition who demonstrate the same type of disruptive behavior. Generalizations to other teachers, students, and behavioral problems would have to be argued on a logical basis. To do so would require a knowledge of counseling in such situations and the possible effects that might be expected. Since this is an example of action research, the teacher is probably not very concerned about generalization. If Results Pattern 1 had appeared, the teacher would have solved the problem. Other teachers might be interested in the results, and could make inferences to their own situations on a logical basis.

Multiple-Baseline Designs

There is a family of designs called *multiple-baseline designs,* which can be considered modifications of the single-subject designs. These designs use the *A-B* logic, but rather than being limited to one subject, one behavior, and one situation, they involve two or more behaviors, situations, or subjects, or some combinations of these. The multiple baselines are included because they come from the different behaviors, situations, or subjects. Generally, once an experimental treatment is introduced for a subject, it is continued, so these designs apply to studies in which it is undesirable to remove a treatment after it is started.

Multiple-Baseline Across Behaviors. In this design, a single subject is observed on two or more behaviors in the same situation. After the baselines for the behaviors are stable, the experimental treatment is applied to one of the behaviors for a specified time; then it is applied to the second behavior for the same amount of time, and so on. If there is a consistent change in the behaviors after the experimental treatment is applied, a strong case can be made for an experimental effect.

An important consideration in this design is the independence of the behaviors. If the two or more behaviors are related in their occurrence, when the treatment is applied to the first behavior, it may cause change in the remaining behaviors. Thus, this design is best used for situations in which the behaviors are quite discrete and independent.

Multiple-Baseline Across Subjects. This design uses two or more subjects, although they participate in the experiment as individuals. The multiple baselines come from the subjects. After the baseline behavior is stable, the experimental treatment is administered to one subject; then, after a specified period, the second subject begins receiving the experimental treatment, and so on. It is important that the subjects involved are independent in terms of the experimental treatment. That is, applying the treatment to one subject should not affect the others. If a teacher uses this design, it would probably be difficult to maintain independence between subjects unless they were students from different classes.

Multiple-Baseline Across Situations. The baselines for this design come from different situations involving the same behavior and the same subject. The baseline behavior is established and then the experimental treatment is applied in one situation. After a specified period, the treatment is applied in the second situation, and so forth. This design is essentially the same as the multiple-baseline across behaviors, except that situations replace behaviors in being varied. As in the single-subject designs discussed earlier, the multiple-baseline designs have constant periods of time and numbers of observations during the administration of an experimental treatment, at least for any initial administrations of the treatment.

Example 6.8

The example presented here is of a multiple-baseline across situations design. A teacher is planning to use individualized instruction (the experimental treatment) in reading, mathematics, and social studies with a student who is having difficulties in these areas. The individualized instruction will be applied first in reading for a 2-week period, then in mathematics, then in social studies. Once individualized instruction is begun in an area, it is continued for the duration of the study. There are three dependent variables in this study: the student's performances in reading, mathematics, and social studies. Four observations on each variable are taken during each 2-week period. Operationally, the dependent variables are the percentages of instructional objectives attained out of those specified by the teacher.

The design is diagrammed in Figure 6.11. Note that there is an initial baseline period of 2 weeks for all three areas. Then the baseline periods for mathematics and social studies continue for another 2 and 4 weeks, respectively, while the individualized instruction is phased in. The entire study requires 8 weeks.

Example 6.8 Results Pattern.   Since there are three dependent variables and each is measured 16 times, 48 scores are obtained on the subject. There are many possible patterns of results, with a pattern for each dependent variable, since each dependent variable has its own set of 16 scores. Rather than listing 48 scores, a possible pattern of results is given in Figure 6.12.

Interpretation: The experimental treatment (individualized instruction) appears to be having an effect, but the effect is not consistent across situations (subject areas). In reading, there is a positive effect, which shows a gradual increase. In mathematics, the pattern becomes erratic after the experimental treatment is introduced. The increases at O_{11} and O_{14} may have been due to an external variable; perhaps the ob-

Figure 6.11
Diagram of Example 6.8 Multiple-Baseline Across Situations Design

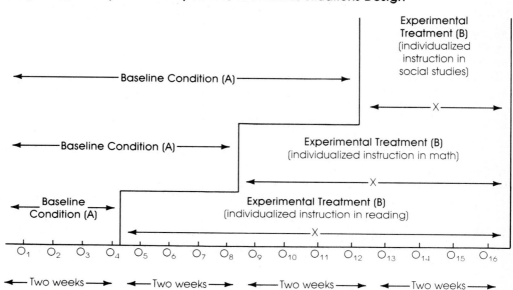

Figure 6.12
Plot of Results Pattern for Example 6.8 Multiple-Baseline Across Situations Design

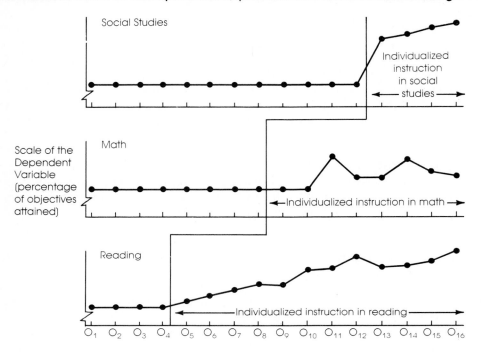

jectives at these points were simply easier for the subject to attain. It is impossible to conclude that those increases are due to the experimental treatment. In social studies, the experimental treatment appears to have an immediate and sustained positive effect. In summary, we can conclude that individualized instruction does have an effect on performance in reading and social studies; the effect is positive for both areas, but more gradual for reading. If there is an effect in mathematics, individualized instruction causes performance to fluctuate and possibly increase slightly.

Multiple-baseline designs can become complicated very quickly, and interpretation may require considerable sorting of results. Depending on the variables studied, the designs can be modified to include reversal of conditions (withdrawal of the experimental treatment), but this complicates the designs even more. For such designs, *A-B-A* or *A-B-A-B* formats would be used. However, because of the complexity, such designs are generally used only if a simpler design cannot be developed for a specific study. Assuming that adequate internal validity can be attained, multiple-baseline designs do tend to have broader external validity than single-baseline designs. This is because of the multiple behaviors, subjects, or situations included in the designs.

SUMMARY

This chapter has discussed quasi-experimental research, which uses designs in which subjects are not randomly assigned or selected. The lack of randomization poses potential problems for establishing the validity of the research. When intact or naturally formed groups are used, there is a possibility of selection bias being introduced, and the similarity (or lack thereof) of the groups must be considered. In single-subject designs, the subject is usually selected because of some problem or condition associated with that subject. Rarely are the subjects used in single-subject designs selected at random.

Although the use of intact groups or specified subjects may pose threats to validity, they can be used effectively if adequate attention is given to the design of the research. In educational research, it is often impossible to apply random assignment when forming groups. Yet intact groups can provide valuable results, provided that they are interpretable.

When two or more intact groups are used, the credibility of the research depends on the extent to which the groups are similar on relevant variables. Relative to randomness, the groups are nonequivalent, but an argument may be made for their similarity. Therefore, it is important to have antecedent information about the groups, preferably through some kind of pretesting. Generalizability is argued on a logical basis.

Single-subject designs apply when the research centers on individuals rather than on groups—for example, when teachers or counselors are working with individual students. These designs involve multiple observations or measurements, taken across the baseline condition and the experimental treatment condition. Single-subject designs are characterized by extensive control over the administration of the experimental treatment and the collection of data on the subject, but since they are usually conducted in a natural setting, extraneous variables may have effects. Such research commonly involves extensive data collection, and the analysis of results may require considerable sorting through the data. It is often helpful to plot the data to identify the dominant pattern.

This chapter and the immediately preceding chapter have dealt with experimental and quasi-experimental research and have discussed the more commonly used designs for such research. However, many variations can be made to accommodate specific research situations. For example, if a time series design were used with random assignment to the groups, we would then have a "true" experimental design, with some type of repeated observation. The important thing is to have a design that fits the objectives of the experiment, one that provides adequate control so that the results can be interpreted with confidence and generalized as intended.

KEY CONCEPTS

Quasi-experimental research
Nonequivalent groups
Posttest-only, nonequivalent
    control group design
Pretest-posttest, nonequiva-
    lent control group design
Time series designs
Single-group time series de-
    sign
Multiple-group time series
    design
Single-subject designs

Single-variable rule
Baseline
A-B design
A-B-A design
A-B-A-B design
Multiple-baseline designs
Multiple-baseline across be-
    haviors
Multiple-baseline across sub-
    jects
Multiple-baseline across sit-
    uations

EXERCISES

6.1 The most desirable procedure for obtaining groups for an experiment is random selection or assignment of subjects, yet at times it is necessary to use intact groups and a quasi-experimental design. Discuss some of the difficulties that may be introduced when intact groups are used.

6.2 A biology teacher has three sets of laboratory materials available and decides to use one set with each of three classes over the period of one semester. The research question of interest is whether or not the different materials have differing effects on attainment of laboratory concepts, as measured by a section of the final examination given at the end of the semester. The score on this section of the test is the dependent variable. The classes are heterogeneous in ability, although students have not been randomly assigned to classes. The teacher decides to use a posttest-only, nonequivalent control group design. Diagram the design. How could the teacher apply a pretest-posttest, nonequivalent control group design, and what advantages would this design have over the posttest-only design? What are possible threats to the internal validity of this study? How generalizable are the results?

6.3 A study is conducted in three elementary schools on the effects of individual versus massed practice on fifth-grade spelling achievement. The fifth-grade teachers are allowed to use the method they prefer, but any one teacher uses only one method. After an 8-week period, the students are given a common spelling test. Discuss possible problems in interpreting the results of this experiment. Comment on both internal and external validity.

6.4 A teacher conducts a study on third-grade reading achievement with a class. Two methods of instruction are used, but not simultaneously. The students are tested every 2 weeks, and a particular method is used for each 2-week period. The methods are randomly assigned to the 2-week periods, and the study continues for an 18-week semester. Diagram this study as a time series design. Discuss its strong points and potential weaknesses. What might be a special measurement problem?

6.5 A study is conducted using intact groups to determine the effects of three different training programs. The groups are pretested, and the training programs are implemented for 6 weeks. The groups are posttested immediately following completion of the programs and again 6 weeks later. The design can be diagrammed as follows:

$$G_1 \qquad O_1—X_1—O_2\text{———}O_3$$
$$G_2 \qquad O_4—X_2—O_5\text{———}O_6$$
$$G_3 \qquad O_7—X_3—O_8\text{———}O_9$$

Interpret the following sets of results. Consider each independently.

a. $O_1 = O_4 = O_7 = O_3 = O_6 = O_9$, and O_2 is greater than O_1, and O_5 is greater than O_4, and O_8 is greater than O_7, but O_2 is greater than O_5, which is greater than O_8.

b. $O_1 = O_4 = O_7$, and $O_2 = O_5 = O_8 = O_3 = O_6 = O_9$, but $O_1, O_4, O_7 \neq O_2, O_5, O_8, O_3, O_6, O_9$.

c. $O_1, O_4,$ and O_7 are not equal to each other, in that O_1 is greater than O_4, which is greater than O_7; O_2 is greater than O_5, which is greater than O_8, but $O_3 = O_6 = O_9$.

d. Assuming that there is an experimental treatment effect immediately after the program is completed, what comparisons would be made to determine whether there are long-term experimental treatment effects?

e. Is there any way to check on whether or not there is an effect of pretesting in this design? If so, how would it be checked; if not, why not?

6.6 A two-group time series design is used in a health education study in which two senior high school classes participate. The dependent variable is attitude toward health maintenance habits; it is measured at the beginning of the semester and every 3 weeks during the 18-week semester. Thus, each class is measured seven times. An experimental treatment (X), which consists of showing a series of films about the medical effects of poor health habits, is randomly inserted in one 3-week period for one of the classes. The design can be diagrammed as follows:

$$G_1 \qquad O_1{-}O_2{-}O_3{-}X{-\!-\!-}O_4{-\!-\!-}O_5{-\!-\!-}O_6{-\!-\!-}O_7$$
$$G_2 \qquad O_8{-}O_9{-}O_{10}{-\!-\!-\!-\!-\!-}O_{11}{-}O_{12}{-}O_{13}{-}O_{14}$$

Interpret the following possible patterns of results:

a. $O_1 = O_2 = O_3 = O_8 = O_9 = O_{10} = O_{11} = O_{12} = O_{13} = O_{14}$, and O_4 is greater than O_3, but O_4 is less than O_5, which is less than O_6, which is less than O_7. The greater the score on the dependent variable, the more positive the attitude.

b. $O_1 = O_8$, and $O_2 = O_9$, and $O_3 = O_{10}$; none of O_8 through O_{14} are equal, and the pattern is such that the scores increase consistently from O_8 through O_{14}; O_4 is greater than O_3 and O_{11}; O_5 is greater than O_{12}, but $O_6 = O_{13}$, and $O_7 = O_{14}$.

c. What comparisons would be made to check whether or not the normal class instruction is having an effect independent of X?

6.7 A guidance counselor is working with a high school student who, though an able student according to Scholastic Aptitude Test results, is having difficulty in all subjects. The counselor has been meeting with the student once a week for 4 weeks. The counselor decides to have the student keep a detailed log of how his time is spent when not in school. These logs are then used in the counseling sessions in an attempt to get the student to concentrate more on his subjects. Each week, the counselor receives reports from the student's teachers and synthesizes this information. The logs are used for a 4-week period, so this is an *A-B* design. Diagram the design. What pattern of results would be indicative of an experimental treatment (the use of the logs) effect? If there was an experimental treatment effect, how would the patterns of results differ if it was a one-time effect versus a consistent, accumulative effect? Present a pattern of results from which no conclusion could be drawn.

6.8 Describe a situation in an area of your own interest for which a single-subject design would apply. What are the advantages if an *A-B-A* or *A-B-A-B* design can be used instead of an *A-B* design? What are the advantages of going to a multiple-baseline design? Diagram your design.

6.9 Describe the differences between the following designs: (1) multiple-baseline across behaviors, (2) multiple-baseline across subjects, and (3) multiple-baseline across situations.

NOTE

1. The *A-B-A-B* design discussed in the next section is also referred to as a reversal or withdrawal design, since there is a reversal of conditions in that design, too.

REFERENCE

Campbell, D. T., & Stanley, J. C. (1963). Experimental and quasi-experimental designs for research on teaching. In N. L. Gage (Ed.), *Handbook of research on teaching* (pp. 171–246). Chicago: Rand McNally.

7

Ex Post Facto and
Survey Research

The preceding two chapters have dealt with experimental research. It was noted that for a research project to be an experiment, at least one independent variable must be manipulated by the researcher according to some preconceived plan. However, many variables in educational settings do not lend themselves to deliberate manipulation. For example, intelligence, aptitude, and socioeconomic background cannot be randomly assigned to individuals and manipulated in an experiment.

Generally, there tends to be less control in nonexperimental research than in experimental research; therefore, interpretation of nonexperimental results may be less straightforward and more susceptible to ambiguity. But this is more a function of the general conditions under which nonexperimental research is conducted than a consequence of one or more independent variables being manipulated in an experiment. Nonexperimental research is generally conducted in a natural setting, with numerous variables operating simultaneously. Nevertheless, nonexperimental research can be carefully designed, which enhances not only completion of the research but also interpretation of the results. It is the research problem and the conditions of the research that determine the appropriate methodology.

There are different types of nonexperimental research; in this chapter, two closely related types, ex post facto research and survey research, will be considered. These nonexperimental approaches to research are used extensively in education. The survey is probably the single most widely used approach in educational research.

The distinctions between different types of nonexperimental research are generally not as clear-cut as the distinction between experimental and nonexperimental research. At least this is so for the distinction between ex post facto and survey research. Ex post facto research may deal with variables whose data are collected through survey procedures, and when interpreting results of a survey, a researcher often takes an ex post facto approach, but it is useful to consider both types of research.

Ex Post Facto Research: A Definition

Kerlinger (1973) defines *ex post facto research* as "systematic, empirical inquiry in which the scientist does not have direct control of independent variables because the manifestations have already occurred or because they are inherently not manipulable." He notes further that "inferences about relations among variables are made, without direct intervention, from concomitant variation of independent and dependent variables" (p. 379). The term *ex post facto* means "from a thing done afterwards"; it implies some type of subsequent action. The variables are studied in retrospect, in search of possible relationships or effects.

The independent variables of an ex post facto study usually are identified before the data are collected and are of such a nature that they have occurred in the situation. Socioeconomic level is an example of a possible independent variable in an ex post facto study. A researcher cannot randomly assign socioeconomic level to individuals. In essence, individuals have "self-selected" themselves into the socioeconomic categories. A researcher can randomly select individuals from the categories, so that the categories are appropriately represented, but there may be factors associated with the way individuals get into the categories initially that are certainly not randomly distributed across the categories.

Ex post facto research should be carried on in the framework of the research problem statement and related hypotheses. Unfortunately, this is not always the case. Sometimes data are collected with apparently no more direction than to see what appears. Then some type of retrospective search begins to determine, if possible, what variables exist that might be the basis for some hypotheses. Although the definition of ex post facto research states that the independent variables have already occurred and do not lend themselves to manipulation, that does not mean that the researcher is ignorant or oblivious of them when planning the research. The variables should be considered in the context of the research that is being planned.

> *Ex post facto research* is systematic and empirical inquiry in which the independent variables have already occurred and are inherently not manipulable by the researcher. Inferences about relationships among variables are made without direct intervention.

Example 7.1

In a large senior high school, a study is being conducted on the reading achievement of the students. The research problem can be stated as follows:

A study of factors related to the reading performance of students in ABC Senior High School.

The dependent variable is performance on an appropriate standardized reading achievement test.

A number of independent variables could be considered in this study, including the following:

1. The sex of the student
2. The overall grade point average (GPA) of the student
3. The elementary school attended by the student
4. The grade level of the student: sophomore, junior, senior
5. The type of program in which the student is enrolled: college prep, general, specific vocational

A number of hypotheses could be generated for these independent variables and the dependent variable, reading performance. For illustration, one hypothesis will be provided for each independent variable:

Hypothesis 1: *Reading performances of boys and girls are the same.*

Hypothesis 2: *As a student's GPA improves, reading performance increases.*

Hypothesis 3: *The students from the different elementary schools differ in reading performance.*

Hypothesis 4: *The reading performance by grade level differs, with seniors having the greater performance and sophomores the lesser.*

Hypothesis 5: *Type of program in which enrolled is related to reading performance, with college prep students showing the highest performance.*

These hypotheses deal with the independent variables singly, but there may be more complex hypotheses involving the independent variables in combination. For example, a pattern of reading performance might be hypothesized for the grade-level and type-of-program variables. In essence, there may be an interaction between these two variables when they are combined. An example of such a hypothesis might be:

The reading performance of sophomores in the college prep program exceeds that of juniors and seniors enrolled in the general and specific vocational programs.

A hypothesis such as Hypothesis 3 might be further described to indicate an anticipated pattern of results. For example, rather than simply hypothesizing differences among students from different elementary schools, the hypothesis could be:

The reading performances of the students from the different elementary schools differ in such a way that students from schools located in higher socioeconomic areas demonstrate the higher performance.

Thus, several hypotheses may be used in a single study, including hypotheses of varying complexity, depending on the variables of the study.

A random sample of students can be selected from the student population and tested on reading performance. The sample might be a simple random sample, but more likely it would be some type that ensures adequate representation from the students in the various programs, grade levels, and so forth. (Sampling designs are discussed in Chapter 10.) The design for the study, including the independent variables, is diagrammed in Figure 7.1. GPA is separated into four categories, as indicated in the figure. There are four elementary schools in the high school's district.

In the selection of the sample, it is desirable to have each student selected fit one (and only one) category of each independent variable. This condition would be met for all independent variables except, possibly, the elementary school attended. In most high schools, there are transfer students who did not attend an elementary school in the district. One approach would be to exclude such students from the sample. Another approach would be to have a category of "other" for the elementary school attended. For the purposes of the example, students who did not attend one of the four elementary schools will be excluded. There may also be students who attended more than one of the elementary schools. They could either be deleted or classified according to the most recent elementary school attended.

As the sample is selected, we would not expect equal numbers for the categories of the independent variables, unless equal numbers were deliberately selected for some variables. For example, if the total sample size were 300, there might be 100 of each grade level and 50 boys and 50 girls per grade level.

Figure 7.1
Design of Example 7.1 Ex Post Facto Study of Reading Performance

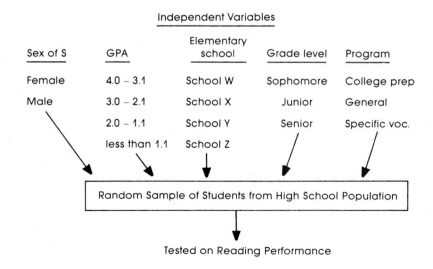

There are many possible combinations of independent variables in the design—288 to be exact ($2 \times 4 \times 4 \times 3 \times 3$). However, there may be some combinations across all five independent variables that would be missing. For example, there may be no sophomore girls with a GPA less than 1.1 from School W in the college prep program. For the purposes of the study, this would cause no difficulty.

Although the hypotheses deal with possible relationships as reflected in reading performance, cause and effect are not hypothesized. For example, Hypothesis 5 indicates a pattern between reading achievement and program, but the researcher is not hypothesizing that reading performance is causing students to go into certain programs or that the programs are causing the reading performance. There may be other variables or factors operating that cause this relationship.

Setting and Scope

Ex post facto research can be of almost any magnitude. The preceding example involved a relatively large senior high school. A study could involve only a single classroom—or even part of a classroom—and the relationship between achievement and attitude toward school could be studied for a segment of the class. Or an entire school or school district could be included, perhaps involving such sociological variables as socioeconomic status. A study could even be international in scope, involving several countries, such as the *International Study of Achievement in Mathematics* (Husen, 1967).

Guidelines for Ex Post Facto Research

Ex post facto investigations can be improved by adhering to some relatively simple guidelines. Hypotheses should be stated and tested whenever possible; the study should also state other plausible hypotheses (possibly supplementary hypotheses) and, if possible, these hypotheses should be tested as well. When other hypotheses are tested and refuted, the remaining hypotheses are strengthened as plausible explanations of the results. The procedure of testing multiple hypotheses and zeroing in on the plausible explanations through elimination of refuted hypotheses has been referred to as "strong inference" (Platt, 1964).

The interpretation of the results of an ex post facto study, as with any type of research results, should be supported by knowledge of the independent and dependent variables—their possible relationships and effects. Such knowledge will tend to guard against profuse and improper interpretations. For example, it may be found that student achievement and teachers' salaries are related, but it would be difficult to argue that one causes the other. A third factor or combination of factors related to both of these variables would likely cause this result.

Any conjecture should be recognized as just that. The researcher should recognize the empirical results of the study and should limit the discussion to these results in preference to pursuing conjectures for which there is little or no basis.

An ex post facto study often involves several analyses, as well as different analysis procedures. In this way, the results can be synthesized and interpretation is usually enhanced. A specific result may suggest another analysis or another way of combining data that will assist in interpreting results. The analysis should not be arbitrarily restricted, but the researcher should be alert for possible supplementary analyses as the results are considered.

A potential weakness of ex post facto research is lack of control, but this should not be interpreted as a reflection on the value of ex post facto research. Many educational research problems, especially those involving social and psychological variables such as aptitude, teacher characteristics, and school climate, are primarily ex post facto in nature and thus must be researched in an ex post facto manner. Many of these variables are certainly important factors in the educational setting, and the importance of ex post facto research could be argued solely from that fact.

Survey Research: A Definition

Studies in education conducted to determine the status quo go by such names as *school surveys, status surveys,* or just *surveys.* Such studies are concerned with the gathering of facts rather than the manipulation of variables. A school survey may be taken to determine the number of students who eat in the school cafeteria or ride the buses, the average student load per teacher, and so on. Such surveys provide important and useful information for the educational enterprise.

Status studies are not the only educational research endeavors to come under the survey umbrella. Survey has a broader meaning, and there are different types of survey studies. Since both surveys and ex post facto research are nonexperimental, the difference between them is not as distinctive as, for instance, the difference between experimental and ex post facto research. Basically, surveys deal with research questions of "What is?" with, possibly, some emphasis on attempting explanation. A sample research question that could be studied through survey research is, "What are the patterns of disruptive behavior and student performance in school?"

Survey research can also deal with the incidence and interrelationships of sociological and psychological variables, usually as they occur in some educational context. Such studies deal with how people feel or perceive, how they behave, or their role or group status. The objectives of a survey research study might be to determine how the psychological and sociological variables are related. Often, the relationships among the psychological (or sociological) variables are studied as well.

Survey research can include a status quo study or a study in which the interrelationships of sociological or psychological variables are determined and summarized.

Classification of Survey Studies

To enhance definition and understanding, it is helpful to classify types of survey research. The classifying scheme used here includes two criteria, quite arbitrarily chosen. These criteria apply whether a survey consists of a status study or whether it includes the interrelationships of sociological or psychological variables.

One criterion for the classification of surveys is the group measured—a sample or a population. We shall refer to these as a *sample survey* and a *population survey*. Population surveys (sometimes called *censuses*) can be used effectively with small populations, but they are rarely used with large ones. It may be physically or financially impossible to include an entire population. In the case of large populations, the time involved in measuring the entire population might actually reduce the accuracy of measurement; that is, during the extended time required for measurement, the population might change with respect to the dependent variable, and the passing of time would reflect a change in the measurement between individuals measured earlier in the survey and those measured later. Thus, a random sample could actually provide greater accuracy than measurement of the entire population, because it would not contain this effect of the longer time span.

A sample survey involves the selection of a subset of the population, called a *sample,* to be measured. The sample selected is usually some type of random sample. The method of choosing the sample may be quite complex; different sampling designs will be discussed in a later chapter. When a sample is used, the researcher attempts to generalize from the sample observations to the population from which the sample was selected.

> One criterion for classifying surveys is the group measured—whether it is an entire population or a sample.

The second classification for surveys is the method of data collection. There are numerous approaches to data collection in educational research, but for surveys, the data collection generally falls into three categories: the personal interview, the written questionnaire, and controlled observation. Interviews may be conducted in person or by telephone. Questionnaires and interviews used as data collection instruments are of varying length; they are usually constructed specifically for the study being conducted. They consist of items, often in question form, to which the individual responds. Controlled observation in its simplest form consists of collecting data from such sources as school records. It also includes collecting data using measuring instruments such as achievement tests, attitude inventories, or physical performance tests. Another type is represented by the trained observer who goes into a classroom or other natural setting to observe the incidence of some phenomenon, perhaps something as complex as the interaction of students and teachers. In controlled observation, the measurement or data collection is controlled directly by the researcher to a greater extent than with interviews and questionnaires. It should be noted that the control here is on the observation or measurement, not on the independent variables in an experimental sense.

A second criterion for classifying surveys is the method of data collection: interview, questionnaire, or controlled observation.

The two criteria proposed here can be combined into a 3 × 2 classification system for surveys, as illustrated in Figure 7.2. When the categories are taken in all combinations, a classification system with six mutually exclusive categories or cells is formed. Any survey fits into only one of the classifications of each criterion; placing a survey into one of the six cells identifies it in terms of both criteria.

The two criteria used in the classification scheme in Figure 7.2 define the group measured and the method of data collection, two very important factors in any survey. The group measured will influence the quantity of data collected and also the interpretation of results, whether or not they are intended to generalize to the population. Since data collection is usually a major portion of the effort in a survey, it influences the specific procedures that will be conducted. It also determines whether instruments such as questionnaires must be constructed or whether available instruments, such as achievement tests, can be used.

Interview and Questionnaire Studies

Most people are aware of large-scale surveys conducted by survey organizations, such as the surveys developed by George Gallup. Such surveys are especially visible

Figure 7.2
Diagram of a 3 × 2 Classification of Surveys

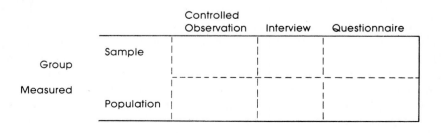

around the time of national elections. Polling organizations usually have extensive resources, however, and not many graduate students can acquire such resources for conducting research. Nevertheless, major polls do provide methodological suggestions regarding appropriate sampling, good item construction, and procedures for enhancing response, which can be applied to any survey.[1] Survey organizations typically use both interviews and questionnaires (not necessarily in the same study), although they tend to use interviews more extensively than graduate students do. Because of time and cost factors, graduate students (and others) are more likely to use mailed questionnaires.

Although interviews and questionnaires have similarities as data collection instruments, they also have some important differences. The interview, conducted in person or by telephone, is an oral exchange between an interviewer and an individual or group of individuals. The questionnaire is a list of questions or statements to which the individual is asked to respond in writing; the response may range from a checkmark to an extensive written statement. In an interview, the response may be limited to a single word (for example, yes or no), or it may require a rather lengthy oral discussion. A questionnaire is sometimes referred to as a written, self-administered interview, and by the same token an interview could be considered an oral questionnaire. Both the interview and questionnaire can include open-ended items—items for which the individual constructs the response rather than select it from a list of options. The interview provides further flexibility in that the interviewer can pursue the response with the individual and can ask for an elaboration or redefinition of the response if it appears incomplete or ambiguous. The response may also reveal factors or feelings the interviewer may choose to pursue and probe, or it may reveal things that would not be touched on in a questionnaire.

Flexibility is basically a matter of item structure. Items allow varying degrees of flexibility, on a continuum from unstructured to completely structured. An example of an unstructured item is:

What do you think of the honors program in mathematics?

A corresponding partially structured item is:

What do you think about the effectiveness of the mathematics honors program relative to advanced placement in college?

A structured item is:

Do you feel that the present honors program in mathematics should be:
a. continued without modification?
b. continued but modified?
c. discontinued?

In this example, the term *honors program in mathematics* would refer to a specific program with which the respondent is familiar.

The foregoing questions could be asked in either an interview or a questionnaire, but the unstructured items would more likely be used in an interview than a questionnaire. The reason for this is that unstructured items leave much more interpretation to the respondent. In an interview, this interpretation can be somewhat controlled and directed, but with a questionnaire such direction is not possible, and the respondents may make unintended interpretations that can lead to an undesirable variety of responses, some of which may be confusing. For example, if the foregoing unstructured item were used in a questionnaire, respondents might interpret the item differently, one commenting on the content of the honors program and another commenting on the usefulness of the program.

> In contrast to a questionnaire, an interview provides the option of elaborating or clarifying items after they are presented to the respondent.

The interview has a particular advantage over the questionnaire: If an interviewee grants the interview and if the interviewer is adequately skilled, there should not be any missing or unusable data. Questionnaires are susceptible to nonresponse and, usually to a lesser extent, unusable data. The latter occurs when a questionnaire is incorrectly completed or the items are misinterpreted. Questionnaire studies are generally much less expensive and less time-consuming than interviews, because interview studies require trained people for administration and questionnaires do not. Both interview and questionnaire studies can vary considerably in the number and extent of items included. However, interviews are usually not conducted unless a substantial quantity of data is to be collected. On the other hand, brevity in a questionnaire encourages response. Thus, interviews generally tend to be more extensive than questionnaires.

Interviews have another advantage over questionnaires: They can be used with individuals from whom data cannot otherwise be obtained, such as an illiterate or nearly illiterate person who could not respond to a questionnaire. A study involving the responses of educationally disadvantaged adults might require an interview, since such persons might lack the motivation to respond to a questionnaire, even if the items were written in an understandable manner.

Conducting an Interview

Although the interview is well suited to probing the feelings and perceptions of the individual, the items of the interview itself do not ensure accurate measurement of those feelings. The individual must be able and willing to respond accurately with adequate oral expression, and difficulties arise if the individual does not have the information necessary to answer the question or if there is an uneasy feeling about divulging the information. An individual may misunderstand the question or misinterpret the type of response needed. The interviewer must be able to recognize misunderstanding and uneasiness and make on-the-spot decisions about any additional probing that may be desirable.

The data of the interview are the responses of the individual being interviewed, and the accuracy of these data depends on the truthfulness of the respondent. Good rapport is necessary between the interviewer and the respondent. Usually, the interviewer begins by gathering factual information about the respondent, and it is during this period that the rapport of the interview is established. Personal and controversial questions generally appear later in the interview, if they appear at all; the timing and inclusion of such questions must be left to the judgment of the interviewer. The interviewer should proceed in a businesslike manner in a friendly atmosphere, but excessive informality should be avoided.

Since an interview is a social encounter, respondents will tend to respond in a socially acceptable or socially desirable way. An individual may respond in what is perceived to be a socially or professionally preferable manner, regardless of his or her true feelings. Personal or controversial information may not be readily forthcoming. There is no methodological technique that can ensure the accuracy of the data, but it may be possible to enhance truthful responses and to construct somewhat crude checks. The interviewer must be careful not to imply that there are preferable responses, and controversial questions should be avoided until the proper background and rapport have been established. In the context of the interview, the interviewer may form an opinion of whether the respondent is telling the truth, and it may be possible to construct questions that check on the consistency of responses. In so doing, the interview contains questions that ask essentially the same information, but in somewhat different form or wording, and appear at different points in the interview.

The data-recording procedures used in the interview should be efficiently structured so that they do not interfere with the process of conducting the interview. A tape recorder can retain the entire oral communication, but the interviewer should get the respondent's consent before using one. If taping an interview is not practical or feasible, shorthand records of the interview must be developed. Structured questions may require only a checkmark indicating one of several alternative responses, whereas responses to unstructured questions must be recorded briefly but completely, covering all main points. The recording of data should be as inconspicuous as possible and should not arouse suspicion in the respondent; for example, if a short response is given, the interviewer should not engage in extensive writing.

The interview should be structured to obtain the necessary information efficiently in a friendly but businesslike atmosphere. If possible, there should be some accuracy checks on the responses.

Interviewers must be well trained in the procedures for conducting an interview. For a particular survey, they should be well informed about the variables under investigation so that they can make perceptive probes. Almost without exception, interviewers benefit from a training period in interviewing techniques. If there is no training period, the early interviews essentially become the training sessions, and they may differ in style and efficiency from later interviews by the same interviewer. Interviewers should understand the importance of a high response rate and should know how to conduct the interview effectively. For example, responses should be strictly confidential, and the respondent should understand that this is so.

When two or more interviewers are used, attention must be given to training for interviewer consistency. Each interviewer should conduct a number of practice interviews (depending on the complexity of the interview schedule) until the procedure has been mastered. If possible, practice interviews should be recorded and then reviewed by the interviewers. The results can then be compared, differences discussed, and the process repeated until consistency or agreement is judged adequate. An agreement of 90% or so on the interpretation of responses may be set as a criterion for adequacy. All of this training may require considerable time and effort, but it is essential if the data are to be collected properly and if the results are to be interpretable.

Training the interviewer is a necessity. When two or more interviewers are used, their consistency in conducting the interview must be checked. In any event, an interviewee's responses should not be the function of the specific interviewer.

To schedule the interview, a mutually convenient time for the potential respondent and the interviewer must be identified. Interviewers should have flexible schedules so that they are available at times convenient for the respondents. For example, if those surveyed are not available during the day, it is necessary to concentrate on evenings and weekends for the interviews.

After the interview is scheduled or initiated, it is necessary to obtain the respondent's cooperation. An advance letter informing the respondent about the study can be effective in obtaining cooperation. Such a letter is not only informative but it can reassure respondents, especially those who are concerned about their personal safety when admitting a stranger. The respondents should be informed about the purposes of the study and the importance of their contributions. Respondents should not be threatened by the interview or the subsequent use of the data. Making the respondent informed and comfortable about the interview does much to enhance cooperation.

Interview Items

Generally, each respondent in a survey using an interview is asked the same set of questions. Wording could vary slightly to accommodate different respondents—for example, if students, teachers, and principals were being interviewed in the same study. There are generally two types of item format: *forced-response* and *open-ended*. These formats are exactly what their names imply. In a forced-response format, the respondent is asked to select a response from two or more alternatives; with the open-ended format, the respondent is allowed to construct the response. Both types are often used in a single interview.

Whether items require an open-ended response or a forced response, they should be clearly stated in complete question form, with unambiguous terms that are meaningful to the respondent. Also, terms should have consistent meaning across respondents. The item should give the respondent adequate direction. Sometimes, optional wording or optional probes are given with items, but these should be used with caution. Consider the following open-ended item:

What do you like best about the schools in this district?

If the respondent hesitates, an optional probe might be given, such as:

We are interested in things such as the facilities, the quality of instruction, the schedule, the administration, whatever.

If this optional probe is used, those respondents who hesitate are answering a somewhat different question than those who do not receive the optional wording. At least, those who hesitate would be given more structure through the cues. A better approach would be to provide the same amount of structure for all respondents, such as:

Of the following, which do you feel are strong points of the schools in this district?
a. quality of instruction
b. facilities
c. schedule
d. central office administration
e. school (building) administration

Respondents could be invited to list others after the structured list is exhausted.

Items within sections of an interview are often sequential in nature. For example, in the Gallup (1981) poll, two questions were asked to gain insight into the public's attitudes toward nonpublic schools. The first question asked:

In recent years the number of nonpublic schools, that is, private and church-related schools, has increased in many parts of the nation. Why do you think this has happened?

This question was followed by a second question:

> In general, do you think this increase in nonpublic schools is a good thing or a bad thing for the nation? (p. 37)

The first question is open-ended. Although a respondent could indicate "no idea" about the increase in nonpublic schools, most respondents volunteered one or more reasons. The second question is forced-response, although one option was "no opinion." Note that these items are complete questions. The first, in essence, contains a definition of nonpublic schools, so there is no confusion about what nonpublic schools are.

Interviewers may have a tendency to present forced-response items as incomplete questions, and as has been indicated, all items should be stated as complete questions. For example, "How many children?" is an incomplete question for an interview. It might be stated as:

> *How many of your children are enrolled in the ABC Elementary School?*

The order of content in the stem of an item is also important. Consider the following poorly written item:

> *Please rate different characteristics of your school as excellent, good, fair, or poor. Please think carefully about each characteristic as I read it.*
> *a. central administration*
> *b. quality of instruction*
> *c. facilities, etc.*

A better wording for this item would be:

> *I am going to ask you to rate different characteristics of your school. Please think carefully about your answers. How would you rate [characteristic]—excellent, good, fair, or poor?*

Note that the respondent is given the options immediately after the characteristic to be rated. The subsequent characteristics can simply be inserted.

> Interview items should involve complete questions, whether the item is open-ended or forced-response.

Telephone Interviews Versus Face-to-Face Interviews

In recent years, the use of the telephone has increased in survey research. Of course, the telephone has long been used to make advance appointments for face-to-face interviewing. This reduces travel time and enhances the likelihood that those to be interviewed will be available. However, for some studies, the telephone can be used to conduct the entire interview. Many survey or polling organizations now use computer-assisted telephone interviewing (CATI), with very sophisticated equipment. CATI uses the computer memory, and it is possible to have relatively complex skipping and branching of questions.

The big advantage of telephone interviews over face-to-face interviews is cost; they are only about one-half to one-third as expensive. Generally, the lack of a telephone by potential respondents is no longer a problem (households in some rural areas might be an exception), and certainly not with populations of professional respondents. Sudman (1981) found that cooperation rates are about the same for telephone and face-to-face interviews, with possibly a slightly higher refusal rate for telephone interviews. However, the telephone is more effective in locating hard-to-reach respondents.

Groves and Kahn (1979) found some evidence that respondents do not put quite as much effort into the task when interviewed by telephone rather than face-to-face. This was indicated by a slightly higher percentage of "don't know" responses over the telephone. There was also a tendency for shorter responses to open-ended items in the telephone interview.

Face-to-face interviews provide greater flexibility in conducting the interview than telephone interviews. Visual cues, such as graphs and pictures, can be used in face-to-face interviews. However, if the study requires respondents to react to some written material, this can be accommodated in a telephone interview by first sending the material to the respondent and then obtaining responses by telephone. Surveys that require such materials are seldom used with the general public; they are more applicable to institutions or populations of specialized professionals.

Consider an example. Suppose that a survey is being conducted of the school superintendents in a state. This is a specialized, professional population. A random sample is selected for the interview. Rather than travel around the state conducting interviews, the superintendents selected for the sample could be sent necessary materials in advance and interviewed by telephone at mutually convenient times. The telephone interview would be less costly than a face-to-face interview.

In summarizing the comparison between telephone interviews and face-to-face interviews, Sudman (1981) concluded:

> Response differences between phone and face-to-face procedures are small and can be ignored for most research applications. Using the appropriate methods and experienced interviewers, initial cooperation is the same on telephone and face-to-face interviews. There may be slightly higher refusal or don't know

responses and shorter answers to open-ended questions on the phone because respondent suspicions may be higher while motivations to talk are not as great. (p. 8)

Thus, telephone interviews are certainly worth considering as an alternative to face-to-face interviews. They may not be quite so effective with sensitive or controversial questions, but this may be countered by the savings in effort, time, and costs.

> Telephone interviews are less costly than face-to-face interviews. They can be used effectively under conditions that do not require a face-to-face encounter. There is no evidence that cooperation is greatly reduced by the telephone approach.

The Use of Mailed Questionnaires

The mailed questionnaire is quite commonly used as a data collection technique for surveys conducted in education, since it is less costly than the interview. Yet it often comes under severe criticism for a variety of reasons, including the following:

1. There is excessive nonresponse.
2. Items are poorly constructed or organized.
3. Respondents are not truthful in their responses.
4. Questions deal only with trivial information.
5. Data from different questions are difficult to synthesize.

Unfortunately, these are often valid criticisms of surveys involving questionnaires; the criticisms generally can be summarized as (1) the questionnaire is poorly conceived and constructed or (2) it is used in a situation for which it is not applicable.

The difficulty of poor questionnaire construction can be overcome by careful and thorough construction of questionnaire items that deal with a meaningful research problem and by providing a clear definition of the necessary data. Constructing an adequate questionnaire is no easy task; sometimes, however, questionnaires appear to have been developed and thrown together during a coffee break. A common error is construction of items before the research problem has been properly identified. If this is done, the entire study is usually beset with inefficiency and confusion.

Certain situations in survey research are simply not amenable to the use of questionnaires, possibly because the data required do not lend themselves to being collected in this manner, or because the amount of necessary data may be excessive. If the population or sample from which the data are required is not likely to respond, there is no point in attempting to use a questionnaire. Most researchers have some idea of how well people will respond, and although some nonresponse can usually be tolerated, a questionnaire should not be used if excessive nonresponse is anticipated. There is no point in attempting to conduct an impossible study.

> Questionnaires require careful construction and organization, and they should not be used if nonresponse is likely to be excessive.

The following discussion describes several steps that can be taken to enhance the success of a study involving questionnaires.

Item Construction

If a research problem has been adequately formulated and appropriate hypotheses or questions have been developed, all items should relate to the research problem and, as a composite, they should produce the necessary data. The burden of communication is on the questionnaire constructor, who must eliminate ambiguities and transmit the intended meaning of the item. Several principles should be considered when constructing questionnaire items.

As with interview items, questionnaire items are generally of two types: forced-response and open-ended. Both types may be used in a single questionnaire; to the extent possible, items of a similar format are usually grouped together.

Forced-response items enhance the consistency of response across respondents. Data tabulation generally is straightforward and less time consuming. Forced-response items have the disadvantage of possibly "boxing-in" the respondent on the breadth of the response, but if the forced-response items produce the required data, this is not a problem. Adequately constructing forced-response items generally requires more time and effort, primarily because more of them are needed to cover a research topic, question, or hypothesis. But this time is usually well spent and is more than made up when the responses are tabulated and interpreted.

Open-ended items allow the individual more freedom of response, because certain feelings or information may be revealed that would not be forthcoming with forced-response items. A disadvantage of open-ended items is that responses tend to be inconsistent in length, and sometimes in content, across respondents. Both questions and responses are susceptible to misinterpretation. In any event, responses to open-ended items are usually more difficult to tabulate and synthesize than responses to forced-response items. Forced-response items should be used to the extent that they can obtain relevant information. They also require less effort from the respondents, since they do not need to construct the responses, and responding can be done in shorter time.

Figure 7.3 contains examples of forced-response items selected from a questionnaire used in a doctoral dissertation (Bowdouris, 1984). These items are on what is called a five-point Likert scale. (More will be said about Likert scales in Chapter 11.) The research for this dissertation involved a survey of elementary and secondary science teachers in Ohio, and it focused on instructional practices and teacher perceptions of the National Aeronautics and Space Administration (NASA) Aerospace Education Program. The instructions for responding are given before the items, as they would be in any questionnaire.

Overall, perceptions about a program such as the Aerospace Education Program of NASA are usually best obtained through the use of forced-response items. Such items provide a context for the respondent, and they focus response on concepts of interest to the researcher. If open-ended items were used, there would be fewer items, but they would probably generate a greater variety of responses. Some examples of open-ended items in such a survey would be:

1. *Please describe what you feel are the strong points of the NASA Aerospace Education program relative to teaching science in the elementary and secondary schools. You may consider factors such as the availability of materials, the relevance of the concepts to science, and the usefulness of materials.*

2. *Please list what you feel are obstacles to incorporating the concepts of space exploration into science instruction at the level you teach.*

In the first item, the respondent is given some cues that might also be relevant for the second item. One difficulty with open-ended items is that some responses may be incomplete simply because the respondent does not give adequate thought to the responses. Another possible difficulty is that the respondent might take an undesirable direction when responding. These difficulties tend to be avoided by providing increased structure for responding to the item, as was done in the first item.

Different types of forced-response items may require different ways of indicating the response, although a consistent method of response should be used in a single questionnaire or at least in each section of a questionnaire. Responses can be checked or circled. In some cases, the respondent may be asked to give a numerical rating— perhaps from 1 to 5 or from 1 to 10. Respondents can also be asked to rank things such as concepts, ideas, or problems, although directions must be given carefully to indicate the direction of the ranking. For example, a respondent could rank a list of educational issues in order of importance.

Items should not ask for the answer to more than one question in a single response—for example, "Are you in favor of team teaching and the use of computer-assisted instruction?" If the respondent says no, it is unclear whether he or she is not in favor of team teaching or of the use of computer-assisted instruction, or both. The respondent may also misinterpret the question to mean that if either or both are favored, the response should be yes. Items should be phrased and partitioned so that the response can be definite and the meaning is not confusing.

The question of whether or not the item might convey a meaning different

Figure 7.3
Sample Questionnaire Illustrating Forced-Choice Response Items

PERCEPTIONS ABOUT AEROSPACE EDUCATION
AND THE PROGRAMS OF NASA

BELOW ARE SOME STATEMENTS ABOUT AEROSPACE EDUCATION AND SPACE
EXPLORATION. PLEASE RESPOND TO EACH OF THESE STATEMENTS BY
CIRCLING THE LETTER REPRESENTING YOUR PERCEPTION.

(SA) - STRONGLY AGREE   (A) - AGREE   (U) - UNDECIDED   (D) - DISAGREE
(SD) - STRONGLY DISAGREE

- -

172.	TEACHERS HAVE A RESPONSIBILITY TO TEACH BASIC FACTS ABOUT THE AEROSPACE PROGRAMS AND SPACE EXPLORATION IN THEIR CLASSROOMS.	SA	A	U	D	SD
173.	RAPID PROGRESS IN THE AEROSPACE PROGRAM REQUIRES PUBLIC SUPPORT.	SA	A	U	D	SD
174.	A MAJOR PURPOSE OF THE AEROSPACE PROGRAM IS TO HELP MAN LIVE MORE COMFORTABLY.	SA	A	U	D	SD
175.	THE AEROSPACE PROGRAM IS DEVOTED TO THE EXPLORATION OF SPACE FOR THE BENEFIT OF ALL MANKIND.	SA	A	U	D	SD
176.	THE VALUE OF THE AEROSPACE PROGRAM LIES IN ITS USEFULNESS IN SOLVING PRACTICAL PROBLEMS.	SA	A	U	D	SD
177.	MOST PEOPLE ARE ABLE TO UNDERSTAND THE WORK OF THE AEROSPACE PROGRAM.	SA	A	U	D	SD
178.	I AM ACADEMICALLY PREPARED TO TEACH ABOUT THE AEROSPACE PROGRAM AND SPACE EXPLORATION IN MY CLASSROOM.	SA	A	U	D	SD
179.	SPACE EXPLORATION AND ITS RELATED TECHNOLOGIES ARE SO DIFFICULT THAT ONLY HIGHLY TRAINED SCIENTISTS CAN UNDERSTAND THEM.	SA	A	U	D	SD
180.	THE PRODUCTS OF THE AEROSPACE PROGRAM ARE MAINLY USEFUL TO SCIENTISTS AND NOT VERY USEFUL TO THE AVERAGE CITIZEN.	SA	A	U	D	SD
181.	I WOULD WELCOME A TEACHING ASSIGNMENT THAT INCLUDED AEROSPACE EDUCATION CONCEPTS.	SA	A	U	D	SD
182.	I UNDERSTAND THE CONCEPTS OF AEROSPACE EDUCATION.	SA	A	U	D	SD
183.	MOST PEOPLE ARE NOT ABLE TO UNDERSTAND THE WORK OF THE AEROSPACE PROGRAM AND THE RESULTS OF SPACE EXPLORATION.	SA	A	U	D	SD
184.	TEACHERS HAVE A RESPONSIBILITY TO TEACH THE BENEFITS OF SPACE EXPLORATION TO MANKIND.	SA	A	U	D	SD

Figure 7.3
(continued)

185.	NASA SCIENTISTS ARE ALWAYS INTERESTED IN IMPROVING THEIR EXPLANATION OF NATURAL EVENTS.	SA	A	U	D	SD
186.	MOST SCIENCE TEACHERS DO NOT HAVE THE SCIENTIFIC BACKGROUND TO UNDERSTAND THE AEROSPACE PROGRAM OF NASA.	SA	A	U	D	SD
187.	PEOPLE NEED TO UNDERSTAND THE NATURE OF THE AEROSPACE PROGRAM AND SPACE EXPLORATION BECAUSE IT HAS A GREAT EFFECT ON THEIR LIVES.	SA	A	U	D	SD
188.	MOST TEACHERS DO NOT WANT TO TEACH ABOUT THE AEROSPACE PROGRAM OF NASA.	SA	A	U	D	SD
189.	I BELIEVE THAT I UNDERSTAND THE BASIC CONCEPTS OF THE AEROSPACE PROGRAM OF NASA.	SA	A	U	D	SD
190.	I DO (WILL) NOT TEACH ABOUT THE AEROSPACE PROGRAM OF NASA IN MY SCIENCE CLASSES.	SA	A	U	D	SD
191.	SPACE EXPLORATION IS RELATIVELY EASY TO UNDERSTAND.	SA	A	U	D	SD
192.	AS A TEACHER, I DO NOT WANT TO TEACH ABOUT SPACE EXPLORATION.	SA	A	U	D	SD
193.	I DO NOT UNDERSTAND THE CONCEPTS OF SPACE EXPLORATION.	SA	A	U	D	SD
194.	STUDENTS WILL BE MOTIVATED TO STUDY THE PRINCIPLES OF SCIENCE BY THE INCLUSION OF AEROSPACE CONCEPTS IN THE SCHOOL CURRICULUM.	SA	A	U	D	SD
195.	STUDENTS ARE VERY INTERESTED IN THE STUDY OF SPACE.	SA	A	U	D	SD

Source: This scale was developed by George Bowdouris (1984), based on items from an attitude inventory, "What is your attitude towards science and science teaching?" by R. W. Moore. Used by permission of the author.

from the intended meaning should be considered. For example, if the item asks where an individual teaches, one respondent may conclude that the type of school—elementary, high school, inner city, or suburban—is the required response. Another respondent may conclude that a geographical region is wanted, and a third respondent may give the name and address of a specific school. A fourth individual, responding hurriedly, may simply state "in a classroom." Such an item would be improved by rephrasing the question as: "List the name and address of the school in which you teach." Or, if the type of school is desired, it would be well to provide a set of alternative responses, such as (1) elementary, (2) junior high, (3) senior high, thus avoiding confusion about what criterion was being used to define "type."

> Items should include only one concept or question, and there should be no ambiguity regarding the type of response intended.

Other desirable item characteristics are as follows:

1. Items should not be personally offensive or embarrassing to the respondents.
2. All items should fit the informational background of the respondents.
3. Items should not raise suspicions; there should be no indication of hidden motives for securing information.
4. Items should not suggest a preferred response.
5. Item checklists or categories for response should be exhaustive; different possible responses should be mutually exclusive.
6. The form of item response being solicited should be straightforward and uniform.
7. For some items, it is necessary to provide a middle-of-the-road or neutral response, such as "no definite feeling" or "undecided," to avoid forcing the respondent to make an undesirable response.

The items of a questionnaire should be arranged in a manner that facilitates data tabulation. Many times this is simply a mechanical matter of allowing the appropriate amount of space on the questionnaire. Anticipated coding schemes should be developed, such as assigning responses on a five-point ordinal scale to certain numerical codes. The space allotted for open-ended items should conform to the extent of the anticipated response; the respondent may take a cue from the space regarding the expected length of response. Although specified space lessens the likelihood of a rambling response, the amount of space should be adequate so that the respondent does not feel restricted in responding.

It is very important to decide exactly how the questionnaire data are to be summarized, including any graphical representation that may be used, the descriptive or inferential statistics to be computed, and the form the results will take in the final report. If these factors are considered when the questionnaire is in draft form—that is, well before it is printed—it usually is relatively easy to make the appropriate revisions. Failure to consider these matters early, when the questionnaire is being developed, is one of the most common sources of difficulty and distress for the researcher.

Questionnaire items should ask only for information that cannot be obtained elsewhere. Extraneous or superficial information should not be collected, because it tends to lengthen the questionnaire needlessly and may irritate the respondent. The researcher should know in advance how the information from each item will be used; if there is no need for certain information, the item should not be included. Sometimes, potentially sensitive information (for example, age and income) can be obtained through an indirect rather than a direct question. For example, instead of asking a teacher's age, asking for years of teaching experience may provide the necessary information. Just one or two unnecessary or sensitive questions may cause the respondent to discard the entire questionnaire, thus reducing the response rate and the credibility of the study.

Formulating items is essentially a matter of common sense. The law of parsimony applies: Keep things as simple as possible to obtain the necessary data.

The preceding discussion focused on technically well-constructed items, but no matter how well constructed they are, items should not come out of the blue. Identifying the research problem and hypotheses is no less important in questionnaire studies than in any other type of research. There may be a tendency in questionnaire studies to begin generating items without adequately identifying the problem. This results in "items in search of a problem"—a very undesirable situation—and also tends to produce an excessive number of poorly organized items, some of which will generate data that will not be used.

To avoid an "items in search of a problem" situation, the research problem and hypotheses should be identified explicitly, and only necessary items should be developed from the hypotheses. The item format used should facilitate response and generate the required data—that is, the data necessary to test the hypotheses. More than one item format can be used if this is desirable, but to the extent possible, the items should be forced-response. After the items are generated, they can be revised and reorganized so that completing the questionnaire is a logical and straightforward process.

Figure 7.4 contains an example of items generated from a research problem and related hypotheses. In an actual study, more items would likely be included for the example hypotheses. Also, since the research problem implies a survey of specialized professionals, more hypotheses would be included in the study.

The construction of items is a time-consuming task, but all item construction does not have to begin at ground zero. Sources of information are available that can provide ideas and beginning points for item construction. The Institute for Social Research (ISR) at the University of Michigan, for example, conducts much survey research and can provide many useful publications.[2]

A Pilot Run of the Items

Before preparing the final form of the questionnaire, the items should be tried out with a small group in a *pilot run*. The group need not be a random sample of prospective respondents, but the members of the group should be familiar with the

Figure 7.4
Example of Research Problem, Hypotheses, and Questionnaire Items*

Research Problem
A study of professional preparation and activities of the personnel in college counseling centers in Ohio private colleges.

Hypotheses (examples)
1. The primary function of counselors is that of one-to-one counseling of students with academically related problems.
2. (a) The majority of counselors (50% or more) have an earned masters degree in a social services or professional area.
   (b) The majority of counselors have less than three years counseling experience at the college level.
3. The work load in the centers is such that the average number of hours per week spent in center activities exceeds 50 (pro-rated on a full-time basis).

These hypotheses imply questions about the functions of the centers, questions about the preparation of the professionals in the center, and questions about the work load.

With surveys involving questionnaires, it is sometimes convenient to develop related research questions rather than specific hypotheses. Examples of questions corresponding to the three hypotheses above might be:

1. What are the professional functions of counselors in the counseling centers?
2. What is the distribution of highest earned degrees among the counselors in the centers? What is the distribution of counseling experience at the college level?
3. What is the distribution of work loads for counselors in the centers, and how is the work load partitioned among the professional functions?

Related Items (for each hypothesis [question], two example items are presented)

Hypothesis 1: I-1 Please check the one function that you perceive is your primary professional function in your counseling center.
——— a. Group counseling of students on nonacademically related problems.
——— b. Individual counseling of students on nonacademically related problems.
——— c. Group counseling of students on academically related problems.
——— d. Individual counseling of students on academically related problems.
——— e. None of the above.

I-2 Please rank the following functions in order of importance using rank 1 as most important and rank 5 as least important.
——— a. Group counseling
——— b. Individual counseling
——— c. Preparation for counseling sessions
——— d. Follow-up after counseling sessions
——— e. Routine paperwork associated with counseling sessions

Hypothesis 2. II-1 Check the highest degree earned.
——— Bachelors
——— Masters in an academic discipline
——— Masters in a professional area, including social services
——— Doctorate

II-2 Indicate the number of years of counseling experience at the college level that you had as of July 1, 1985.
——— none
——— one or less

Figure 7.4
(continued)

_____   more than one but less than three
_____   three or more

Hypothesis 3. III-1 Indicate the total hours per week spent counseling clients—direct contact with clients.

_____   less than 10
_____   10–20
_____   21–30
_____   31–40
_____   41–50
_____   more than 50

III-2 During a typical week, indicate in the space provided the number of hours you spent in all center (professional) activities.

*Of course, in the actual questionnaire, there would be more items, many more if this were a comprehensive study. The above items also illustrate different forms of response, select one of several options, ranking, and a short answer, although all are short responses and, with the exception of III-2, for Hypothesis 3, forced-choice. III-2, Hypothesis 3, could have included a number of item responses such as less than 10 hours, 11–15 hours, etc. However, it would be difficult to compute an average using such categories.

The items would not likely be consecutive in the questionnaire. The items for Hypothesis 2 could be placed with the background information of the respondent. If it were an extensive questionnaire, the items could be placed under headings such as "Functions of Professional Center Personnel" and "Work Load of Center Professionals."

variables under study and should be in a position to make valid judgments about the items. A class of students, possibly graduate students, can often serve effectively as a pilot run group. The results of the pilot run should identify misunderstandings, ambiguities, and useless or inadequate items. Additional items may be suggested, and mechanical difficulties in such matters as data tabulation may be identified. Difficulties with the directions for completing the questionnaire may also be uncovered. On the basis of the pilot run results, necessary revisions should be made for the final form of the questionnaire.

Besides eliminating ambiguities and clarifying directions, a pilot run can avoid results that provide little or no information. The following item, used in a pilot run with results as indicated from 25 respondents, is an example:

Please indicate your years of teaching experience (to the closest whole year) by checking the appropriate category.

0–10 __21__   11–20 __3__   21–30 __1__   _more than 30_ __0__

These results provide little information, because the response categories do not separate the respondents. The possible responses might be changed, with the following results:

0–2 __7__   3–5 __5__   6–8 __4__   9–11 __5__   _more than 11_ __4__

Now the response categories have provided much more information about the years of experience of the respondents.

The questionnaire as a whole should be attractive and easily read. Multicolored printing can be used, although there is little evidence that such printing has much effect on the respondent's motivation. The questionnaire should not be so long that it makes responding a tedious or burdensome task or makes unreasonable demands on the respondent's time. For many questionnaires, the items follow a logical sequence that can enhance the interest of the respondent.

Procedures for Increasing Response Rate

One of the persistent problems with questionnaire studies is the possibility of a high rate of nonresponse. The validity of survey research involving questionnaires depends on the response rate and the quality of response. *Response rate* is the percentage of respondents returning the questionnaire, and *quality of response* depends on the completeness of the data. The problem with nonresponse is that it introduces the possibility of bias, since the respondents might not be representative of the group intended to be surveyed.

> The possibility of nonresponse is a problem with questionnaire studies because nonresponse may introduce bias into the data.

Of course, the greater the response rate, the better the survey. Most surveys can tolerate some nonresponse, but what are acceptable rates of response? Writers differ on suggested minimum response rates, and the rates may also vary somewhat depending on the population being surveyed. Generally, however, when surveying a professional population, 70% is considered a minimum response rate. When surveying the general public, more nonresponse can probably be tolerated because the primary reasons for nonresponse may be apathy and lack of interest. For surveys conducted in the Austin (Texas) Independent School District, Jackson and Schuyler (1984) reported typical response rates for staff surveys from the high 70s to low 90s. Response rates of parents were in the 60s, and those of graduates were in the 60s and 70s, with a few lower.

Essentially, individuals will respond to questionnaires if the perceived cost of responding (in terms of time and effort) is low relative to the perceived reward. Dillman (1978) identifies the rewards a researcher can offer as follows:

1. being regarded positively by another person
2. expressing appreciation to the respondent, and
3. being consulted on an issue of importance to the respondent. (p. 13)

Of course, monetary rewards have also been used on occasion, but these are not often feasible because of the cost. An important question of any survey involving a questionnaire is, "What can be done to motivate individuals to respond?" A number of procedures can be used, although none of them will guarantee a high response rate. The effectiveness of the following procedures may vary with specific characteristics of the population being surveyed.

The Cover Letter.   The cover letter is an essential part of any survey involving a questionnaire. It is the mechanism for introducing individuals to the questionnaire and motivating them to respond. Rewards, either implied or explicit, are mentioned in the cover letter. The letter should be straightforward, explaining the purposes and potential value of the survey and transmitting the message that an individual's response is important. There should be nothing in the cover letter to arouse suspicions about the purpose or nature of the survey. The individual should be assured that the researcher is interested in the overall responses of the group and that individual responses will not be singled out. A procedure may be set up by which replies remain anonymous, but in any event the individual should be assured that all responses are confidential.

The matter of who signs the cover letter can be of some importance. Response may be improved if the cover letter carries the signature of someone who is (or appears to be) associated in some way with the respondents. For example, the cover letter of a questionnaire being sent to guidance counselors about guidance institutes might carry the signature of the institute director on the staff of a university that conducts such institutes. A graduate student who sends out a questionnaire with a cover letter stating his purpose to be data collection for a thesis can expect a limited and disappointing response.

Figure 7.5 contains the cover letter of the survey conducted by Bowdouris (1984), which was mentioned earlier in connection with item construction. The letter states the purpose of the survey, and the *implied* reward is that the respondent is being consulted on an issue of importance to the respondent. (A better understanding of NASA's educational endeavors and an assessment of practices and perceptions may be helpful in improving science education.) A tangible reward is mentioned in the final paragraph.

Anonymity of response is assured, and the respondent is given a deadline (about two weeks from the mailing) for returning the questionnaire. The letter indicates that a follow-up will be forthcoming to nonrespondents. The individual is asked to return the questionnaire in an enclosed self-addressed, stamped envelope, a very simple procedure. The cover letter was signed by the Chief of the Educational Services of the Lewis Research Center, a part of NASA.

The cover letter in Figure 7.5 is approaching the maximum length of a cover letter, in that a cover letter should not exceed one page. The cover letter should be concise, but it must contain the necessary information. The overall response rate of the Bowdouris survey was 72%.

Figure 7.5
Cover Letter Used with Doctoral Dissertation Questionnaire

National Aeronautics and
Space Administration

Lewis Research Center
Cleveland, Ohio
44135

NASA

JANUARY 5, 1984

DEAR COLLEAGUE:

THIS YEAR MARKS THE 25TH ANNIVERSARY OF THE CREATION OF THE NATIONAL AERONAUTICS AND SPACE ADMINISTRATION (NASA). AN IMPORTANT PART OF THE NASA STORY RELATES TO NASA'S SUPPORT TO EDUCATORS. FROM TIME TO TIME, THE EDUCATIONAL SERVICES OFFICE AT LEWIS RESEARCH CENTER PARTICIPATES IN RESEARCH EFFORTS TO BETTER UNDERSTAND THE EFFECTS OF NASA'S EDUCATIONAL ENDEAVORS. AS A RESULT, WE HAVE AGREED TO PARTICIPATE IN A STUDY THAT WILL ASSESS THE PRACTICES AND PERCEPTIONS OF TEACHERS IN THE STATE OF OHIO AS THEY RELATE TO THE EDUCATIONAL SERVICES PROVIDED TO TEACHERS BY THE LEWIS RESEARCH CENTER OF NASA.

YOU HAVE BEEN RANDOMLY SELECTED TO PARTICIPATE IN THE STUDY BECAUSE YOU WERE EMPLOYED AS A PUBLIC SCHOOL TEACHER DURING THE 1982-83 SCHOOL YEAR.

PLEASE COMPLETE THE ENCLOSED QUESTIONNAIRE AND RETURN IT IN THE SELF-ADDRESSED STAMPED ENVELOPE. ALTHOUGH THE QUESTIONNAIRE HAS BEEN PRE-NUMBERED, THE NUMBERING SYSTEM IS SOLELY A BOOKKEEPING PROCEDURE TO PROVIDE A RECORD OF RETURNS TO FACILITATE THE MAILING OF FOLLOW-UP QUESTIONNAIRES TO ACHIEVE A MAXIMUM RATE OF RETURN. YOUR REPLY WILL BE ANONYMOUS AND NO ATTEMPT WILL BE MADE TO IDENTIFY ANY RESPONSE WITH ANY SPECIFIC TEACHER.

FOR PARTICIPATING IN THIS STUDY, WE HAVE ENCLOSED A PAMPHLET FROM NASA WHICH WE HOPE YOU WILL FIND INTERESTING AND VALUABLE AS YOU BEGIN THE NEW YEAR. PLEASE RETURN SURVEY TO ME BY **JANUARY 20, 1984.**

SINCERELY,

R. LYNN BONDURANT, JR.
CHIEF, EDUCATIONAL SERVICES OFFICE

ENCL.

Source: Bowdouris (1984). Reproduced by permission of the author and R. Lynn Bondurant, Chief, Educational Services Office, NASA Lewis Research Center, Cleveland, OH.

Follow-ups.   Follow-ups are a must for almost all questionnaire surveys. They should come shortly after the initial mailing and, as the original cover letter, should encourage the individual to respond immediately. Follow-ups should be planned in advance; in some cases, two or more follow-ups may be desirable. The follow-up letter should be pleasant but firm. Jackson and Schuyler (1984) found that fewer responses were received from graduates who received cute reminders than from those whose reminders were more businesslike. Figure 7.6 contains the follow-up letter of the Bowdouris (1984) study. It was sent about two and a half weeks after the original mailing. Another copy of the questionnaire was included, along with an

Figure 7.6
Follow-up Letter Used with a Doctoral Dissertation Questionnaire

National Aeronautics and
Space Administration

NASA

Lewis Research Center
Cleveland, Ohio
44135

JANUARY 16, 1984

DEAR COLLEAGUE:

TWO WEEKS AGO, YOU RECEIVED A QUESTIONNAIRE DESIGNED TO DETERMINE TEACHER PRACTICES AND PERCEPTIONS RELATED TO THE AEROSPACE PROGRAMS OF NASA.

FROM RESPONSES RECEIVED TO DATE, MY RECORDS SHOW THAT I HAVE NOT RECEIVED YOUR COMPLETED QUESTIONNAIRE. IN CASE YOUR LETTER AND QUESTIONNAIRE WERE MISPLACED OR LOST, I HAVE ENCLOSED A NEW ONE FOR YOUR COMPLETION. YOUR RESPONSES WILL BE KEPT CONFIDENTIAL.

PLEASE RETURN THE COMPLETED SURVEY IN THE ENCLOSED SELF-ADDRESSED STAMPED ENVELOPE. PLEASE TAKE A FEW MINUTES AND COMPLETE THE QUESTIONNAIRE.

YOUR CONSIDERATION AND PROMPT RETURN WILL BE APPRECIATED. THANK YOU FOR YOUR VALUABLE CONTRIBUTION.

SINCERELY,

R. LYNN BONDURANT, JR.
CHIEF, EDUCATIONAL SERVICES OFFICE

ENCL.

Source: Bowdouris (1984). Reproduced by permission of the author and R. Lynn Bondurant, Chief, Educational Services Office, NASA Lewis Research Center, Cleveland, OH.

envelope. Sometimes, a postcard reminder can be used effectively, but if so, it is sent within a week or 10 days of the original mailing. Of course, it is not possible to include another questionnaire with the postcard, and this is a disadvantage. The individual is more likely to respond if a questionnaire is at hand, rather than having to find the one from the original mailing.

> In most studies involving questionnaires, a follow-up letter is necessary; it should be planned for in advance.

There are two approaches to a follow-up: (1) send a letter (or postcard) only to individuals who have not responded, or (2) send a blanket follow-up to everyone. The former approach is much preferred, because it is less expensive and eliminates the possibility of receiving two completed questionnaires from the same person. The latter approach should be used only if the nonrespondents cannot be identified. If the latter approach is used, the individuals must be told not to respond a second time if they have already responded.

Telephone calls, telegrams, or special-delivery letters may also be used for follow-up. However, they are expensive in terms of time and costs and therefore are not used extensively.

The cover letter and follow-up letter in Figures 7.5 and 7.6 use a general salutation. If equipment such as an information processor is available, each salutation can be personalized, which may have a positive effect. Note that both letters were signed by the same individual.

Use of Rewards.   Earlier, it was mentioned that the respondent should perceive some reward connected with completing the questionnaire. Even token monetary incentives can increase the response rate. In a survey of young adults who had been undergraduate students at a large postsecondary educational institution and then had voluntarily withdrawn, Zusman and Duby (1984) found that including one dollar with the questionnaire made a difference of almost 19% in the response rate—the group receiving the dollar having the higher rate. There was no evidence that the use of the token reward introduced any response bias.

The effects of implied rewards are far from conclusive. In a study using four types of reward conditions—(1) egotistic (your opinion is important), (2) social utility (your opinion provides useful information), (3) help the sponsor (we need your assistance), and (4) no implied reward—Tollefson, Tracy, and Kaiser (1984) found that the reward condition had no substantial effect on the return rate. Yet in educational research surveys of professional populations, appealing to an individual's professional commitment would seem to have a positive effect. The professional commitment implication is basically an implied egotistic reward.

Other Factors That May Affect Response Rate. Certainly, characteristics of the population surveyed will have an impact on response rate. If a professional population is being surveyed and the content of the questionnaire is professionally relevant, the response rate is usually greater than when the general public is surveyed. Tollefson et al. (1984) used three time-cue conditions—(1) 30 minutes, (2) 15 minutes, and (3) no information—for completing a questionnaire that required about 28 minutes for completion in field testing. They found the highest return rate with the 30-minute cue, which led them to conclude:

> While time cues increase the response rates, the time cues need to be matched to the average time required to complete the questionnaire. (p. 9)

It can be inferred that individuals will not be tricked by an unrealistic time cue. Although reduced time for completing the questionnaire may increase the return rates, any time cues should be realistic.

Different sizes of paper may be used; for example, the physical size of a questionnaire can be reduced to make it appear shorter. Multicolored printing may also be used to enhance the attractiveness of the questionnaire. There is little evidence, however, that these procedures increase response rate. In fact, Kanuh and Berenson (1975) concluded:

> Despite the large number of research studies reporting techniques designed to improve response rates, there is no strong, empirical evidence favoring any techniques other than the follow-up and the use of monetary incentives. (p. 451)

Thus, for most educational surveys requiring questionnaires, the researcher is well advised to construct an attractive, concise questionnaire with an informative cover letter and to provide for timely follow-up. If time cues are given, they should be realistic. A monetary incentive is helpful if this is an option.

Of the procedures used to increase the response rate, follow-ups and monetary incentives seem to be most effective, according to the results of empirical studies.

Identifying Sources of Nonresponse

The difficulty with a high rate of nonresponse is that the data may be biased. If this happens, they will not represent the group under study. A survey on the need for mathematics teachers, conducted on a statewide basis with the following response, illustrates this point. The central administrations of almost all large school systems responded, but for some reason, those in small school systems did not return the questionnaire. The data on the returned questionnaires therefore indicated an average need for mathematics teachers in excess of the total number of mathematics teachers in most schools throughout the state. Thus, nonresponse can result in a data gap that markedly distorts the real situation. It is very tenuous to assume that nonresponse is randomly distributed throughout the group.

Nonresponse is something that does *not* exist, so it cannot be put into an analysis directly, but it should not be ignored. At the very least, the researcher should be able to identify the sources of nonresponse in terms of respondent characteristics that may be related to the variables under study. Do certain subgroups of individuals—for example, men, junior high school teachers, suburban teachers, superintendents of small school systems—have a high nonresponse rate? It is generally not satisfactory to use a questionnaire without having a way of knowing who has returned it. Sources of nonresponse are identified by determining the response rates for categories of demographic variables—for example, secondary teachers versus elementary teachers.

Identifying subgroups with high nonresponse rates does not reveal the feelings of the nonrespondents, but it does identify the nonresponding groups. If nonresponse is associated with a certain type of feeling toward the questionnaire items—that is, nonrespondents have unfavorable attitudes toward them—the sample of responses will definitely be biased, since response and nonresponse are associated with the variables under study. A check of subgroups may indicate such a phenomenon, but it will not eliminate or correct it. The researcher must take this into consideration when interpreting results. It may be possible to interview a sample of nonrespondents to acquire useful information about their characteristics and their reasons for not returning the questionnaire.

> Nonresponse cannot be ignored, and the researcher must know the sources of the nonresponse. To the extent possible, it is important to determine the reasons for nonresponse.

One way a researcher can deal with nonresponse when discussing results is to calculate what the effect would have been if all nonrespondents had responded in a manner that causes the greatest change in the results. This would be relatively easy to do for items that have only two alternative choices. For example, if an item has yes-no alternatives, if 800 of 1,000 questionnaires sent had been returned, and if 500, or 62.5%, of the 800 had responded yes, the extremes would be either that the 200 nonrespondents all would have responded yes or that they all would have responded no. If all had responded yes, the yes responses would have totaled 700 out of 1,000, or 70%. If all had responded no, there still would have been a 500 out of 1,000, or

50%, yes response. Therefore, although the observed percentage of response was 62.5%, the interval of 50% to 70% includes the possible extremes. The researcher would take this into consideration when reporting the pattern of results.

Demographic Information

Most surveys involving questionnaires include in the questionnaire a section on respondent background, or demographic information. This section provides information on variables associated with the respondent, such as sex, position, and degrees. The typical pattern in organizing a questionnaire is to place the demographic information section early in the questionnaire, usually right after the cover letter. To enhance the transition from the cover letter to the questionnaire, it may be better to place the demographic information section at the end of the questionnaire. The cover letter usually describes the purposes of the survey, and the first items encountered in the questionnaire should focus on what is described in the cover letter. This organization provides for better transition and does not break the respondent's train of thought.

Items dealing with demographic information are usually straightforward and brief. The amount of necessary background information varies, depending on the survey, but only information necessary for the study should be requested. Figure 7.7 contains items on demographic information from the Bowdouris (1984) study. Note that the items request personal information about the teacher, information about the teaching situation, and information about the school. The respondent was requested to circle only the number or letter of the appropriate response, making it easy to respond and eliminating self-constructed responses.

Sequential Activities of a Questionnaire Study

Thus far in our consideration of the use of questionnaires, we have discussed various characteristics and activities. As in any research study, these activities must be put together into a comprehensive project. To a large extent, the activities are sequential, although some may be done concurrently. Figure 7.8 illustrates the logistical procedures *directly* related to the questionnaire in a commonly followed order. As in any research project, there would also be other activities, such as the review of the literature, which are not shown in the figure.

The activities move from left to right in the figure, in order of occurrence. Activities listed vertically may be done concurrently. Any activity, such as sample selection, may occur at any time prior to the mailing but should not be left to the last minute. An accurate and complete record—including mailing dates, destinations, dates of return, and by whom returned—should be kept of outgoing and incoming

Figure 7.7
Sample Section of Questionnaire for Respondent Demographic Information

TEACHER PERCEPTIONS AND INSTRUCTIONAL PRACTICES
CONCERNING AEROSPACE EDUCATION

PART I: BASIC DATA.

DIRECTIONS: PLEASE CIRCLE THE NUMBER OR LETTER THAT IS APPROPRIATE FOR EACH
ITEM.

1.   SEX. (A) MALE   (B) FEMALE

2.   DISTANCE YOUR SCHOOL DISTRICT IS FROM CLEVELAND, OH

(A)   50 MILES OR LESS   (B) 51 - 100 MILES   (C) 101 - 150 MILES
(D)   151 - 200 MILES   (E) 201 MILES OR MORE

GRADES CURRENTLY TEACHING:

3.   GRADES 3 - 4   6.   GRADES 9 - 10
4.   GRADES 5 - 6   7.   GRADES 11 - 12
5.   GRADES 7 - 8

8.   YEARS OF FULL-TIME TEACHING EXPERIENCE:

(A) 1-4   (B) 5-8   (C) 9-16   (D) 17-20   (E) 21+

9.   NUMBER OF SECONDARY CLASSES TAUGHT DAILY:

(A) 1   (B) 2   (C) 3 or 4   (D) 5 OR MORE   (E) NONE

10. APPROXIMATE NUMBER OF MINUTES YOU TEACH SCIENCE IN GRADES 3-6, NOT
INCLUDING HEALTH.   (A) 80 MIN. OR LESS   (B) 81 TO 100   (C) 101 TO 120
(D) 121 TO 140   (E) 141 OR MORE

11. TOTAL SCHOOL ENROLLMENT:

(A) UNDER 200   (B) 200-400   (C) 401-600   (D) 601-1,000   (E) 1,000+

TYPE OF TEACHER CERTIFICATION: (CIRCLE ALL THAT APPLY):

12. ELEMENTARY 1-8   16.   CHEMISTRY
13. GENERAL SCIENCE 7-12   17.   EARTH SCIENCE
14. COMPREHENSIVE SCIENCE   18.   PHYSICS
15. BIOLOGICAL SCIENCE   19.   NONE OF THE ABOVE.

COLLEGE/UNIVERSITY ATTENDED:

20. UNDERGRADUATE STUDY: (A) PUBLIC INSTITUTION (B) PRIVATE INSTITUTION

21. GRADUATE STUDY: (A) PUBLIC INSTITUTION (B) PRIVATE INSTITUTION (C) NONE

22. HIGHEST DEGREE EARNED: (A) BS/BA   (B) MA/M.ED.   (C) PH.D./ED.D.

23. HIGHEST DEGREE IN A SCIENCE FIELD: (A) BS/BA (B) MA/MS (C) PH.D. (D) NONE

Source: Bowdouris (1984). Reproduced by permission of the author.

Figure 7.8
Sequential Activities of a Questionnaire Study That Are Directly Related to the Questionnaire

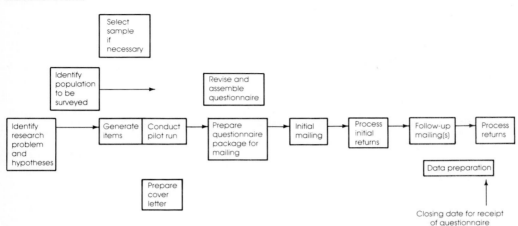

questionnaires. Incoming questionnaires should be inspected for ambiguous and incomplete responses, and those that are returned late after repeated follow-ups should be kept separate and checked against the early responses for any bias due to persistence. Reluctant respondents who return their questionnaires late may differ in their responses from earlier respondents; if this occurs, it should be noted and considered in the interpretation of results. Data preparation can begin as the returns come in, or it can be delayed until the close or near the close of the receipt of questionnaires.

A definite closing date for the receipt of questionnaires should be established. Any questionnaires received after that date would be discarded. Unless there are unusual mailing circumstances, such as international mailings, the closing date should be approximately ten days after the final follow-up mailing. If two follow-up mailings are used, this would put the closing date approximately thirty days after the initial mailing.

Surveys involving questionnaires sometimes receive "bad press." When this happens, it is usually because of (1) a poorly constructed questionnaire or (2) excessive nonresponse. As with most research, surveys require considerable effort. Careful planning and attention to detail will do much to enhance the survey and to avoid potential pitfalls. Although a recipient of a questionnaire cannot be forced to respond, as indicated earlier, several things can be done to encourage response. The next section discusses data collection through controlled observation, for which nonresponse is generally not a problem.

Controlled Observation

When controlled observation is used in a survey, the data collection and type of response are more directly controlled by the observer than they are with an interview or a questionnaire. For controlled observation, the individual may respond to a written inventory, such as an achievement test or attitude measure. The standardized testing that occurs in many school systems each April or May is an example of a survey using controlled observation. Sometimes an observer produces the data by observing an event, such as a teacher conducting a class, but *observation* is used here in a general sense to mean the collection of data. Often, available measuring instruments are used so that it is not necessary to construct instruments, as it is with interviews and questionnaires.

> *Controlled observation* usually involves the use of an available instrument, such as a test or attitude inventory. Data collection is highly structured and controlled.

Controlled observation in survey research can include numerous measurement forms. Because measurement is discussed in detail in Chapter 11, we will not dwell on it at this point. The following examples focus on the nature of the research.

Example 7.2

Griswold (1984) conducted a survey of the attitudes of fourth- and fifth-graders who did or did not participate in computer-assisted instruction (CAI). The research problem, posed as a question, was as follows:

> Assuming a cognitive, social-psychological model of school learning, which has as key components school-related attitudes and social interaction, does the growing use of computers in the classroom, by affecting social interaction, alter student attitudes and thus the learning process? (paraphrased, p. 737)

The dependent variables were scores on a 40-item attitude inventory and selected subscales of the inventory. The inventory addressed attitudes toward school and toward math, reading, and language arts, and it also provided scores on self-esteem and locus of control. Data were collected on 155 students, and the independent variables of the study were minority status, gender, achievement (in reading and math), and CAI.

Although this research study was a survey, it also involved ex post facto research, because the relationships among the variables were studied. The results are too numerous to report here, but with respect to CAI, the following was concluded:

Analysis indicated that CAI (independent of gender, minority status, and achievement) accounted for significant amounts of variation in self-responsibility for success and academic self-confidence, but not for attitudes toward school or math. (Griswold, 1984, p. 737)

Example 7.3

Shifting to a somewhat different example involving the measurement of teacher performance, Dickson and Wiersma (1984) reported the results of a survey of student teacher performance using an observation inventory called Classroom Observations Keyed for Effectiveness Research (COKER). The COKER instrument is an observation inventory used for measuring teacher and student behaviors in the classroom. It is described more fully in Chapter 11.

The COKER instrument can be used to measure teacher competencies. At the University of Toledo, it was used to measure the performance of student teachers relative to identified competencies (Dickson & Wiersma, 1984). Mean scores on competencies were computed for student teachers at different levels: elementary, secondary, and special education. Means for eight sample competencies are given in Table 7.1. These competencies were classified under a general teaching skills topic:

Table 7.1
COKER Scores for Student Teachers on Eight Selected Teacher Competencies, by Level Taught

| Competency | Level Taught | | |
	Elementary	Secondary	Special Education
1. Provides group communication (cooperation, interaction, learning from others)	43.26	41.48	40.70
2. Uses a variety of functional verbal and nonverbal communication skills with students	50.93	52.56	51.83
3. Gives clear directions and explanations	60.07	59.76	60.48
4. Motivates students to ask questions	27.46	27.06	27.88
5. Uses questions that lead students to analyze, synthesize, and think critically	29.10	29.15	26.71
6. Accepts varied student viewpoints and/or asks students to extend or elaborate answers or ideas	5.06	4.31	4.66
7. Demonstrates proper listening skills	56.81	56.97	57.79
8. Provides feedback to learners on their cognitive performance	6.97	6.17	8.36

Source: G. E. Dickson & W. Wiersma, *Research and Evaluation in Teacher Education: Empirical Measurement of Teacher Performance* (Toledo, OH: University of Toledo, 1984), p. 88.

"Communication with Learners." The number of student teachers measured was 169, including 106 elementary, 45 secondary, and 18 special education. The scoring system is such that scores should not be compared across competencies, but they can be compared across levels taught.

There are several instruments that can be used for observing phenomena such as student–teacher interaction and teacher behavior. Simon and Boyer (1974) have presented a rather comprehensive anthology of such instruments. Survey research using controlled observation applies in projects of varying extensiveness. It could be used with a single class simply to determine some of the characteristics of the students. Testing a class early in the fall semester essentially fits this situation. The foregoing examples each involved measurement of fewer than 200 individuals measured, but there are also examples of extensive projects, such as the National Assessment of Educational Progress Project.[3] Wainer (1984) conducted a study of Scholastic Aptitude Test (SAT) performance in which the data from thousands of students were analyzed. Thus, although studies vary in magnitude, they have several factors in common: measurement is highly controlled—in many cases, standardized—and there is no experimental manipulation of variables.

> Survey research using controlled observation has many applications, and projects can vary greatly in magnitude.

Survey Designs and Methodology

A number of design options are available to anyone anticipating doing a survey. These general designs are more commonly used with samples than with entire populations. The two characteristics that distinguish the designs are (1) the points at which data collection takes place and (2) the nature of the sample (or population, if an entire population is measured).

Longitudinal Designs

Longitudinal designs involve the collection of data over time and at specified points in time. Some longitudinal studies are of short duration, and others span a long period, possibly several years. In any event, data for such studies are collected at two or more points in time.

One type of longitudinal design is the *trend study*. In a trend study, a general population is studied over time. If sampling is involved, random samples are taken at various points. Different samples are selected at different times, but the samples represent the general population. Trend studies are often used for studying attitudes over an extended period. For example, in a study of a community's changing attitude toward the schools, the general population would be the members of the community. Each time (possibly yearly) attitude is measured, a random sample would be selected from the general population. An individual might be selected for more than one sample. The Gallup polls conducted over the course of a political campaign are an example of a trend study.

A *trend study* is a longitudinal study in which a general population is studied over time. Usually, the population is sampled, and random samples are measured.

A variation on the trend study is the *cohort study,* which is also a longitudinal design. In a cohort study, a specific rather than a general population is studied, usually by drawing random samples at different points in time rather than including the entire population. The difference between trend and cohort studies can be shown by an example. A researcher is interested in studying the attitudes of the teachers in Region A toward professional unions. The attitudes are surveyed every 3 years for 15 years. At any given time, the random sample of teachers surveyed is selected from the teacher population at that time. The membership of the population would have changed, at least partly, from the previous time, but at any particular time it is *the* teacher population (in this case, called a general population). A survey conducted in this manner would be an example of trend study.

If the researcher were interested in studying the attitudes toward professional unions of the beginning teacher population in Region A in 1986, this would involve studying a specific population. Three years later, the next random sample would be drawn from what remains of this population, which in 1989 would be teachers with 3 years' experience. Although some of the original beginning teachers would have left teaching along the way, the study would include only the attitudes of the population of teachers who were beginning teachers in 1986. A survey conducted in this manner would be an example of a cohort study.

A *cohort study* is a longitudinal study in which a specific population is studied over time, usually through sampling.

In some populations that turn over rapidly, the actual members of the population may change almost entirely over time. For example, if a survey of undergraduate attitudes at a college were conducted every 4 years, there would be a large percentage of change in the actual members of the undergraduate population. However, the undergraduates at each point in time would still be the general population under study.

Trend and cohort studies enable the researcher to study change and process over time. However, because different random samples are selected each time data are collected, the trends are studied for the group, not for individuals. If changes are taking place, the researcher cannot specifically determine which individuals are causing the changes.

One variation on longitudinal designs, the *panel study,* involves collecting data on a sample of individuals at different times. The sample of individuals used is called the *panel,* which should be randomly selected at the outset of the study. Panel studies very rarely include an entire population. In fact, trend and cohort studies rarely include an entire population.

A *panel study* is a longitudinal study in which the same sample is measured two or more times. The sample can represent either a specific or a general population.

One advantage of panel studies is that they enable the researcher not only to measure net change but also to identify the source of change in terms of the specific individuals who are changing. Panel studies can also provide information on the temporal ordering of variables. Such information is important if the researcher is attempting to establish cause and effect, because an effect cannot precede its cause. Suppose that we were interested in attitudes toward the central administration and promotion patterns among college professors. If a full professor has an excellent attitude, is it because of promotion, or was the attitude there before promotion, and did it have some effect on whether or not promotion took place? Without some kind of ordering of what occurred first, there is no way to establish a possible cause and effect. (The ordering does not necessarily establish cause and effect; it merely indicates whether or not a cause–and–effect relationship is possible.)

Panel studies have some definite disadvantages, an obvious one being attrition in the panel across the data collection points. Therefore, panel studies tend to be of relatively short duration compared to other longitudinal studies. Another disadvantage is that the panel study is demanding for both the panel members and the researcher, who must follow up and locate panel members. If the population from which the panel was selected is highly mobile and changing, the original panel may no longer be representative of that population at later data collection points. Panel studies are most applicable with static populations over short time periods. For example, surveying school board members quarterly over one calendar year might involve a panel study. Another possible disadvantage is that the panel members might become conditioned to certain variables so that they are better at recall or exceptionally skilled in responding. Conditioning can also work the other way, causing panel members to become fatigued, bored, or careless.

Longitudinal designs are used for studying change or status over a period of time. The length of time and the number of data collection points involved in a specific longitudinal design depend on the objectives of the study. For sampling, the trend study involves different random samples from a general population, the cohort study involves different random samples from a specific population, and the panel study involves a single random sample measured at several times.

Cross-Sectional Designs

In contrast to longitudinal designs, *cross-sectional designs* involve the collection of data at one point in time from a random sample representing some given population at that time. A cross-sectional design cannot be used for measuring change of an individual, because an individual is measured only once. However, differences between defined groups in the cross-sectional study may represent changes that take place in a larger-defined population. Consider the following example.

Suppose that a researcher is conducting a survey of mathematics achievement of senior high school students (grades 9–12) in a city school system or in a geographical region. Mathematics achievement is operationally defined as performance on a comprehensive, standardized mathematics test. (This is an example of controlled observation.) A random sample is selected that includes tenth-, eleventh-, and twelfth-graders, and each individual is identified in terms of grade level. Another way of viewing the sampling is that random samples are selected from each grade level. The sample is tested, and the researcher now has data on all three grades.

Even though the data are collected at the same point in time, because the three grade levels are represented, the data represent the pattern of mathematics achievement in senior high school. The differences between the grade levels represent gains in mathematics achievement across the three years. However, instead of using a single, grade-level population of students and measuring them three times longitudinally as they progress through the grades, three different grade levels are studied simultaneously.

A *cross-sectional design* involves data collection at one point in time from a sample or from more than one sample representing two or more subpopulations.

Selecting samples from two or more populations simultaneously and conducting a study related to the same research problem is called a *parallel-samples design*.

Parallel-samples designs usually appear as cross-sectional designs, although they can be longitudinal. In the latter case, there would be two or more data collection points, separated by a time interval.

As an example, a parallel-samples design used in a study of attitudes toward professional unions might include samples of teachers, school administrators, and school board members. Each of these three samples could respond to similar, if not identical, attitude inventories or questionnaires. The results of the different samples could then be compared.

Characteristics of different survey designs are summarized in Table 7.2. The cross-sectional designs have some logistical advantages over the longitudinal designs. Data collection is not spread over an extended time period, and potentially difficult follow-up of individuals is not necessary, as it is in a panel study. For these reasons, cross-sectional designs are more practical than longitudinal designs for master's thesis and doctoral dissertation research. If the time interval between data collection points is very short—for instance, less than three months—a longitudinal design may be feasible for dissertation research. Most longitudinal studies are relatively large-scale, however, and many take on the characteristics of continuing research that is conducted over a period of years. The characteristics of longitudinal and cross-sectional designs can be combined into a complex design that includes sampling two or more subpopulations (or populations) at two or more times. Comparisons could then be made at a given point in time and also across data collection times.

The Methodology of Survey Research

The methodology involved in conducting a survey involves a series of detailed steps, each of which should be carefully planned. The initial step is to define the research problem and to begin developing the survey design. The definition of the research problem should include a good background in the variables to be studied, which of course includes a review of the literature. Variables included in the survey must be operationally defined, and the investigator should have information about the rela-

Table 7.2
Characteristics of Survey Designs

Design	Population Studied	How Sampled
Longitudinal	(Two or more data collection times)	
Trend	General	Random samples at each data collection time
Cohort	Specific	Random samples at each data collection time
Panel	General or specific	The initial random sample is used throughout the data collection times
Cross-sectional	General or specific, and could include subpopulations*	Random samples from all subpopulations at one point in time

*If two or more populations are studied simultaneously, this becomes a parallel-samples design.

tionships of the sociological and psychological variables from past studies. This information is valuable in constructing the items for the measuring device.

The next step is the development of the sampling plan, if it has been decided to sample rather than measure the entire population. Various factors must be considered. The population to be sampled must be defined and described in detail. (Chapter 10 describes approaches to sampling that are applicable for surveys.) The sample selection must be conducted in such a manner that valid inferences can be drawn to the population and to any subpopulations.

Although some activities can be conducted simultaneously, the next major step is the preparation for data collection. For surveys involving interviews or questionnaires, this is a major step, because the instruments must be constructed. When controlled observation is used, it is more likely that an available test or inventory will be selected; it must then be obtained. It may also be necessary to train observers or testers.

Certainly, it is necessary to identify the specific types of data that will be generated by the questionnaire early in the construction of the items, but it is also necessary to consider how data will be tabulated, summarized, and analyzed. The procedures by which data are to be analyzed should be specifically identified. The items must produce data that can be used to test the research hypotheses or answer the questions raised by the research problem.

Background information about the respondent is important in that it identifies the individual in terms of classifying variables for the analysis. For example, if the responses of men and women are to be analyzed separately or comparatively, it is essential to know the sex of the individual.

When the measurement instrument is judged to be satisfactory, the data collection begins. The researcher should adhere to the sampling plan in collecting the data. If interviews are used, there should be some provision for systematically checking the interviewers. This may be accomplished by having multiple interviews (usually no more than two) of the same interviewees by different interviewers; for example, every fifteenth interview could be checked by having two interviewers interview the same individual. Such a measure of consistency is called *interrater reliability*. For certain types of interviews, it is also well to get a measure of the consistency of a specific interviewer, which is called *intrarater reliability*. This can be accomplished by taping responses and having the interviewer record the responses on two independent occasions.

The data analysis depends on several factors, but the responses must first be translated into a quantified form, such as assigned numbers to responses, that can be analyzed. Responses must be categorized, and for open-ended questions, category systems will have to be constructed. Such systems may be based on a content analysis or on an a priori analysis of responses. The translation of data is known as *coding*. This task is greatly facilitated if the information from the questionnaire or interview form can be put directly into the computer.

The data and corresponding analyses ultimately must take forms that allow for testing of hypotheses and answering the research questions of the survey. If inferences are to be drawn to populations, the analyses should provide for them. A number of separate analyses are commonly conducted on the data of a single survey, and separate analyses as well as different types of analyses may be in order. For example, data composed of frequencies on factual information items would be analyzed differently than data of an attitude scale. The former might involve proportions, whereas the latter would most likely involve frequencies or means. Analyzing survey data often involves several different analyses, rather than a large single analysis.

Figure 7.9 summarizes the steps in the methodology of conducting a survey.

Figure 7.9
Flowchart for the Steps in Conducting a Survey

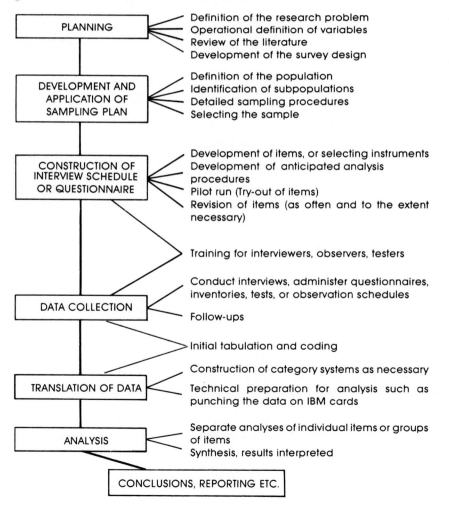

The left side of the figure includes the major steps, and the right side shows the activities that come under each step. In some cases, activities overlap into two steps. Not all activities would necessarily be applicable for a specific survey; for example, training of interviewers is necessary only for studies involving interviews.

The successful completion of a survey is not a simple task. Several possible pitfalls and problems can sabotage the survey. One common problem is the failure to allow enough time and resources for the various steps. The sampling procedure can break down, or there may not be enough resources to test and revise the items adequately. The items of the interview or questionnaire may be poorly constructed, resulting in unusable data. Failure to provide for follow-ups is a very obvious but common difficulty, and inadequate procedures for assembling and tabulating the data as the questionnaires are returned are often sources of inefficiency and confusion. Failure to consider nonrespondents may bias the results and lead to unwarranted generalizations. Finally, if the researcher reports results as separate, isolated analyses without some synthesis, it is likely that the maximum information is not being obtained from the survey. Careful planning is essential for a successful survey; although such planning will not guarantee success, it will go a long way toward attaining this goal.

SUMMARY

This chapter has discussed the methodology of ex post facto and survey research, two closely related types of nonexperimental research. More attention was devoted to survey research than to ex post facto research, because it takes on a greater variety of forms. Also, the distinction between ex post facto and survey research is not always clear-cut. Many times when data from surveys are interpreted, the studies take on the characteristics of ex post facto research.

Survey research is undoubtedly the most widely used nonexperimental type of educational research. It is used in a wide variety of situations to investigate a large number of different research problems. Questionnaires are commonly used in surveys—more so than interviews because of the time and effort required in conducting interviews. Questionnaire studies have many parts, from the identification of the research problem to the analysis and interpretation of the data. For some studies, it may be feasible to use the telephone for interviewing or for making arrangements for an interview. The telephone can also be used to provide advance notice that a questionnaire is on the way. To a limited extent, telephone calls may also be used for follow-up.

Surveys involving controlled observation were also discussed. With controlled observation, available tests or inventories are often used for the data collection. They are commonly administered in a controlled data collection situation, rather than having individuals respond at their own convenience.

Survey and ex post facto research deal with the variables as they are found. There is no manipulation of any experimental variables.

KEY CONCEPTS

Ex post facto research
Status survey
Sample survey
Population survey
Controlled observation
Forced-response items
Open-ended items
Telephone interviews
Pilot run
Response rate

Nonresponse
Cover letter
Follow-up letter
Survey designs
Survey methodology
Longitudinal designs
Trend study
Cohort study
Panel study
Cross-sectional designs

EXERCISES

7.1 A researcher is interested in the effects of location of school, grade level, and sex of the student on performance on a critical thinking test. A random sample is selected and measured using a published critical thinking test. Discuss why this is an example of ex post facto research rather than an experiment. Identify the independent and dependent variables. Grades seven through nine are included, and students are selected from two locations—rural and urban. Diagram the research study in terms of the variables being studied.

7.2 The director of institutional research at a college is concerned about the reasons why undergraduates drop out before graduation. Each student who drops out is sent a questionnaire as soon as it is known that the student is not returning. Construct items that might be used in this questionnaire. Discuss the reasoning that would go into your items. Suggest possible checks on the truthfulness of responses. Is nonresponse likely to be a problem? What information could be obtained about those who do not respond? Classify this type of survey in the classification scheme presented in this chapter.

7.3 The Department of Guidance and Counseling in a state department of education is planning to survey the secondary guidance counselors of the state in an attempt to determine their specific professional duties and the time spent weekly on each duty. A random sample of guidance counselors will receive the three-page questionnaire by mail. Prepare a cover letter for this questionnaire. Whose signature (the position, not the individual) would you suggest for the cover letter?

7.4 Suppose that for the survey in Exercise 7.3 a random sample of 100 guidance counselors was selected. Under what conditions would it be possible to conduct the survey by telephone? What would be the advantages of doing the survey by telephone? What would be the disadvantages?

7.5 A survey is made of teacher opinion toward the concept of minimum competency testing for promotion to grades five and nine and for graduation from high school. A brief one-page questionnaire is sent to a random sample of teachers in a tristate area. Construct three or four items for the questionnaire to determine the policy or policies for implementing minimum competency testing that are most acceptable to the teachers. Discuss the provisions you would make before sending the questionnaire for identifying sources of nonresponse.

7.6 Suppose that the study in Exercise 7.5 were changed to a status survey, involving the same sample and a questionnaire, with the purpose of determining the number of teachers and the extent to which teachers favor minimum competency testing. Construct a short questionnaire (one page or less) of items whose responses are fixed and easily tabulated. With this change in the purpose of the study, do you think your nonresponding group would change? If so, how?

7.7 Discuss the advantages and disadvantages of using an interview for survey research. Do the same for the questionnaire, and then compare the circumstances under which each would be the preferable technique.

7.8 In a liberal arts college of approximately 6,000 undergraduate students, a study of student attitudes toward the general education requirement is to be conducted. The researcher is also interested in the change of attitude throughout students' college careers. One approach would be to design a longitudinal study, beginning with the present freshman class and surveying a sample of this population at four yearly points. Another approach would be to use a cross-sectional design, selecting random samples from the four undergraduate class populations and surveying them at one point in time. Discuss the merits and disadvantages of the two types of designs.

7.9 An educational products publishing firm is conducting a 5-year longitudinal survey of teacher opinion and use of its products. The survey is conducted in a large city system, and a random sample of teachers is selected to serve as a panel for a panel study. Data will be collected from the panel every 6 months. What is to be gained by using a panel study as the longitudinal design? Discuss some disadvantages and potential difficulties of this panel study.

7.10 The parents of the students in a single school are to be surveyed about their opinions of a new grading system and report card. Under what conditions would you suggest a longitudinal design over a cross-sectional design, and vice versa? Assume that the school has about 350 students. Would you suggest selecting a random sample of parents or surveying the entire parent population? Why?

NOTES

1. See, for example, G. H. Gallup, "The 16th Annual Gallup Poll of the Public's Attitudes Toward the Public Schools," *Phi Delta Kappan, 66,* No. 1, Sept. 1984, pp. 23–38. This 16th poll was financed by Phi Delta Kappa. The questions in this annual poll are not copyrighted; they may be used by local educators and there are no special limits placed on the use of information from these polls. Within recent years, results of the annual poll have appeared in the September issues of *Phi Delta Kappan.* Another example in which a sample from a professional population was surveyed is Alec Gallup, "The Gallup Poll of Teachers' Attitudes Toward the Public Schools, Part 2," *Phi Delta Kappan, 66,* No. 5, Jan. 1985, pp. 323–330.

2. Surveys often involve the measurement of attitudes, and one of ISR's publications is J. P. Robinson and P. R. Shaver, *Measures of Social Psychological Attitudes* (Rev. ed, 1973). ISR periodically publishes a brochure listing its books in print; the address is Institute for Social Research, University of Michigan, P.O. Box 1248, Ann Arbor, MI 48106.

3. See, for example, S. J. Rakow, "Student Achievement in Science: A Comparison of National Assessment Results (Data from 9–13, and 17-year-olds)." *Science Education, 68* (Oct. 84), 571–578.

REFERENCES

Bowdouris, G. J. (1984). *An assessment of Ohio public school teacher instructional practices and perceptions towards aerospace education as related to the educational services provided to teachers by the NASA Lewis Research Center: A federal government influence on public school curriculum.* Doctoral dissertation, University of Toledo, 1984.

Dickson, G. E., & Wiersma, W. (1984). *Research and evaluation in teacher education: Empirical measurement of teacher performance.* Toledo, OH: University of Toledo.

Dillman, D. A. (1978). *Mail and telephone surveys: The total design method.* Toronto: Wiley.

Gallup, G. H. (1981). The 13th annual Gallup poll of the public's attitudes toward the public schools. *Phi Delta Kappan, 63*(1), 33–47.

Griswold, P. A. (1984). Elementary students' attitudes during 2 years of computer-assisted instruction. *American Educational Research Journal, 21*(4), 737–754.

Groves, R. M., & Kahn, R. L. (1979). *Surveys by telephone: A national comparison with personal interviews.* New York: Academic Press.

Husen, T. (Ed.). (1967). *International study of achievement in mathematics: A comparison of twelve countries* (2 vols.). New York: Wiley.

Jackson, E. E., & Schuyler, N. B. (1984, April). *Practice makes perfect? Skills gained in seven years of questionnaires.* Paper presented at the AERA annual meeting, New Orleans.

Kanuh, L., & Berenson, C. (1975). Mail surveys and response rates: A literature review. *Journal of Marketing Research, 12,* 440–453.

Kerlinger, F. N. (1973). *Foundations of behavioral research* (2nd ed.). New York: Holt, Rinehart & Winston.

Platt, J. R. (1964). Strong inference. *Science, 146*(16), 347–353.

Simon, A., & Boyer, E. G. (Eds.). (1974). *Mirrors for behavior III: An anthology of observation instruments.* Wyncote, PA: Communications Materials Center.

Sudman, S. (1981, April). *Telephone methods in survey research: The state of the art.* Paper presented at the AERA annual meeting, Los Angeles.

Tollefson, N., Tracy, D. B., & Kaiser, J. (1984, April). *Improving response rates and response quality in educational survey research.* Paper presented at the AERA annual meeting, New Orleans.

Wainer, H. (1984). An exploratory analysis of performance on the SAT. *Journal of Educational Measurement, 21*(2), 81–92.

Zusman, B., & Duby, P. B. (1984, April). *An evaluation of the use of token monetary incentives in enhancing the utility of postsecondary survey research techniques.* Paper presented at the AERA annual meeting, New Orleans.

8

Historical Research

Historical research deals with the meaning of events. It has been defined by Borg and Gall (1983) as involving

> the systematic search for documents and other sources that contain facts relating to the historians' questions about the past. (p. 800)

The process of historical research is one of critical inquiry, and the product of this research is the narration or description of past events and facts. Since historical research involves a description of past events, there is no possibility of control or manipulation of variables in the experimental sense. As control and manipulation of variables are essential to the experimental approach, so is critical inquiry essential to historical research.

A review of related literature is necessary for any research study, and in a sense this itself is historical research. To be sure, it may be a relatively modest portion of the overall research project, but nonetheless, a review of related literature serves an important function. Essentially, it provides a context for conducting the research and interpreting the results. On a larger scale, a research study consisting entirely of historical research provides a perspective for interpreting a part of the contemporary educational context. Historical research provides information that aids in making educational decisions. To meet this function adequately, the information must be accurate and must be viewed in the context of when the events occurred. Although the nature of historical data—that is, events that cannot be observed firsthand—often makes it more difficult to meet these standards, historical research still requires standards of objectivity that are as demanding as those for other methods of educational research.

> Historical research is the process of critical inquiry into past events to produce an accurate description and interpretation of those events.

Sources of Information in Historical Research

Because historical research concerns the critical evaluation and interpretation of a defined segment of the past, it is necessary to acquire some records of the period under study. The most common source is some type of written record of the past, such as books, newspapers, periodicals, diaries, letters, minutes of organizational meetings, and so on. However, written documents are not the only sources. Physical remains and objects (relics) of the past are other possible sources. Information may be orally transmitted through such media as folksongs and legends, and pictures, records, and various other audiovisual media can also serve as sources of information about the past.

The sources of historical information are commonly classified as primary and secondary. A *primary source* is an original or firsthand account of the event or experience. A *secondary source* is an account that is at least once removed from the event. A court transcript of a desegregation hearing would be an example of a primary source for a study involving a desegregation problem; a newspaper editorial concerning the problem would be a secondary source. In a study including, among other things, the relationships between teachers and community members in nineteenth-century America, Clifford (1978) used teachers' written accounts of living with community families. These accounts were primary sources. A report on the same topic by another author would be a secondary source. The writings of John Dewey are primary sources of his views, whereas an interpretation by his students would be considered a secondary source.

Primary sources are firsthand accounts of the event or experience under study; *secondary sources* are accounts at least one step removed from the event or experience.

The Methodology of Historical Research

The methodology of historical research can be summarized in four steps. As is true with any type of research, the steps in conducting historical research tend to have some overlap. They begin with the identification of the research problem, which may include the formulation of hypotheses or questions, and they conclude with analysis, interpretation, and drawing conclusions. The four steps are diagrammed in Figure 8.1.

Identification of the Research Problem

The statement of the research problem may be such that hypotheses or questions are formulated along with the problem. If hypotheses are stated, they can be viewed as

Figure 8.1
The Four Steps in the Methodology of Historical Research

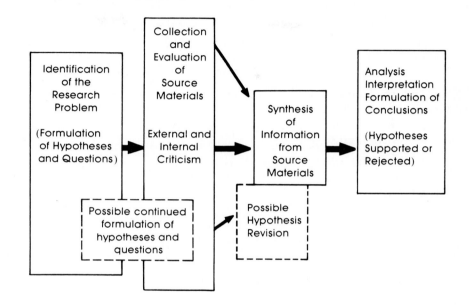

answers to implicit (or explicit) questions, or the problem may be stated as the purpose of the research without an explicitly stated hypothesis or question. An example of the latter is found in a study by Langdon (1978), entitled "The Jesuits and French Education: A Comparative Study of Two Schools, 1852–1913." In the first paragraph of the report, the author clearly identifies the purpose of the study, which is stated in neither hypothesis nor question form but directly implies certain questions:

> . . . presents a detailed comparison of career preferences of graduates of the two most prestigious Jesuit schools of the period. Studying the progress of alumni of the College de l'Immaculée-Conception and of the École Sainte-Genevieve de la rue des Postes, permits an examination of similarities and ddifferences between the two schools. It also provides a statistical basis for conclusions regarding the impact of this institution on French society. (p. 49)

This statement of purpose implies these questions:

1. What were the similarities between the two schools?
2. What were the differences between the two schools?
3. What impact did the schools have on French society?

The statement of purpose provided adequate direction for the study.

Berkeley (1984), in a study of public education and women's rights, used questions effectively, interspersing them throughout the report. After introductory comments, the questions appear at three points, as follows:

> Did Superintendent Mitchell and those following him have cause to worry about the attrition of their male teaching staff? If the answer is yes, then was it because ambitious men viewed the teaching profession as a temporary stepping stone to more lucrative and satisfying ventures? (p. 49)

> What factors accounted for the school board's ability to pursue a discriminatory salary policy which favored men over women? Why was it not until the 1870s that an organized, collective struggle by women for "equal pay for equal work" appeared in Memphis? (p. 49)

> What then enabled the women teachers in Memphis to overstep the bounds of female propriety during the 1872–73 school year by agitating for "equal pay for equal work?" (p. 51)

After questions are raised, answers are presented and defended on the basis of a historical perspective. More than 60 references were used in this report, not only to provide the context of the study but also to defend the conclusion. The use of questions in this manner enhanced the continuity of ideas in the report.

When hypotheses are stated, they usually are not stated in a statistical sense, although statistical information from the past could be used to support or refute hypotheses. Rather, in historical research, hypotheses are conjectures about the characteristics, causes, or effects of the situation, issue, or phenomenon under study.

Suppose that a study is being conducted on the decline of the humanistic curriculum during the seventeenth and eighteenth centuries. Undoubtedly, this decline was due to a combination of factors. One hypothesis might be that the elevation of the common person and his/her vernacular through the Industrial Revolution reduced the importance of the humanities as an avenue to culture. A second hypothesis might be that the advances of science made unwelcome inroads into the curriculum, and this was detrimental to the humanities.

It should be noted that these hypotheses rest on an assumption of fact—that is, that the humanistic curriculum did decline during this period. If this assumption were not correct, the hypotheses would have no basis. Having established any necessary assumptions (or facts) and stated the hypotheses, the researcher would then set out to assemble the necessary information to confirm or refute the hypotheses. In the foregoing example, when dealing with the initial hypothesis, the researcher would look for increased use of the common vernacular in the curriculum materials of the period. Different avenues to culture that developed during the period and the relationships between these and the humanities could be investigated. On the bases of the evidence, the hypothesis could be retained or discarded.

Another example would be a study of the historical development of professional education in the United States, specifically as it relates to secondary teachers. Undoubtedly, there would be several hypotheses; one might be that the teachers college developed as an outgrowth of the normal school, due primarily to the inadequate supply of teachers produced by the colleges and universities. The researcher would then collect evidence about the various possible factors that influenced the development of the teachers college. Information would be needed about the supply and demand of secondary teachers and how this was related to the numbers of teachers produced by colleges and universities. The hypothesis is based on the assumption that the teachers college was an outgrowth of the normal school and considers the inadequate supply not only as a factor, but as the primary factor.

The matter of basing hypotheses on accurate assumptions may seem obvious, but failure to do so can occur, and a false assumption is almost certain to lead to an erroneous conclusion. For example, in the late nineteenth century, many liberal arts colleges took the position that it was unwarranted to grant a baccalaureate to graduates of professional schools. This position was based on the assumption that it was not in the tradition of higher education to award bachelors degrees for the profession of education. Careful historical research would have revealed that the arts degree of the medieval university originated almost exclusively for teaching purposes.

Collection and Evaluation of Source Materials

The collection of source materials does not consist of simply assembling all available documents that appear to have some relevance to the research problem. A basic rule of historical research is to use primary sources whenever it is possible to locate them. The researcher must decide which are primary and which are secondary sources. This requires an analysis of the sources.

External Criticism.   Source materials must be subjected to *external criticism,* the tool for establishing the validity of the document. The question to be answered is, "Is the document genuine, authentic, and what it seems to be?"

External criticism in historical research evaluates the validity of the document—that is, where, when, and by whom it was produced.

Establishing the validity of materials involves several possible factors, any of which could make the document invalid. With written material, the status of the author in the context of the event is important. Was the author in a position to make a valid record of the event? Was the author an on-the-spot observer, if the document appears to be a primary source? Are factors such as time and place consistent with what is known about the event?

Since the practice of using ghost writers is common, a document that appears to be the product of a direct observer may in fact be a secondary source. The ghost writer's unique contributions may inadvertently or deliberately threaten the validity of the document, and there are also possibilities of inadvertent mechanical errors. A word may be mistranslated or an error made in typing or transcribing documents. For source materials produced before the advent of printing, copy errors in reproduced documents are not unusual. Printing has not eliminated the possibility of such errors, but it has reduced their likelihood.

Internal Criticism.   The second part of critical evaluation is *internal criticism,* which establishes the meaning of the material along with its trustworthiness. There may be some overlap between external and internal criticism, but the shift in emphasis is from the actual material as a source to the content of the material. To some extent, external criticism precedes internal criticism in the sequence, since there is little point in dealing with the content of the material if its authenticity is doubtful. However, consider the external criticism directed toward the author of what appears to be a historical document. In establishing the author's status, it may very well be necessary to evaluate some of the content. This essentially becomes internal criticism.

Internal criticism in historical research evaluates the meaning, accuracy, and trustworthiness of the content of the document.

The author is an important factor in evaluating the content of a document as well as in establishing the authenticity of the document. A pertinent question of internal criticism is whether the author was predisposed, because of position or otherwise, to present a biased rather than an objective account. Biographies and autobiographies may tend to shift the emphasis from the event to the person. Fictitious details may be included by the author because of some personal factor. An author who was opposed to an existing educational policy might have emphasized different factors than one who was favorable toward the same policy at the same time. For these kinds of situations, the position or status of the author is very important in ascribing meaning to the content.

An analysis of the author's style and use of rhetoric is important for internal criticism. Does the author have a tendency to color the writings by eloquent but misleading phrases? Is part of the writing figurative rather than a record of the real event? If the question of figurative and real meaning arises, the researcher must be able to distinguish between the two. Does the author borrow heavily from documents already in existence at the time of his/her writing? If so, is the document an objective restatement of the facts, or do the author's own interpretations come into the writings? The latter is more likely the case. The researcher should check the reporting of the author for consistency with the earlier sources. This process should also give indications of the separation of fact and interpretation.

The concern for accuracy is basic to all internal criticism (as well as external criticism). There are two parts of the question of the accuracy of a specific author: Was the author competent to give an accurate report and, if competent, predisposed to do so? A competent reporter may, for some reason, give a distorted account of an event. In checking several authors, there may be inconsistencies even about such facts as the date of a specific event. In such a case, the researcher must weigh the evidence and decide which account is more accurate.

A single document, even a primary source, can seldom stand on its own. Internal criticism involves considerable cross-referencing of several documents. If certain facts are omitted from an account, this should not be interpreted to mean that the author was unaware of them or that they did not occur. Each document should be evaluated in its chronological position—that is, in the light of the documents that preceded it, not in the light of documents that appeared later. If several sources contain the same errors, they are likely to have originated from a common erroneous source. If two sources are contradictory, it is certain that at least one is in error, but it is also possible that both are in error. The discounting of one account does not establish the trustworthiness of another. A specific document may prove valuable for certain parts of the overall research problem and essentially useless for other parts.

Both external and internal criticism are necessary for establishing the credibility and usefulness of the source. If the source is not authentic, it cannot be used. Even if it is authentic, if its content is not relevant to the research problem, it would be useless. The functions of external and internal criticism are summarized in Figure 8.2.

Figure 8.2
External and Internal Criticism in the Evaluation of Source Materials for Historical Research

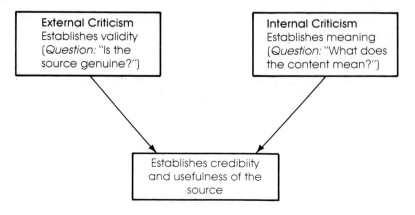

Synthesis of Information

Internal criticism carries over into the third step of the methodology—synthesis of the information. The materials have now been reviewed and their authenticity established, at least to the satisfaction of the researcher. The relative value of the various sources must be considered. For example, a primary source may be considered more important than a secondary one. If contradictory accounts appear, the inconsistencies must be resolved, which may require developing a case for discounting one version of the event.

Central ideas or concepts must be pulled together and continuity between them developed. If a substantial period of time—say, several years—is covered by the research study, the ideas can often be organized chronologically. In fact, chronological ordering is often required to avoid confusion between possible cause and effect among events. Several accounts of the same event may be included in the source materials. If the accounts are consistent, they provide historical support, and the researcher can summarize the information from these accounts with respect to the point being made.

As the researcher reviews the source materials and synthesizes the information from them, it may be necessary to formulate additional hypotheses or revise initial ones. Evidence may appear that refutes initial hypotheses; unanticipated information may support new hypotheses; and the materials may also generate new questions relevant to the research problem. If hypotheses and questions are not included but the research proceeds from a statement of purpose, it may be advantageous to introduce hypotheses when synthesizing the information. In any event, hypotheses should be introduced when they prove useful, especially as they provide direction for the research and assist in synthesizing information.

Analysis, Interpretation, and Formulating Conclusions

The final step of historical research methodology is characterized by decision making about the research problem. Historical research relies heavily on a logical analysis of the information from the documents. This may include statistical information from the period under study. Such information occasionally is generated by random samples of documents from the period. As an example, in a study reported by Ringer (1978), a random sample of entries was selected from major biographical encyclopedias for Germany, France, England, and the United States. The entries were those for males born between 1810 and 1899 who might have reached advanced educational institutions between 1830 and 1930. All possible entries could not have been checked because of time limitations, so a random sample was used.

At the final step, the conclusions are formulated, and any hypotheses introduced earlier are either supported or rejected. Of course, it is necessary to make interpretations of the information, and the researcher should recognize the possibility of alternative explanations of the results if such explanations are reasonable. A case should be made for the most likely interpretation, but if other possible interpretations exist, they should at least be recognized. For all interpretations, the author should remain as objective as possible.

Comments on the Reporting of Historical Research

In contrast to the reports of experimental or survey studies, which typically include generally accepted headings, reports of historical research often take the form of an unbroken narrative. For reporting historical research, it is often easier to enhance the continuity of ideas by not dividing the report. The research problem is usually identified early in the report, with a supporting context. Hypotheses or questions may be included, or a proposition (which is basically a hypothesis) may be presented that will be supported or refuted. Then the evidence is provided, synthesizing information from several sources. Finally, conclusions are presented, based on the evidence.

Reports in Professional Journals

A number of professional journals devote at least part of their space to reports of historical research. Probably the most obvious journal is the *History of Education Quarterly,* published by the History of Education Society. Numerous other journals also publish reports of historical research, although they are not limited to this area. These journals include:

> *Educational Studies,* published by the American Educational Studies Association
> *Comparative Education,* published by the World Council of Comparative Education Societies
> *Comparative Education Review,* published by the University of Chicago Press
> *Harvard Education Review,* published by Harvard University Press

Although it may be useful to illustrate some points from a research literature example, it is not necessary to reproduce an entire report from one of the professional journals. In a study entitled "Origins of the Modern Social Studies: 1900–1916," Lybarger (1983) focuses on the work of the Committee on Social Studies, a committee of the Commission on the Reorganization of Secondary Education. The committee acknowledged a pedagogical debt to Hampton Institute of Hampton, Virginia. The relationship between the work of the committee and Hampton Institute is considered in the context of the following questions:

> What view of society did the early social studies reflect?
> Whose view was this?
> What counted as social studies knowledge?

Whose knowledge was this?
What forms of social action did this knowledge legitimate, and what forms did it proscribe? (p. 456)

Lybarger then proceeds to develop answers to these questions. The report contains 65 notes or citations, many from primary sources such as *Social Studies in the Hampton Curriculum,* by Thomas Jesse Jones, the chairman of the Committee on Social Studies. Of course, the committee report, *The Social Studies in Secondary Education,* was used as a primary source. Numerous other sources were also used, including histories of black education. The report establishes the content and context of the Hampton Institute social studies and then examines the extent to which they were reflected in the recommendations of the committee.

Reports of historical research in professional journals often tend to be somewhat longer than those of experiments or surveys, because historical research requires information from numerous sources that must be included with considerable detail. The information cannot be simply referred to and stated in a sentence or two. Historical research studies usually cover periods of several years (or longer) or deal with issues that involve considerable information. Using all of this information effectively, with good continuity of ideas, tends to increase the length of the report.

Why Do Historical Research?

Since historical research deals with something that is over and done with, why do it at all? The reason is that historical research in education is useful in a number of ways. It can provide a perspective for decision making about educational problems, and it assists in understanding why things are as they are. Educational reform and even social reform are functions often served by historical research. Issues are often better understood—and probably better dealt with—if the historical perspective is known. Historical research can also be useful for predicting future trends. There is an old adage that those who are unfamiliar with the mistakes of history are doomed to repeat them. Thus, historical research can provide information necessary to avoid previous mistakes.

Graham (1980) argues for the contribution that the study of history makes to the process of policy making. Policy making is principally concerned with two questions: "What is right? and What will work?" (p. 21). Answering these questions—that is, the formulation of policy—is often done through a judgment call, with the hope that a wise decision has been made. Graham concludes:

I believe that history, perhaps more than any other academic discipline does make a valuable, though partial, contribution. . . . I believe that history's contribution is twofold: perspective and prevention. (p. 22)

Educational research problems investigated by historical research can cover a variety of areas: general educational history, the history of an issue, the history of educational legislation, institutional history, and many others. In some manner, the problems generally deal with either policy or practices, and the nature of history and historical inquiry places this limitation on historical research. In a certain sense, the problems investigated by historical research have an ongoing characteristic. Many of the important educational issues are initially dealt with by relying on the perspective supplied by the history of the issue. Curriculum change is often viewed in the light of past philosophy, ideas, developments, and curriculums, and historical research is necessary to define the situation of the past and its meaning in the light of the present problem. Interpretations based on historical research thus can aid in defining a course of action for dealing with a present educational problem.

The historical researcher may be looking for any one or a combination of things. The accuracy of the facts alone may be involved, but more likely there will be a search for cause-and-effect relationships of the past. The interactions of two or more relevant factors that were present during the period under study may be scrutinized. A valid and adequate interpretation, whether old or new, of some event or idea may be the purpose of the research. As in any research study, what is done depends on the objectives of the specific research.

SUMMARY

Historical research, like any type of research, has some unique characteristics. It is nonexperimental research, so no variables are directly manipulated by the researcher. Historical research relies heavily on source materials from the past. External and internal criticism are used to establish the authenticity and usefulness of the materials. Historical research is a systematic process of reconstructing what happened and interpreting the meaning of events.

As with any period, there presently are many educational issues before the profession and before the public. Historical research in education can provide a perspective for issues, including information that can be used to avoid mistakes. Policy makers at any level in education can benefit from the contributions of historical research in arriving at decisions.

KEY CONCEPTS

Critical inquiry
Source materials
Primary source
Secondary source

External criticism
Internal criticism
Policy making

EXERCISES

8.1 Select an article from a professional journal that reports on a historical research study. Review the article carefully, focusing on the author's procedures for collecting information. Consider such things as whether or not primary sources were used. Is there an adequate continuity between ideas? Did the author use hypotheses, either explicitly stated or implicit in the statement of the research problem? If so, what are they? Did the evidence used in making decisions about the research problem (or hypotheses) seem adequate?

8.2 For each of the following examples, indicate what type of research is most likely called for: experimental, ex post facto, survey, or historical:

a. An indicator of the likelihood of passing a school district's bond proposal.

b. The effects of drill exercises on the development of computation skills in arithmetic.

c. The basis for the age-graded school.

d. The relationship between psychomotor skills and achievement in academic success.

e. Precedents for the establishment of a dress code.

f. The effect of attitude toward school on achievement in science.

g. The attitude toward school of students enrolled in science courses.

8.3 Suppose that you are interested in the history of graduation requirements for graduation from elementary school that involved passing a common test of some kind. The period to be covered is 1900–1940, and the history within a single state is being studied. To some extent, this is a study of minimum competency testing of the past. What sources would you use for information? What are possible primary and secondary sources? Would there be any merit in reviewing educational legislation passed at the state level during the period?

REFERENCES

Berkeley, K. C. (1984). The ladies want to bring about reform in the public schools: Public education and women's rights in the post–Civil War South. *History of Education Quarterly, 24*(1), 45–58.

Borg, W. R., & Gall, M. D. (1983). *Educational research: An introduction* (4th ed.). New York, Longman.

Clifford, G. J. (1978). Home and school in 19th century America: Some personal history reports from the United States. *History of Education Quarterly, 18*(1), 3–34.

Graham, P. A. (1980). Historians as policy makers. *Educational Researcher, 9*(11), 21–24.

Langdon, J. W. (1978). The Jesuits and French education: A comparative study of two schools, 1852–1913. *History of Education Quarterly, 18*(1), 49–60.

Lybarger, M. (1983). Origins of the modern social studies: 1900–1916. *History of Education Quarterly, 23*(4), 445–468.

Ringer, F. K. (1978). The education of elites in modern Europe. *History of Education Quarterly, 18*(2), 159–172.

9
Ethnographic Research

In recent years, ethnographic research in the educational context has been receiving increasing attention. Part of this attention has been generated by the discussion of quantitative versus qualitative research, an issue that has considerable confusion associated with it. Another contributing factor to the interest in ethnographic research has been the realization that there may be problems in education that can best be attacked, and possibly can only be attacked, through an ethnographic research approach. Ethnographic research sometimes goes by other names, such as *field research* or *qualitative research*. However, these terms are not entirely synonymous with ethnographic research, and their substitution may lead to confusion about the nature of ethnographic research. In this chapter, the nature of ethnographic research is discussed, along with procedures used in ethnographic studies. Also discussed are examples of educational research using ethnographic methodology.

The Nature of Ethnography in Education

The term *ethnography* comes to us from anthropology. The *Random House Dictionary of the English Language* defines *ethnography* as follows:

> A branch of anthropology dealing with the scientific description of individual cultures.

Anthropology is considered a science—specifically, the science that deals with the origins, development, and characteristics of humankind, which includes such factors as social customs, beliefs, and cultural development.

If we project this definition of ethnography into educational research, we can describe ethnographic research as follows:

> *The process of providing scientific descriptions of educational systems, processes, and phenomena within their specific contexts.*

This is a broad definition, which is necessary because ethnographic research can be applied in a variety of situations. Note that the definition does not limit ethnographic research to either qualitative or quantitative data; however, there are implied characteristics of this approach to research.

As stated earlier, ethnographic research is sometimes referred to as field research. Although not all field research is necessarily ethnographic research, all ethnographic research is conducted in the educational context under study. In that sense, it is a field-study approach. The term *field research* is used by anthropologists and sociologists; it means research conducted in a naturalistic setting. In the study by Becker, Geer, Hughes, and Strauss (1961), "Boys in White: Student Culture in Medical School," the researchers collected their data in a medical school by observing the day-to-day activities of the medical students. The study was not based on a simulation of medical school or on accounts from secondary sources about the nature of medical school life. Similarly, an ethnographic study of social interaction among students in an integrated school would require the observation of student behavior in the school. It could not be limited to teachers' opinions or to theory from social psychology.

A related characteristic of ethnographic research is the characteristic of *contextualization,* which requires that all data be interpreted only in the context of the situation or environment in which they were collected. Although all of educational research has a contextual emphasis to some extent, ethnographic research is probably more sensitive to context than other approaches. This has implications for the generalizability of research results. Ethnographic researchers are often not concerned about generalizability; to them, accurate and adequate description of the situation being studied is paramount. Of course, generalizability of results depends on the correspondence between the context under study and other situations.

> Ethnographic research involves *field research* and requires *contextualization—* the interpretation of results in the context of the data collection.

The Qualitative Nature

Ethnographic research involves some qualitative data, but it should not be inferred that ethnographic research is limited to qualitative data; nor is all educational research that involves qualitative data ethnographic research. The emphasis in ethnographic research is on describing the context in qualitative terms without superimposing the researcher's (observer's) own value system on the situation. Thus, ethnographic research takes a qualitative-phenomenological approach.

Phenomenology is the study of phenomena; it stresses the careful description of phenomena in all areas of experience. Phenomenologists do not assume that they know what things mean to the people they are observing, but they emphasize the subjective aspects of people's behavior. Thus, rather than simply tabulating that a certain behavior has occurred, the ethnographic researcher attempts to understand what that behavior means to the persons under study. Such understanding requires, at least in part, placing qualitative meaning on the behavior.

The Participant-Observer

Data collection in ethnographic research involves observation of what is occurring in the situation under study. An observer may be identified openly as a researcher or may be in a disguised role. Whatever the case, observers try to be as unobtrusive as possible so that they do not interfere with normal activities. An important part of observation relates to the idea of contextualization; that is, to understand behavior, the observer must understand the context in which individuals are thinking and reacting. The observer must have the option of interpreting events. Thus, observation extends beyond objective recording of what happens. The participant-observer attempts to assume the role of the individuals under study and attempts to experience their thoughts, feelings, and actions.

Not all data collection in an ethnographic study is necessarily conducted through participant-observation. Interviews may be conducted with key individuals, and data may be collected through a survey that may support or refute information collected through observation. On occasion, the ethnographic researcher may conduct some observation as a complete outsider—that is, a nonparticipant. However, in any ethnographic study, data must somehow be generated from the insiders' perspective.

> The *participant-observer* attempts to generate the data from the perspective of the individuals being studied.

The Holistic and General Perspective

Experimentation and survey research traditionally have involved a priori hypothesis formation, followed by specific procedures designed to test hypotheses. In contrast, ethnographic research proceeds from the position that hypotheses may emerge as the data collection occurs. The observer attempts to suspend any preconceived ideas or notions that might undesirably influence the interpretation of what is being observed. The observer wishes to concentrate on the entire context and thus maintains a holistic view, rather than focusing on bits and pieces. The ethnographic researcher attempts to maintain a perspective on the totality of the situation. If hypotheses emerge from the data collection, they are retained for the time being, but an ethnographic researcher is willing to abandon tentative hypotheses if subsequent data collection fails to support them.

With such a general and holistic approach, ethnographic research does not often proceed from a strong theoretical base, nor is it much concerned with theory testing. There may be theory develoment, but formal theory enters into the research only after its relevance has been established or has become apparent. The results of prior research are also held in abeyance until the researchers are convinced of their relevance to the research situation at hand.

Ethnographic research takes a general and holistic perspective. Hypotheses are more likely to emerge from the data than to be formulated prior to the research. Theory is considered only as it appears relevant.

Given these characterists, we can see that ethnographic research consists of naturalistic inquiry with a holistic emphasis. It is a phenomenological approach, emphasizing the subjective nature of behavior. Ethnographic research is conducted in the field setting, based on the premise that the situation influences people's interpretations, thoughts, and actions. The researcher attempts to interpret the situation from the perspective of the individuals being studied, and the researcher is involved in the situation as a participant-observer. Geertz (1973) characterized the task of ethnography as "thick description."

The methodology of ethnographic research is different from that of experimental research. For example, statistical procedures for analysis are usually not so complex, nor are they so clearly specified beforehand as they are in experimental and survey research. However, ethnographic research does involve certain procedures and it has a general orientation or focus.

A Conceptual Schema for Ethnographic Research[1]

Before considering specific procedures and examples of ethnographic research, it is worthwhile to consider concepts that provide a general context for ethnographic research. What elements are present in a situation that lends itself to ethnographic research? What kinds of research problems are attacked through ethnographic research?

We will consider the second question first. Typical ethnographic studies in education might have the following research statements:

1. *A study of life in an urban classroom.*
2. *A study of decision making in an inner-city high school.*
3. *A study of student life in law school.*
4. *A study of student relations in an integrated school.*
5. *A study of peer interactions in racially mixed classrooms of a suburban high school.*
6. *A study of racial attitudes of children in a desegregated elementary school.*
7. *A study of interaction patterns among faculty in a private prep school.*
8. *A study of instruction in writing in the elementary school.*
9. *A study of socialization within a rural high school.*

Note that these statements are general. They do not contain phrases such as "the effects of," nor do they imply cause-and-effect relationships. As research statements, they lack specificity, which would be undesirable if an experiment or a survey were anticipated. But ethnographic research does not begin from specified, preconceived hypotheses; it relies heavily upon description as the research proceeds. The foregoing sample statements clearly imply description.

Another commonality among ethnographic research studies is that they focus on an *organization*—usually a social organization—or some part of it. For example, a school is a social organization, as is a classroom. We think of an organization as defined groups of people who interact in regular and structured ways. There is collective social action, based on rules and relations that have been developed by consensus. The behavior of any one group is influenced by how that group interacts with the other groups. Furthermore, individuals in an organization tend to behave as the members of the groups to which they belong.

> Ethnographic studies focus on *organizations,* which consist of defined groups of people who interact in regular and structured ways.

In our conceptual schema, we can now begin breaking down an organization into its parts. There are a number of ways this can be done, depending on the criteria used. We will consider two divisions: cultures and perspectives.

An organization can be viewed as consisting of *cultures.* For example, a school has a student culture (possibly more than one student culture), a faculty culture, an administrative culture (assuming that the school is large enough), and possibly a teacher aide culture and a maintenance personnel culture. A culture consists of the collective understandings among the members of a group that are related to their particular role. Whatever makes up the parts of a culture, there is coherence and consistency among these parts. We will call the parts that make up a culture *perspectives*.

Perspectives direct the behavior of individuals and groups; usually in ethnographic research, group perspectives are studied. The coordinated set of ideas and actions utilized by an individual in dealing with a situation is the individual's perspective. Thus, perspectives are situation-specific. A group perspective consists of ideas and actions developed by a group that faces a common problematic situation. Ideas include beliefs and attitudes as well as conceptual schemes about how to deal with the problem.

Organizations are considered to be composed of *cultures*, and cultures are made up of *perspectives*.

To understand an organization or some part of it, ethnographic research is conducted from the inside, outward. That is, the researcher begins with the perspectives of one or more defined groups and uses them to describe one or more cultures. The purpose of the research may be to describe only one culture or to describe some aspect of one or more cultures in the organization. Unless the organization is small and sociologically simple, describing the entire organization might be quite ambitious. In the research statements listed earlier, the first implies description of an entire organization, the urban classroom. The second focuses on decision making, an aspect that cuts across cultures in a high school. The third focuses on student culture.

The relationship of perspectives, cultures, and organization is illustrated in Figure 9.1. The perspectives form the cultures, and the cultures make up the organization. The arrow indicates the direction of ethnographic research, beginning with perspectives to describe the cultures, which in turn describe the organization or some part of it.

Figure 9.2 illustrates an application of the conceptual schema to an ethnographic study of student life in law school. As indicated, three cultures are considered. These cultures may be made up of different numbers of perspectives—hence the use of k and k' and k''. This study focuses on a particular culture—the student culture—which is indicated by bold lines. The other two cultures are included because they are likely to affect student culture, although they are not the cultures of primary interest.

Thus far, we have discussed ethnographic research primarily in terms of generally conceptualizing the nature of such research. The process has been alluded to, but specific procedures have not been described. At this point, we turn to the process and procedures of conducting ethnographic research.

Figure 9.1
Conceptual Schema of a General Context for Conducting Ethnographic Research

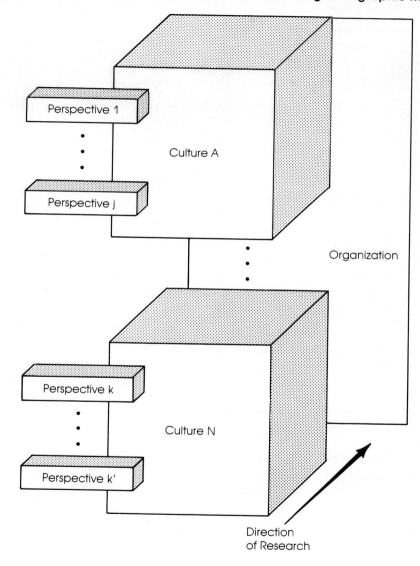

The Process of Ethnographic Research

One characteristic of the process of ethnographic research is that the activities or procedures are more integrated than the procedures of other research methodologies. In Chapter 1, a sequential pattern of general activities for conducting research was

Figure 9.2
Sample Application of the Conceptual Schema to an Ethnographic Study of Student Life in Law School

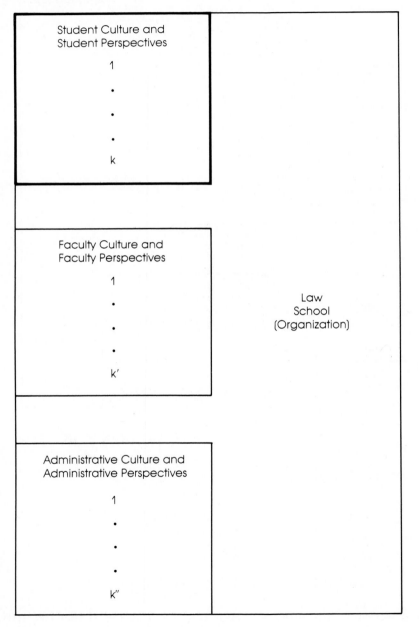

discussed. The activities were quite distinct, generally proceeding from identifying the research problem through drawing conclusions. Although we can identify specific procedures in ethnographic research, the procedures tend to run together or overlap throughout the process. For example, hypotheses may be generated throughout the entire data collection process rather than being listed first and then having the data collected to test them. Thus, the ethnographic researcher is little concerned with sequencing specific procedures.

> The process of ethnographic research is an integrated process in which procedures are conducted concurrently.

The activities of the ethnographic research process are diagrammed in Figure 9.3. The layering of the activities in the figure indicates that they overlap and that they may be conducted concurrently. Although ethnographic research does not have distinct sequencing of activities, there is a starting point and an ending point. The identification of the phenomenon to be studied is the starting point, and the study terminates when the final conclusions are drawn. The activities will be described and illustrated here in the context of a hypothetical study.

Identification of the Phenomenon to be Studied

Suppose that a study is conducted on:

The social interaction of students in a desegregated urban high school.

This statement identifies the phenomenon to be studied as social interaction of high school students, specifically in a desegregated school. This is a general statement with little restrictions, but it does provide a starting point. If stated in question form it would be, "What happens socially to students in a desegregated urban high school?"

Such a statement usually implies what are called *foreshadowed problems*—somewhat specific research problems that provide a focus for the study. Essentially, there may be any number of foreshadowed problems, depending on the nature and extent of the study. The following are foreshadowed problems associated with the foregoing statement:

1. *Interaction among the students across races.*
2. *Interaction among the students across the sexes.*
3. *Faculty social systems.*
4. *Role of the faculty in the social interaction of students.*

Figure 9.3
The Activities of the Ethnographic Research Process

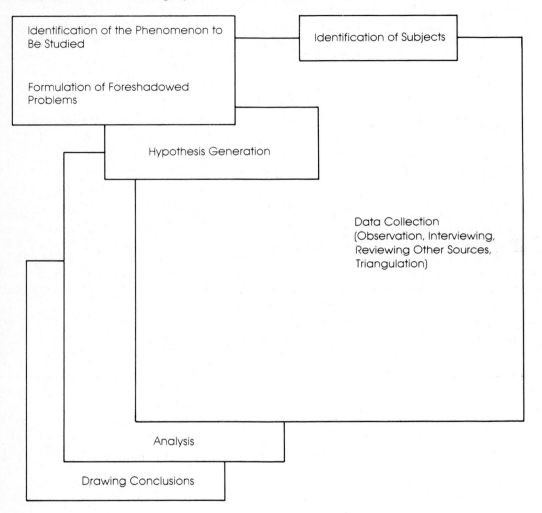

5. *Established policies that encourage or discourage social interaction.*
6. *Acceptable codes of social behavior among students.*

Foreshadowed problems provide the researcher with something to look for. They provide direction, but they should not be considered restrictive. For example, as the study progresses it might become apparent that grouping patterns for instructional purposes are also relevant, so these patterns would then be analyzed and discussed.

> *Foreshadowed problems* follow from the more general statement of the phenomenon to be studied; they provide a focus for the researcher.

Identification of Subjects

Because the example problem deals with social interaction of students, students are the subjects of interest. However, it is impossible to observe every student in the high school, so possible conditions must be considered. Will students be observed:

1. as one class followed through 4 years, or as four classes simultaneously?
2. from the time they enter the school in the morning until they leave at night, or only for a specified segment of the day?
3. in class and out of class, participating in such activities as clubs and athletics, or only in specified activities?
4. only in instructional situations and in situations such as eating lunch or walking in the halls, or in all the situations of the school day?

These questions illustrate the kinds of things that need to be considered to conduct the data collection. Decisions about conditions are somewhat arbitrary. The study must be feasible, but it would be undesirable to have restrictions that might distort or mask the phenomenon under study. For the example, the four classes would likely be observed simultaneously; following one class through 4 years would require a long study. Students would be observed in any situations that involve social interaction. They would be observed in large groups and small groups, some as small as one-on-one interchanges. To facilitate data collection, groups of students (possibly even individuals) would be selected and then observed for a specified period, such as a day or a week. Groups for observation might be selected randomly or on the basis of some other criteria. For example, a group might be included because it contains both boys and girls of both races in a relatively informal setting.

Although the students are certainly the subjects of major concern in this example, other subjects, such as faculty members, may also be observed or interviewed. Faculty may affect the social interaction of the students, and they are a source of information. Essentially, the research is a study of the student culture, with a focus on social interaction, but other cultures in the school would undoubtedly contribute relevant information.

> Subjects to be studied must be identified; this often includes specifying conditions so that the study is feasible.

Hypothesis Generation

As the data collection proceeds in an ethnographic study, hypotheses may be formulated and modified. A study may begin with few if any specific hypotheses, but the data may imply hypotheses as the study goes along. The ethnographic researcher is very amenable to introducing new hypotheses and discarding hypotheses that are not supported. There are no a priori limits on the number or nature of hypotheses.

A hypothesis that might be formulated in the social interaction example is, "Social interaction across racial lines increases as students become older." Initial data might support such a hypothesis, but it might be modified later to state, for example, that the increase occurs only within the sexes. The hypothesis modification procedure may become a process of successive approximations in an attempt to describe the phenomenon under study accurately.

Hypothesis generation is a continuing activity throughout an ethnographic study. Unlike survey research or experimentation, for which hypotheses are initially specified and then tested, ethnographic research may begin with no hypotheses, and hypotheses may be formulated and modified along the way.

Data Collection

In the earlier discussion of the characteristics of ethnographic research, it was mentioned that data collection involves participant-observation. However, the data collected are not limited to those obtained through participant-observation. Interviewing may be used, and supportive quantitative data may be brought to bear from internal or external sources. Whatever the source, however, the data should reflect the perspectives of the subjects under study.

Observation. Observation in ethnographic research is comprehensive—that is, continued and total. The observer attempts to record all relevant information in an unobtrusive way. Consequently, observation is quite unstructured. It is not likely that an observer conducting ethnographic research would have a structured observation inventory. The emphasis is on capturing the perspective of the individuals being observed, which requires careful listening to pick up subtle cues and nuances. Observation is a continuing process; it is not limited to one or two sessions. In the social interaction example, observers would likely be in the school situation every day, all day, for an extended period—possibly an entire school year.

The recordings made by the observer while actually conducting the observations are called *field notes*. The content of field notes may be somewhat unorganized and rough. Immediately following observation, the observer should synthesize and summarize the field notes, include any interpretations that come to mind, and record any questions that may be implied. Any observation record should be carefully identified in terms of when, where, and under what conditions it was made.

> *Observation* in ethnographic research is continuing and total. It is quite unstructured. Field notes should be synthesized and summarized immediately after the observation.

Figure 9.4 contains a partial observation record that might apply to the social interaction example. The field notes are written as a narrative; if the observer were rushed while recording, they might consist of phrases. A partial synthesis is provided in the lower part of the figure.

Figure 9.4
Example of a Partial Observation Record: Upper Part, Field Notes; Lower Part, Summary

Time: 11:45 a.m., January 15, 1986
Location: School Cafeteria, Ninth-Grade Students' Lunch Period

The groupings for lunch follow pretty much along sex lines: small groups of boys and small groups of girls. There were only two or three groupings of couples, in all cases both members of the same race (white). There was no mixing of the races for girls, but there was some for boys. In two instances there were white and black boys in groupings, and these boys were recognized as some of the aspiring athletes of the school. Students were orderly regardless of their groupings. . . .

After the observation—part of the summary and synthesis:
It appears that boys are more likely to interact socially across racial lines than girls. This difference may stem from the differences in traditional sex roles for students at this age of development. Girls tend to have a heightened interest in their appeal to the opposite sex and probably have little concern about making social contacts across races but of the same sex. Boys tend to be interested in factors such as physical competition; hence the groupings of athletes across racial lines. Question: In other situations, will groupings of boys occur along other factors? . . .

Interviewing.   Interviewing might be quite casual and informal, or it might be quite structured. Casual and informal interviewing can be done when an occasion presents itself during observation. Questions might be asked of those being observed in an attempt to clarify what is happening or in an attempt to capture the feelings of those observed.

Formal, structured interviews may be conducted with a predefined set of questions. In the social interaction example, a number of students might be interviewed. Faculty and administrators might also be interviewed. Other people, such as cooks, lunchroom attendants, and janitors, might be interviewed to obtain their perceptions of the students' social interaction. Such interviews would be helpful in determining the tone of the social interaction, which might not be entirely apparent from observing behavior.

Reviewing Other Sources.   There may be other sources of data that reflect on the research problem under study. These other sources often consist of records maintained on a routine basis by the organization in which the study is being conducted. In the example, records of the incidence of discipline infractions involving interchanges between two or more students would be of interest. Such records might support (or fail to support) the observation data and the perceptions of the researchers.

Triangulation.   Triangulation is qualitative cross-validation. It can be conducted among different data sources or different data collection methods. As Denzin (1978, p. 308) points out:

> Triangulation can take many forms, but its basic feature will be the combination of two or more different research strategies in the study of the same empirical units.

Figure 9.5 illustrates triangulation in two cases—one involving data sources and the other involving data collection methods. The figure applies to the social interaction example.

Basically, triangulation is comparison—comparison of information to determine whether or not there is corroboration. It is a search for convergence of the information on a common finding or concept. To a large extent, the triangulation process assesses the sufficiency of the data. If the data are inconsistent or do not converge, they are insufficient. The researcher is then faced with a dilemma regarding what to believe.

Triangulation is qualitative cross-validatiton. It assesses the sufficiency of the data according to the convergence of multiple data sources or multiple data collection procedures.

Figure 9.5
Triangulation (the Process of Qualitative Cross-Validation) for the Social Interaction Example

Triangulation Involving Multiple Data Sources

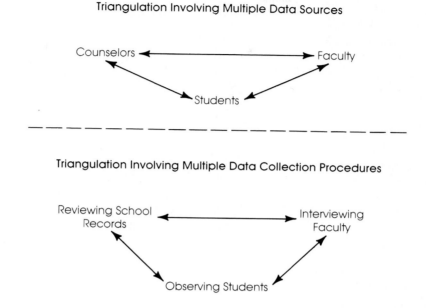

Triangulation Involving Multiple Data Collection Procedures

Consider an instance of triangulation from the social interaction example. The observation data in Figure 9.4, concerning ninth-grade students, led the researcher to a tentative hypothesis that there was more social interaction across the races for boys than for girls at this age. Some information collected from individual interviews with a ninth-grade boy and a ninth-grade girl was as follows:

Ninth-grade boy: *Yes, I do things at school with both black and white boys. We practice basketball together and sometimes eat lunch together. When we talk in the halls it is mostly about sports. There are not many white kids in my neighborhood, but sometimes on Saturday we get together on one of the playgrounds at the big park and shoot baskets, and the white guys come over. One time a bunch of us went to a movie that the coach wanted us to see, but only guys went.*

Ninth-grade girl: *The black girls in school pretty much stick together. We have nothing against the white girls, but they do different things. If we have a party or something outside of school, it's for the neighborhood which is mostly black. Sometimes in science class the teacher has us do projects together, and I might work with a white girl or guy, which is OK.*

This information from the interviews supports the hypothesis based on the observation data.

In reviewing school records, one type of information checked was the composition of the races in extracurricular activities, such as athletics and clubs. For activities in which ninth-grade students participated, the records showed that the proportional incidence of both black and white ninth-grade boys being involved in predominantly male-oriented activities was greater than the corresponding proportional incidence for black and white ninth-grade girls in predominantly female-oriented activities. Although this was relatively weak supportive evidence for the hypothesis, there was no data to refute the hypothesis. The results of the triangulation appear to be consistent.

Analysis

Analysis in ethnographic research consists of synthesizing the information from the observations, interviews, and other data sources. Analyses tend to be less statistically oriented than analyses of experimental or survey data. However, there are proportions and percentages that can be computed, based on classifications of items from interviews or types of activities and events observed.

Becker et al. (1961) suggest a number of ways information can be classified, including the following:

1. Dichotomous categories indicating whether information obtained was directed by the observer's activities or was volunteered spontaneously by those being studied
2. Number of responses to direct queries
3. Dichotomous categories indicating whether information was obtained in the presence of the observer alone or when other individuals were present
4. Proportions of information that consist of activities observed versus statements made

For analysis purposes, it may be helpful to present results in tabular form, giving both frequencies and proportions. A format for the social interaction example is shown in Figure 9.6.

The analysis in ethnographic research relies heavily on description; even when statistics are used, they tend to be used in a descriptive rather than an inferential manner. Inferential statistics might be appropriate if random sampling of events or of some characteristic of the study had been done. But we would not expect the research context to be a random sample of some larger population of contexts. The ethnographic researcher is probably more willing than other types of researchers to accept the uniqueness of the research context and its conditions.

Drawing Conclusions

Experimental and survey research typically leave drawing conclusions as one of the final steps. In ethnographic research, drawing conclusions is integrated much more

Figure 9.6
Sample Format for Presenting Results for Analysis in the Social Interaction Example

Statements	Volunteered	Directed	Total
To observer alone			
To other students with observer present			
To other students with observer and faculty present			

Activities	Same Race	Mixed Race
With one other student		
With more than one other student		
With one or more faculty		
With both other student(s) and faculty		

with the other parts of the research process. This is partly because of the successive approximation procedure of coming to conclusions when conducting ethnographic research. Tentative hypotheses, theories, and conclusions are generated during the research, but the ethnographic researcher guards against drawing the final conclusions prematurely.

Connecting the Example and the Conceptual Schema

What value has the conceptual schema for ethnographic research, discussed earlier, to the example of the study of social interaction in a desegregated high school? Essentially, schema helps clarify the components of the research. In the example, the organization in which the study is conducted is the desegregated high school. Several cultures are involved, including the student culture, the faculty culture, and administration culture. But in this example, neither the organization nor a culture is of primary interest. The focus of interest is a part of the student culture—basically, the group perspectives of the students as they affect the social interaction. The perspectives are the modes of thought and action developed by the students as they deal with social interaction situations.

> The conceptual schema for ethnographic research helps clarify the compo-
> nents involved in a specific study and aids in identifying the focus of the
> research.

Examples of Ethnographic Research in Education

There are classic examples of ethnographic research, such as the Becket et al. (1961) study, "Boys in White: Student Culture in Medical School." More recently in ed-ucation, the comprehensive reports on the American high school by Boyer (1983) and Sizer (1984) are based on ethnographic research studies. However, not many educators are likely to conduct studies of such magnitude—not even for a doctoral dissertation. The extensive classic studies can provide useful information about meth-odology, but at this point, it should be helpful to consider examples of less extensive studies—those that are feasible for the practicing educator. Sitton (1980) and Strahan (1983) have noted that the teacher is in an advantagous position as an ethnographer. Part of the teacher's role is that of classroom observer, which can help in conducting ethnographic research.

Ethnographic research, by its every nature, requires a considerable time com-mitment. The phenomena under study often require extensive observation if they are to be understood. If teachers conduct ethnographic research alone in their own classrooms, the studies will necessarily be of limited focus. Therefore, teachers will probably find their most useful roles in ethnographic research as collaborators with others. Kantor, Kirby, and Goetz (1981, p. 305) emphasize this point:

> Experienced teachers have knowledge of children and classroom settings which
> makes them potentially strong researchers; ethnography allows them to use
> that knowledge and opens opportunities for dialogue between teachers and
> researchers. Especially promising are collaborative efforts between teachers and
> researchers.

Example from Elementary School Writing Instruction

Florio and Clark (1982) conducted a study on the functions of writing in an elemen-tary classroom. The following is a brief overview of the study, with emphasis on its ethnographic nature.

The report of the research was based on a 2-year study undertaken in two classrooms: one, a second/third-grade open-space classroom in an elementary school, the other, a sixth-grade middle-school classroom. The report, published in the May 1982 issue of *Research in the Teaching of English,* focuses on the second/third-grade class.

The study was interdisciplinary, in that methodology from ethnographic re-search was used, incorporating ideas from cognitive psychology along with percep-tions of experienced teachers. Data were obtained from the following sources:

1. ethnographic field notes of extensive participant observation in each class-room,
2. selected video tapes of everyday life in the classroom,
3. weekly journals kept by the local teachers describing their instruction and the teaching of writing in particular,
4. interviews with teachers about the content of journals and videotapes, and
5. collection of student written work and discussion with students about their work. (p. 118)

The classroom occupied an entire wing of the school. It was a unique room in the school, designed to accommodate open-classroom, cross-age instruction. The room was described in the report, with special emphasis on the area used for writing instruction. Such description is important for an understanding of the instructional context.

Based on the data collected and interpretation, four writing functions were identified:

1. writing to participate in community,
2. writing to know oneself and others,
3. writing to occupy free time, and
4. writing to demonstrate academic competence. (p. 120)

The community referred to is the group involved in the writing instruction as it is conducted in the classroom.

In the process of conducting the research, the authors state:

Fieldworkers did not limit their insights to activities explicitly involving writing and its instruction. Instead, pains were taken to spend considerable time in the school and classroom, observing and sharing in the round of daily activities and gradually noting patterns in the use of writing by teacher and students. Similarly, when teacher and students were asked questions about writing in both formal and informal interviews, the questions came at first in terms of the larger context of their classroom life. Finally, in the same spirit, student writings and drawings were collected widely and in large quantity. (p. 121)

This statement summarizes the ethnographic research methodology. In the report, the four functions are then examined closely, and examples of writing and observers' interpretations are presented. Then the report is drawn to a close by summarizing the conclusions, one of which was stated as follows:

One very promising function of writing observed was perhaps the most challenging pedagogically—it was the writing that started with the real experiences of children and was organized both to have legitimacy as a school event and to offer children considerable control and influence on the process. (pp. 128–129)

The authors conclude by commenting on the viability and the value of this type of research in the study of writing instruction.

Example from Bilingual Education

Ethnography has sometimes been proposed as an approach to evaluation, especially program evaluation. Masemann (1978) reports on an evaluation of the bilingual/ bicultural education program of the Milwaukee Public Schools, as applied with Spanish-speaking students, in which ethnographic research techniques were used. The program, as applied at the elementary school level, had seven goals:

1. to achieve the basic skills of understanding, speaking, reading, and writing two languages, one of which is English,
2. to develop a bilingual readiness in Spanish-speaking and English-speaking children,
3. to stimulate Spanish-speaking children to understand and communicate in English,
4. to cultivate in Spanish-speaking pupils a pride in their native language and culture, and a more positive self-image as they make the transition to another language and culture,
5. to enable Spanish-speaking pupils, by the end of grade six, to achieve such general proficiency in their first language that they can pursue their studies with about equal ease in their first and second languages,
6. to promote in the English-speaking children a personal awareness and respect for the cultural values of the Spanish-speaking people, and
7. to enable pupils in the above classes to progress in school so that by the end of grade six they will reach grade level achievement in all their subjects. (Milwaukee Bilingual Education Project, 1977, p. 39)

A reflection on these goals, especially numbers 3, 4, and 6, indicates ambitious types of outcomes, which would be difficult to assess through available quantitative measures. However, in the project evaluation, the focus was on the following questions:

1. To what extent are these goals reflected in classroom practice?
2. Do social processes in the classroom facilitate or hinder the reaching of these goals?
3. What actually happens in bilingual classrooms? (Masemann, 1978, p. 299)

An ethnographic research study was conducted using four classrooms in the Milwaukee schools, with observation taking place during the fall semester. Three of these classrooms were bilingual and one was monolingual, the latter being used for comparison purposes. Classrooms were described comprehensively in terms of a number of variables, such as percentage of Spanish-surnamed students in the school and teacher ethnicity.

Observation provided detailed descriptions of classroom climate and activities. Use of time, space, and language in spoken interaction were used as central categories of observation as indicated in the following excerpt from an observation:

> In the first classroom, the young male anglo teacher was the most formal of any of the teachers in his use of classroom time and space, and in his specification of the appropriate times and places at which Spanish or English was to be used. . . . The Classroom I teacher divided the school day into segments of time in which only one language was spoken or taught, with all formal or informal language interaction in the appropriate language. (Masemann, 1978, p. 302)

Of course, the observation data were analyzed and synthesized for the individual classrooms and across the four classrooms.

The following is one of the conclusions drawn from this study:

> The "language climate" of the classroom is greatly influenced by the techniques a teacher uses to organize the classroom day, whether in terms of time, or the use of classroom space, or the role of the teacher's aide, or the way in which children are assigned to tasks, individually or in groups. (Masemann, 1978, p. 306)

The author recognizes that, as ethnographic studies go, this was a limited study, at least in terms of the length of time during which observation was conducted. Nevertheless, because of the stability of instruction in a specific elementary school classroom, the observation was considered adequate. Note that the ethnographic research procedures were directed to the three questions, which reflect the goals of the project but are not the project goals. The ethnographic research focused on the instructional process. For example, the research did not test whether or not goal number 7 had been attained. The attainment of that goal would be checked through achievement testing.

Other Considerations

Thus far, we have discussed the nature of ethnographic research, its methodology, and examples of its use in education. Before summarizing the chapter, it is appropriate to comment on other considerations associated with ethnographic research—the reliability and validity of such research and the use of quantitative procedures.

The Reliability and Validity of Ethnographic Research

As indicated in Chapter 1, the *reliability* of research involves the extent to which studies can be replicated. The concept applies to both procedures and results. If a study is reliable, another researcher who uses the same procedures, variables, measurement, and conditions should obtain the same results. The *validity* of research involves the interpretation of research results with confidence and the generalizability of the results. The former is called internal validity and the latter, external validity. Reliability and validity influence the credibility of the research and the confidence that can be placed in the findings.

Reliability is concerned with replicability of both procedures and findings. *Validity* refers to the interpretation and generalizability of results.

Reliability. Goetz and LeCompte (1984) distinguish between two types of reliability in ethnographic research—external and internal. External reliability involves the extent to which independent researchers working in the same or similar contexts would obtain consistent results. Internal reliability involves the extent to which researchers concerned with the same data and constructs would be consistent in matching them. Because it is conducted in naturalistic settings and often focuses on processes, ethnographic research is susceptible to problems of replication. However, these problems have been addressed and procedures have been suggested for averting them.

Ethnographic research is usually focused not on the tabulation of frequencies of events or behaviors, but on obtaining an accurate description of the phenomena under study. In a specific study, internal reliability would depend on the extent to which two or more observers agree on what they saw and how they interpret what they saw. How can observers be made to agree? Basically, the way to enhance reliability (and validity, for that matter) in ethnographic research is no different from the way to do so in any other type of research—that is, through applying good methodology.

Ethnographic researchers may not be able to begin a study with as much design specificity as exists for other research, but the context of the research and the overall problem addressed should be specified as much as possible. The status of the observers in the situation should be well defined. The use of multiple data collection procedures, along with triangulation, tends to enhance internal reliability. The extensive description used in ethnographic research is a plus in terms of internal reliability; if there seems to be a lack of observer agreement, the source of disagreement can be identified from the description. If observers are in disagreement, there should always be an opportunity for discussion to resolve the disagreement. Ethnographic research is often a cooperative effort among several individuals; as such, it provides excellent oportunities for teachers and university faculty to participate jointly in research studies. There should always be opportunities for sharing insights, discussing interpretations, and reviewing the descriptions of others. If situations are video-taped, the tapes can be viewed and any discrepancies in what is seen can be discussed.

External reliability is a matter of degree, and some would argue that nothing can be replicated exactly. Many ethnographic researchers are not very concerned about whether or not others could replicate their studies. But because ethnographic procedures are varied and are applied with varying degrees of sophistication, the ethnographic researcher must be particularly comprehensive in describing the methodology. It is not sufficient to use a shorthand description and then assert that data collection and analysis were carefully conducted. Goetz and LeCompte (1984, p. 217) summarize this point:

> The researcher must clearly identify and fully discuss data analysis processes and provide retrospective accounts of how data were examined and synthesized. Because reliability depends on the potential for subsequent researchers to reconstruct original analysis strategies, only those ethnographic accounts that specify these in sufficient detail are replicable.

Validity.   Attaining reliability does not assure the validity of research—either internal or external. For example, observers could agree on their conclusions and yet the conclusions could be in error. If conclusions cannot be drawn in confidence, there are deficiencies in the research procedures, and the study lacks internal validity. If the results of a study do not generalize, the study lacks external validity, even if results were consistent internally and the study is replicable.

A research study may be both internally and externally reliable yet lack validity.

Consider internal validity first. In experimental design, we control extraneous variables to the extent possible—for example, through randomization or by including additional independent variables into the design. Because ethnographic research is conducted in the natural setting, it does not have this option of control. Ethnographic studies often cover a relatively long time period, which increases the possibility of extraneous effects. However, longevity in the research context does enhance the search for causes and effects. The temporal ordering of events, the perspectives of various informants, and the possible effects of confounded variables are examples of factors that may affect internal validity, yet they are factors that tend to become better understood with exposure in the situation. Establishing internal validity is a process that involves both deduction and induction; the researcher systematically reasons through the possible causes responsible for the data.

The concern of external validity is generalization; to what populations, conditions, and so forth, do the results generalize? LeCompte and Goetz (1982, p. 51) identify the problem as one of demonstrating "the typicality of a phenomenon, or the extent to which it compares and contrasts along relevant dimensions with other phenomena." In educational research, random sampling is often not a feasible option, and representativeness has to be argued on a logical basis. When generalizing from an ethnographic research study, it is important to specify the conditions of the setting and the methodology, so that the bases for comparison (or lack thereof) can be established.

External validity can be strengthened by multisite studies. If a phenomenon seems to be consistent across a number of studies, its generalizability is increased. Even if there is inconsistency in the phenomenon, a study of the differences between the sites may reveal the limitations or special conditions of generalization. Certainly, not all ethnographic studies in education can be multisite studies; in fact, few would meet that criterion. But the external validity can be enhanced by including variations of the research context in the same study. For example, if writing instruction in the elementary school is being studied, including two or more elementary classrooms in the same study would enhance external validity.

Absolute reliability and validity in any research study are impossible to attain, regardless of type. Yet researchers establish reliability and validity by a careful balancing of the variables and effects operating in the research context. This general strategy also applies to ethnographic research.

Quantitative Methodology

Ethnographic research is considered to be qualitative in nature, and some writers argue that qualitative and quantitative research differ in so many fundamental ways that integrating methodology from the two types is difficult, if not impossible. Schofield and Andersen (1984) present a convincing argument that methodology can be integrated and present examples for incorporating selected quantitative methodology into qualitative studies such as ethnographic studies. The methodology described here is taken from the Schofield and Andersen paper.

Use of Numbers. In qualitative research, terms such as *large, a long time,* or *quite rapid* are often used in describing phenomena. For certain types of phenomena, such as length of time, quantitative measures are available, and their use can increase the precision of the description. To say that the observation periods averaged about 3 hours is more precise than saying that they were "quite long" or that they lasted "most of the afternoon." In a study of high schools, if size of class is a characteristic used in the description, numbers such as averages are more informative than simple descriptive terms.

Ethnographic researchers engage in what is sometimes called *ballparking*—providing a very rough estimate of a phenomenon. An example of ballparking is, "Many students engaged in conversations in the halls involving students of both sexes." For some activities and situations, it is impossible or undesirable to obtain numerical estimates, and ballparking is adequate. However, confusion can be introduced if numbers are specified when in fact they represent only ballpark estimates. Researchers should be clear about whether numbers are ballpark estimates or more specific estimates. If they are ballpark estimates, they may be indicating only order of magnitude.

Researchers should use caution in classifying individuals on variables whose frequency or existence involves a subjective perception. Schofield and Andersen (1984, p. 13) cite an example of ethnic identity, which is described as follows:

> Ethnic identity is, after all, a construct referring to one's subjective sense of self rather than to certain physical or cultural criteria that someone else might use to label one as belonging to a particular group.

A problem arises when certain counts or categorizations are based on operational definitions that are not in agreement with the perceptions of the individuals being studied. For example, "official classification" may not be in agreement with the way individuals studied perceive themselves, in which case numbers based on official classification would be misleading.

> Numbers are useful in ethnographic research for providing more specific information than descriptive terms alone. Researchers must be clear about the level of precision contained in the numbers.

Use of Sampling Procedures.   Random sampling is commonly associated with research studies that involve quantitative methodology. Random selection ensures representativeness within the constraints of sampling fluctuation. Ethnographic research studies usually focus on a specific situation or context, yet not every possible part of a phenomenon is observed or checked, so some selection is involved.

Most ethnographic research studies are conducted on a single site, or possibly on a small number of sites; unless an extensive study is being done, random selection of sites would not be applicable. For example, if a large study were being done on the senior high schools of a state, and 20 sites were to be involved, the sites could be randomly selected from the population of senior high schools of the state. More likely, in studies of lesser magnitude, random sampling would be more applicable at the site.

Consider again the example introduced earlier of social interaction at a desegregated high school. It is not likely that all of the classes and other gatherings will be observed or that all students and faculty will be interviewed. Therefore, selection must be done. Individuals might be randomly selected for interviewing. There might be random selection of classes, activities, or blocks of time for observing. Selection might be done not through simple random sampling but through a more complex sampling plan. Random sampling increases the validity of the study and would be unlikely to compromise the flexibility of conducting the research.

> *Random sampling* can be used effectively in some ethnographic research studies, more likely at the site than in site selection.

Use of Questionnaires, Observational Inventories, and Content Analysis. Questionnaires and structured observational inventories are usually associated with survey research. They commonly provide data that are analyzed by usual quantitative procedures. In an ethnographic research study, questionnaires might be used to supplement the data from interviews, for example, since the items of the questionnaire are more structured than the open-ended items of the interview.

Many indices and inventories are available that attempt to provide quantitative measures of such phenomena as teacher–pupil interaction and social interaction patterns. The Classroom Observations Keyed for Effectiveness Research (COKER) inventory was used by Dickson and Wiersma (1984) to assess the demonstration of student teacher competencies. The COKER instrument also provides a picture of the classroom interaction in a way that quantifies the behaviors that occur in the classroom. Schofield and Sagar (1977) discuss the coding of cafeteria seating patterns and the use of indices of racial clustering in their study of peer interaction patterns. These are examples of procedures that generate data that can be analyzed using quantitative methodology, the results of which may be useful in an ethnographic study.

Data from formal content analysis may be used as supplementary data in an ethnographic research study. Content analysis involves coding into specified categories. There might be content analysis of material at the observed site, such as bulletin board content in elementary school classrooms. Curriculum materials or course syllabi might be analyzed if they are relevant to the study. Content analysis should focus on supplementary sources of data; as Schofield and Andersen (1984) point out, problems arise if content analysis is attempted with the ethnographer's field notes. The field notes record only a portion of the events that occurred in the observed setting, and after-the-fact content analysis may lead to erroneous conclusions.

> Questionnaires, observational inventories, and content analysis can provide supplemental quantitative data in an ethnographic research study.

SUMMARY

This chapter has discusssed ethnographic research in education—its rationale and methodology. Ethnographic research has received increasing attention over the past decade. Numerous writers have argued for its application and benefits (see, for example, Smith, 1982), especially when conducting research in naturalistic educational settings. The emphasis in ethnographic research is to understand the phenomenon under study from the perspective of those being studied.

Hypotheses in ethnographic research result from immersion in the research context, which is a field setting. They generally are not specified a priori and are not based on a theory. Data are collected in the field, which necessitates on-site observation using field-based instruments. The processes of generating hypotheses, collecting data, and drawing conclusions are highly integrated. The objective is to attain a holistic description of the phenomenon under study.

Ethnographic research is generally viewed as qualitative research, and therefore the methods used are varied and often somewhat unstructured. As Rogers (1984) suggests, this creates some difficulty in developing adequate definitions of qualitative research techniques. Yet ethnographic research focuses heavily on observation and interviewing, with supportive data coming from other available resources. As discussed in this chapter, ethnographic research, though primarily qualitative in nature, should not exclude the use of quantitative methodology if it is applicable and useful.

A conceptual schema for ethnographic research was discussed, involving the concepts of perspectives, culture, and organization. Such a conceptual schema aids in understanding the general characteristics of an approach to research. The methodological steps in ethnographic research include data collection, analysis, and so forth. These steps or activities tend to overlap more and are more extensively integrated than they are in other types of research. For example, an experimenter typically begins with a specified set of hypotheses that will be tested by conducting the experiment. In contrast, the ethnographic researcher identifies the phenomenon to be studied and then develops hypotheses through the data collection. Subsequently, the hypotheses may be retained, modified, or discarded.

Ethnographic research lends itself to the study of phenomena in classrooms. For this reason, and because teachers are the on-site observers of classroom behavior (certainly, they are participant-observers), teachers can effectively participate in ethnographic research. Because research is a demanding and time-consuming task, teachers will probably find that participating on a team of researchers is more feasible than conducting research alone, although the latter is certainly a possibility.

Arguments about the relative merits of quantitative versus qualitative research abound in the literature. Taking an either-or position is probably not very fruitful. It is more useful to recognize that there are different approaches to research and that each can make its contribution where applicable. Of course, whatever research methods are used, reliability and validity of the research must be considered, and the methods should be used correctly.

KEY CONCEPTS

Ethnography
Field research

Triangulation
Reliability

Contextualization   *Validity*
Phenomenology   *Ballparking*
Participant-observer   *Random sampling*
Culture   *Perspective*
Organization   *Foreshadowed problems*
Observation   *Field notes*

EXERCISES

9.1 Contrast the nature of ethnographic research and the nature of experimental research. Identify differences in orientation and methodology. What are some conditions under which each type is appropriate?

9.2 If we identify the conceptual components of ethnographic research as perspectives, cultures, and organizations, describe how these components are related or connected. Select an example (either real or hypothetical) of ethnographic research in education, and identify these components for the example.

9.3 Define the process of triangulation. Suppose that a researcher is conducting ethnographic research on instruction in elementary school mathematics. Describe how triangulation might be used.

9.4 A study is being conducted on student life in a private, residential prep school (assume grades 9–12). Identify the perspectives, cultures, and organization for this study. Develop two or more sample hypotheses that might be generated, based on the observation.

9.5 Distinguish between the reliability and the validity of ethnographic research.

9.6 Why is it sometimes difficult to establish external validity of ethnographic research? What can be done to enhance external validity in ethnographic research?

9.7 Select an article dealing with ethnographic research from a professional journal. Review the article carefully, identifying the research problem and the hypotheses generated. Is the methodology described in adequate detail so that the reader can understand how the study was conducted? Do the conclusions follow from the results?

NOTE

1. The schema discussed in this section is based on concepts discussed in Becker et al. (1961), *Boys in White: Student Culture in Medical School* (Chicago: University of Chicago Press).

REFERENCES

Becker, H. S., Geer, B., Hughes, E. C., & Strauss, A. L. (1961). *Boys in white: Student culture in medical school.* Chicago: University of Chicago Press.

Boyer, E. L. (1983). *High school: A report on secondary education in America.* New York: Harper & Row.

Denzin, N. K. (1978). *The research act: A theoretical introduction to sociological methods* (2nd ed). Chicago: Aldine.

Dickson, G. E., & Wiersma, W. (1984). *Research and evaluation in teacher education: Empirical measurement of teacher performance.* Toledo, OH: University of Toledo.

Florio, S., & Clark, C. M. (1982). The functions of writing in an elementary classroom. *Research in the Teaching of English, 16* (2), 115–130.

Geertz, C. (1973). Thick description: Toward an interpretive theory of culture. In *The interpretations of cultures.* New York: Basic Books.

Goetz, J. P., & LeCompte, M. D. (1984). *Ethnography and qualitative design in educational research.* New York: Academic Press.

Kantor, K. J., Kirby, D. R., & Goetz, J. P. (1981). Research in context: Ethnographic studies in English education. *Research in the Teaching of English, 15* (4), 293–309.

LeCompte, M. D., & Goetz, J. P. (1982). Problems of reliability and validity in ethnographic research. *Review of Educational Research, 52* (1), 31–60.

Masemann, V. (1978). Ethnography of the bilingual classroom. *International Review of Education, 24* (3), 295–307.

Milwaukee Bilingual Education Project. (1977). *Application for Continuation, ESEA Title VII Funding, Fiscal Year 1977–78.* Milwaukee Public Schools.

Rogers, R. R. (1984). Qualitative research—Another way of knowing. In P. Hosford (Ed.), *Using what we know about teaching.* Alexandria, VA: Association for Supervision and Curriculum.

Schofield, J. W., & Andersen, K. (1984, April). *Integrating quantitative components into qualitative studies: Problems and possibilities for research on intergroup relations in educational settings.* Paper presented at the annual meeting of the American Educational Research Association, New Orleans.

Schofield, J. W., & Sagar, H. A. (1977). Peer interaction patterns in an integrated middle school. *Sociometry, 40* (2), 130–138.

Sitton, T. (1980). The child as informant: The teacher as ethnographer. *Language Arts, 57* (5), 540–545.

Sizer, T. (1984). *Horace's compromise: The dilemma of the America high school.* Boston: Houghton Mifflin.

Smith, M. L. (1982). Benefits of naturalistic methods in research in science education. *Journal of Research in Science Teaching, 19* (8), 627–638.

Strahan, D. B. (1983). The teacher and ethnography: Observational sources of information for Educators. *Elementary School Journal, 83* (3),194–203.

10

Sampling Designs

The preceding chapters have emphasized research design for various types of studies and have mentioned samples and random assignment. This chapter considers various procedures for obtaining random samples. On occasion, an entire population of individuals may be included in a research study, but in many educational research studies, it is simply not feasible to include all members of a population. The time and effort required would be prohibitive. This is certainly true in survey research when large populations are concerned. Thus, a sample is used much more commonly.

A sample is a subset of the population to which the researcher intends to generalize the results. To do this, the researcher wants the sample, or the individuals actually involved in the research, to be representative of the larger population, and this generally requires some aspect of random selection. A sample either is or is not random. Obtaining a random sample may be a relatively complex procedure, especially if large (and possibly diverse) populations are to be sampled. For some studies, the selection and acquisition of the sample may be a major activity of the research study.

The Concept of a Random Sample

A random sample involves what is called *probability sampling,* which means that every member of the population has a nonzero probability of being selected for the sample. In other words, all members of the population have some chance of being included in the sample. In complex sampling designs, the probabilities of selection may *not* be the same for all members, but the probabilities are all nonzero. A simple random sample is such that when it is selected, all members of the population have the same probability of being selected.[1]

A *random sample* is an unbiased sample, which means that those individuals selected vary only as they would due to random fluctuation. There is no systematic variation in the sample that would make this sample different from other samples. Of course, a random sample is representative of the population from which it was selected.

> A *random sample* is a probability sample in that every population member has a nonzero probability of selection. In a simple random sample, this probability is the same for all population members.

Random Selection and Random Assignment

Random selection and random assignment are not quite the same, but they are both used to obtain representativeness and eliminate possible bias. In *random selection,* the individuals are randomly selected as representing a population; in *random assignment,* commonly used in experiments, the individuals are randomly assigned to different groups or treatments. They may or may not have been initially selected from a larger population to participate in the experiment. Some examples follow.

An institutional researcher at a university selects a random sample of 250 from the freshman class of 6,821 students, who are then surveyed about their attitudes toward certain factors of college life. This example involves random selection. The 250 students of the sample are representative of the 6,821 in the freshman class.

A psychologist has 90 students in a sophomore-level psychology course. The psychologist is conducting a learning experiment using three different types of materials. All 90 students will participate, and 30 will be randomly assigned to each of the types of materials. In this way, the three groups of students assigned to the different materials vary only on a random basis. As the students are assigned, any student has the same probability of being assigned to any one of the three materials—namely, one-in-three or one-third.

In the latter example, what population do these 90 students represent? They were not randomly selected from a larger population. Their reason for participating in the experiment is that they enrolled in the psychology course. In a sense, they have self-selected themselves. In this situation, the psychologist would likely argue that the 90 students are representative of young adults attending college. If sophomore students at this university are much like those at other universities, the results may generalize to other populations of university students. It is not likely that the results would generalize to all young adults everywhere. Often, in studies of this type, representativeness is argued on a logical basis, depending on the individuals and variables involved. This is true of quasi-experimental research, as was discussed in Chapter 6.

The contrast between random selection and random assignment is diagrammed in Figure 10.1. When a defined group (such as the psychology class) is used, and the members are randomly assigned to treatments, there is no question about the unbiasedness of the assignment or the results generalizing to the group involved. But the generalizability of the results to larger populations is done on a logical basis, in which questions of unrepresentativeness may be raised. Of course, this is a matter of external validity, and the extent of representativeness and, correspondingly, the

Figure 10.1
Contrast Between Random Selection and Random Assignment

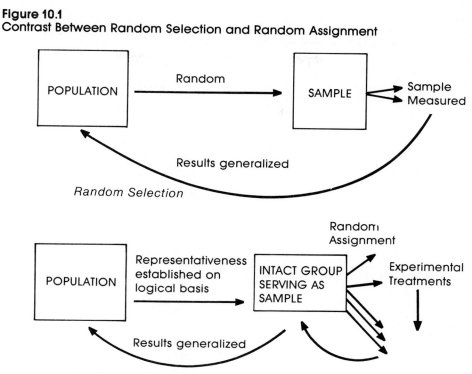

generalizability is always a matter of degree. Yet random assignment is commonly used in this way in educational research. Knowledge about the variables and individuals of the study is then used to make valid generalizations.

It might be mentioned that in a situation in which the number of individuals in the intact group does not equal the number required, the excess individuals are eliminated at random. (This is conceptually the same as selecting those for inclusion at random.) In the learning experiment example, if there were 94 students in class and only 90 were required, 4 would be randomly selected *not* to participate. To avoid causing any apprehension, the psychologist could use all 94 in the experiment and then randomly eliminate the data of 4 individuals with the condition that each type of material would still have the data of 30 individuals.

Use of a Random Number Table

A simple random sample can be obtained by using a table of random numbers. (Table 10.1 is a sample page from a random number table.) Each member of the finite population is assigned a number, and then as many numbers as comprise the sample

Table 10.1
Sample Page from a Table of Random Numbers

	50-54	55-59	60-64	65-69	70-74	75-79	80-84	85-89	90-94	95-99
00	59391	58030	52098	82718	87024	82848	04190	96574	90464	29065
01	99567	76364	77204	04615	27062	96621	43918	01896	83991	51141
02	10363	97518	51400	25670	98342	61891	27101	37855	06235	33316
03	86859	19558	64432	16706	99612	59798	32803	67708	15297	28612
04	11258	24591	36863	55368	31721	94335	34936	02566	80972	08188
05	95068	88628	35911	14530	33020	80428	39936	31855	34334	64865
06	54463	47237	73800	91017	36239	71824	83671	39892	60518	37092
07	16874	62677	57412	13215	31389	62233	80827	73917	82802	84420
08	92494	63157	76593	91316	03505	72389	96363	52887	01087	66091
09	15669	56689	35682	40844	53256	81872	35213	09840	34471	74441
10	99116	75486	84989	23476	52967	67104	39495	39100	17217	74073
11	15696	10703	65178	90637	63110	17622	53988	71087	84148	11670
12	97720	15369	51269	69620	03388	13699	33423	67453	43269	56720
13	11666	13841	71681	98000	35979	39719	81899	07449	47985	46967
14	71628	73130	78783	75691	41632	09847	61547	18707	85489	69944
15	40501	51089	99943	91843	41995	88931	73631	69361	05375	15417
16	22518	55576	98215	82068	10798	86211	36584	67466	69373	40054
17	75112	30485	62173	02132	14878	92879	22281	16783	86352	00077
18	80327	02671	98191	84342	90813	49268	95441	15496	20168	09271
19	60251	45548	02146	05597	48228	81366	34598	72856	66762	17002
20	57430	82270	10421	05540	43648	75888	66049	21511	47676	33444
21	73528	39559	34434	88596	54086	71693	43132	14414	79949	85193
22	25991	65959	70769	64721	86413	33475	42740	06175	82758	66248
23	78318	16638	09134	59880	63806	48472	39318	35434	24057	74739
24	12477	09965	96657	57994	59439	76330	24596	77515	09577	91871
25	83266	32883	42451	15579	38155	29793	40914	65990	16255	17777
26	76970	80876	10237	39515	79152	74798	39357	09054	73579	92359
27	37074	65198	44785	68624	98336	84481	97610	78735	46703	98265
28	83712	06514	30101	78295	54656	85417	43189	60048	72781	72606
29	20287	56862	69727	94443	64936	08366	27227	05158	50326	59566
30	74261	32592	86538	27041	65172	85532	07571	80609	39285	65340
31	64081	49863	08478	96001	18888	14810	70545	89755	59064	07210
32	05617	75818	47750	67814	29575	10526	66192	44464	27058	40467
33	26793	74951	95466	74307	13330	42664	85515	20632	05497	33625
34	65988	72850	48737	54719	52056	01596	03845	35067	03134	70322
35	27366	42271	44300	73399	21105	03280	73457	43093	05192	48657
36	56760	10909	98147	34736	33863	95256	12731	66598	50771	83665
37	72880	43338	93643	58904	59543	23943	11231	83268	65938	81581
38	77888	38100	03062	58103	47961	83841	25878	23746	55903	44115
39	28440	07819	21580	51459	47971	29882	13990	29226	23608	15873
40	63525	94441	77033	12147	51054	49955	58312	76923	96071	05813
41	47606	93410	16359	89033	89696	47231	64498	31776	05383	39902
42	52669	45030	96279	14709	52372	87832	02735	50803	72744	88208
43	16738	60159	07425	62369	07515	82721	37875	71153	21315	00132
44	59348	11695	45751	15865	74739	05572	32688	20271	65128	14551
45	12900	71775	29845	60774	94924	21810	38636	33717	67598	82521
46	75086	23537	49939	33595	13484	97588	28617	17979	70749	35234
47	99495	51434	29181	09993	38190	42553	68922	52125	91077	40197
48	26075	31671	45386	36583	93459	48599	52022	41330	60651	91321
49	13636	93596	23377	51133	95126	61496	42474	45141	46660	42338

Source: Reprinted by permission from *Statistical Methods* (6th ed.), by G. W. Snedecor and W. G. Cochran, © 1967 by the State University Press, Ames, Iowa.

size are selected from the table. If there is a population of 70 members and 10 are to be selected at random, each of the 70 members is assigned a number from 1 to 70. The first 10 numbers that appear, wherever one begins in the random number table, determine the 10 sample members. Since there are only 70 members in the population, two-digit random numbers are used. Beginning with the first row in Table 10.1 and going across, taking two-digit numbers in sequence gives the following 10 numbers:

59, 39, 15, 80 (which is ignored, since our highest number is 70), 30, 52, 09, 88 (also ignored), 27, 18, 87 (also ignored), 02, and 48.

If a number exceeding 70 appears, it is ignored. If a number appears that has already been selected, it, too, is ignored, because a single member of the population is not included twice in the sample. Any kind of sequencing in the table is random, and it is not necessary to go across the rows. The numbers could be selected in columns or by blocks. In Table 10.1, the numbers are grouped by fives to make it easier to locate them.

The random number table can also be used for random assignment. If 10 individuals are to be assigned at random, 5 to each of two treatments, single–digit numbers can be used, since (instead of 10) zero can be assigned to one individual. Using the random numbers of Table 10.1, if one begins with the first row of the second major block of five rows, the individuals with the first five numbers would be assigned to Treatment 1: 9, 5, 0, 6, 8. This leaves the individuals with the following numbers for Treatment 2: 1, 2, 3, 4, and 7. If an individual's number repeats, it is passed over, because an individual can be assigned to only one treatment.

Random number tables can be used for random selection and random assignment.

Criteria for a Sampling Design

There may be any number of reasons why a researcher would depart from simple random sampling to use a more complex sampling design. Probably the most common reason is that the population from which the sample is to be selected is so large that simple random sampling cannot be conducted. The population may also be quite diverse and may consist of several subpopulations. Populations whose members are grouped or clustered are more readily sampled than individual members. If the population is very heterogeneous, an alternative to simple random sampling will tend to control some of the sampling variation.

Whatever the reason for using a more complex sampling design, a good sampling design should meet certain requirements. Kish (1965) has identified four broad criteria for a good sampling design: (1) goal orientation, (2) measurability, (3) practicality, and (4) economy.

The first criterion, goal orientation, means that the sampling design should be tailored to the research design and should be based on the study's goals or objectives. The measurement necessary to obtain the data and the anticipated analyses, based on the research problem, also have important implications for sampling. These factors are considered in deciding what sampling design will best meet the goals and objectives of the study.

The criterion of measurability means that the sampling design provides the data for the necessary analyses. If a design has measurability, valid estimates of sampling variability, which are essential for the use of inferential statistics, can be made. (Inferential statistics are discussed in Chapter 12.) Measurability enables valid inferences to be made from the sample data to the population from which the sample was selected.

It is one thing to sketch a sampling design on paper theoretically and another to apply the design in a real situation. The criterion of practicality means that the actual activities of applying the sampling design have been identified and are feasible in the real situation. Practicality also means attempting to anticipate problems and devising methods for avoiding or circumventing them, and it involves making the conceptual design conform with the actual situation.

The criterion of economy is largely self-explanatory. Expenditures for educational research projects are usually limited, and economy requires that the research objectives be met with available resources: time, financial, personnel, and so on. Since obtaining data for a research project can be time-consuming and expensive, a good sampling design is not wasteful of data collection efforts.

Because it is not likely that all four criteria can be met maximally, attempting to meet these four criteria when developing a sampling design often becomes a matter of balance. For example, to enhance measurability, the researcher may increase the sample size to the extent that some economy is sacrificed. It may not be possible to anticipate all problems, but even with problems a design may be feasible and thus attain adequate practicality. The important overall criterion is that the design be feasible and adequately accommodate the research problem.

Stratified Random Sampling

Before discussing stratified random sampling, it is necessary to define the *sampling fraction*. This fraction is the ratio of sample size to population size, often designated n/N. Thus, if a sample of size 300 is selected from a population of size 2,000, the sampling fraction would be 300/2,000 or 3/20, which equals .15. For a simple random sample, the sampling fraction equals the probability of any member of the population being selected for the sample.

The *sampling fraction* is the ratio of sample size to population size, expressed as n/N.

In some cases, the population to be sampled is not homogeneous but, in essence, consists of several subpopulations. Rather than selecting randomly from the entire population, the researcher might divide such a population into two or more subpopulations, called *strata*. This approach to sampling is called *stratified random sampling* because the population is stratified into its subpopulations. All strata are represented in the sample, and the sample members are selected from each stratum at random. Thus, the condition of random selection is included by the selection within the strata.

Allocation of Sample Size Among Strata

The decision must be made as to the numbers (that is, allocations) that will be selected from each stratum for the sample. One method of allocation, called *equal allocation,* is to select equal numbers from the strata. Thus, if there were five strata, one-fifth of the sample would be selected from each stratum. Unless the strata had equal population sizes, the sampling fraction would vary among strata.

A more commonly used method is *proportional allocation,* whereby each stratum contributes to the sample a number that is proportional to its size in the population. The allocation of strata members in the sample is proportional to the numbers of members in the strata of the population. Suppose that there are k strata to be sampled and that the respective population sizes of the strata are N_1, N_2, . . . , N_k. Total population size can be indicated by N and total sample size by n. We can let n_1, n_2, . . . , n_k be the sample sizes for the respective strata. Then:

$$\frac{n}{N} = \frac{n_1}{N_1} = \frac{n_2}{N_2} = \ldots = \frac{n_k}{N_k}$$

where $N_1 + N_2 + \ldots + N_k = N$ and $n_1 + n_2 + \ldots + n_k = n$. The sampling fraction is n/N, and this fraction (proportionality) is held constant for the allocation of the sample to the k strata.

Stratified sampling guards against wild samples, ensures that no subpopulation will be omitted from the sample, and avoids overloading in certain subpopulations. Stratified random samples are sometimes called *self-weighting samples*. Simple random samples have a tendency to distribute themselves according to the population proportions, and stratified random sampling with proportional allocation will build this proportionality into the sample.

> *Proportional allocation* in stratified random sampling distributes the sample in such a way that the sampling fraction is the same for all strata.

A third method of allocation is *optimum allocation,* in which the strata contributions to the sample are proportional to the product of the strata population sizes and the variability of the dependent variable within the strata. Large strata and strata with large variability will have the larger allocations to the sample. Optimum allocation is used infrequently, primarily because it requires good estimates of the population variability of the dependent variable. Such estimates are seldom available before the sample is selected.

Both proportional allocation and optimum allocation have an advantage over equal allocation and simple random sampling in that they control part of the variability in the dependent variable. This is a statistical advantage and may make analyses more sensitive to differences. The three types of allocation are summarized in Table 10.2

Example 10.1

We will present an example using proportional allocation. The director of institutional research at a university is conducting a survey of student opinion on the adequacy of facilities—the student union, the library, and so forth. The questionnaire is quite extensive, so rather than administer it to all students, a 5% stratified random sample will be selected. The university contains seven colleges, with a total enrollment of 15,823 students. The definition of an enrolled student is one who is presently

Table 10.2
Three Types of Allocation in Stratified Random Sampling

Type	Characteristics
Equal	All strata contribute the same number to the sample. If there are k strata, each contributes n/k members to the sample. The sampling fraction varies among strata.
Proportional	Sample allocation is proportional to the strata population sizes. The sampling fraction is constant for all strata and equals n/N. The larger the stratum, the more members it contributes to the sample.
Optimum	Sample allocation is proportional to the product of the strata population sizes and variability. The larger and more variable the stratum, the greater will be its contribution to the sample. The sampling fraction varies among strata.

registered to be taking at least one course for degree credit. College is the stratifying variable, and proportional allocation will be used. Since a 5% sample is selected, the sampling fraction is 1/20, or .05. The information for this sampling example is presented in Figure 10.2.

Note that all strata (colleges) contribute to the sample. The sample members for each college are randomly selected within the college. Since colleges vary greatly in size, equal allocation would not be desirable if the opinions varied considerably among colleges. Since the variability of opinion within college is not known prior to sample selection, optimum allocation is not an option.

The question might be raised, "What variables and how many can be effectively used for stratification?" More than one stratifying variable could be used, but this can substantially increase the number of strata because it involves combinations of the two variables. In the example, if the colleges of Arts and Sciences, Business Administration, Education, and Engineering have graduate as well as undergraduate programs, it might be desirable to stratify on the dichotomous variable undergraduate-graduate in these four colleges. Law would likely be considered a graduate program and thus would have no undergraduates. Community Services and Pharmacy have only undergraduates. If stratification were done in this manner, there would be 11 instead of 7 strata.

Figure 10.2
Sample Selection Using Proportional Allocation—University Example

Strata (college)	Strata sizes		Sample size by strata
Arts & Sciences	5,461		273
Business Administration	1,850		93
Community Services	2,092	A 1/20 random sample is selected from each stratum	105
Education	3,508		175
Engineering	2,112		106
Law	318		16
Pharmacy	482		24
	15,823 = N		792 = n

.05 of the total university population equals 15,823 x .05 = 791.15. The n of 792 includes any rounding off.

The number of strata that can be conveniently accommodated depends to some extent on the sample size. The larger the sample size, the more strata can be used. However, strata are not identified simply for the sake of having a large number of them. Unless a large survey is being conducted, stratification seldom involves more than two stratifying variables (usually only one), and the total number of strata would seldom exceed 20 and usually is considerably less.

Cluster Sampling

When the selection of individual members of the population is impractical or too expensive, it may be possible to select groups or clusters of members for the sample. *Cluster sampling* is a procedure of selection in which the unit of selection, called the cluster, contains two or more population members. Each member of the population must be uniquely contained in one, and only one, cluster. Cluster sampling is useful in situations where the population members are naturally grouped in units that can be conveniently used as clusters. For example, pollsters doing surveys sometimes use city blocks as the cluster unit for selecting a sample. In educational research, a class can serve as a cluster. A school building, or possibly even a school system, might serve as a cluster in a large-scale study.

Cluster sampling differs from stratified random sampling in that the random selection occurs not with the individual members but with the clusters. The clusters from the sample are randomly selected from the larger population of clusters, and once a cluster is selected for the sample, all the population members in that cluster are included in the sample. This is in contrast to stratified random sampling, in which the individual members within strata are randomly selected. In clustering sampling, before selecting the sample, not only must all population members be identified in their clusters, but all the clusters must be identified. It is not necessary that all clusters have the same number of population members.

> *Cluster sampling* involves the random selection of clusters from the larger population of clusters. All the population members of a selected cluster are included in the sample.

In cluster sampling, the exact sample size may not be known until after the sample is selected. This is because clusters usually are not the same size, and the final sample size depends on those clusters that are randomly selected. However, clusters are often somewhat similar in size, and if the researcher has a sample size in mind, the number of clusters required can be estimated.

Example 10.2

An example of a research situation for which cluster sampling would be appropriate is a survey of fourth-grade achievement in mathematics, using a standardized achievement test, conducted by the research director of a city system that contains 33 elementary schools. It is too expensive to administer the test to all fourth-graders in the system, and the logistics of selecting a simple random sample and administering the test would be quite extensive. Stratified random sampling might be feasible, but it has one disadvantage: the fourth-graders are in classes, and it is inconvenient to test some members of the class and not others. Since the fourth-graders are "naturally" assembled in classes, cluster sampling is to be used, using class as the sampling unit. Then all students in a selected class are to be tested.

There are 83 fourth-grade classes throughout the system, with an average enrollment of 27.3 students per class. A sample size of approximately 550 students is desired, so it is decided to select 20 classes or clusters. The sampling design is diagrammed in Figure 10.3.

All members of the 20 selected classes are tested on mathematics achievement. It so happens that 561 students are tested, which is a slightly larger than anticipated sample. (Some students may be absent on the testing day, but this is of no concern if the absence pattern is typical.)

The tendency is for cluster sampling to be used with large populations. Whatever the sampling unit, it is usually something that groups the population members naturally. As the size of the clusters increases, however, the sample size also becomes large, since all members of a selected cluster are in the sample. The sampling unit should be carefully selected and well defined so that there is no confusion as to what comprises a cluster. Cluster sampling has implications for the analysis of data in that the cluster may be used as the unit of analysis.

Figure 10.3
Sample Selection Using Cluster Sampling—Fourth-Grade Example

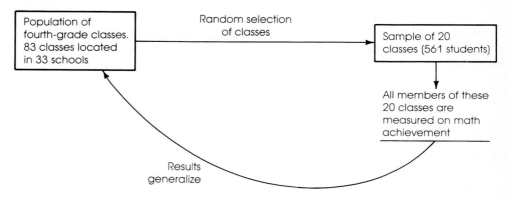

Sampling Through an Intermediate Unit

Sampling through an *intermediate unit* applies to relatively large-scale projects in which the members of the population to be sampled are found in large groups or units and in which it is undesirable to include all members of a selected unit, as in the case of cluster sampling. The members of the population in these intermediate units are called *primary units*. Thus, the probability of a primary unit being selected becomes the product of two probabilities: (1) the probability that its intermediate unit will be selected and (2) the probability that it will be selected if its intermediate unit has been selected.[2] Sampling through an intermediate unit is a form of *two-stage sampling*, since two sampling steps are required in obtaining the sample. It is also considered a form of multistage sampling.

> In sampling through an intermediate unit, in which the primary units are contained within intermediate units, the intermediate units are randomly selected, and then the primary units are randomly selected within the previously selected intermediate units.

Selection Procedure

The selection of the sample when sampling through an intermediate unit requires information about the number of primary units in each of the intermediate units of the population. One selection procedure is to list all the intermediate units and select the sample of intermediate units with probability proportional to size. The larger the intermediate unit, the more likely it is to be selected. With a little algebra, it can be shown that this selection procedure requires the selection of an equal number of primary units from each of the intermediate units selected.

The order of listing the intermediate units prior to their selection requires some aspect of randomization. If there are stratifying variables that subdivide the intermediate unit population, it may be well to order the intermediate units by strata. The order within strata should be random. The stratifying procedure will ensure that no strata are inadvertently missed and also that the strata will have proportional representation.

The procedure of selecting intermediate units with probability proportional to size and then selecting the primary units can be summarized by the following steps. (The notation of k, N, I, n, and N_i is introduced for convenience. These symbols represent certain numbers as defined.)

1. Determine the number of intermediate units (k) to be included in the sample. This is often an arbitrary decision based on available resources.

2. Let N equal the number of primary units in the population—that is, total population size of primary units—and, correspondingly, N_i the number of primary units in the ith intermediate unit; determine N/k, which we will call a sampling interval, and let $N/k = I$.

3. List all the intermediate units of the population in random order or some determined grouping if stratification is used with random order with strata. Determine the cumulative frequencies of the N_i's. Each intermediate unit thus has a number (cumulative sum) associated with it consisting of the sum of its N_i and all preceding N_i's.

4. Select a number (j) at random from the number 1 through I, inclusive. The first intermediate unit selected is the one in whose cumulative sum j falls. Subsequent units are selected by determining the numbers $j + I$, $j + 2I$, and so forth, and the units that these numbers "hit." When the process has been applied to the entire list, the k intermediate units have been selected. (Using the cumulative sums as described here has provided selection of the intermediate units with probability proportional to size—that is, the number of primary units they contain.)

5. Randomly select n/k (n is total sample size) primary units from each of the k selected intermediate units.

This five-step procedure completes the selection process for both intermediate and primary units. As presented for the general case, the procedure may seem somewhat abstract and complex. However, it is quite straightforward to apply, because the numbers k, N, and N_i are integers. The procedure will be illustrated in an example later in this section.

Potential Problems and How to Deal with Them

Special problems may arise, especially if the intermediate units vary greatly in size—that is, in the number of primary units they contain. One potential problem is that a selected, small intermediate unit might not have sufficient primary units. (It contains less than n/k primary units.) The usual solution is to include all the primary units and make no other adjustments. If it were necessary to obtain n/k scores from every selected intermediate unit, the additional required scores could be randomly selected repetitions of the available primary unit scores. However, this procedure is seldom used.

Another potential problem is that a very large intermediate unit might be selected or "hit" twice. To keep the sample size intact, a double sample of primary units can be selected, and this is certainly an option. A single sample may be selected, but if this is done, another intermediate unit is usually included to retain the original sample size.

Intermediate units may be institutions or organizations, such as schools, school districts, colleges, or hospitals. In a large-scale study, it may be that not all intermediate units selected will choose to participate. In such situations, a selection procedure for alternates is necessary. If the intermediate units have been ordered by strata and then randomly listed within strata, and if an intermediate unit chooses not to participate, it can be replaced by the unit immediately following it on the list. This retains the unit within the original stratum. If the intermediate unit being replaced happens to be the final unit of the stratum, the immediately preceding unit can be used as a replacement if the researcher wants to make the selection within the same stratum. If the problems described here are a possibility, they should be considered prior to the sample selection, and the specific procedures for dealing with the problems should be identified.

Example 10.3

A researcher conducts a survey of knowledge in the fine arts of seniors in private colleges in a six-state region. An acceptable 1-hour written test is available to measure knowledge in the fine arts. There are 208 private colleges in the six-state region, and the numbers of seniors enrolled by college are known. College is the intermediate unit and college senior is the primary unit. The colleges are stratified by state before selecting the sample.

Resources are available to conduct testing in 25 colleges, and a total sample size of 875 is desired. Thus, 35 seniors will be tested within each selected college. (In this example, $k = 25$ and $n/k = 35$.) The total population of seniors in the 208 colleges is 107,120. To determine I, $I = N/k = 107,120/25 = 4,284.8$, which can be rounded to 4,285. Next, a number is selected randomly between 1 and 4,285. Suppose that this number is 1,710. (In the general notation, this number is j.) Then the first college selected would be the one whose cumulative frequency contains 1,710. The next college selected would be the one whose cumulative frequency contains 5,995 (1,710 + 4,285); the third college selected would be the one whose cumulative frequency contains 10,280 (1,710 + 2 × 4,285); and so forth until the 25 colleges are selected. The sampling design is diagrammed in Figure 10.4.

Sampling through an intermediate unit, with the intermediate units stratified, has some of the characteristics of both stratified random sampling and cluster sampling. As in stratified random sampling, all strata will be represented. Intermediate units appear somewhat like clusters, but unlike cluster sampling, all the primary units of an intermediate unit are not included. This can be an advantage when intermediate units vary greatly in size. If cluster sampling is used and clusters vary greatly in size, large clusters selected tend to dominate the sample, and sample size may be markedly increased. Sampling through an intermediate unit also tends to enhance the logistics of data collection from the sample. In the private college example, if a listing of all the seniors in the 208 colleges were available, it would be relatively easy to select a simple random sample, but the logistics of testing a simple random sample of seniors spread through 208 colleges would be very difficult if not impossible to implement. Sampling through an intermediate unit organizes and concentrates the data collection.

Figure 10.4
Sample Selection Using Sampling Through an Intermediate Unit—Private College Example

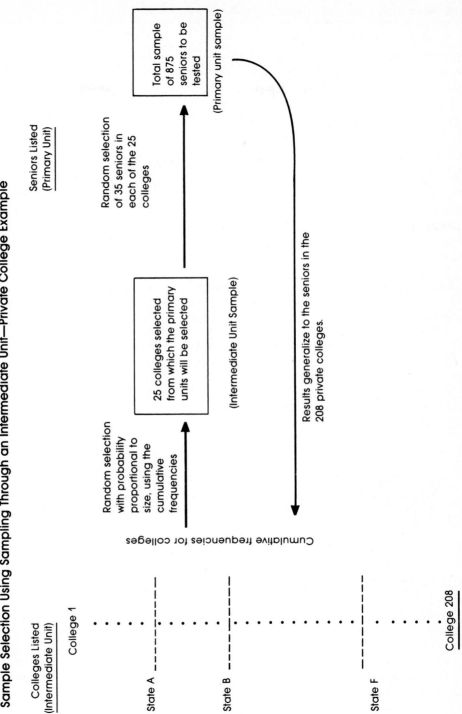

As indicated earlier, sampling through an intermediate unit applies to large-scale studies, and it would be quite rare to find this sampling design used for the research for a master thesis or a doctoral dissertation. Publishers of standardarized tests often use this sampling design when selecting normative groups, and this approach was also used in the National Assessment of Educational Progress study.[3]

Systematic Sampling

The use of systematic sampling is quite common in educational research where large populations are studied and alphabetical or possibly other lists of the population members are available. Directors of institutional research often use this technique in selecting a sample. The primary advantage of systematic sampling in educational research is convenience.

Systematic sampling is a procedure by which the selection of the first sample member determines the entire sample. The population members (that is, their names or type of identification) are in some type of order; for example, the names of the population members may be placed in alphabetical order on a list. The sample size is chosen and the sampling fraction determined. If the sampling fraction is 1/10, the first member of the sample is randomly selected from the first ten names on the list. Following this first selection, every tenth member of the population is selected for the sample. In the general case, if the sampling fraction n/N equals $1/k$, the first member of the sample is randomly selected from the first k names on the list, and after that, every kth name on the list is selected. When the list is exhausted, the sample will have n members.

Systematic sampling involves randomly selecting the first member of the sample from a list and from that point on taking every kth name on the list if $1/k$ equals the sampling fraction.

The Possible Problem of Periodicity

Although the first member of a systematic sample is randomly selected, it is possible that this sampling design will yield a biased sample. The most serious and really the only threat of bias in systematic sampling is the existence of some type of periodicity in the ordering of the population members. *Periodicity* means that every kth member of the population has some unique characteristics that are related to, or have an effect on, the dependent variable. In that case, the sample becomes biased.

The likelihood of periodicity entering a list is generally quite small, though it could enter inadvertently. The following example illustrates how that might occur.

Example 10.4

A sample of fifth-graders is being selected from a large school system population. The sample is to be measured on an ability test to estimate the ability level of the fifth-grade population of the school system. The researcher in charge of the study decides to take a 1-in-30 sample and notes that class lists can be used conveniently, since the fifth-grade classes all contain about 30 students. The researcher calls for class lists, but instead of sending alphabetical lists, the fifth-grade teachers send lists on which the student names in each class are arranged from high to low according to performance on a recent achievement test. The researcher puts the lists together, one class following another, and selects the systematic sample. Since achievement and performance on an ability test are quite conclusively related, periodicity has entered into the sampling list. If the first random selection gives the third name on the list, it would mean that the third, thirty-third, sixty-third, and so forth, students on the list would comprise the sample. This sample would differ from other samples, especially, for example, one beginning with the twenty-sixth name on the list. Whatever sample is selected would have the effect of periodicity in it.

The foregoing example of periodicity, though possible, is quite unlikely, because for that type of research situation, another sampling design, possibly cluster sampling, would likely be used. Systematic sampling is convenient, for example, for an institutional researcher in a university who is to survey the student body (or some part of it) with a brief questionnaire to be returned by mail. Alphabetical lists of students for whatever population is being surveyed could be used.

Systematic sampling provides the condition of sampling throughout the population due to its spacing of selections over the entire list. A definite advantage of systematic sampling over, say, simple random sampling is that it requires less work. However, the researcher should be aware of how the list is ordered and check for the possibility of periodicity.

Considerations in Determining Sample Size

Several factors can influence the size of the sample used in a research study, but with the exception of cost, information about such factors is often incomplete and it becomes difficult to set an exact sample size. Cost refers not only to the expenditure of money but also to the time and effort required to obtain the sample data. In any survey, the actual cost of obtaining the data per unit in the sample should be estimated as accurately as possible. If standardized tests are used, what is the cost per test? How much does it cost to score the tests and summarize the data? What, if any, costs will be encountered in locating the sample for testing? What is the cost of test administration? These are all examples of questions that can be raised. A researcher who is securing funds for a project from a funding agency is usually required to produce quite accurate cost estimates. Researchers who are university professors (and possibly graduate students) often receive funds from a funding agency or from a source within the university; thus, cost estimates are required. Even in the rare instances when facilities and resources are available through a university at no hard-dollar costs, costs of proposed projects should be estimated; at least time and man-power estimates should be made.

Sample size also relates to what might be called the precision of statistical analyses. This deals with the concept of the magnitude of the differences between statistics necessary to attain statistical significance (discussed in Chapter 12). If enough prior information is available about the characteristics of the dependent variable, it may be possible to estimate the sample size necessary for a desired level of precision. Multiple factors must be considered simultaneously. Hinkle and Oliver (1983) discuss the determination of sample size given certain conditions. Generally, increasing sample size enhances statistical precision.

However, it should not be inferred that it is always desirable to increase the sample size to its maximum, since this may be unduly costly and wasteful of effort and information. For some surveys, the time required for the data collection of large samples may be so long that the timeliness of the results is ruined. Increasing sample size is not necessary to attain adequate representation. The method of sampling with the characteristic of random selection is the important determiner of attaining adequate representation. In the presidential election of 1936, the *Literary Digest* magazine predicted a victory for Republican Alfred Landon (which turned out to be a disastrous prediction). The survey was based on a poll involving 2.4 million people. George Gallup, using a sample of only 3,000 from the population surveyed by the *Digest,* predicted what the *Digest* predictions would be. Of course, there were serious errors in the sampling procedures used by the *Digest.* Freedman, Pisani, and Purves (1978) have provided an excellent description of the polls taken for that election and of how Gallup predicted the Roosevelt victory using another sample. The annual Gallup polls of the public's attitudes toward the public schools are national surveys, yet the 16th annual poll, for example, was based on a sample size of 1,515 adults (Gallup, 1984, p. 24).

With some types of research studies, there is the possibility that data will not be obtained from all sample members. Questionnaires mailed in survey research are susceptible to nonresponse, and studies conducted in a laboratory may lose subjects because of inability to perform. It has been noted that uncooperative intermediate units can be replaced. However, if the likelihood of substantial nonresponse or non-participation by sample members is great, a certain percentage of oversampling may be included. This, of course, has direct implications for sample size. The percentage of oversampling to be used in a specific project will need to be estimated, possibly on the basis of previous experience or information from the research literature. It should be noted that oversampling does not solve the problem of possible bias caused by nonresponse; it only tends to keep the amount of data at an originally desired level.

> A number of factors may affect the sample size; in educational research, available resources of time, money, personnel, and facilities are often the most influential.

SUMMARY

Sampling is an important consideration in any research study designed to generalize from a sample to a population. When surveys are conducted, it often is necessary for logistical and analytical reasons to use some approach other than simple random sampling. This chapter has described a number of approaches to sampling, all of them involving some aspect of randomization. A summary of the general characteristics of the designs is provided in Table 10.3.

The matter of randomization is important in justifying the representativeness of the sample. Representativeness deals with the populations to which a researcher

Table 10.3
Summary of General Characteristics of Sampling Designs

Design	Random Selection	Other Characteristics
Simple random sampling	Sample members individually from the population.	The entire population serves as a single unit from which the sample is selected.
Stratified random sampling	Sample members individually within each of the subpopulations or strata.	All strata are represented in the sample; strata are allocated sample members, usually by one of three allocation systems: equal, proportional, or optimum. Proportional allocation is most frequently used.
Cluster sampling	Clusters of members selected from the larger population of clusters.	All members of a selected cluster are included in the sample. Not all clusters are included. Clusters need not be of equal size.
Sampling through an intermediate unit	Intermediate units selected from population of intermediate units; primary units selected from those intermediate units selected.	This is two-stage sampling in that both intermediate and primary units are sampled. Intermediate units may be stratified prior to selection.
Systematic sampling	The initial sample member is individually selected.	The population is ordered in some manner and the designation of the initial sample member designates the entire sample.

intends to generalize results. But what about the use of nonrandom samples? Are they representative? Strictly in a technical sense, they are not. However, there is no general answer to these questions. If a nonrandom sample is used, the researcher is required to make the case for representativeness, usually on a logical basis. How well this case can be made depends on the specifics of the situation.

The foregoing discussion is essentially an overview of some of the more common sampling designs used in educational research. Sometimes the technical and logistical aspects of sampling can become complex. Entire books are written on sampling; if more detailed coverage is required, the reader is referred to texts such as that by Sudman (1976). The discussion here was intended to provide the researcher with a basic knowledge of design characteristics, differences among designs, and the conditions under which they might be applied.

KEY CONCEPTS

Random sample	*Optimum allocation*
Random selection	*Cluster sampling*
Random assignment	*Intermediate unit*
Stratified random sampling	*Primary unit*
Sampling fraction	*Two-stage sampling*
Proportional allocation	*Systematic sampling*
Equal allocation	*Periodicity*

EXERCISES

10.1 Suppose that a researcher has a population of 839 members, and a simple random sample of size 50 is to be selected. Discuss how you would use a random number table for selecting the sample. Use Table 10.1 in this chapter to select the first ten members of the sample.

10.2 Describe the procedures involved in stratified random sampling using proportional allocation. Provide an example of a situation for which this sampling procedure might be used.

10.3 A study is proposed to determine the mathematics achievement of high school seniors in a statewide area. A sample of seniors is to be measured. Discuss some of the sampling difficulties that would be likely with such a large population. Discuss the possibilities of using stratified or cluster sampling. What would be possible stratifying variables if a stratified random sample were selected?

10.4 Discuss how the condition of random selection differs between stratified random sampling and cluster sampling in terms of including strata, clusters, and the members of the strata or clusters.

10.5 A population is divided into four strata. The population sizes of the four strata are 830, 660, 480, and 1,030 for stratum 1 through stratum 4, respectively. A sample of size 450 is to be selected, using stratified random sampling with proportional allocation. What is the sampling fraction? Distribute the sample among the four strata using proportional allocation.

10.6 A school board is interested in surveying the attitudes of the district's voters toward a school bond issue. The district comprises a city of approximately 300,000 population. A random sample of voters is to be selected. If stratified random sampling were used, what would be possible stratifying variables? Discuss the advantages and disadvantages of selecting a systematic sample. What kinds of lists would be used if a systematic sample were to be selected?

10.7 An educational psychologist has a population of 690 undergraduates available for participation in a concept-attainment experiment to be conducted in the learning lab. The experiment requires 120 individuals, including 60 men and 60 women. The population contains 381 women and 309 men. Describe how the individuals would be randomly selected for participation in the experiment. Suppose that the experimental variable has four levels and that equal numbers of men and women are to be assigned to each level. Describe how the individuals would be randomly assigned to levels.

10.8 The state department of a state containing approximately 500 school districts is planning a survey of the reading achievement of entering senior high school students (tenth grade). A sample of students is to be tested around mid-September. Discuss the relative merits and disadvantages of using (1) cluster sampling, or (2) sampling through an intermediate unit. Identify possible cluster units and intermediate units. Overall, which approach do you think would be the most efficient and acceptable method? Why? Assume that the total sample size of students tested would be the same regardless of the method used.

10.9 A researcher in health education is interested in surveying the health maintenance habits of adults in a city of 30,000 population. A one-page questionnaire is to be used, and a sample of size 200 is desired. One approach is to mail the questionnaire. Discuss how the sample might be selected for such a mailing. What sources of information could be used for identifying the population? Suppose that instead of mailing the questionnaire, the researcher went to a local clinic and gave the questionnaire to the first 200 adult patients willing to complete it. What is wrong with this approach to sampling and what are the possible sources of bias if it were used? It probably would be difficult to get the general population to respond to a mailed questionnaire on this topic. Suppose that the city had one large shopping mall and the researcher decided to select a random sample of shoppers to complete the questionnaire. Discuss how the random selection might be done. Are there any potential problems with this sample being representative of the intended population? What could be done to enhance representativeness?

NOTES

1. If sampling is from a finite population without replacement, a slight adjustment in the definition is necessary. A sample is then considered to be a simple random sample if it is drawn in such a way that all possible samples of a given size have the same probability of being selected.

2. This is somewhat analogous to the situation in which the probability of getting two consecutive 6's on two rolls of a single unbiased die is determined. This probability is 1/6 times 1/6, or 1/36. If we do not get a 6 on the first roll, we have no chance of getting the two 6's. By the same token, if a primary unit's intermediate unit is not selected, the primary unit can no longer get into the sample. If we have a 6 on the first roll, we still need a 6 on the second roll to meet the criterion of two 6's. If an intermediate unit is selected, the primary unit must still be selected to get into the sample.

3. See W. Greenbaum, M. S. Garett, and E. L. Solomon, *Measuring Educational Progress: A Study of the National Assessment* (New York: McGraw-Hill, 1977). Sampling is discussed in Chapter 7, pp. 132–139.

REFERENCES

Freedman, D., Pisani, R., & Purves, R. (1978). *Statistics.* New York: Norton.

Gallup, G. H. (1984). The 16th annual poll of the public's attitudes toward the public schools. *Phi Delta Kappan, 66* (1), 23–38.

Hinkle, D. E., & Oliver, J. D. (1983). How large should the sample be? A question with no simple answer? Or . . . *Educational and Psychological Measurement, 43,* 1051–1060.

Kish, L. (1965). *Survey sampling.* New York: Wiley.

Sudman, S. (1976). *Applied sampling.* New York: Academic Press.

11

Measurement and Data Collection

A large variety of measurement devices are used in educational research—tests, inventories, observation schedules, and others. In some research projects, the measurement requirements can readily be met through the use of existing tests or instruments. For others, developing adequate measurement procedures may involve a substantial portion of the research effort. But whatever the case, the measurement instruments must adequately measure the variables, concepts, or phenomena under study. Operationally, measurement generates the required data for the research study.

The areas of educational measurement—indeed, the measurement of educational variables such as achievement and attitudes—are of themselves disciplines of study. It is the intent of this discussion to provide an overview of measurement as it is a part of conducting research, including basic measurement concepts. The questions of measurement as related to research are basically twofold: What is to be measured and how is it to be measured? This chapter will present examples of the more commonly used measurement instruments in educational research.

Concepts of Measurement

A straightforward and widely accepted definition of measurement is given by Kerlinger (1973, p. 426):

The assignment of numerals to objects or events according to rules.

A numeral is a symbol, such as 1, 2, 3, that is devoid of either quantitative or qualitative meaning unless such meaning is assigned by a rule. The rules for a particular measurement are the guides by which the assignment of numerals proceeds. These may include, for example, the assignment of points for certain kinds of responses or the summing of numerals that have been assigned to the responses of two or more items.

> Measurement is a process of assigning numerals according to rules. The numerals are assigned to events or objects, such as responses to items, or to certain observed behaviors.

Types of Measurement Scales

The four general types or levels of measurement scales—nominal, ordinal, interval, and ratio—were defined in Chapter 2. They will be briefly reviewed here. The four scales comprise a hierarchy of measurement levels based on the amount of information contained in the score or the measure generated by the scales. The scales go from nominal to ratio in order from least to most information contained. The four scales are defined as follows; in each case, an example of a variable that could be measured by the type of scale is given:

Nominal: This gives categorization without order; whatever is being measured is categorized into two or more classifications that indicate only differences with respect to one or more characteristics. Example: sex of the individual.

Ordinal: In addition to indicating difference, this scale also orders the scores on some basis, such as low to high or least to most. Although the scores are ordered, equal intervals between scores are not established. Example: attitude toward school.

Interval (also called equal unit): In addition to order, equal units or intervals are established in the scale such that a difference of a point in one part of the scale is equivalent to a difference of one point in any other part of the scale. Example: temperature.

Ratio: In addition to an equal unit, the scale contains a true zero point that indicates a total absence of whatever is being measured. Example: monetary expenditures for various school functions.

Many educational variables cannot be easily categorized into the hierarchy of scales, especially into ordinal and interval scales. Sometimes it is difficult to define the equal unit or interval absolutely. Rather, the intervals are established on the basis of convention and usefulness. An interval scale provides the option of more powerful statistical analyses, but that is not the criterion that establishes the type of scale. The basic concern is whether the level of measurement is meaningful. For example, suppose that there are 20 items that reflect a student's attitude toward school, each item scored 1 to 5 on a scale from "strongly dislike" to "strongly like." The items are all in the same direction such that a high score indicates the more positive attitude. If the item scores are summed (the numerals assigned to responses), does this sum represent interval scale measurement? Some writers would argue that it does, and it does if appropriate meaning can be ascribed to the sum. The meaning depends on the conditions and variables of the specific study.

A great variety of variables are measured in educational research. In many cases, they are human characteristics, attributes, or traits that are somewhat subtle. However, whatever is being measured must be defined operationally. This means that the variable will be represented or described by the score of the test or whatever measurement device is used. For example, mathematics achievement may be defined as the mathematics subtest score on the Iowa Test of Basic Skills. A student's perception of instruction may be the score on a ten-item rating scale developed specifically for the instruction under consideration. In doing research, such variables are defined in terms of what is used to measure them.

> The operational definition specifies the instrument or the operations to be used for measuring the variable.

Reliability of Measurement

Two essential characteristics of measurement that must be considered in establishing the appropriateness and usefulness of measurement instruments are reliability and validity. In a word, *reliability* means consistency—consistency of the instrument in measurement whatever it measures. It is the degree to which an instrument will give similar results for the same individuals at different times. In a conceptual sense, an observed score can be seen as consisting of two parts, one part, the individual's "true" score and the other part, an "error" score, which is due to the inaccuracy of measurement. Reliability is related to these parts. If scores have large error components, reliability is low, but if there is little error in the scores, reliability is high. Reliability is a statistical concept based on the association between two sets of scores representing the measurement obtained from the instrument when it is used with a group of individuals. *Reliability coefficients* can take on values from 0 to 1.0, inclusive. Conceptually, if a reliability coefficient was 0, there would be no "true" component in the observed score. The observed score would consist entirely of error. On the other hand, if the reliability coefficient was 1.0, the observed score would contain no error; it would consist entirely of the true score. Clearly, in educational measurement, it is desirable to obtain high-reliability coefficients, although coefficients of 1.0 are very rare indeed.

> *Reliability* is the consistency of the instrument in measuring whatever it measures. Reliability coefficients can take on values of 0 to 1.0, inclusive.

Empirical Procedures for Estimating Reliability

Several procedures can be used to estimate reliability. All of them have computational formulas that produce reliability coefficients. The commonly used procedures are described as follows:

Parallel forms or alternate forms: This procedure involves the use of two or more equivalent forms of the test. The two forms are administered to a group of individuals with a short time interval between the administrations. If the test is reliable, the patterns of scores for individuals should be about the same for the two forms of the test. There would be a high positive association between the scores.

Test-retest: In this procedure, the same test is administered on two or more occasions to the same individuals. Again, if the test is reliable, there will be a high positive association between the two scores.

Split-half: This procedure requires only one administration of the test. In computing split-half reliability, the test items are divided into two halves, with the items of the two halves matched on content and difficulty, and the halves are then scored independently. If the test is reliable, the scores on the two halves have a high positive association. An individual scoring high on one half would tend to score high on the other half, and vice versa.

Kuder-Richardson procedures: Two formulas for estimating reliability, developed by Kuder and Richardson (1937), require only one administration of a test. One formula, KR-20, provides the mean of all possible split-half coefficients. The second formula, KR-21, may be substituted for KR-20 if it can be assumed that item difficulty levels are similar.

Cronbach alpha: A formula developed by Cronbach (1951), based on two or more parts of the test, requires only one administration of the test.

Although all reliability coefficients are estimates of test consistency, there are different types of consistency. Procedures that involve only one test administration (split-half, KR-20, KR-21, Cronbach alpha) generate coefficients of internal consistency.

When two or more parallel forms of the test are used, the reliability coefficient is a coefficient of equivalence—the extent to which the forms are equivalent. Using the test-retest procedure gives a reliability coefficient that is a coefficient of stability—the extent to which the scores on the single test remain stable. Coefficients of equivalence and stability are based on more than one test administration.

> There are a number of procedures by which the reliability can be empirically estimated. Those procedures that involve only one test administration give reliability coefficients of internal test consistency. If there is more than one test administration, the reliability coefficients are estimates of test equivalence or stability.

If published tests or inventories are used, the accompanying manuals should contain information about reliability, such as the type of reliability and the size of the reliability coefficients. When locally constructed instruments are used, reliability estimates should be computed. For example, suppose that a group of teachers is conducting a study on student attitude toward school, measured by a locally constructed attitude inventory. The reliability of interest would most likely be internal consistency reliability. If the inventory contained 40 items, they could be divided into two halves of 20 items each, and the scores on the two halves could be correlated (correlation procedures are discussed in the next chapter). The correlation coefficient between the scores on the two halves would then be used for estimating the reliability of the attitude inventory.

Expected Reliability Coefficients for Various Types of Tests

Although it is desirable to obtain reliability coefficients as close to 1.0 as possible, reliability is affected by a number of factors. One factor is the length of the test. Increased length tends to increase reliability, which is one reason why total test reliability tends to be greater than the reliability of subtests that may be contained in the total test.

Size of the reliability coefficient is also affected by the variable being measured. Achievement tests in academic and skills areas, for example, tend to have higher reliability than interest and attitude inventories. Table 11.1 contains examples of typical reliability coefficients found with selected tests and inventories. When a range is given for the reliability coefficient (r), it indicates reliability estimates from multiple administrations of the test.

Validity of Measurement

Another essential characteristic of a measurement is *validity*—the extent to which an instrument measures what it is supposed to measure. Simply stated, validity of mea-

Table 11.1
Examples of Reliability Coefficients Reported for Selected Tests and Inventories

Test	r
Metropolitan Readiness Test	.90
Psychological Screening Inventory	.66–.95
Wechsler Memory Scale	.68–.94
Cooperative Preschool Inventory—English	.92
Wallace Self-Concept Scale	.81
Learning Style Inventory (Kolb's)	.55–.72
Standardized Test of Essential Writing Skills	.97
Minnesota Multiphasic Personality Inventory	
Family Problems Scale	.71
Family Attachment Scale	.65
Graduate Management Aptitude Test	
Reading Comprehension	.77
Data Sufficiency	.81
Computer Attitude Scale	
Computer Anxiety	.86
Total Score	.95
Beck Depression Inventory	.86–.88
Jackson Vocational Interest Survey	
Basic Interest Scales	.70–.91
Higher-Order Occupational Themes	.82–.92

Source: These coefficients were obtained from a number of sources: *Educational and Psychological Measurement, 44* (1984); *Journal of Educational Measurement, 21* (1984); *Journal of Clinical Psychology, 40* (1984); and *Journal of Consulting and Clinical Psychology, 52* (1984).

surement deals with the question, "Does the instrument measure the characteristic, trait, or whatever, for which it was intended?" Validity refers to the appropriateness of the interpretation of the results of a test or inventory, and it is specific to the intended use. A test may be highly valid for some situations and not valid for others. For example, a science achievement test may be valid for measuring science knowledge but not valid for measuring logical reasoning skills.

There are basically two approaches for determining the validity of an instrument. One is through a logical analysis of content or a logical analysis of what would make up an educational trait, construct, or characteristic. This is essentially a judgmental analysis. The other approach, through an empirical analysis, uses criterion measurement, the criterion being some sort of standard or desired outcome. The criterion measure might be performance on a task or test, or it could be a measure such as job performance. Validity is then a measure of the association or correlation between the test being validated and the criterion measure.

The traditional view of validity has been that there are basically three different types of validity—content, criterion, and construct—with two variations of criterion validity, concurrent and predictive. A more current view (Gronlund, 1985) is that validity is a unitary concept but that there are different types of evidence of validity.

This is essentially a conceptual difference; the procedures for establishing validity are the same whether we consider different types of validity or different types of evidence for establishing validity. In the following discussion, the types-of-evidence view is used.

> *Validity* of measurement is the extent to which the instrument measures what it is designed to measure.

Content-Related Evidence. Content validation is the process of establishing the representativeness of the items with respect to the domain of skills, tasks, knowledge, and so forth, of whatever is being measured. Thus, content-related evidence deals with the adequacy of content sampling. Content validation is a logical analysis of the items, determining their representativeness. Validity of achievement tests is commonly based on content-related evidence.

Criterion-Related Evidence: Concurrent and Predictive. Criterion validation establishes validity through a comparison with some criterion external to the test. The criterion is, in essence, the standard by which the validity of the test will be judged. If the scores of the measure being validated relate highly to the criterion, the measure is valid. If not, the measure is not valid for the purpose for which the criterion measure is used.

Concurrent and predictive validation are empirical approaches to establishing validity in which the relationship between the test scores and measures of performance on an external criterion are determined. Concurrent validation is used if the data on the two measaures, test and criterion, are collected at or about the same time. Predictive validation involves the collection of the data on the criterion measure after an intervening period—say, 6 months—from the time of data collection for the test being validated. This is the basic operational distinction between the two. There is also a distinction in the objectives of validation. Concurrent validation is based on establishing an existing situation—in other words, what is—whereas predictive validation deals with what is likely to happen. Specifically, the question of concurrent validation is whether or not the test scores estimate a specified present performance; that of predictive validation is whether or not the test scores predict a specified future performance.

The criterion measure of concurrent validation is not necessarily the score on another test given at the same time as the test being validated. It may consist of concurrent measures, such as job success or grade-point average. The criterion measures used with predictive validation are often some types of job performance—certainly subsequent performance. Predictive validation is especially relevant when test results are used for the selection of personnel to fill positions. In school, predictive validation is associated with reading readiness tests, algebra aptitude tests, and foreign language aptitude tests.

Construct-Related Evidence. Construct validation can involve both logical and empirical analyses. The term *construct* refers to the theoretical construct or trait being measured, not the technical construction of the test items. A construct is a postulated attribute or structure that explains some phenomenon, such as an individual's behavior. Because constructs are abstract and are not considered to be real objects or events, they are sometimes called hypothetical constructs. Theories of learning, for example, involve constructs such as motivation, intelligence, and anxiety.

Quite often, one or more constructs are related to behavior, in that individuals are expected to behave (or not behave) in a specified manner. A theory of frustration might include specific behavior patterns. For example, frustration increases as the individual unsuccessfully persists in a problem-solving task. The construct may be informally conceptualized with only a limited number of propositions, or it may be part or all of a fully developed theory. When using construct validation, the researcher initially suggests which constructs might account for test performance based on a logical analysis. Empirical procedures of construct validation involve relating scores on the test to scores on other tests that reflect the same general theory or constructs. Personality tests are examples of tests that commonly are validated on the basis of construct-related evidence.

The different types of evidence all have their functions in educational measurement, and correspondingly in educational research as measurement is involved. If published tests or inventories are used, validity information should be provided in the accompanying manuals. However, published tests, especially those for school-age children, are often prepared for broad populations, and the validity (and reliability) information may not be generalizable to the subjects of the research study. Researchers should determine the validity and reliability of the test for the specific situation. The types of validity evidence and their characteristics are summarized in Table 11.2.

Reliability is a necessary but not sufficient condition for validity. That is, a test or measuring instrument could be reliable but not valid. In that case, it would be consistently measuring something for which it was not intended. However, a test must be reliable to be valid. If it is not consistent in what it measaures, it cannot be measuring that for which it was intended.

The discussion of reliability and validity in this chapter is only an overview and is necessarily brief. Although procedures have been named and described, no computational examples have been given. Specific procedures can be quite extensive and can be found in several measurement and testing books.[1]

The Variables Measured in Educational Research

Since educational research covers a broad spectrum of phenomena, many different variables are measured. Research on student learning often focuses on student achievement in cognitive and skills areas, intelligence or some measures of inherent

Table 11.2
Types of Evidence and Their Characteristics Used in Establishing Validity

Type	How Analyzed	Example of Use
Content	Logical analysis of item content	Achievement tests in academic and skills areas; a test of computational skills in fifth-grade mathematics
Criterion		
Concurrent	Empirical analysis—establishing the relationship between scores on the test and those on another measure obtained at the same time	Validation of a short history test against a long, standardized history exam that is known to be a valid measure of history achievement
Predictive	Empirical analysis—establishing the relationship between scores on the test and those on another measure obtained at a later time	A comparison of performance on a screening test for stenographers to a measure of job performance taken 6 months later
Construct	Logical and empirical analyses	Analysis of a personality test to determine whether it measures the major traits of a neurotic personality

ability, and student attitudes. Sometimes, observations are made of student behavior in a classroom. The variables measured may include different behaviors that occur as well as the frequency of occurrence of certain behaviors. Educational research is often concerned with the measurement of opinions or perceptions. Some examples are studies of teachers' perceptions of administrative practices and student opinions of teaching effectiveness.

Sometimes, attempts are made to measure relatively abstract phenomena, such as how individuals learn to learn or how an individual's personality develops and changes. Many times, what is measured is very specific to the study. This is especially characteristic of surveys in which self-constructed questionnaires are used. Sometimes, physical skills or characteristics are measured. For example, a survey might be conducted on differences in personal habits related to health promotion. The list could go on. Individuals in practically any age range might be included in the measurement, although those measured are often of school age.

Tests and Inventories Used for Measurement

The types of tests and inventories commonly used in obtaining the data for educational research studies will be discussed in this section. Often, an available test or measuring instrument can be used; if this can be done, it greatly reduces the effort required to prepare for data collection. Many tests are available through commercial publishers of educational tests, including achievement tests, intelligence tests, attitude inventories, self-concept inventories, and personality tests, among others. Sometimes, measuring instruments are available from other researchers who are working with similar variables.

In many situations, however, the researcher must construct an instrument because of the specific nature of the dependent variable. Sometimes, an existing instrument can be modified by changing the content of items, or a general format for the items can be used with only the content of the items being specific to the study. For example, a general form for an attitude scale may be used, but the items must be constructed for the study. In this section, some general forms will be described and examples will be included. Since construction of items for questionnaires was given considerable attention in Chapter 7, that discussion will not be repeated here. However, a questionnaire might include several items comprising an attitude scale, for example, and the comments on attitude scales would be relevant for a questionnaire as well as for an inventory administered in a classroom.

Achievement Tests in Academic and Skills Areas

Because achievement (or lack of it) is one of the principal outcomes of schooling, much research is done on this topic. Multitudes of *achievement tests,* commonly known as standardized achievement tests, are commercially available. These are generally norm-referenced tests; that is, performance on the tests is compared to the performance of some group, called the *normative group.* Information about the normative group is contained in the manual accompanying the test.

When a researcher uses a published test for a research study, the task is to select a test that measures what the researcher wants to measure. This requires a careful review, preferably of the potential tests themselves, but at least of sources that describe the test. The typical college library contains a number of sources that describe available tests.

One of the most extensive sources of information about tests are the publications of the Buros Institute of Mental Measurements at the University of Nebraska-Lincoln. *Tests in Print III,* edited by Mitchell (1983), catalogs 2,672 tests, many of them achievement and scholastic tests. For example, the entries include 74 achievement batteries and 199 English tests (p. xxvi). Figure 11.1 contains a sample entry from *Tests in Print III* and a brief explanation of its contents. (The entry contains 259 references, which are not included in the figure.)

The *Mental Measurement Yearbook* provides reviews and information that are useful in evaluating tests. The *Eighth Mental Measurement Yearbook* (Buros, 1978) contains descriptions of more than 1,000 commercially available tests. The two volumes exceed 2,100 pages, and they include information about other tests than achievement tests.

When using a standardized achievement test, the researcher should check carefully to determine the appropriateness of the test. If the researcher intends to use normative data, the manual should be carefully reviewed to make certain the norms are appropriate. Often it is not necessary to have norms, since comparisons are made between or among groups in the study, not with external groups.

Figure 11.1
Sample Entry from *Tests in Print III*

[1192]

*Iowa Tests of Basic Skills, Forms 7 and 8.
Grades kgn.1–1.5, kgn.8–1.9, 1.7–2.6, 2.7–3.5, 3, 4, 5, 6,
7, 8–9; 1955–79; ITBS; previous edition still available;
A. N. Hieronymus, E. F. Lindquist, H. D. Hoover, and
others; Riverside Publishing Co.*

a) PRIMARY BATTERY: LEVELS 5–8. Grades kgn.1–1.5,
kgn.8–1.9, 1.7–2.6, 2.7–3.5; 1978–79.
 1) *level* 5. Grades kgn.1–1.5; 5 scores: listening,
 vocabulary, word analysis, language, mathematics.
 2) *level* 6. Grades kgn.8–1.9; 6 scores: listening,
 vocabulary, word analysis, reading, language, mathematics.
 3) *level* 7. Grades 1.7–2.6; 2 batteries.
  (*a*) Basic Battery. 9 scores: vocabulary, word
  analysis, reading comprehension (pictures, sentences,
  stories), language skills (spelling), mathematics skills
  (concepts, problems, computation).
  (*b*) Complete Battery. 15 scores: 9 scores from Basic
  Battery plus listening, language skills (capitalization,
  punctuation, usage), work study skills (visual materials, reference materials).
 4) *level* 8. Grades 2.7–3.5; details same as for Level 7.
b) MULTILEVEL EDITION: LEVELS 9–14. Grades 3, 4, 5,
6, 7, 8–9; 1978–79.

For additional information and reviews by Larry A.
Harris and Fred Pyrczak of Forms 5–6, see 8:19 (58
references); see also T2:19 (87 references) and 6:13 (17
references); for reviews by Virgil E. Herrick, G. A. V.
Morgan, and H. H. Remmers, and an excerpted review
by Laurence Siegel of Forms 1–2, see 5:16. For reviews of
the modern mathematics supplement, see 7:481 (2
reviews).

Information in entry[a]

*Name of the test, forms, grades for which appropriate, date of publi-
cation, acronym, authors, and publisher. The * indicates the test has been
revised since its last listing. The closing * indicates that the entry was prepared from a firsthand examination.

a (1–4) and *b* provide information about levels, subtests, special editions,
etc.

The final paragraph contains additional information; for example, the
reviews by Harris and Pyrczak are referenced "see 8:19." This means see
Test 19 in the *Eighth Mental Measurements Yearbook,* another publication
of the Buros Institute.

Source: Mitchell (1983), p. 190 (references not included).

[a]The introductory section of *Tests in Print III* contains a detailed description of the information in
the entry.

> Published standardized tests can often be used effectively for research in achievement. The content of the test should be reviewed, as should any norms that may be used.

Published achievement tests are usually very well constructed—at least technically—and of course their use greatly reduces the effort needed to prepare for the measurement, compared to a study for which the test must be constructed. However, in some studies, the researcher may want to measure achievement in a very limited area for which a test is not readily available. Also, it may be that the standardized test is much longer than is actually needed and therefore would not be desirable. A self-constructed achievement test may then be used.

When a self-constructed achievement test is used, the items of the test should very closely reflect the objectives of the research. Usually, in achievement testing, this is not very difficult, since validity can be established through a logical analysis (content analysis). However, if at all possible, a pilot run of the test should be made, and reliability should be checked prior to the use of the test for the project. Then reliability can be checked using the research data. If reliability has not been previously checked and then turns out to be undesirably low, the entire project is in jeopardy.

Achievement tests are usually made up of objectively scored items that can adequately measure the acquisition of factual knowledge. Other outcomes of learning, such as the application of concepts, can also be measured by using such items. Achievement tests need not be limited to short items; free-response items of varying types and lengths can also be used. For example, in geometry achievement, the individual might be required to produce an entire proof of a theorem. Such an item could be objectively scored, although scoring time would be increased. Less objective items can also be used in achievement tests, although the use of such items might raise some difficulties relative to validity and reliability.

Attitude Inventories

Achievement tests are generally designed to measure an individual's best or maximum performance, whereas an attitude inventory is intended to measure typical performance. Attitudes involve an individual's feelings toward such things as ideas, procedures, and social institutions. Note that the attitude is *toward* something. Most people think of attitudes in such terms as acceptance-rejection or favorable-unfavorable; however, the intensity of a person's feeling usually is not dichotomous but is on a continuum between the extremes. Measurement of the attitude is intended to place individuals on this continuum.

Attitude inventories are available from commercial publishers. The sources for information about tests discussed in the preceding section also contain information about available attitude inventories. However, it is usually more difficult to find an available attitude inventory than an achievement test for a research project. This is because attitude inventories used for research tend to be quite specific, and more general inventories may not be adequate. Often, it is necessary to construct an attitude scale. Several item formats may be used.

Likert Scale.[2] The *Likert scale* is a scale with a number of points, usually five, in which the spaces between the points are assumed to be equal. A set of related responses, one for each point, is provided. The individual responds by checking a point or circling a letter representing a point on the scale. These points are assigned numerical values, 1 to 5 or 0 to 4, which are then totaled over the items to give the individual an attitude score.

There are any number of possible sets of Likert responses. The important characteristic of a set is that the responses be appropriate for the items. The following are some sample sets of Likert responses:

Very satisfactory	Very good
Satisfactory	Good
Undecided	No opinion
Unsatisfactory	Poor
Very unsatisfactory	Very poor
Highly appropriate	Highly favorable
Appropriate	Favorable
Neutral	No opinion
Inappropriate	Unfavorable
Highly inappropriate	Highly favorable
Very supportive	Definitely yes
Supportive	Probably yes
Neutral	Uncertain
Unsupportive	Probably no
Very unsupportive	Definitely no

When scoring a Likert scale, it is important to note the direction of the item. Usually, the items are scored so that the greater the score, the more positive the attitude. If a five-point scale from "strongly agree" to "strongly disagree" is used, for some items the more positive attitude is indicated by the "strongly agree" end of the scale and for others it is indicated by the "strongly disagree" end. Figure 11.2 contains seven items from a 20-item scale used to measure student attitude toward learning mathematics.

These items were scored 1 to 5, so that the greater the score, the more positive the attitude. Items 14–17 and 20 were scored with "strongly agree" high (score of 5). Items 18 and 19 were scored with "strongly disagree" high. Since the scale

Figure 11.2
Sample Items Using a Likert Scale

Note: Circle the appropriate letter(s) to indicate how you feel. (SA strongly agree, A agree, U undecided, D disagree, SD strongly disagree).

SA A U D SD   14. Math is fascinating and fun.

SA A U D SD   15. I feel at ease in math and I like it very much.

SA A U D SD   16. It is fun to work math puzzles.

SA A U D SD   17. My parents like math.

SA A U D SD   18. I do not like to work fraction problems.

SA A U D SD   19. My parents do not think math is very important.

SA A U D SD   20. If I were helping someone with schoolwork, I would like to
         do it in math.

Source: "Student Interest Inventory—Learning Mathematics—Grades 7–8." Used in Project IMMPACT, Sandusky County Schools, Fremont, Ohio.

contained 20 items, possible scores ranged from 20 to 100—the greater the score, the more positive the attitude.

> A *Likert scale* consists of a number of points on a scale, and the intervals between the points are assumed to be equal. Usually, five points are used, with designations such as "strongly agree" to "strongly disagree."

Constructing an attitude inventory using Likert scale items requires identifying the major topics or points to be addressed by the scale and then generating statements. These will undoubtedly need some revision to ensure clarity and relevance. Usually, items of both directions are used to provide more variety and breadth in the items. It may also make the items more interesting for the respondents. A pool of items is generated, and these items should be administered in a pilot test. On the basis of the pilot test, items can be put into final form and those items identified that will be used in the inventory.

Unlike achievement tests, it is possible for a respondent to fake responses when taking an attitude inventory. The direction of the more positive attitude can usually be identified from the item, and the respondent could deliberately respond in that direction regardless of true feelings. However, if the researcher is primarily interested in groups of scores, such as those for a class, and the respondent is aware of this, there is no reason to fake. Sometimes, very similar items are put in different parts of the inventory so that the consistency between responses can be checked.

Some respondents may develop a response set or tendency to respond in a certain manner as a reaction to the construction of the scale, independent of the item content. For example, the middle-of-the-roader will respond near the center of the scale regardless of his or her true feelings. Sometimes, reversing direction of items is used as a deterrent against response set.

It should be noted that Likert scales can be used for measurements other than attitude inventories. For example, the Likert scale presented in Chapter 7 was part of a questionnaire designed to measure teacher perceptions.

Semantic Differential. The *semantic differential* (Osgood, Suci, & Tannenbaum, 1957) is a measuring instrument that focuses on a single word or concept at a time to measure the connotative meaning of that concept. Then a series of bipolar adjective scales are given, and the respondents are asked to indicate their feelings (perceptions) on each scale with respect to the word or concept. Figure 11.3 contains a sample semantic differential. The concept being considered is "Mathematics and Me." There are 15 bipolar adjective scales. This particular example is appropriate for measuring the attitude toward mathematics of elementary school students in grades 4–6. The instructions given in the figure that show the students how to respond according to their feelings are worth noting.

The *semantic differential* provides a series of bipolar adjective scales relative to a word or concept; the respondents indicate their feelings on the continuum of each scale.

Scoring of the semantic differential can be done in different ways. The important thing about scoring is that it is consistent and meaningful. The usual scoring procedures are such that the greater the score, the more positive the attitude.

Hopkins and Stanley (1981, p. 300) suggest listing all pairs of adjectives in a consistent direction, usually low to high or negative to positive. The position of the adjectives (whether the right or left side is negative) is an arbitrary choice, but if the negative adjectives are on the left and the positive ones on the right, then the values 1-2-3-4-5-6-7 are assigned to the slots from left to right. Values of -3, -2, -1, 0, $+1$, $+2$, $+3$ could also be used, although this gives a possibility of a total score that is negative. Either way, the score is the sum of the values across the pairs of adjectives.

In the example in Figure 11.3, the adjective pairs are listed in both directions. For example, items 8 and 9 have reversed directions. Scoring can be done by reversing the direction of assigning the numerical values, always keeping the 7 on the positive end and the 1 on the negative end.

Figure 11.3
Sample Semantic Differential

STUDENTS: We are interested in how you feel about mathematics. At the top of the next page you will see the words "Mathematics and Me" and beneath it a list of word pairs that look like this:

good _____ : _____ : _____ : _____ : _____ : _____ : _____ bad

If you feel mathematics is **very** good, place an X near good:

good ___X___ : _____ : _____ : _____ : _____ : _____ : _____ bad

Or if you feel mathematics is **very** bad, place an X near bad:

good _____ : _____ : _____ : _____ : _____ : ___X___ : _____ bad

If you don't feel mathematics is either **very** good or **very** bad, place an X closer to the middle but toward the side you favor.

IMPORTANT 1. Place your X in the center of the spaces, not on the boundaries.
2. Be sure you mark an X for every word pair.
3. Make only **one** X on a word pair.

MATHEMATICS AND ME

1. dull _____ : _____ : _____ : _____ : _____ : _____ : _____ interesting

2. slow _____ : _____ : _____ : _____ : _____ : _____ : _____ fast

3. enjoyable _____ : _____ : _____ : _____ : _____ : _____ : _____ distasteful

4. positive _____ : _____ : _____ : _____ : _____ : _____ : _____ negative

5. low _____ : _____ : _____ : _____ : _____ : _____ : _____ high

6. unpleasant _____ : _____ : _____ : _____ : _____ : _____ : _____ pleasant

7. good _____ : _____ : _____ : _____ : _____ : _____ : _____ bad

8. worst _____ : _____ : _____ : _____ : _____ : _____ : _____ best

9. strong _____ : _____ : _____ : _____ : _____ : _____ : _____ weak

10. fair _____ : _____ : _____ : _____ : _____ : _____ : _____ unfair

11. like _____ : _____ : _____ : _____ : _____ : _____ : _____ dislike

12. easy _____ : _____ : _____ : _____ : _____ : _____ : _____ hard

13. boring _____ : _____ : _____ : _____ : _____ : _____ : _____ fascinating

14. usual _____ : _____ : _____ : _____ : _____ : _____ : _____ unusual

15. worthless _____ : _____ : _____ : _____ : _____ : _____ : _____ valuable

Another scoring procedure can be used in which the values 7-6-5-4-3-2-1 are assigned left to right regardless of item direction. Then the score for the item is weighted either positive or negative, depending on its direction. For example, in the semantic differential in Figure 11.3, items 1 and 2 would have negative weightings and items 3 and 4 would have positive weightings. The total score would be the sum of these weighted scores, with a constant added to avoid any negative totals. Again, this procedure for scoring is such that the greater the score, the more positive the attitude.

The semantic differential in Figure 11.3 would generate a single score. Sometimes, semantic differentials are constructed to contain two or more subscales, called *dimensions* or *constructs*. For example, a semantic differential could be constructed to measure teachers' professional attitude that might contain a subscale on feelings toward children and a subscale on feelings toward the school administration. A subset of the items in the semantic differential would make up the items for a subscale. Subscale scores would be generated in a manner similar to generating a total score. Of course, a subscale would involve fewer items than the total scale.

Aptitude Tests

Aptitude is considered to be the potential for achievement. Although actual achievement and the potential ability for achievement are not the same thing, operationally they may be difficult to separate. Intelligence tests are the most commonly known measures for aptitude in academic and skills areas, but other terms such as *general scholastic ability* and *general mental ability* are being used increasingly to replace the term *intelligence*. The difficulty with the term *intelligence* comes with the long-standing belief that intelligence tests somehow measure an inborn capacity, regardless of the individual's background, experience, and the like. Cronbach (1984, p. 198) comments on the problem with this perception of intelligence:

> In British and American discourse, "intelligence" seemed usually to refer to potentiality as if the test score foretold what level the person would reach if given every educational advantage. The evidence is necessarily one-sided. Good ultimate performance proves capacity, but poor performance does not prove incapacity. The typical school-age test is best identified as a "test of general scholastic ability." It measures a set of abilities now developed and demonstrated (not a "potential"). It emphasizes abilities helpful in most schoolwork.

The importance of Cronbach's remarks to the educator is that one must be cautious when using an aptitude test and not assume that the test is measuring inherent ability independent of other factors, such as existing achievement (or the lack thereof). When diverse groups, possibly those from subcultures within the larger culture, are being measured by aptitude tests, it should not be assumed that the tests are equally valid for all groups.

Aptitude tests come in a variety of forms, commonly designated as individual or group tests. Individual tests tend to be more elaborate and may involve manipulation of objects, whereas group tests are usually limited to items on paper. The Wechsler Adult Intelligence Scale is an example of an individual test, and the California Test of Mental Maturity is an example of a group test.

The tests mentioned here are largely designed to measure global intelligence or ability. There are also aptitude tests that focus more on specific abilities. For example, the Scholastic Aptitude Test is highly oriented to the types of abilities learned in formal schooling, with an emphasis on verbal and mathematical abilities. There are numerous batteries of aptitude tests that measure multiple aptitudes through a series of subtests or subscores, an example being the Differential Aptitude Test. Such tests contain subtests of abilities, such as mechanical reasoning, numerical ability, and spatial relations, to mention just a few.

Scores on aptitude tests are sometimes used in educational research as control variables. For example, scores on an aptitude test may be used to classify individuals according to levels of ability if ability is used as an independent variable in the research design. Aptitude test scores may also be used as statistical controls.

The development of an aptitude test is a difficult task that requires a good deal of information, effort, and measurement expertise. For this reason, aptitude tests are seldom self-constructed for a research project. There are numerous aptitude tests available for both general and specific aptitudes. Information about specific aptitude tests can be found in sources such as the *Mental Measurements Yearbook,* mentioned at other points in this chapter.

Aptitude is the potential for achievement. It may be difficult in the measurement to separate potential from actual achievement. In essence, an aptitude test gives indirect evidence of the existence of the potential.

Personality Measures

When characteristics such as motivation, attitudes, and emotional adjustment as a whole are considered, we are focusing on the individual's personality. Personality tests generally are designed to measure the affective or nonintellectual aspects of behavior.

The measurement of personality has certain inherent difficulties—for example, what to measure. Although there is some ambiguity associated with the term, the consensus is that personality measurement deals with the measurement of traits. In this sense, a trait is a tendency for the individual to respond to situations in a certain way. For example, a pessimistic individual will tend to respond by emphasizing the unfavorable aspects of almost any situation, and an honest person will tend to respond consistently in a certain manner in situations testing honesty. However, a trait is not usually so "pure" that one response is consistent for all situations. Thus, a foremost problem of measuring personality is validity—the question of whether one is measuring what one intends to measure.

There are generally two kinds of personality tests: projective and nonprojective. *Projective tests* use a word, a picture, or some stimulus to elicit an unstructured response. A respondent might be asked to develop a story about a picture or to indicate what is seen in an ink blot. The response must then be interpreted by someone who scores the responses. The Thematic Apperception Test is an example of a projective test.

Nonprojective tests are paper-and-pencil tests that require the individual to respond to statements by selecting an option from a number of possible responses. The score is then generated from the options selected and certain patterns of options selected, or scores are indicative of identified personality characteristics. The Minnesota Multiphasic Personality Inventory is an example of a nonprojective test.

> Personality tests are generally of two types—projective and nonprojective.

Constructing personality inventories is not a task for the novice. It requires extensive psychological knowledge and sophisticated psychometric methods. Satisfactory personality tests are usually commercially available. Personality tests are often listed and reviewed in psychological measurement publications. In educational research, which commonly includes normal individuals, traits are broadly defined—such as personal adjustment or social adjustment. Published inventories are available for measuring such broad traits.

Rating Scales

Rating scales are measurement devices used quite frequently in educational research to collect data on a variety of variables. A rating scale presents a statement of some type (possibly just one word), and the respondent is asked to make a judgment of categories on a scale that most closely fits the statement. Rating scales may have three, four, five, or conceivably any finite number of points. Quite often, there are five points or categories on a scale, each representing a possible description of the concept contained in the statement. The scale may contain an odd number of points so that there is a middle point, although this is not a requirement.

Any number of variables can be measured using rating scales, including instruction, facilities, effects of programs, and so forth. The descriptors used for the categories of the scale are selected to fit the particular variable being rated. Rating scales can also be used by observers who are observing an activity such as teaching.

Rating scales can vary in length, but usually they contain several statements, called *items,* that use the same descriptors and relate to a single concept, activity, phenomenon, experience, or physical object. Sample items from a rating scale are given in Figure 11.4. These items were part of a 40-item scale used in a community survey of the schools. Respondents were asked to rate the extent to which they felt the characteristics of the items were true. Although there were several schools in the district, respondents were asked to rate the specific school in their area.

Rating scales are much like Likert scales; in fact, they can be considered a special case of a Likert scale, one that requires a rating by the respondent. If it is desirable to obtain a total score over all items or groups of items, this can be done in the usual manner. For the example in Figure 11.4, the characteristics of the 15 items are all positively stated; if the item scores were summed, the greater the score, the higher would be the respondent rating of the school on these characteristics.

Figure 11.4
Sample Items from a Rating Scale

Directions: Below are some statements about ABC Elementary School. For each statement, indicate how true you think it is by circling one of the numerals. Please use the code listed below and respond to *all* statements.

How True
4 = Almost Always   2 = Sometimes
3 = More Often than Not   1 = Almost Never

Statement	How True?			
1. Students are enthusiastic about the school and teachers.	4	3	2	1
2. Students respect their teachers.	4	3	2	1
3. Students respect the principal.	4	3	2	1
4. School personnel are enthusiastic about working with students.	4	3	2	1
5. School personnel respect students.	4	3	2	1
6. The teachers get along well with students.	4	3	2	1
7. School personnel respect cultural differences.	4	3	2	1
8. Students respect cultural differences.	4	3	2	1
9. The atmosphere for learning at the school is generally positive.	4	3	2	1
10. School expectations are understood and accepted by both students and staff.	4	3	2	1
11. Academic standards are high enough.	4	3	2	1
12. Students are learning basic reading skills.	4	3	2	1
13. Students are learning basic mathematics skills.	4	3	2	1
14. Students are learning basic communication skills.	4	3	2	1
15. Students are learning basic human relations skills.	4	3	2	1

> *Rating scales* contain items related to a concept, phenomenon, activity, or physical object; the respondent is asked to select a descriptor on a scale that most closely approximates the content of the item.

Observation Systems

Tests and inventories used for measuring achievement, attitudes, and so forth, are for the most part paper-and-pencil instruments, many of them administered simultaneously to an entire group. There are also educational research situations in which the data are collected through an *observation system*—a procedure by which an observer records what is occurring in some situation or setting, such as a classroom.

Several observation systems have been developed recently for measuring teacher and/or student behavior. One such system is the Classroom Observation Keyed for Effectiveness Research (COKER) system.[3] This is an objectively administered, low-inference system for recording teacher–student interactions and transactions in the classroom. It is a composite instrument derived from five objective, systematic, direct-observation instruments used in a 2-year study of teaching: the Spaulding Teacher Activity Recording Schedule (STARS), formerly the Spaulding Teacher Activity Rating Schedule (Spaulding, 1970); the Coping Analysis Schedule for Educational Settings (CASES) (Spaulding, 1969); the Observation Schedule and Record 5V (OScAR 5V) (Medley, 1973); the Florida Climate and Control System (FLACCS) (Soar, Soar, & Rogosta, 1971); and the Teacher Practices Observation Record (TPOR) (Brown, 1968).

The COKER system is a relatively comprehensive system that includes both student and teacher behavior as classroom interaction takes place and is appropriate for elementary or secondary level classes. An observation consists of a 5-minute recording period coded on a one-page schedule, a copy of which appears in Figure 11.5. *Coding* is the process of recording the occurrence of behaviors into categories. The behaviors to be observed have been selected prior to the observation. An observation system so used is also called a *coding system*.

> An *observation system* is used for recording preselected behaviors in an attempt to quantify behavior in the situation being observed.

Collecting data through observation is a relatively demanding task. It requires considerable training of observers, who must be consistent in recording what they observe. Thus, agreement of observation is always a concern, not only between

Figure 11.5
The Classroom Observations Keyed for Effectiveness Research (COKER) Instrument—Section A

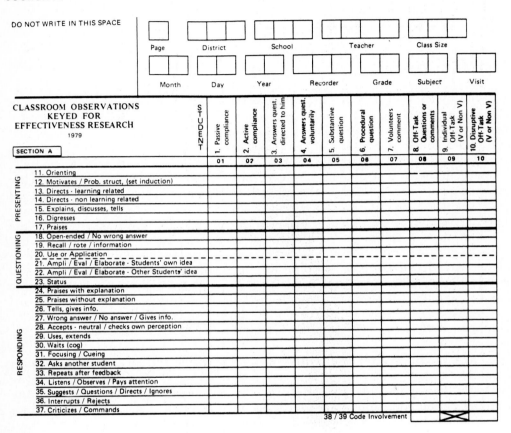

Source: Used with permission of the authors.

different observers, but also between the different observations of a single observer. For the COKER system, a minimum of 40 hours of observer training is suggested. Subsequent agreement checks are also made.

An inspection of the COKER instrument in Figure 11.5 shows that it has two sections of some complexity. Section A consists of a two-dimensional matrix, with teacher behavior on one dimension and student behavior on the other. Thus, behaviors recorded in this section represent joint occurrence. Section B contains student and teacher behaviors separately; the intent here is simply to indicate that specific behaviors occurred or did not occur. In an attempt to illustrate and to explain the

Figure 11.5 Continued
COKER—Section B

| SECTION B |

STUDENT

40. Enthusiastic
41. Praises another
42. Pats, hugs / Pos. horseplay
43. Laughs, smiles
44. Shows pride
45. Agrees, V or NV
46. Friendly, V or NV
47. Helps / Shares / Consider V or NV
48. Code Involvement (40 · 47)
49. Intense Involvement
50. Leadership
51. Follows Routine WO Rem.
52. S. answers another S.
53. Works w/social
54. Collab. work/play
55. Compet. · work/play
56. Confused
57. Self-directed; Inappro.
58. Wanders about
59. Pouts, withdraws
60. Shows fear, shame
61. Makes face, frowns
62. Tattles
63. Teases
64. Resists
65. Picks at another / Neg. horseplay
66. Dem / Com / Boss / Con
67. Disr / Annoy / Interferes
68. Takes / Damage / Stamp / Throws
69. Crit / Disparages
70. Att / Hit / Hurt / ·agg
71. Code Involvement (61 - 70)
72. Code Interest/Attention

COMMENTS:

TEACHER

METHODOLOGY

Motivation	73. Intrinsic Immed
	74. Intrinsic Future
	75. Extrinsic
Student	76. S no choice
Choice	77. S lim choice
	78. S free choice
	79. Aloof, detached
	80. Observes, Monitors
Super-	81. Joins, partic.
vision	82. Manages simul. Act
	83. Close superv.
Focus	84. T. Q. Prob.
	85. S. Q. Prob.
Source	86. Text, pkg. res.
	87. Multiple res.
Differ/	88. Same mat/eval.
Evaluation	89. Indiv. mat/eval.
	90. S. partic./eval.
Student	91. Discourages
Expres.	92. Encourages
Student	93. Prevents
Perpl.	94. Fosters
Mis-	95. Accepts
inform	96. Corrects
	97. Inductive
Strategy	98. Deductive
	99. Transductive
	100. Expository
Cogn.	101. Simple
Level	102. Complex
Use of	103. T. assigns SA
Student time	104. Indep. work

AFFECT   NON-VERBAL   CONTROL

105. Warm, cong.	
107. Nod, smiles	108
109. Tou / Pat / Hug	110
111. Pause	112
113. Eye contact	114
115. Ignore	116
117. Gestures / Sig'l / Raps	118
119. Shakes head / shh	120
121. Takes something	122
123. Glares, Frowns	124
125. Holds, Pushes	126

VERBAL

127. Praise, non-sub	128
129. Agrees, Supports	130
131. Pos. Indiv. Attn.	132
133. Reminds	134
135. Says stop	136
137. Firm / Sharp	138
139. Sco / Warns / Pun	140

GROUPING (circle dominant mode)

	Non-pres		No. of Stu.	Prescribed		
	WT.	WOT		WT.	WOT	
141	146		1	150		155
142	147		2-3	151		156
143	148		4 -½	152		157
144	149		½ +	153		158
145			ALL	154		159

SUBJECT KEY:

01. — Music & Art	06. — Science
02. — Lang. Arts	07. — Soc. Stu.
03. — Literature	08. — Planning
04. — Math	09. — Transition
05. — Reading	10. — Other

Joan G. & Homer Coker
P. O. Box 1017
Carrollton, Georgia 30117

use of the COKER, the following description is excerpted from the *Observer Training Manual* (Coker & Coker, 1982, p. ii):

> *Section A:* This section [Items 1 through 39] consists of a matrix of numbered cells designating specific teacher and student transactions or interactions. The matrix is designed to accommodate one 5-minute observation. When an interaction represented by a numbered cell occurs, the cell should be marked. For example, if a teacher is "Directing-learning related" (13) and a student is "passively complying" (01), code the appropriate cell (13/01). Each cell is coded only once in a given 5-minute observation period even though the behavior may occur numerous times. When using a sign system, code as many items as seen during a given coding period.
>
> *Section B:* This section [Items 40 through 140] is designed to record specific student and/or teacher cognitive and affective behaviors as well as teaching

strategies which occurred during the previous 5 minutes. These behaviors may or may not be interactions. Code this section from memory.

Grouping: This section [items 141 through 159] refers to the organizational plan or method used by the teacher, and whether the activities are prescribed by the teacher or not.

The following are examples of the kinds of interactions or behaviors that would be coded in a certain way; one example is from Section A, the other from Section B. They are coded in numbers 28 and 67, respectively.

28. *Accepts—neutral; checks own perception:*

Teacher accepts or rephrases student's substantive work or comment, is neutral in response, keeps the idea in discussion. Teacher is accepting with no commitment as to whether the response is accurate or not. Or rephrases, checking the teacher's own perception.

Examples: "Jimmy says if Columbus hadn't discovered America, someone else would have." "Did you say the 'a' in apple is short?" (p. 8)

67. *Disrupts, annoys, interferes:*

Student intentionally disrupts, annoys, or interferes with classroom activities, getting the attention of the teacher or classmates through inappropriate behavior.

Examples: Student sings, claps hands loudly, and rocks back and forth to imaginary musical beat. Student yells, talks loudly, calls out. (p. 17)

Instruments used for observation are not limited to matrices or category systems that require coding. Rating scales using items similar to those of a Likert scale could be used. The observer would then complete the items. The number of points or intervals on the scale is somewhat arbitrary; usually, an odd number is used, such as five, seven, or nine. A sample item from a rating scale used for classroom observation might be:

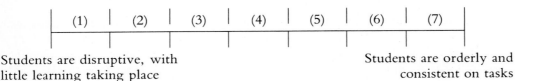

Students are disruptive, with little learning taking place

Students are orderly and consistent on tasks

Scoring over a number of items can then be done, as with any rating scale.

Collecting data through observation requires careful preparation and planning. When classroom observation is to be done, the principal and teachers should be well informed about why the observation is being done, and they should participate in making the arrangements. While observation is being done, the observer should keep a low profile, which means being as unobtrusive as possible. There should be no participation in activities or interaction with those being observed.

Where to Find Test Information

There are a number of sources for information about tests and inventories in almost all areas of education. Some of these, such as *Tests in Print III* (Mitchell, 1983) have already been mentioned in connection with achievement testing; *Tests in Print III* also contains information about other types of tests, including 245 intelligence and scholastic aptitude tests and 576 personality inventories.

The *Mental Measurements Yearbook* reviews a large variety of educational and psychological measures. The Buros Institute of Mental Measurements, located at the University of Nebraska-Lincoln, plans to publish new editions (beyond the eighth) of the yearbooks. This institute also provides a computerized database service, Biographic Retrieval Service, Inc. (BRS), which is useful for obtaining information about new and revised tests. Libraries that offer the BRS service can conduct computer searches of the database.

Other sources of test information are available—for example, *Tests in Education* by Levy and Goldstein (1984). This volume provides information and reviews about tests used in the British educational system. Nearly 200 tests are evaluated, grouped under the following headings:

Early Development (including Reading and Number)

Language

Mathematics

Composite Attainments

General Abilities

Personality and Counseling

Miscellaneous Topics

Although this volume deals with tests used in the British Isles, sources such as this may contain information about tests that can be used for research purposes.

A volume referenced in Chapter 7 that merits repeating here is *Mirrors for Behavior III* (Simon & Boyer, 1974). This is an informative anthology of observation instruments focusing on teacher and student behavior. There are 99 instruments listed and described, many highly specific, such as the Biology Teacher Behavior Inventory and the Medical Instruction Observation Record. The description of an instrument is complete, including information about the conditions of its use. The volume contains an extensive bibliography.

Many test publishers provide promotional brochures and catalogues about their tests. An example is the Publishers Test Service of CTB/McGraw-Hill. Educational Testing Service of Princeton, New Jersey, maintains a test collection of more than 10,000 tests and publishes a monthly newsletter, *News on Tests,* which describes revised tests or new tests added to the collection. The newsletter also includes references to reviews and general news about testing.

Virtually all tests are accompanied by a manual, which is a valuable source of detailed information about the test under consideration. Many school systems and universities have counseling centers or testing centers where such manuals and sometimes examples of tests are available.

Information about tests is contained throughout the periodical literature. Tests are occasionally reviewed in professional journals. Journals such as the *Journal of Educational Measurement* often contain reports about the use of exploratory approaches to measurement. Thus, there is a good deal of test information available, much of which can be located through the use of indices (see Chapter 3).

Data Preparation

After the data have been collected, tabulation is necessary, and it may also be desirable to make some type of data transformation in preparation for analysis. If answer sheets or tests are to be hand-scored, routine precautions would include supervised practice for scorers and accuracy checks while the actual scoring is being done.

Research projects that include the collection of considerable data using standardized tests probably would use machine-scored answer sheets. Companies such as IBM and National Computer Systems sell standardized machine-scored answer sheets. It is possible to have special-purpose machine-scored answer sheets developed, but the process is quite expensive. Test-scoring machines not only provide the actual scores, they commonly provide tabulations, summaries, and conversions to various types of standard scores. In some cases, the machines are connected to a computer to provide certain kinds of analyses.

Machine scoring of tests is usually less expensive than hand scoring and more accurate and (if necessary) makes it easier to prepare the data for computer analysis. Not all educational research data are collected in a form that can be machine-scored, however, and the organization of data for analysis when a machine is not to be used to transmit data from the answer sheet to the computer is an important part of the research procedure.

Coding Data

With the general availability of computers, any research project involving even a small amount of data or requiring anything but very simple statistical analysis should allow for the use of a computer. Data must be transmitted from data sheets to the computer, either through the use of data cards or through a computer terminal.

Within recent years, the use of data cards has declined with the increasing availability of computer terminals and microcomputers.

Whether a data card is used or data are transmitted directly through a terminal, the format for the data must be specified. The standard IBM data card contains 80 columns, and usually the information for one individual is contained on a card. It is not necessary to use all 80 columns.

A computer terminal screen contains rows that correspond to data cards, and the spaces in the rows correspond to columns. However, there may be fewer than 80 spaces available in a row (for example, 72 spaces). Whether or not cards are used, the process of developing the format for identifying the information in each column is called *coding* the data. Information is commonly of two types—identification and scores or responses. The identification information consists of such things as the individual's classification on the independent variables, an identification number, and sex. Usually, the identification comes in the early columns, although this is not required. The scores, commonly the scores on the dependent variables, are entered using as many columns as necessary. A two-digit score, for example, requires two columns. If there are ten different tests, each giving a two–digit score, these data would require 20 columns. If tests with varying numbers of digits in the scores are used, the number of columns used for each score is sometimes held constant—that is, the greatest number of digits for any score. This may facilitate setting up the analysis. If the data for an individual require more than the number of columns in the row, simply use additional rows (if using cards, additional cards) for that individual.

Coding data consists of developing a system by which the data and identification information are specified and organized in preparation for the analyses.

An example of coding information is presented in Figure 11.6. This is a sample data layout. The information is from a research study involving an experimental and a traditional reading program in 14 elementary schools. The first ten columns contain identification information. The first two columns identify the school, and the next two columns the class in the school. Since no school contains more than 1,000 students, three columns are reserved for the student identification number. Columns 8, 9, and 10 contain classifying information. If the numbers in the first ten columns were

1 1 0 6 1 3 1 1 5 1

Figure 11.6
Sample Coding of Information

Column Number	Column Information
1, 2	School code; 14 numbers possible
3, 4	Class number in the school
5, 6, 7	Student identification number
8	Sex 1 = female, 2 = male
9	Grade level 3, 4, 5, or 6
10	Type of reading program 1 = experimental 2 = traditional
11, 12	Number in class
13, 14, 15	Score on recent IQ test
16, 17, 18	Score on attitude toward school inventory
19, 20	Total score on reading test
21, 22	Reading comprehension subscore
23, 24	Reading word attack subscore
25, 26	Score on comprehension math test involving written or "story" problems
27, 28	Score on science test
29, 30	Score on social studies test
31, 32	Score on English usage test
33, 34	Score on logical reasoning test

Remaining columns blank

these mean: student 131 from school 11 in class 6, who is a fifth-grade girl in the experimental reading program. Columns 11 and 12 contain the number in the class, information that may be used in analyses. The remaining 22 columns contain the various test scores.

An Example of a Data File

The data should be organized so that minimum effort is required to transmit the data from its original form to the computer. Sometimes data can be transmitted directly from the measuring instrument to the computer. If this is not convenient, because reorganization of the data is necessary or the process is too complex, a computer recording form can be used, which is readily available at computer centers and stationery stores. Either way, the data for each individual should be presented in a line or a row in the exact order they are to be transmitted. It is inefficient to be fishing around for information when transmitting data. When data have been transmitted, either through a computer terminal or onto cards, they should be checked for possible errors. When all the data have been transmitted into the computer, we have a data file.

Suppose that a school system has 54 teachers in grades 3–6 and a study is being conducted on the extent to which these teachers demonstrate six selected teaching competencies. The six competencies are as follows:

C-1 Uses a variety of instructional strategies.
C-2 Uses convergent and divergent inquiry strategies.
C-3 Develops and demonstrates problem-solving skills.
C-4 Establishes transitions and sequences in instruction which are varied.
C-5 Modifies instructional activities to accommodate identified learner needs.
C-6 Demonstrates ability to work with individuals, small groups and large groups.

The teachers are observed using a classroom observation inventory (such as the COKER), and scores are obtained for each teacher on the six competencies.

The data are recorded on a computer recording form, as illustrated in Figure 11.7. Teachers are identified only by number; the information for six teachers is given in Figure 11.7. The coding is straightforward: the first two columns are for identification, and then the six competency scores are given in order. The scores are two-digit numbers, and one-column spaces (which are not necessary) are inserted between scores for easier reading. Thus, the identification number, the scores, and the spaces use 20 columns. The data for each teacher are placed on a row.

When putting the data into the computer, we create a data file. Whether this is done through cards or directly through a computer terminal, the file needs a name. This file will be called **FILE: TCHRCOMP DATA.** Usually, the name is descriptive of the data and is used in locating the file for future analyses. Abbreviations are used because there usually is a limit on the number of characters that can be used in a file name. The data file is given in Figure 11.8. Note that there are 54 rows, one for the data on each teacher, and that the format for the rows is consistent. The file is now ready to be used in analyzing data; we will use it for a sample analysis in Chapter 12.

If the data are to be analyzed using a hand or desk calculator, it is important to classify and organize all scores so that there is no confusion as to the identification

Figure 11.7
Sample Computer Recording Form Used for Coding Data

CODING FORM

ID	C-1	C-2	C-3	C-4	C-5	C-6
0 1	6 1	3 6	3 5	4 9	4 0	6 1
0 2	5 3	4 9	6 1	4 7	5 4	5 8
0 3	5 7	4 8	4 6	5 1	5 1	5 8
0 4	3 4	5 1	5 0	4 7	3 8	3 8
0 5	5 8	4 5	4 7	4 5	5 1	4 1
0 6	5 3	3 5	3 4	4 5	5 2	5 5

Figure 11.8
Sample Data File for the Six Competency Scores of 54 Teachers

```
FILE: TCHRCOMP DATA
      A     UNIVERSITY OF TOLEDO TIME-SHARING SYSTEM

01 61 36 35 49 40 61          28 36 43 53 43 37 47
02 53 49 61 47 54 58          29 42 71 56 45 42 51
03 57 48 46 51 51 58          30 55 51 56 43 67 56
04 34 51 50 47 38 38          31 39 55 39 57 45 36
05 58 45 47 45 51 41          32 48 50 55 47 43 38
06 53 35 34 45 52 55          33 52 67 50 45 65 80
07 39 62 51 49 43 56          34 58 45 46 28 54 56
08 44 46 43 32 48 76          35 36 43 43 43 45 41
09 58 61 66 56 72 66          36 46 53 49 69 44 47
10 56 73 59 79 56 44          37 40 44 68 43 56 52
11 53 36 36 43 50 36          38 36 38 43 49 39 54
12 53 42 36 45 41 37          39 48 47 54 75 74 55
13 45 49 40 45 61 50          40 52 61 76 79 59 45
14 40 37 39 45 38 50          41 88 75 66 61 75 60
15 41 38 48 45 66 49          42 42 49 37 47 47 56
16 61 65 53 49 40 58          43 55 63 62 51 52 46
17 57 60 73 51 53 52          44 49 47 57 51 53 52
18 51 41 39 47 38 38          45 61 50 52 54 50 44
19 51 47 44 43 53 47          46 53 67 52 51 41 52
20 56 45 41 45 48 39          47 45 49 49 47 60 64
21 66 43 54 45 64 52          48 49 44 46 49 48 44
22 38 51 39 43 39 45          49 58 59 48 74 50 48
23 38 45 54 45 37 69          50 52 45 55 47 42 34
24 36 56 54 47 36 36          51 55 47 45 65 47 43
25 43 47 44 43 60 45          52 58 54 63 49 58 53
26 58 49 63 49 47 56          53 63 51 50 49 48 57
27 35 42 40 45 40 45          54 49 31 38 57 44 37
```

Note: These are hypothetical data.

of a score. The scores should be presented so that errors are minimized in transmitting them from data sheets to the calculator. The computations on the calculator should be performed in such a manner that several internal checks can be made during the calculations.

Ethical Considerations in Conducting Research

Much educational research involves the use of human participants, who may be involved in experiments in which they have certain treatments administered to them.

In the case of a survey, it is usually the human participant from which the data are collected. Sometimes, school or other records are used as sources of data that, of course, contain information about people. Since human participants are involved at the point of data collection, ethical considerations are discussed in this chapter.

Within the past 15 years or so, increased attention has been given to the ethical and legal considerations of conducting research involving human participants. The National Research Act of 1974 deals with these matters, and Michael and Weinberger (1977), among others, have commented on the meaning of the act. One stipulation of the act is that universities and agencies engaging in research with human participants have an institutional review board for proposals. The board must approve the proposal and certify that the project will be conducted in accordance with the law. Universities have committees through which such proposals must be channeled, and school systems often have defined procedures of approval for any proposed research or data collection. Any researcher doing research with human participants at a university or in a school system must follow the institution's rules and procedures.

The American Psychological Association (APA) has issued a monograph, developed by the Committee on Ethical Standards in Psychological Research, entitled *Ethical Principles in the Conduct of Research with Human Participants* (Washington, D.C.: American Psychological Association, 1973). This is probably the most comprehensive statement on ethics involved in research with human participants. The content is relevant for educational research, since, like psychological research, it often involves human participants. More recently, the APA has published ten ethical principles for conducting research with human participants. These are summarized in the *American Psychologist* (1981).

An editorial in the *Educational Researcher* (vol. 2, no. 2, February 1973), "Ethical Standards for Research in Education," by Richard Schultz, discusses the content of the APA monograph in relation to education. It also discusses ethical standards for research with children as presented by the Society for Research in Child Development. Fowler (1984) discusses ethical considerations when conducting survey research. He identifies eight procedures for protecting respondents:

1. All people who have access to the data or a role in the data collection should be committed in writing to confidentiality.
2. Minimize links between answers and identifiers (of respondents).
3. Completed interview schedules or questionnaires should not be accessible to nonproject members.
4. Identifiers should be removed from completed questionnaires if they are looked at by nonstaff people. Remove them as soon as possible in any case.
5. Individuals who could identify respondents from their profile of answers should not be permitted to see the actual questionnaire responses.
6. The link between the ID number of a respondent and identifiers should not be available to general users of the data file.
7. During analysis, researchers should be careful about presenting data for very small categories of people who might be identifiable.

8. When a project is completed or the use of the actual questionnaire is over, it is the responsibility of the researcher to see the eventual destruction of the completed instruments or their continued, secure storage. (p. 137, with paraphrasing)

Although real risks to respondents or interviewees in a survey are small, the foregoing precautions and procedures should be followed.

Several important points are made in the legislation and related publications, including the following: The researcher must protect the dignity and welfare of the participants. The individual's freedom to decline participation must be respected, and the confidentiality of research data must be maintained. The researcher must guard against violation or invasion of privacy. The responsibility for maintaining ethical standards remains with the individual researcher, and the principal investigator is also responsible for actions of co-workers or assistants.

Most educational research studies focus on group data rather than individual data. For example, an experiment may emphasize how the groups receiving different treatments differ in performance, not the performance of a particular individual. Yet to collect the group information, data must be collected from individuals. However, individuals should not be specifically identified with their data unless it is necessary, and then only after the individuals have given consent.

There has been much written on this topic, and it is not necessary to review all of it here. Protecting the rights of individuals in research is, to a large extent, a matter of common sense and respect. But all researchers may not have the same concept of respect. Almost all educational research is conducted under the auspices of some institution, such as a university, school system, or related agency. When human participants are involved, the rules and procedures of that institution must be reviewed and followed. Generally, these will be in keeping with the intent of federal and, possibly, other legislation.

SUMMARY

This chapter has provided an overview of some of the more common types of measurement used in educational research. For many research studies, adequate measurement devices—in the form of tests, inventories, scales, or observation schedules—are available, and suggestions were provided about information sources. Because the measurement instruments used provide the operational definition of the data, their selection merits attention.

Because some research projects have measurement needs that cannot be met readily by existing instruments, it is sometimes necessary to construct the instruments, and this increases the total research effort. Commonly constructed instruments such as rating scales were discussed. Before embarking on the development of an instrument, however, the researcher should check for available instruments and estimate the magnitude of the development task. In some areas, such as the measurement of personality, instrument development requires sophisticated knowledge and skills.

The concepts of reliability and validity of measuring instruments were discussed. Whenever an instrument is used, its validity in the context of its use must be considered. There are a number of procedures for establishing reliability.

Since education includes so many variables, measurement is very broad and varied. Entire books are written on even limited areas within measurement, so this chapter has not gone into detail about the theoretical concepts of measurement or some of the infrequently used procedures. How much effort must be put into obtaining the measurement instrument and collecting the data depends on the conditions of the specific research study.

It is important to plan the data collection carefully and to identify the specific measurement requirements of the research study. Collecting a mass of data and then trying to fit a research problem to it is not acceptable practice. After data are collected, they must be assembled for analysis. Coding and construction of a data file were illustrated in this chapter; these procedures are done so that analysis can proceed in an appropriate and efficient manner. Although good measurement does not ensure good research, it is a necessary but not sufficient condition for good research.

KEY CONCEPTS

Measurement	*Achievement tests*
Scales of measurement	*Aptitude tests*
Reliability of measurement	*Personality measures*
Parallel forms procedures	*Projective tests*
Split-half procedure	*Nonprojective tests*
Kuder-Richardson	*Likert scale*
procedures	*Semantic differential*
Cronbach alpha procedure	*Rating scales*
Reliability coefficient	*Observation systems*
Validity of measurement	*Test information sources*
Content-related evidence	*Coding data*
Criterion-related evidence	*Data file*
Construct-related evidence	*Ethical considerations*

EXERCISES

11.1 Discuss the distinction between the concepts of validity and reliability. Why do we say that measurement can be reliable without being valid, but that the reverse cannot be true?

11.2 A researcher plans to do a study about the extent of hostility in upper elementary classrooms taught by teachers classified as autocratic or democratic.

Discuss the problem of establishing validity in measuring hostility. Assume that hostility can go both ways: from students to teachers and vice versa. What are possible approaches to measuring hostility? For example, would observation be used? If so, what would be included in the observation schedule? What is a possible operational definition of hostility? Is it possible to quantify hostility in any way?

11.3 Suppose that a guidance counselor wants to do a study on the attitudes of junior high students toward a compulsory "orientation to the school" program. Students who have completed the program are to respond to an attitude inventory. Construct five items for such an inventory. Designate the scoring for your items.

11.4 A researcher is doing research on the science achievement of students in grades five through seven. Another researcher is doing research on personality characteristics of junior high students. Contrast the measurement of these two research studies with respect to:

a. The availability of published measuring instruments.

b. The type of validity of major concern.

c. The data collection procedures.

11.5 Suppose that a researcher is doing research on the attitudes of junior high school students toward their teachers. Construct a semantic differential that might be used to measure such attitudes.

11.6 Construct five items for a rating scale that might be used with high school teachers to measure faculty perceptions of the central administration of the school system.

11.7 Contrast the use of a Likert scale and a semantic differential. In what ways are they operationally different in terms of the manner in which an individual responds? Describe any differences and similarities in the scoring procedures.

11.8 A research director for a large city school system conducts an extensive study of achievement in grades three through eight. Achievement in several areas is measured, with subscores in the areas so that there are 18 different achievement scores for each participating student. Ten of the scores require two digits each and the remainder three digits each. The sample of students is drawn form 74 city schools. The total sample size is over 1,000, and each student in the sample is to be identified by a number. In addition to the specific school and grade level, the students are classified according to sex. The student's age is recorded to the nearest month. There are nine high schools in the city, and each of the 74 elementary schools is in only one high school district. This information is also recorded in terms of the high school district in which the student's school is located. Develop a possible coding scheme that includes all of the foregoing information. Consider the number of columns you would use for identification information and achievement scores. The order of providing information is somewhat arbitrary, but identify a specific order. Assume that the data will be put into the computer through a terminal and that 72 columns are available. Would it be necessary to use more than one row for the data of a single student?

11.9 Select an article from a professional journal that involves the measurement of attitudes or personality characteristics. Read the article carefully and check to see whether the author discusses such things as validity, reliability, and type of measuring device. Are the data quantified in some way? Were standardized tests used for the study? If so, were norms available?

11.10 In the research literature on teacher effectiveness, locate two or more studies using classroom observation systems. If the observation systems are reproduced, inspect them for similarities and differences. If they are not reproduced, there should at least be descriptions of the system. Identify the specific classroom interaction variables measured by the systems. Is any reliability information provided? You might want to check *Mirrors for Behavior III* (Simon & Boyer, 1974) to see if the observation system is described in that volume.

NOTES

1. See for example, W. Wiersma and S. Jurs, *Educational Measurement and Testing* (Boston: Allyn and Bacon, 1985); or T. Kubiszyn and G. Borich, *Educational Testing and Measurement* (Glenview, IL: Scott, Foresman, 1984).

2. The terms *index* and *scale* are commonly used interchangeably, although some authors make a technical distinction between them. Both scales and indices are composite measures of variables based on responses to more than one item, and both typically provide ordinal measurement, at least for the individual items. An index is obtained through the simple cumulation of scores to responses over the items. A scale is obtained through the assignment of scores to response patterns, thus taking into account any intensity structure that may exist in the items. By these technical definitions, most of the scales used in educational research are indices, but this discussion will continue with the more common term, *scale*.

3. See J. G. Coker and H. Coker, *Classroom Observations Keyed for Effectiveness Research: Observer Training Manual* (Rev. ed.) (Atlanta: Georgia State University, 1982). The *User's Manual*, written by the same authors and also published by Georgia State University, contains descriptions about the rationale and uses of the observation inventory.

REFERENCES

Brown, B. B. (1968). *The experimental mind in education.* New York: Harper & Row.

Buros, O. K. (1978). *Eighth mental measurements yearbook* (2 vols.). Highland Park, NJ: Gryphon Press.

Coker, J. G. & Coker, H. (1982). *Classroom observations keyed for effectiveness research: Observer training manual* (Rev. ed.). Atlanta: Georgia State University.

Committee on Scientific and Professional Ethics and Conduct. (1981). Ethical principles of psychologists. *American Psychologist, 36,* 633–638.

Cronbach, L. J. (1951). Coefficient alpha and the internal structure of tests. *Psychometrika, 16,* 297–334.

Cronbach, L. J. (1984). *Essentials of psychological testing* (4th ed.). New York: Harper & Row.

Fowler, F. J., Jr. (1984). *Survey research methods.* Beverly Hills, CA: Sage.

Gronlund, N. E. (1985). *Measurement and evaluation in teaching* (5th ed.). New York: Macmillan.

Hopkins, K. D., & Stanley, J. C. (1981). *Educational and psychological measurement and evaluation* (6th ed.). Englewood Cliffs, NJ: Prentice-Hall.

Kerlinger, F. N. (1973). *Foundations of behavior research* (2nd ed.). New York: Holt, Rinehart & Winston.

Kuder, G. F., & Richardson, M. W. (1937). The theory of the estimation of test reliability. *Psychometrika, 2,* 151–160.

Levy, P., & Goldstein, H. (Eds.). (1984). *Tests in education.* New York: Academic Press.

Medley, D. M. (1973). *Observation Schedule and Record, Form 5 verbal (OScAR 5V).* Charlottesville: University of Virginia.

Michael, J. A., & Weinberger, J. A. (1977). Federal restrictions on educational research: Protection for research participants. *Educational Researcher, 6,* 3–7.

Mitchell, J. V. (Ed.). (1983). *Tests in print III.* Lincoln: University of Nebraska Press.

Osgood, C. E., Suci, G. J., & Tannenbaum, P. H. (1957). *The measurement of meaning.* Urbana: University of Illinois Press.

Simon, A., & Boyer, E. G. (Eds.). (1974). *Mirrors for behavior III: An anthology of observation instruments.* Wyncote, PA: Communications Materials Center.

Soar, R. S., Soar, R. M., & Rogosta, M. (1971). *Florida Climate and Control System (FLACCS): Observer's manual.* Gainesville: University of Florida, Institute for Development of Human Resources.

Spaulding, R. L. (1969). *Classroom behavior analysis and treatment.* Durham, NC: Duke University, Education Improvement Program.

Spaulding, R. L. (1970). *Spaulding Teacher Activity Rating Schedule (STARS).* San Jose, CA: San Jose State University.

Weinberger, J. A., & Michael, J. A. (1976). Federal restrictions on educational research. *Educational Researcher, 5* (1), 3–8.

Weinberger, J. A., & Michael, J. A. (1977). Federal restrictions on educational research: A status report on the privacy act. *Educational Researcher, 6* (2), 5–8.

12

The Analysis of Data

After the research design has been implemented and the data have been collected, the next step in the research process is analysis. Data consist of scores, frequencies, or some type of responses in the form of numbers. They usually have quantitative meaning of some sort, and the usual approach is to perform an appropriate type of statistical analysis.

The term *statistics* has multiple meanings in educational research, but probably its simplest meaning is "bits of information." If one says that 632 students are enrolled in a specific school, this can be considered a statistic. The salary schedule and the numbers of teachers at each salary level for a district are sometimes called salary statistics.

Statistics has a much broader meaning than simply bits of information, however. It also refers to the theory, procedures, and methodology by which data are summarized. It has been suggested that to some people, the terminology of statistics seems like a foreign language; although this may be true, the understanding and use of statistics is not so much a matter of identifying new terminology and symbols for already known concepts as it is a way of reasoning and drawing conclusions. Although the layperson often views statistics as an accumulation of facts and figures, the researcher sees statistics as the methods used to describe data and make sense out of them.

Many different specific statistical analyses are available to the educational researcher, but it is not the intent of this discussion to cover statistical analysis in detail. Rather, the following two purposes will be addressed: (1) to provide the reasoning underlying the use of statistical analysis and (2) to list the more commonly used statistical procedures and the conditions under which they apply. The discussion is intended to emphasize the logic of analysis, not computational procedures.

Descriptive Statistics

After values or scores on some variable have been collected, one of the first tasks is to describe these scores. If 50 fourth-grade students have been tested on arithmetic achievement and their 50 scores comprise the data of the reseach study, how will these scores be described? Simply listing them on a sheet of paper is not adequate.

They must be summarized somehow. Certain information is generated that describes these scores as a group. This information and the process by which it is obtained are called *descriptive statistics*.

Distributions

The group or set of all scores or observations on a variable is called a *distribution*. The 50 arithmetic achievement scores mentioned earlier would be a distribution. If measurement were on an interval scale, rather than listing all 50 scores individually, one would tabulate them according to frequency. That is, each possible score would be listed, and the frequency of its occurrence would be listed, as in Table 12.1. The *f* stands for frequency, and the content of Table 12.1 is called a *frequency distribution*.

Arranging the scores as in Table 12.1 does not provide much information. The largest and smallest scores, 60 and 99, can be determined, and they cover a total of 40 points on the scale of measurement. Thus, the scores have a range of 40 points. Instead of a tabular form, the scores could be put into graphic form by indicating frequency on the vertical axis and the values of the scores on the horizontal axis. Such a representation is called a *histogram*. The histogram for the arithmetic test scores is quite flat and spread out because of the relatively small frequencies and wide range of scores. The histogram brings out the general shape of the distribution, as illustrated in Figure 12.1.

Describing a Distribution of Scores

Although a frequency distribution and a histogram pull together the scores, they are hardly adequate for describing a distribution. All research results cannot be reported by merely producing frequency distributions and constructing related histograms. Measures that more efficiently and fully describe a distribution are needed.

Table 12.1
Frequency Distribution of Arithmetic Test Scores

Score	f	Score	f	Score	f	Score	f
60	1	70	0	80	2	90	1
61	1	71	0	81	2	91	1
62	0	72	4	82	3	92	1
63	0	73	0	83	2	93	2
64	0	74	2	84	2	94	1
65	0	75	3	85	1	95	2
66	3	76	1	86	2	96	0
67	1	77	1	87	1	97	1
68	0	78	2	88	0	98	2
69	1	79	1	89	2	99	1

Figure 12.1
Histogram for the Frequency Distribution of the Raw Scores on an Arithmetic Test

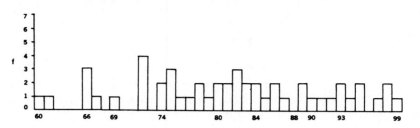

Basically, there are three requirements for describing a distribution of scores or observations. One is that something must be known about where the distribution is located on the scale of measurement. Second, there must be information about how the distribution is spread out—how it is dispersed. The third requirement is the identification of its shape.

> To describe a distribution is to provide information about its location, dispersion, and shape.

Statistics called *measures of central tendency* indicate the location of a distribution. Correspondingly, statistics can be computed to indicate the dispersion of the distribution; these are called *measures of variability*. A histogram could be generated to determine the shape of a distribution, but it would be more common to infer a shape from knowing something about the variable under study. Many educational variables—for example, achievement scores in academic areas—tend to have symmetrical, bell-shaped distributions, which approximate what is known as a normal distribution.

Measures of Central Tendency. Measures of central tendency are commonly referred to as *averages*. In this sense, they give an indication of what a typical observation in the distribution is like. Measures of central tendency are locators of the distribution; that is, they locate the distribution on the scale of measurement. They are points in the distribution that derive their name from a tendency to be centrally located in the distribution.

The mean, median, and mode are the most commonly used measures of central tendency. *Mean,* used in this context, refers to the arithmetic mean. The mean is determined by simply adding the scores in a distribution and dividing by the number of scores in the distribution. The *median* is the point on the scale of measurement below which one-half of the scores of the distribution lie. The *mode,* which is used infrequently, is simply the score with the greatest frequency.

The following illustrates the idea of a locator. There are two distributions of weights, one for adult men and one for adult women. The mean weight of the distribution is 170 pounds for the men and 132 pounds for the women. Both distributions have the same measurement scale—pounds—and both can be located on the measurement scale by their means. If the distributions are set on the measurement scale, the distribution for the men would be located to the right—that is, farther up the scale—than the distribution for the women.

Measures of *central tendency* are points in the distribution used to locate the distribution. The *mean* is the most commonly used measure of central tendency; it is the arithmetic average—the sum of all the scores divided by the number of scores. The *median* is the point below which one-half of the scores lie.

Measures of Variability. In describing a distribution, it is also necessary to know something about its dispersion, or spread of the scores; dispersion is indicated by measures of *variability*. In contrast to measures of central tendency, which are points, measures of variability are intervals (or their squares); that is, they designate a number of units on the scale of measurement.

There are several measures of variability. The *range* is a crude measure, since it provides little information. It gives the number of units on the scale of measurement necessary to include the highest and lowest scores, but it provides no information about the pattern of variation between these scores.

The measures of variability most commonly used are the *variance* and the *standard deviation*. Before these measures can be defined, the meaning of a deviation must be considered. *Deviation* means the difference between an observed score and the mean of the distribution. To determine the variance, the squares of these deviations are summed and divided by the number of scores.[1] If n is the number of scores and $\overline{X}$ (read "X bar") the mean of the distribution, the variance is then given in symbol form by:

$$\text{Variance} = \frac{\Sigma(X_i - \overline{X})^2}{n}$$

That is, the deviation of each score from the mean is squared, the squares of these deviations are then summed, and this sum is divided by the number of observations in the distributions. Thus, the variance is the average of the squared deviations from the mean. The *standard deviation* is defined as the positive square root of the variance.

> The *variance* and the *standard deviation* are the most commonly used measures of variability. They are intervals (or their squares) on the scale of measurement, and they indicate the dispersion in the distribution.

This discussion of measures of central tendency and measures of variability has indicated the need for both types of measures, as well as knowing something about the shape, for describing distributions. When distributions are described as being alike, for example, it is important to specify in what way they are similar. Figures 12.2 and 12.3 illustrate distributions that are alike in one respect yet very different in the other.

Shapes of Distribution.   Distributions may take on a variety of shapes. The shape of the histogram in Figure 12.1 has no specific name, but there are distributions whose shapes have been named. A distribution that (at least theoretically) occurs frequently in educational research is the *normal distribution*. The normal distribution is not a single distribution with a specific mean and standard deviation. Rather, it is a smooth, symmetrical distribution that follows the general shape of the distributions in Figure 12.4 (sometimes called bell-shaped). The specific normal distribution depends on characteristics such as its variability.

When considering the shape of a distribution of scores comprising the data of some research study, the important consideration is not identifying the exact shape of the distribution. Histograms, for example, are seldom actually constructed. The important questions about the distribution's shape are: Theoretically, what shape should the data from this variable take? Can it be assumed that a variable will maintain a specified shape if all possible scores for the group under study are known? What kind of assumed distribution is required for the intended procedures to be

Figure 12.2
Distributions with Like Central Tendency but Different Variability

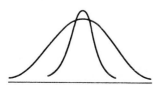

Figure 12.3
Distributions with Like Variability but Different Central Tendency

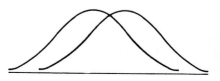

Figure 12.4
Examples of Normal Distributions

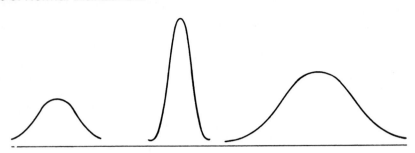

applied to the data? These are the relevant questions to be raised about the shape of the distribution of observed scores. In contrast to working with measures of central tendency and variability, for which the specific values are computed, a researcher usually is less concerned with the actual shape of the distribution of observed scores and more concerned with its assumed or theoretical shape.

Correlation—A Measure of Relationship

Thus far, this discussion has been concerned mainly with describing the scores on a single variable, those of one distribution or set of data. However, in education, researchers are often interested in two variables simultaneously, to determine how they relate to one another. An example might be the relationship between student achievement in language arts and scores on a self-concept inventory.

This extent of relationship is approached through the distributions of scores that represent the two variables. The two distributions are commonly made up of paired scores from a single group of individuals. In any event, the distributions make up sets of ordered pairs of scores. The researcher is interested in how the scores in the distributions correlate or covary. To *covary* means to vary together—high scores with high, low with low, high with medium, whatever the case may be. The relationship between the two distributions (and, hence, the variables represented by the distributions) is based on how the pairs of scores vary together—that is, how changes in one variable compare with changes in the other variable. The degree of relationship or association between two variables is referred to as *correlation*. Thus, correlational studies are concerned not with a single distribution but with two distributions of scores.

The measure of correlation is called the *correlation coefficient* or the *coefficient of correlation*. The correlation coefficient is an index of the extent of relationship between two variables, which can take on values from -1.00 through 0 to $+1.00$, inclusive. The greater the absolute value of the coefficient, the stronger the relationship. The end points of the interval indicate a perfect correlation between the variables, whereas a correlation of 0 indicates no relationship between variables, in which case it is said that the variables are independent. The sign on the coefficient, plus or minus, indicates the direction of the relationship. If the sign is plus, high scores on one variable go with high scores on the other variable. The same is true for low scores on both variables going together. If the sign is minus, the relationship is reverse. That is, low scores on one variable go with high scores on the other variable, and vice versa.

> The *correlation coefficient* is a measure of the relationship between two variables. It can take on values from -1.00 to $+1.00$, inclusive. Zero indicates no relationship.

A plot of the scores of the two variables in a two-dimensional space or plane illustrates the concept of correlation. Each individual has two scores, one for each variable. For the scores to be plotted, the scale of one variable is assigned to the horizontal axis and the scale of the other variable to the vertical axis. The variables may be called X and Y, and each individual's pair of scores may be plotted as a point in the plane. There will be as many points as there are individuals measured on both variables. Such a plot is called a *scattergram*.

Figure 12.5 illustrates a positive relationship between variables and, hence, a positive correlation coefficient. The high values of variable X are associated with high values of variable Y. The opposite situation is true for a negative correlation; that is, high values of variable X go with low values of variable Y, and vice versa, as shown in Figure 12.6. To have a perfect correlation ($+1.00$ or -1.00), the points of the scattergram must fall on a straight line, although such a relationship is extremely rare in education.

For example, intelligence and achievement in science are two variables that seem to be positively correlated; that is, students who score high in IQ tests tend to

Figure 12.5
Scattergram Indicating a Positive Correlation Coefficient

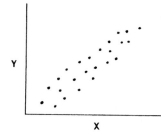

Figure 12.6
Scattergram Indicating a Negative Correlation Coefficient

be the highest scorers on science tests. An example of a negative correlation coefficient might be the relationship between intelligence scores and time to perform a learning task. That is, the more intelligent individuals should tend to perform the task in less time. Two variables that probably have zero correlation are foot size of 14-year-old girls and performance on a mathematics test.

The scatter or dispersion of the points in the scattergram gives an indication of the extent of relationship. As the positions of points tend to deviate from a straight line, the correlation tends to decrease. If a relationship exists but is not +1.00 or −1.00, the points generally fall in an elliptical ring. As the ring becomes narrower—that is, approaches a straight line—the relationship becomes stronger, and the absolute value of the correlation coefficient increases. The direction of the ring indicates whether the relationship is positive or negative, lower left to upper right being positive and upper left to lower right being negative. When the points of the scattergram fall within a circle, there is a correlation of zero. Figure 12.7 presents some examples of scattergrams, with the corresponding magnitude of the correlation coefficient given by r.

The correlation coefficient does not necessarily indicate a cause-and-effect relationship between the two variables. That is, it does not necessarily follow that one variable is causing the scores on the other variable. For example, there usually exists

Figure 12.7
Examples of Scattergrams and Corresponding Correlation Coefficients

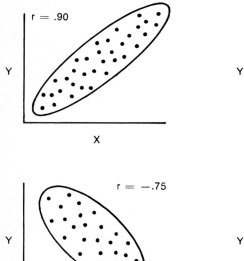
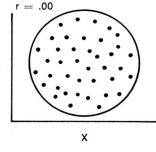
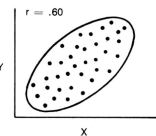

a positive correlation between the salaries paid teachers and the percentage of graduating seniors going on to college in a particular school or system; that is, schools with higher teachers' salaries tend to have greater percentages of graduating seniors going on to college. However, it would be difficult to argue that paying higher teachers' salaries is causing greater percentages of seniors to go on to college or, conversely, that sending seniors to college increases teachers' salaries. A third factor or a combination of external but common factors may be influencing the scores on both variables. Multiple causation is not uncommon when dealing with educational variables.

Uses of Correlation

The correlation coefficient is used extensively as a descriptive statistic to describe the relationship between two variables. It is also used for *prediction*—the estimation of one variable from a knowledge of another variable. The variable from which one predicts is called the *predictor variable,* and the variable being predicted is called the *criterion variable.*

For a prediction study, an equation of the form $Y = bX + a$ can be developed, in which Y is the criterion variable and X is the predictor variable. This is the equation of a straight line that is fit to the scattergram of points representing the scores of the two variables. (It is also called the equation of the regression line of Y on X.) The values of b and a are constants for a given set of data.

The correlation between X and Y has a definite effect on the prediction—specifically, the errors of prediction. The greater the absolute value of the correlation coefficient, the more accurate the prediction. What is meant by accuracy of prediction? Consider the criterion variable, Y. For each Y score, there is a paired X score that can be used in the prediction equation to generate a predicted score, say $\hat{Y}$. Then the difference between the observed and predicted criterion scores can be considered. Such a difference would be symbolized by $(Y - \hat{Y})$, and this difference is an error in prediction. If all the errors of prediction are computed, these would comprise a distribution of error scores. This distribution has a standard deviation, called the *standard error of estimate*. The smaller this standard deviation, the more accurate the prediction. Correspondingly, the greater the correlation between the criterion and predictor variables, the smaller the standard deviation of the distribution of error scores.

Prediction is the estimation of one variable from a knowledge of another. Accuracy of prediction is increased as the correlation between the predictor and criterion variables increases.

Prediction in education is used in a multitude of ways—for example, predicting achievement (criterion) from scores on an intelligence test (predictor). Guidance counselors often use prediction equations composed of more than one predictor variable in attempting to predict success in college or success on a job. Scores on tests such as the Scholastic Aptitude Test (SAT) and the American College Testing (ACT) program are considered predictors of success in college. Often, predictor variables are used in combination rather than singly; for example, SAT score and high school grade point average are used to predict success in college. The correlation coefficient can also be used in inferential statistics, which will be discussed later in the chapter.

Different Correlation Coefficients

Although the concept of correlation is consistent, different correlation coefficients are used under varying conditions. The most commonly used correlation coefficient is the *Pearson product-moment,* which requires at least interval scale measurement, because the means of the distributions must be computed. The most important consideration affecting the choice of a coefficient is the level of measurement of the variables. Table 12.2 lists five of the more commonly used correlation coefficients and the minimum measurement scales required of the variables being correlated.

Example 12.1: Use of Descriptive Statistics

Three sixth-grade teachers in a school are conducting a study involving two types of instruction: individualized and traditional. Both boys and girls are involved in the study; thus, type of instruction and sex of the student are independent variables. The dependent variable is score on a reading achievement test.

The purpose of the study is to describe the distributions of reading achievement scores. It would be important to know the means of those distributions to determine the relative positions. However, knowledge about the variability or dispersion of the distributions is also important. It may be that individualized instruction spreads

Table 12.2
Correlation Coefficients and Minimum Required Measurement of the Variables

Correlation Coefficient	*Measurement of Variables (minimum required)*
1. Pearson product-moment	1. Both variables on interval scales.
2. Spearman rank order	2. Both variables on ordinal scales.
3. Point biserial	3. One variable on interval scale; the other a genuine dichotomy on a nominal or ordinal scale.
4. Biserial	4. One variable on interval scale; the other an artificial dichotomy on an ordinal scale. The dichotomy is artificial because there is an underlying continuous distribution.
5. Coefficient of contingency	5. Both variables on nominal scales.

out the students more than traditional instruction. This would be evidenced by a greater standard deviation for the distribution of reading test scores of those taught by individualized instruction. The research questions can be stated as follows:

1. *What are the means and standard deviations of the distributions of reading test scores for type of instruction: individualized and traditional?*
2. *What are the means and standard deviations of the distributions of reading test scores for sex: boys and girls?*
3. *What are the means and standard deviations of the distributions of reading test scores for the four types of instruction and sex combinations?*

There is a total of 86 sixth-grade students enrolled in the school, 47 girls and 39 boys. The teachers can accommodate 40 students in the individualized instruction, so 20 boys and 20 girls are randomly assigned to this type of instruction. (This means that the remaining 46 students are also randomly assigned to traditional instruction.) The instruction proceeds and after one semester all students are measured on reading achievement. Since type of instruction is an experimental variable, the research design can be described as a posttest only control group design.

Using the notation developed in the chapter on experimental designs, the experiment can be diagrammed as follows:

$$R \ G_1 \text{ (boys)}. \ \ldots \ldots \ X \ \ldots \ldots \ O_1$$

$$R \ G_2 \text{ (girls)} \ \ldots \ldots \ X \ \ldots \ldots \ O_2$$

$$R \ G_3 \text{ (boys)} \ \ldots \ldots \ldots \ldots \ O_3$$

$$R \ G_4 \text{ (girls)} \ \ldots \ldots \ldots \ldots \ O_4$$

In this design, X represents individualized instruction. Although boys and girls within the type of instruction were not separated, they are in the design to show that sex of the student is an independent variable. The Os represent the measurement on the reading achievement test.

The following results appeared.

Distribution	Mean	Std. Dev.
Individualized inst.—both boys and girls	82.1	12.6
Traditional inst.—both boys and girls	76.0	17.2
Individualized inst.—boys	80.6	14.1
Individualized inst.—girls	83.6	11.3
Traditional inst.—boys	71.8	8.0
Traditional inst.—girls	80.2	6.8
All boys	76.2	16.3
All girls	81.9	12.7

Various combinations generated eight distributions that contained varying numbers of scores. For example, the first distribution, individualized instruction for both boys and girls, contained 40 scores, but the second distribution, for traditional instruction, contained 46 scores.

Although distributions with 40 scores and 46 scores would not be distributed as exact normal distributions, the teachers probably would not be much concerned about the distribution shapes, because there would be adequate evidence from previous use of the reading test that sixth-grade scores tend to be normally distributed. Thus, attention would focus on the location and variability of the distributions of scores.

The scores of those students receiving individualized instruction had a higher mean than the scores of those receiving traditional instruction. Overall, girls had a mean score higher than boys, and this pattern was consistent for both individualized and traditional instruction. However, the gap between boys and girls was much greater for traditional instruction than for individualized instruction, the difference between the means being 8.4 and 3.0 points, respectively.

The scores of the boys were more variable than those of the girls overall, and again this pattern was consistent for the two types of instruction. Considering the distributions of boys and girls singly within the types of instruction, the scores for individualized instruction were more variable. However, when the scores of boys and girls were combined, traditional instruction had the greater standard deviation. This was most likely caused by the fact that within traditional instruction, the girls' performance was considerably higher than that of the boys.

Inferential Statistics—Making Inferences from Samples to Populations

In many research situations, the primary interest is in studying a specific group with the intention of generalizing to some larger group. For example, a research director for a large city school system might set up five third grades and expose them to some experimental treatment with the purpose of generalizing to all third-grade students in the system. In a more ambitious vein, the goal might be to generalize to third-grade students in all school systems. In any event, an attempt is made to infer something about a relatively large group by using a subset of that group. The sample is the subset of the larger group, the population. Data are collected for the sample, and from these data the researcher generalizes to the population.

Thus, the researcher has a distribution consisting of sample scores. The descriptive measures, such as the mean and standard deviation computed from the sample data, are called statistics. Correspondingly, there are descriptive measures of the population (these measures are called *parameters*). Of course, parameters are not computed, because data are not collected from the entire population. Rather, inferences are made and conclusions are drawn about parameters from the statistics of the sample—hence, the name *inferential statistics*.

> In *inferential statistics,* statistics are measures of the sample and parameters are measures of the population. Inferences are made about the parameters from the statistics.

The basic idea in making inferences from statistics to parameters is to obtain the sample distribution and then to use accepted statistical techniques to make the inferences to the population. Statistics are computed from the sample data; on the basis of these statistics, generalizations to the parameters (population measures) are made. The theory and methodology underlying this procedure are known as inferential statistics. To construct the reasoning for inferential statistics, some basic concepts of probability and distributions (for the most part theoretical) related to probability must be employed. In this way, the researcher arrives at an established and conceptually sound procedure for making inferences from research data now summarized by statistics—inferences made from the sample to some larger population.

Testing Hypotheses and Estimating Parameters

In analyzing data by means of inferential statistics, we can use one or both of two general procedures: *testing hypotheses* or *estimating parameters.* Hypothesis testing is the more common procedure reported in the research literature. A hypothesis in the context of inferential statistics is a statement (conjecture) about one or more parameters. The researcher goes through a procedure of testing the hypothesis to determine whether or not it is consistent with the sample data. If it is not consistent, the hypothesis is rejected (note that the sample data are not discarded). If the hypothesis is consistent with the sample data, the hypothesis is retained as a tenable value for the parameter.

> In inferential statistics, a hypothesis is a statement about one or more parameters.

A second general procedure of inferential statistics is estimating a parameter. Given a set of sample data, the question can be asked, "What are tenable estimates of the parameter?" There are actually two types of estimates, a *point estimate* and an *interval estimate,* also called a *confidence interval.* A point estimate is simply a single-value estimate of the parameter. It is the value of the corresponding statistic from the sample. An interval estimate is an interval on the scale of measurement that contains tenable estimates of the parameter. Interval estimation is used much more than point estimation.

Estimating a parameter in inferential statistics can be done by point estimation or interval estimation. Point estimation consists of estimating the parameter by a single value. Interval estimation consists of defining an interval (confidence interval) on the scale of measurement that contains tenable values of the parameter. Either way, the estimate is made from sample data.

The procedures of hypothesis testing and related concepts are discussed in the following section and illustrated with examples.

The Concept of Sampling Distribution

Developing the chain of reasoning in inferential statistics requires some concepts of random sampling fluctuation and probability. For example, a researcher might be asked to determine the mean reading achievement score of a large population of eighth-graders. Rather than measuring the entire population, a random sample of 225 students is selected and administered an appropriate reading achievement test. The mean score for the sample is 55.3, and the sample distribution has a standard deviation of 21. This sample mean is a statistic computed from the distribution of 225 reading test scores.

If the curriculum director in charge of reading for this population of eighth-graders hypothesizes, "The population mean is 90," would the researcher go along with this hypothesis? Most likely not. If the curriculum director hypothesizes that the population mean is 56, would the researcher be supportive of this hypothesis? Very likely so.

Why would the researcher go along with the second hypothesis but not the hypothesis that the population mean is 90? The sample mean of 55.3 reflects the population mean, whatever it is. However, the researcher would not expect it to equal the population mean exactly, because the sample mean also reflects random sampling fluctuation. If a population mean of 56 is hypothesized, getting a sample mean of 55.3 is well within the bounds of sampling fluctuation. However, getting a sample mean of 55.3 if the population mean is 90 is very unlikely, because sampling fluctuation is not likely to account for such a difference. The sample mean of 55.3 is a fact that cannot be thrown away, so the researcher rejects the hypothesis that the population mean is 90. Another way of considering this is, "The probability that a sample mean of 55.3 would appear due to random sampling fluctuation, if the population mean is 90, is too small."

However, more than intuition is needed for deciding whether or not probability is too small. The researcher must connect probability with the statistic, using the concept of the sampling distribution of the statistic.

What is a *sampling distribution?* The sample mean of 55.3 will again be considered. If the means of all possible samples of size 225 of the eighth-grade population are computed, they would make a distribution of means. Conceptually, one mean from this distribution was selected when the sample mean of 55.3 was determined. This distribution of means is the sampling distribution of the sample mean. *Sampling distributions* are distributions of statistics, and for the most part they are theoretical— defined for the researcher by mathematical statisticians. Note that the sampling distribution of the mean is *not* the sample distribution.

Conceptually, a *sampling distribution* consists of the values of a statistic computed from all possible samples of a given size.

Continuing the example, the researcher needs to know about the sampling distribution of the mean, which is to know its shape, location (central tendency), and variability (dispersion). The *central limit theorem* describes the sampling distribution of the mean as follows:

Given any population with mean μ and finite variance σ^2, as the sample size increases without limit, the distribution of the sample mean approaches a normal distribution with mean μ and variance σ^2/n, where n is sample size.

This theorem specifies that the sampling distribution of the mean has a mean equal to the population mean, a variance equal to the population variance divided by the sample size (thus, its standard deviation is $\sigma/\sqrt{n}$), and is normally distributed. Since σ is a parameter, it is usually not known, but it can be estimated by the sample standard deviation.

Probability has traditionally been expressed as a proportion between 0 and +1.00; if something has no chance of happening, the probability is 0. In the flip of an unbiased coin, the probability of obtaining a head is .50, which is also the probability of obtaining a tail. The probability of obtaining either a head or a tail is .50 + .50 = 1.00, since one or the other will happen in the flip.

Knowing the sampling distribution, the researcher can bring in the concept of probability. If the area of the sampling distribution is set equal to 1.00, then any area in the distribution between two points on the scale of measurement would correspond to the probability of selecting a value from the distribution between those two points. For the purpose of testing hypotheses about the mean, the researcher is concerned about area as it is located away from the mean of the sampling distribution, where probability will be small.

A new term associated with testing hypotheses, *significance level* or *level of significance,* is now required. Significance level (also designated alpha level or α-level) is a probability such that if the probability that the statistic would appear by chance (due to random sampling fluctuation) if the hypothesis is true is less than this probability, the hypothesis will be rejected. Thus, a significance level is a criterion used in making a decision about the hypothesis. Commonly used significance levels in educational research are .05 and .01. (Occasionally, .10 will be used as a significance level, and the smaller levels of .001 and .0001 may also appear, but they are rarely used.) The significance level is established by the researcher prior to testing the hypothesis, although some researchers report the smallest level attained after testing one or more hypotheses.

The *significance level* (α-level) is a probability used in testing hypotheses. Commonly used α-levels are .05 and .01.

The sampling distribution can now be connected with the level of significance. In the example, the researcher hypothesized about a population mean. The corresponding statistic is the sample mean, and the central limit theorem describes its sampling distribution (normally distributed, located at μ, with standard deviation $\sigma/\sqrt{n}$). If the α-level is set at .05, 5% of the area in the sampling distribution will be designated as the rejection region for the hypothesis. Since the researcher will reject the hypothesis if the sample mean is much larger or much smaller than the hypothesized value, the rejection region must be placed in both tails of the distribution, 2.5% in each tail. Figure 12.8 illustrates the sampling distribution of the mean, with 2.5% of the area in each tail as a rejection region. Sample means that occur within the central 95% of the area would not result in rejecting the hypothesis.

A question arises: How far from the mean in the sampling distribution must one go to reach the cutoff points or critical values that determine the rejection region? From the central limit theorem, it is known that the distribution is a normal distribution, but there are an infinite number of specific normal distributions, depending on the means and standard deviations. Thus, a conversion procedure is needed by which we can go to a common or *standard normal distribution*. This procedure consists of converting the values in a normal distribution to one that has a mean of 0 and a standard deviation of 1.0. The standard normal distribution is given in Table A of Appendix 4. (It is called the *normal curve* in the table title.) The values or scores in this distribution are given in standard deviation units from the mean, designated by x/σ in the table. The x is a score in deviation form; $x = (X - \overline{X})$, where $\overline{X}$ is the mean of the distribution. Corresponding to the x/σ value is given the area in the

Figure 12.8
Area of the Sampling Distribution of the Mean with a Significance Level of .05

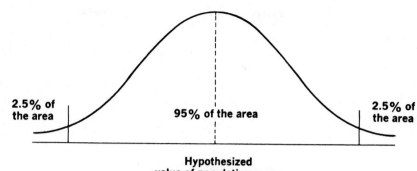

distribution between the mean and the score or value. Thus, if there is a x/σ value (also called a standard score or z-score) of .25, .0987 or 9.87% of the area in the distribution is contained between the mean and a score of .25. With a mean of 0, one-half of the scores in the standard normal distribution will be negative. However, since the normal distribution is symmetrical, the areas for the negative scores will be exactly the same as those for corresponding positive scores, so the table contains only the positive half of the distribution.

> The *standard normal distribution* has a mean of 0 and a standard deviation of 1.0. Scores in the standard normal distribution are given in standard deviation units from the mean.

Why would the researcher reject the hypothesis of the population mean being 90 when the sample mean was 55.3? Recall that the sample distribution had a standard deviation of 21; therefore, the standard deviation of the sampling distribution of the mean[2] is estimated as:

$$s_{\bar{x}} = \frac{s}{\sqrt{n}} = \frac{21}{\sqrt{225}} = 1.40$$

If the hypothesis of the population mean being 90 is true, the sample mean, 55.3, has a standard score of

$$\frac{55.3 - 90.0}{1.4} = -24.8$$

This means that it lies almost 25 standard deviations below the mean. A check of the area in the standard normal distribution shows that it requires 1.96 standard deviation units to leave 2.5% of the area in each tail. Thus, the value of -24.8 is far beyond this criterion or critical value. Therefore, the researcher rejects the hypothesis of the population mean being 90. The probability is less than .05 that a sample mean of 55.3 would appear due to random sampling fluctuation if the population mean is 90. It should be noted that the probability is on the statistic and that the conclusion rests on the hypothesis. In this case, the researcher would say that the statistical test is significant, since the statistic fell in the rejection region as determined by the significance level.

The other hypothesis—of the population mean being 56—can also be considered. If this hypothesis is true, the standard score for the sample mean of 55.3 is:

$$\frac{55.3 - 56.0}{1.4} = \frac{-.7}{1.4} = -.5$$

A check of the normal distribution table shows that a standard score of $-.5$ is well within the standard scores of ± 1.96, which contain the central 95% of the area. Thus, the hypothesis of the population mean being 56 is not rejected; it is tenable. The probability that a sample mean of 55.3 would appear due to random sampling fluctuation if the population mean is 56 is greater than .05. Figure 12.9 indicates the location of the sample mean in the sampling distribution if the population mean is 56.

Building a Confidence Interval—The Example Continued

Developing the concept of sampling distribution was done in the context of a hypothesis testing example. Another procedure in inferential statistics is building a confidence interval, which is an interval estimation of a parameter.

Figure 12.9
Location of the Observed Sample Mean in the Sampling Distribution for the Example

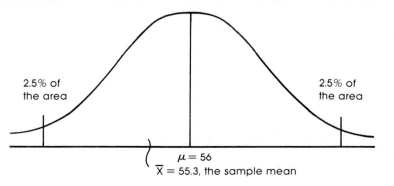

2.5% of the area

2.5% of the area

$\mu = 56$
$\overline{X} = 55.3$, the sample mean

Consider again the example of the 55.3 sample mean on the reading achievement test. Instead of testing hypotheses about the population mean, we want to obtain an interval estimate of it. This requires a confidence level or a confidence coefficient, which is a defined probability that the interval will span the population mean.[3] Commonly used confidence levels in educational research are .95 and .99.

When a confidence interval for the mean is constructed, the interval is constructed symmetrically around the sample mean. If a 95% confidence interval (confidence level .95) for the example is constructed, the researcher wants an interval on the scale of measurement such that it includes 95% of the area of the sampling distribution. Since the sampling distribution is the normal (known from the discussion of hypothesis testing), it is necessary to go 1.96 standard deviation units on either side of the mean. The standard deviation of the sampling distribution of the mean was 1.4. Therefore, to construct the interval, the two points are determined by:

$$55.3 \pm 1.96 \, (1.4)$$

This gives the interval 52.56 to 58.04, and we are 95% confident that this interval spans the population mean.

In general, when constructing confidence intervals, the researcher constructs the interval around the statistic by using the following formula:

$$\text{Statistic} \pm (\text{C.V.}) \, (\text{standard deviation of the statistic})$$

The C.V. is the critical value from the sampling distribution in standard score form, which is necessary to include the proportion of area equal to the confidence level. Then this critical value is multiplied by the standard deviation of the sampling distribution of the statistic to convert from the standard distribution to the scale of measurement for the particular variable. This product is one-half the span of the confidence interval, since its length is contained on either side of the statistic.

Possible Errors in Hypothesis Testing

As mentioned earlier, in inferential statistics a hypothesis is a statement about one or more parameters. The term *null hypothesis* is often used in statistical analysis to describe the hypothesis of no difference or no relationship. (The hypothesis of no relationship is the hypothesis of independence of the variables.) In testing a hypothesis about a population mean, mu (μ), a researcher might have the null hypothesis, H_0: $\mu = 56$, which can be rewritten H_0: $\mu - 56 = 0$, which technically is a hypothesis of no difference. If a researcher is testing a hypothesis about two population means being equal, the hypothesis can be written in the null form as H_0: $\mu_1 = \mu_2$ or H_0: $\mu_1 - \mu_2 = 0$. The null hypothesis is used to locate the sampling distribution for the statistical test.

> The *null hypothesis,* often called a *statistical hypothesis,* is the hypothesis of no difference or no relationship.

Whenever a statistical test is used to test a hypothesis, a decision is made either to reject or not to reject the hypothesis. In either case, there is the possibility that an error has been made becaue the true value of the parameter(s) will not be known, since the entire population is not measured. If a researcher rejects the hypothesis, it is possible that a true hypothesis is being rejected. If a hypothesis is not rejected, it is possible that a false hypothesis is not being rejected.

The test of a specific hypothesis will yield one of four possible results, based on the actual situation in the population and the decision of the researcher. This may be diagrammed in a 2 × 2 table, as in Figure 12.10. The columns in this figure represent the situation in the population, which will never be known for certain. The rows indicate the researcher's decision relative to the hypothesis, and the statements in the box indicate whether the researcher's decision is correct or in error.

If a true hypothesis is not rejected or a false hypothesis is rejected, there is no error. The other two alternatives result in errors—namely, a true hypothesis is rejected or a false hypothesis is not rejected. The error of rejecting a true hypothesis is referred to as a *Type 1* or alpha (α) error. This is because if a null hypothesis is rejected, the probability of having made an error equals the significance (α) level. The error of failing to reject a false hypothesis is called a *Type II* or beta (β) error. Its probability is somewhat complicatd to calculate and depends on a combination of factors. In any one statistical test, there is the possibility of making only one type of error, since the researcher either rejects or fails to reject the hypothesis. Generally, when a statistical test is computed, reducing the risk of one type of error increases the risk of the other type of error.

> In hypothesis testing there are two possible errors, rejecting a true hypothesis or failing to reject a false one. Once the decision is made on the hypothesis, there is the possibility of having made only one type of error.

Figure 12.10
The Four Possible Outcomes in Hypothesis Testing

		True	False
RESEARCHER'S DECISION	Accept	Correct	Error
	Reject	Error	Correct

Inferences from Statistics to Parameters: A Review

Considerable space has been devoted to the discussion of the basic ideas of inferential statistics and relatively elementary examples. The reason for this is that these concepts provide the foundation for testing hypotheses using statistical analyses, which are so extensively used in educational research. There are many specific inferential statistical procedures, and there are numerous statistics texts that describe these very well. Some statistical procedures are quite complex, at least computationally, but whenever inferential statistics are used, the basic reasoning is the same. It is a chain of reasoning used to make decisions when testing hypotheses and estimating parameters. Any reader who masters this reasoning is well on the way to understanding statistical analysis.

When a random sample is used as representative of a population, the inference is from the statistics of the sample to the parameters of the population. The chain of reasoning, illustrated in Figure 12.11, is linked as follows: The researcher has a population and wants to know something about the descriptive measures of this

Figure 12.11
Chain of Reasoning for Inferential Statistics

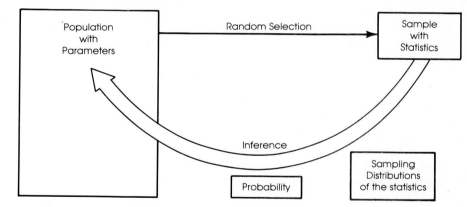

(a) We have a population and we want to make decisions about measures of the population, namely, parameters.

(b) We select a random sample and compute measures of the sample, which are statistics.

(c) The statistics reflect the corresponding parameters and sampling fluctuation.

(d) We observe the statistics, which are the facts that we have, and infer back to the parameters in the light of the sampling distributions and probability.

population—the parameters. It is not feasible to measure the entire population, so a random sample is drawn. The descriptive measures of the sample are statistics, which are calculated. Since the sample is a random sample, the statistics reflect the parameters within the limits of random sampling fluctuation. It is at this point that the sampling distributions of the statistics come in. If the sampling distribution of a statistic is known, it is also known how the statistic behaves—that is, how it fluctuates due to random sampling. The appropriate sampling distribution for a specific statistic has been determined by mathematical theory, and commonly used sampling distributions have been tabled in standard form.

From the information of the statistic and its sampling distribution, we reason back to the parameter. The parameters are never known for certain (unless the entire population is measured, in which case there is no inference or need for inferential statistics). Decisions about parameters are made through testing hypotheses and estimating parameters, usually with a confidence interval.

As mentioned earlier, there are many specific statistical tests used in analyzing data. There are also numerous sampling distributions that are used, depending, of course, on the specific statistic. This is not a statistics text, so it is not intended to develop statistical mastery. However, in the remaining part of the chapter, a compendium of some of the more commonly used statistical procedures is provided. The different statistical tests that apply under different conditions are discussed. Sampling distributions other than the normal distribution are also mentioned as they apply for specific tests. In each case, the hypothesis will be indicated. Most data analyses for research projects are done on a computer, so the important point for any researcher is to understand the analysis.

Parametric Analyses

Undoubtedly the most frequently used analyses in educational research are *parametric analyses,* so called because a set of assumptions, called the parametric assumptions, are required for their application. The example of testing the hypothesis about the reading achievement mean, discussed earlier, involved a parametric analysis.

The parametric assumptions can be summarized as follows:

1. Measurement of the dependent variable, the variable whose data are being analyzed, is on at least an interval scale.
2. The observations or scores are independent, which means that the score of one individual is not influenced by the score of any other.[4]
3. The scores (dependent variable) are selected from a population distribution that is normally distributed. Actually, this assumption is required only if sample size is small—less than 30.
4. When two or more populations are being studied, they have homogeneous variance. This means that the populations being studied have about the same dispersion in their distributions.

With more complex parametric procedures, additional assumptions may be required, but those listed here are the basic assumptions. (Any assumptions involving distributions refer to the population distributions.)

The *t*-Distribution—Another Sampling Distribution

In the discussion about a hypothesized population mean, the normal distribution was used as the sampling distribution of the sample mean—the statistic. Actually, if the sample standard deviation is used to estimate the population standard deviation, the appropriate sampling distribution is not the normal distribution. Rather, it is a family of distributions called the Student *t*-distribution or, simply, *t*-distribution.

The *t*-distributions are identified by *degrees of freedom (df)* values. In an analysis, the degrees of freedom are the number of ways the data are free to vary. Operationally, degrees of freedom are determined by subtracting the number of restrictions placed on the data from the number of scores. When testing a hypothesis about a population mean, the sample mean is computed, which requires the summing of the sample scores. Once $n - 1$ of the scores are determined, the *n*th score, too, is uniquely determined, because it must provide the remainder for the sum. Thus, the degrees of freedom are $n - 1$.

Like the normal distribution, the *t*-distributions are symmetrical and bell-shaped. As degrees of freedom increase, the *t*-distributions become more and more like the normal. Usually, if the degrees of freedom exceed 120, the normal distribution is used as an adequate approximation for the *t*-distribution. Therefore, in the reading achievement example, where sample size was 225, the normal distribution was used as the sampling distribution of the sample mean. The *t*-distributions are given in standard form in Table B of Appendix 4. Degrees of freedom must be considered in their use; this will be illustrated in the following example.

> The *t*-distributions comprise a family of distributions that are the sampling distributions for many statistics. Each *t*-distribution is determined by a degrees of freedom value.

The Difference Between Two Means: An Example Involving the *t*-Distribution. One of the statistical tests for which the *t*-distribution applies is a test for the difference between the means of two independent samples. The previous example involving boys and girls in individualized and traditional instruction will be expanded to illustrate this test. The first assumption is that the individuals represent independent samples selected from their respective populations.

The researcher wants to test the null hypothesis that in the populations, the reading achievement means for boys and girls taught using individualized instruction are equal. Using the Greek letter mu (μ) to represent a population mean, the null hypothesis is written as:

$$H_0: \mu_{IG} = \mu_{IB} \quad \text{or} \quad \mu_{IG} - \mu_{IB} = 0$$

The subscripts on the μ's simply indicate girl and boy, and the I indicates that only individualized instruction is being considered.

Each of these samples contained 20 scores. For each, a mean was computed; therefore, there are $n - 1$ degrees of freedom in each sample. For this particular test, there are $(n_{IG} - 1)$ plus $(n_{IB} - 1)$ degrees of freedom, or $n_{IG} + n_{IB} - 2$. (In general, sample sizes need not be equal.) Therefore, in this example, $df = 20 + 20 - 2 = 38$.

The null hypothesis is: "The populations of boys and girls taught by individualized instruction have equal means, or there is no difference between the population means for boys and girls." Since there are two sample means, the question can be asked, "Is this difference in sample means attributable to random sampling fluctuation?" The statistic to be tested is the difference between the two sample means $\overline{X}_{IG} - \overline{X}_{IB}$, the difference of which equals 3.0 ($83.6 - 80.6$). The standard error of this statistic (the standard deviation of its sampling distribution) is designated by $s_{\overline{X}_{IG} - \overline{X}_{IB}}$, and is found to be 3.24. The appropriate sampling distribution is the t-distribution, with 38 degrees of freedom. The significance level is set at .05.

The computation for the statistical test is:

$$t = \frac{\overline{X}_{IG} - \overline{X}_{IB}}{s_{\overline{X}_{IG} - \overline{X}_{IB}}} = \frac{3.0}{3.24} = .93$$

This computation, which is done here only to illustrate the use of the t-distribution table, provides a value (sometimes called the t-value) in standard score form. It is the standard score of the statistic—in this case the difference between two means—in its sampling distribution.

To check the value of .93 in the table, it is necessary to use the t-distribution for the correct degrees of freedom. The table does not contain 38 df, but 40 is quite close. We look in the column headed .05, level of significance for a two-tailed test, since the null hypothesis of no difference was tested. A critical value of about 2.02 is needed for statistical significance. Since the value of .93 does not reach or exceed this critical value, the statistical test is not significant.

Therefore, the null hypothesis that the population means for girls and boys receiving individualized instruction are equal cannot be rejected. The difference in sample means of 3.0 is well within the limits of random sampling fluctuation. The probability that a difference in sample means of 3.0 would appear by chance if the population means are equal is greater than .05.

Analysis of Variance (ANOVA)

Analysis of variance (ANOVA) is an inferential statistics procedure by which a researcher can test the null hypothesis that two or more population means are equal (H_0: $\mu_1 = \mu_2 = \ldots = \mu_k$). Usually, it is not used for only two means, because a *t*-test for the difference between two means can be used. The sample means, one corresponding to each population mean, are computed and tested simultaneously for any statistically significant differences between them.

The null hypothesis in ANOVA is tested by comparing two estimates of variance.[5] These are put into a ratio form, called the *F*-ratio or *F*-value. The sampling distribution for the ratio of two variances is the *F*-distribution (named after R. A. Fisher). The *F*-distribution is a family of distributions that are generally not symmetrical. They are located between zero and plus infinity, so the numerical values of the distribution are all positive. It requires two degrees of freedom values, one for each of the variance estimates in the ratio, to determine the correct distribution. The *F*-distributions are given in Table D of Appendix 4; their use will be illustrated with a subsequent example.

> ANOVA tests the null hypothesis that two or more population means are equal. A ratio of two variance estimates is computed, and this ratio has as its sampling distribution the *F*-distribution, determined by two degrees of freedom values.

ANOVAs can include one or more independent variables. If one independent variable is included, the ANOVA is a *one-way ANOVA*. If an experiment were conducted in which there were four experimental treatments, there would be the four levels of the independent variable, experimental treatment. The null hypothesis would be, H_0: $\mu_1 = \mu_2 = \mu_3 = \mu_4$; a sample mean for each of the four treatments would be computed and these means would be tested. This would be a one-way ANOVA because only one independent variable is included.

If two independent variables are included simultaneously in an AVOVA, the analysis is called a *two-way ANOVA*. In this case, there is a null hypothesis for each of the independent variables, and an *F*-ratio is computed for each of the groups of sample means from the two independent variables. It may also be possible to compute a statistical test for the interaction between the two independent variables. (Interaction is a combined effect of the independent variables on the dependent variable.) If this is done, the null hypothesis of no interaction is tested. As many *F*-ratios are computed as there are null hypotheses tested. In a two-way ANOVA, there are at most three null hypotheses, one for each independent variable and one for the interaction.

There are also three-way and more complex ANOVAs, which means that more independent variables are included in a single analysis. When more complex ANOVAs are used, increasing numbers of independent variables are included, although in educational research it would be rare to include more than four or five independent variables in a single analysis. The numbers of possible interactions and their complexities (including more than two independent variables in a single interaction) also increases. Data from the factorial designs discussed in the chapter on experimental designs are usually analyzed by what are called *factorial ANOVAs*. This simply means including the two or more independent variables simultaneously in the same analysis.

Example 12.2: One-Way ANOVA

Consider an experiment in which three types of instruction are used for teaching American history—T_1, T_2, and T_3. Random samples of history students are assigned to the three types and, after a period of instruction, are tested on a common history exam. The independent variable is type of instruction. The dependent variable is performance or score on the history exam. The three random samples contain 25, 30, and 33 students, respectively, for T_1, T_2, and T_3.

The null hypothesis is H_0: $\mu_1 = \mu_2 = \mu_3$; that is, the population means of students taught by the three types of instruction are equal. The level of significance is set at .05. The sample means are found to be $\overline{X}_1 = 83$, $\overline{X}_2 = 72$, and $\overline{X}_3 = 80$, and the F-ratio from the ANOVA is $F = 4.93$.

To determine whether or not this F-ratio is statistically significant, we first need to identify the appropriate degrees of freedom associated with it. In this case, the *df* for the numerator of the F-ratio is 2, one less than the number of sample means. In determining the variance among sample means, the mean of all scores (called the *grand mean*) is computed, so one restriction is introduced. In general, for a one-way ANOVA, there are $k - 1$ *df* for the numerator if k is the number of sample means.

The *df* associated with the denominator of the F-ratio is 85. There is a total of 88 scores in the entire ANOVA. When computing the variance estimate for the denominator of the F-ratio, all 88 scores are used, but the mean for each sample is also used in the computation, so three restrictions are introduced. For a one-way ANOVA, there are $N - k$ *df* for the denominator of the F-ratio if N is the total number of scores in the analysis and k is the number of sample means.

Now we have a computed F-ratio of 4.93, with 2 and 85 degrees of freedom. Turning to Table D in Appendix 4, we go down the column for 2 *df* (the *df* for the numerator) to the row for 85 *df* (the *df* for the denominator). There is no row for 85 *df*, but there are rows for 60 *df* and 120 *df*. For each of these *df* values, there are actually four rows of critical values given, one for each of four significance levels. We select α-level .05 and find that the critical value for 60 *df* is 3.15 and that for 120 *df* is 3.07. Since we have 85 *df*, the critical value is about 3.12, based on a straight-line interpolation between the two table values. Our computed F-ratio exceeds 3.12;

therefore, it is statistically significant and the null hypothesis is rejected. The probability statement and the conclusion are as follows:

Probability statement: *The probability that the sample means would have occurred due to random sampling fluctuation, if the null hypothesis is true, is less than .05.*

Conclusion: *The null hypothesis is rejected, and it is concluded that the population means are not all equal. This is the inference to the parameters. The types of instruction are not all equally effective, and we can conclude, at least, that* T_1 *is more effective than* T_2.

If more than two sample means are tested and if the *F*-ratio is statistically significant, the ANOVA does not indicate where the significance lies; that is, only one pair of means may be significantly different, all pairs may be significantly different, or some pairs may be different. We know that at least the two extreme sample means are significantly different (hence, the foregoing conclusion). However, subsequent tests, *post hoc tests,* can be computed to determine specifically which means are significantly different from others. Statistics texts such as those listed near the end of the chapter contain descriptions of such post hoc tests.

Nonparametric Analyses

As indicated earlier, the use of parametric analyses requires certain assumptions about the populations under study. Interval scale measurement is also required so that means can be computed. If these assumptions are not met, it is more appropriate to use nonparametric analyses. These analyses do not require interval scale measurement; ordinal and nominal scale data can be analyzed. Also, for most nonparametric analyses, assumptions about the shape of the population distribution are not required. For that reason, they are often used when small sample sizes are involved.

Nonparametric analyses are part of inferential statistics, so the chain of reasoning for inferential statistics applies. Hypotheses are tested and can be stated in null form. The statistics involved are not means but statistics, such as frequencies. Whatever the case, the statistics are still measures of the one or more samples.

Nonparametric analyses require few if any assumptions about the population under study. They can be used with ordinal and nominal scale data.

The Chi-Square (χ^2) Test and Distribution

The most commonly used sampling distribution for statistics generated by nonparametric analyses is the chi-square (χ^2) distribution. Like the *t*-distribution, the χ^2

distribution comprises a family of distributions, each specific distribution identified by one degrees of freedom value. Unlike the t-distribution, the χ^2 distribution is not symmetrical. Theoretically, it extends from zero to plus infinity. The basic reasoning for using the sampling distribution is the same for the χ^2 distribution as for other distributions, such as the normal and t-distributions. However, because of the non-symmetrical nature of the χ^2 distribution, the rejection region when testing hypotheses is usually contained entirely in the right-hand tail of the distribution.

Numerous hypotheses can be tested by computing a statistic called the χ^2 value. This statistic involves the comparison of observed and expected frequencies—the latter being anticipated on the basis of a null hypothesis—within categories. The χ^2 value is then distributed as the χ^2 distribution with the appropriate degrees of freedom. If a computed χ^2 value exceeds the tabled value (critical value) for a designated significance level, the statistical test is significant and the null hypothesis being tested is rejected. A statistical test involving the χ^2 distribution is commonly called a χ^2 test.

A χ^2 test can be used to test hypotheses about how well a sample distribution fits some theoretical or hypothesized distribution. Such a test is also called a *goodness-of-fit test;* that is, it tests how well the sample distribution fits the hypothesized distribution. For example, we could test a hypothesis that a population distribution from which a sample was selected is normally distributed. The null hypothesis is that the population distribution is normally distributed or is stated as a hypothesis of no difference: "There is no difference between the population distribution and the normal distribution." The statistical test tests whether the sample observations are within random sampling fluctuation of coming from a normal distribution. If the χ^2 value is statistically significant, we would reject the null hypothesis.

One common use of the χ^2 test is with *contingency tables,* which are two-dimensional tables with one variable on each dimension. Each of the variables has two or more categories, and the data are the sample frequencies in the categories. The null hypothesis of independence—that is, no relationship—between the variables is tested. The following example involves a contingency table.

Example 12.3: Contingency Table Using the χ^2 Test

At a liberal arts college, a researcher is interested in student attitude toward compulsory attendance at college convocations. A random sample of students is drawn from each of the four undergraduate classes at the college. Equal numbers need not be selected from the classes. The students in the sample then respond to "agree," "undecided," or "disagree" to compulsory attendance.

The null hypothesis is that the four class populations do not differ in their attitude toward compulsory attendance. Another way of stating the null hypothesis is that class and attitude toward compulsory attendance are independent. This hypothesis does not imply what the extent of agreement or disagreement is; it only implies that the class populations do not differ. Table 12.3 represents sample data in a 3×4 contingency table.

Table 12.3
Observed Sample Frequencies of Response to Compulsory Attendance at College Convoctions

	Category			
Class	Agree	Undecided	Disagree	Total
Freshmen	12	48	20	80
Sophomore	7	20	33	60
Junior	6	19	35	60
Senior	5	3	32	40
Total	30	90	120	240

Table 12.3 contains observed frequencies or sample data. To compute a χ^2 test, expected or theoretical frequencies are required. These expected frequencies are calculated from the sample data by using the marginal totals. The calculations will not be presented here, but Table 12.4 contains these expected frequencies, based on what would be expected if the null hypothesis is true.

In general, contingency tables have $(r - 1) \times (c - 1)$ degrees of freedom, where r and c are the number of rows and the number of columns, respectively, in the contingency table. For the example, the χ^2 test has 6 degrees of freedom. Suppose that we set the significance level at .05. The formula for computing the χ^2 value is given by:

$$\chi^2 = \sum_{i=1}^{k} \frac{(O_i - E_i)^2}{E_i}$$

where O = observed frequency

E = expected frequency

k = number of categories, groupings, or cells.

Table 12.4
Expected Frequencies of Response to Compulsory Attendance at College Convocations

	Category			
Class	Agree	Undecided	Disagree	Total
Freshmen	(12) 10	(48) 30	(20) 40	80
Sophomore	(7) 7.5	(20) 22.5	(33) 30	60
Junior	(6) 7.5	(19) 22.5	(35) 30	60
Senior	(5) 5	(3) 15	(32) 20	40
Total	30	90	120	240

Note: Observed frequencies from Table 12.3 are in parentheses.

When a contingency table is used, $k = r \times c$, the number of cells in the table, which for the example is 12.

The computed χ^2 value for testing the null hypothesis is 33.59, based on the data in Table 12.4. We turn to Table C of Appendix 4, which contains the χ^2 distributions. This table contains critical values. The columns represent area to the right of the critical value point. The rows vary by degrees of freedom. The drawing of the distribution shows how the area is divided.

We set the level of significance at .05, so we go down the column headed .05 to the row corresponding with 6 df and find a critical value of 12.592. Thus, the statistical test is significant and the probability statement and conclusion are as follows:

Probability statement: *The probability that the sample responses would have occurred by chance if class and attitude toward compulsory attendance at college convocations are independent in the population is less than .05.*

Conclusion: *Class and attitude toward compulsory attendance at college convocations are related (not independent) in the college student population. The null hypothesis is rejected.*

An inspection of the frequencies shows that upperclass students tend to have higher frequencies of "disagree" than expected, and lowerclass students have higher frequencies of "undecided" than expected.

The foregoing example illustrates the use of a nonparametric analysis involving the χ^2 test. There are numerous nonparametric analyses, some of which are listed in a table later in this chapter. Specific formulas for computation can be obtained from any applied statistics text. However, the underlying reasoning of inferential statistics still applies.

Correlational Analyses

Correlation was discussed previously as a descriptive statistic that is a measure of the relationship between two variables. Correlational analyses can also be conducted in the context of inferential statistics; that is, hypotheses can be tested about the relationship of the variables in the population based on the correlation coefficient(s) of the sample.

One null hypothesis involving correlation is that the correlation in the population is zero. This is the null hypothesis of independence of the variables in the population, essentially the same as the hypothesis for the contingency table discussed earlier. However, the contingency table itself does not give a measure of the extent of relationship. Also, contingency tables usually deal with ordinal or nominal scale measures, and often the correlation coefficient is a Pearson product-moment coefficient, which has the variables measured on at least an interval scale (see Table 12.2).

The null hypothesis of no relationship between the variables in the population can be tested directly, since the sampling distribution of the sample correlation coefficient is known if this hypothesis is true. The required size of the sample coefficient for a specified significance level depends on the sample size. The larger the sample, the smaller the absolute value of the sample coefficient required to reach statistical significance.

The minimum or critical values of the correlation coefficient required for statistical significance are given in Table E of Appendix 4. Various levels of significance are given in the columns, and degrees of freedom are given on the rows. The degrees of freedom value associated with a particular statistical test is $n - 2$. Two degrees of freedom are lost because a mean is computed for each variable when calculating the correlation coefficient. If the absolute value of the coefficient equals or exceeds the tabled value for the α-level, the null hypothesis is rejected. If not, the null hypothesis is not rejected.

> The hypothesis of independence or no correlation in the population can be tested directly using the sample correlation coefficient.

Example 12.4: Testing the Hypothesis of No Correlation in the Population

The band director of a large high school is interested in whether or not there is a relationship between scores on a divergent thinking test, purported to be a measure of creativity, and scores on a musical aptitude test. The null hypothesis is $H_0: \rho = 0$; that is, the correlation in the population is zero. A random sample of 37 freshmen is selected, and these students are measured using both tests. The level of significance is set at .05.

The sample correlation coefficient, r, equals .21. To test the null hypothesis, we turn to Table E. We use the column headed .05 for level of significance for a two-tailed test, since no direction was hypothesized for the correlation. (It could have been positive or negative.) Since $n = 37$, $df = 35$, we go to the row for 35, and the critical value for the correlation coefficient is .325. The sample r of .21 is less than the critical value; therefore, the null hypothesis cannot be rejected. The probability statement and conclusion are as follows:

Probability statement: *The probability that a sample correlation coefficient of .21 would appear by chance if the correlation in the population is zero is greater than .05.*

Conclusion: *Scores on the divergent thinking test and scores on the musical aptitude test are uncorrelated in the population.*

There are other hypotheses that can be tested about correlation coefficients. One such hypothesis is that the correlation coefficient in the population is a specified value other than zero, which can be written, H_0: $\rho = a$, $a \neq 0$. Another hypothesis is that two population correlation coefficients are equal, which can be written, H_0: $\rho_1 = \rho_2$ or H_0: $\rho_1 - \rho_2 = 0$. However, testing these hypotheses requires a transformation of the statistics, called the Fisher z-transformation, whose sampling distribution is normally distributed. The procedure for testing hypotheses using the Fisher z-transformation is not discussed here but can be found in most applied statistics texts.

Analysis of Covariance

A parametric statistical analysis that involves correlation is the *analysis of covariance*. In Chapter 4, the matter of using a statistical adjustment to enhance control when conducting research was discussed. Analysis of covariance is a procedure for statistical adjustment or statistical control over variation.

Analysis of covariance is closely related to analysis of variance. Essentially, it is analysis of variance with the dependent variable scores adjusted on the basis of the dependent variable's relationship to some other relevant variable. This relationship, of course, involves the correlation between the dependent variable and the other variable. The adjusted dependent variable scores are adjusted so that they are independent of the influence of this other relevant variable, called the *covariate*.

Analysis of covariance is a procedure by which statistical adjustments are made to a dependent variable. These adjustments are based on the correlation between the dependent variable and another variable, called the covariate.

The null hypothesis in the analysis of covariance is that the *adjusted* population means are equal. It can be written as the null hypothesis in analysis of variance, H_0: $\mu_1 = \mu_2 = \ldots = \mu_k$, except that now the μ's represent adjusted population means. As in the analysis of variance, the statistic generated is the ratio of two variances, and the appropriate sampling distribution is the F-distribution. The statistical reasoning is the same, except that conclusions and inferences are now made to adjusted population dependent variable means.

Analysis of covariance is especially useful for situations in which experimental or design control over an extraneous or mediating variable is impossible or undesirable. A researcher, especially one who works in a school setting, often must take intact groups such as classes for research studies. Analysis of covariance may be used to make adjustments, although it should be noted that analysis of covariance does not make the groups equivalent.

Example 12.5: Analysis of Covariance

A researcher is conducting an experiment involving four different types of materials for teaching sixth-grade mathematics. Several sixth-grade classes participate in the experiment, but it is not possible to have random assignment of students to classes or to type of material. Instruction using the materials takes place over one semester, and at the close of this period all participating students are tested by means of a common mathematics test. The intent of the research is to determine whether the different materials have differing effects on mathematics achievement. The null hypothesis is that the means of the populations of sixth-graders taught using the four different materials are equal.

Since there was no random assignment, it is possible that the four groups (samples) taught with the different materials are not equal in academic ability. Thus, if a difference appeared between the group means, it might be due to different abilities rather than different materials, which would be an example of confounding of ability and type of material.

It would be well if the mathematics test scores could be adjusted to remove the effect of different abilities. This could be done through analysis of covariance if a measure of academic ability were available to serve as a covariate. Such a measure would be an IQ test score, preferably one obtained prior to the experiment. (This way the IQ test score could not be affected by the experimental procedure.) The analysis of covariance would adjust the mathematics test score on the basis of the correlation between the IQ test score and the mathematics test score. The null hypothesis tested would be that the adjusted population means are equal. Adjusted means would be those with the effect of academic ability removed. The dependent variable now becomes the math test scores, adjusted for differing IQ test scores.

Using the notation described earlier, this experiment (or quasi-experiment) is diagrammed in Figure 12.12. Note that X_1, X_2 X_3, and X_4 represent the four different types of materials (the levels of the independent variable). There is no random assignment to groups. The Os with odd-number subscripts are measures on the covariate, and the Os with even-number subscripts are adjusted scores on the mathematics test. Actually, the analysis of covariance does the adjusting. The IQ test scores and the mathematics test scores would be entered into the analysis simultaneously.

The study is conducted with 28, 32, 24, and 29 students in groups G_1 through G_4, respectively. Thus, a total of 113 dependent variable scores are analyzed. The level of significance is set at .05 for testing the null hypothesis. Suppose that the following results appear: The adjusted, sample means are $\overline{X}_1 = 78.6$, $\overline{X}_2 = 75.3$, $\overline{X}_3 = 80.4$, and $\overline{X}_4 = 77.1$, and the F-ratio from the analysis of covariance is 1.93. This F-ratio has 3 and 108 degrees of freedom. An additional degree of freedom is lost due to the covariate for the variance estimate of the denominator of the F-ratio, relative to the degrees of freedom had no covariate been used. Referring to Table D of Appendix 4, a critical value of about 2.70 is required for statistical significance. Since the computed F-ratio is less than this critical value, it is not statistically sig-

Figure 12.12
Design of Research Example Involving Analysis of Covariance as a Means for
Adjusting for Possible Initial Differences in the Group

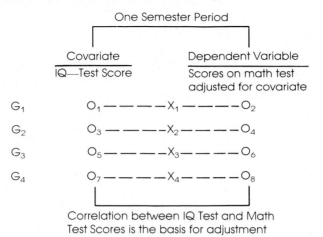

Correlation between IQ Test and Math
Test Scores is the basis for adjustment

nificant and the null hypothesis cannot be rejected. The probability statement and the conclusion are as follows:

> Probability statement: *The probability that the adjusted sample means would appear by chance if the adjusted population means are equal is greater than .05.*

> Conclusion: *The adjusted population means are equal. More generally, the different types of materials have the same effect in the population.*

Choosing the Appropriate Statistical Test

The specific statistical test used depends on the hypotheses being tested, but it is also necessary to meet required assumptions. The levels of measurement of the variables, especially the dependent variable, are important considerations. If we are interested in the relationship of two variables, a measure of the extent of this relationship is a correlation coefficient. The coefficient would be the Pearson product-moment if both variables are at least interval scale measurement. If not, another coefficient appropriate for the measurement would be used.

If the dependent variable is measured on an interval scale and the independent variable is categorical, either ordinal or nominal measurement parametric analyses would be used. Testing hypotheses about means would be examples of using a parametric analysis. When less than interval scale measurement is attained or the parametric assumptions cannot be met, nonparametric analyses are used.

Figure 12.13 contains a somewhat abbreviated decision tree for selecting an appropriate statistical test. By no means does Figure 12.13 exhaust the possibilities of statistical tests, but it does include some of the more commonly used analyses. Also, it indicates the type of hypotheses and conditions that direct the researcher to correlational, parametric, or nonparametric analyses.

Table 12.5 contains a summary of statistical tests and hypotheses that can be tested by the tests. When a *t*-test is indicated, a statistical test involving the *t*-distribution as the sampling distribution is being used. If sample size is large (around 120), the normal distribution is used as an adequate approximation for the *t*-distribution. The table also contains two nonparametric tests not discussed earlier.

Hypotheses, of course, come from the research problem. However, when inferential statistics are used, hypotheses are stated about the population. When the researcher hypothesizes about two population means, for example, two parameters are included in the hypothesis; hence, Greek letters are used in the table.

This discussion of statistical analyses is brief and considers only more commonly used and relatively elementary procedures. Applied statistics texts generally provide specific details about how to conduct analyses. For the interested reader, selected more complex analyses are discussed in Appendix 2. Again, the discussion there provides an overview of the logic and application of the analyses, not computational detail.

The Role of Statistical Analyses

Statistical analyses should be selected to meet the requirements of the research study—describing distributions and relationships, testing hypotheses, estimating parameters,

Figure 12.13
Decision Tree for Selecting an Appropriate Statistical Test

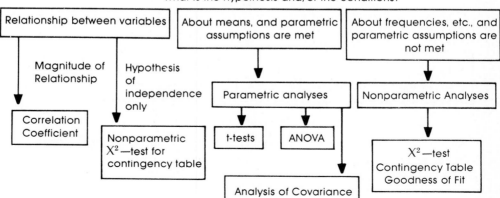

Table 12.5
Some Common Statistical Tests Used in Inferential Statistics

Statistical Test	Hypothesis Tested
Parametric Tests	
t-test (or use of normal distribution)	About a single mean H: $\mu = \alpha$
	Difference between two means H: $\mu_1 = \mu_2$ or H: $\mu_1 - \mu_2 = 0$; used for both independent and dependent samples but formulas differ
Analysis of variance (one-way)	Two or more population means are equal. **H:** $\mu_1 = \mu_2 = \ldots = \mu_k$, from the levels of a single independent variable
Analysis of variance (two-way)	Two or more population means are equal; two independent variables included, and there is a hypothesis for each and their interaction.
Analysis of covariance	Two or more population means are equal after being adjusted for the effect of the covariate.
Nonparametric Tests	
χ^2 test, goodness of fit	A population distribution has a hypothesized shape.
χ^2 test, independence (contingency table)	Two variables are independent in the population.
χ^2 test, median test	The medians of two or more populations are equal.
Mann-Whitney U-Test	There is no difference in the scores from two populations.
Correlational Tests	
t-test (or use of normal distribution)	The population correlation coefficient is zero.
Fisher's *z*-transformation test, which uses the normal distribution	The population correlation coefficient is a specified value. H: $\rho = \alpha$
	Two population correlation coefficients are equal. H: $\rho_1 = \rho_2$ or H: $\rho_1 - \rho_2 = 0$.

and so forth. In essence, analyses assume a service function in the research process. Of course, it is well to plan research so that acceptable analyses can be applied. But a research study should not be done solely because some analysis procedure is available.

> Statistical analyses should not be an end in themselves, but a means to an end. They assume a service function in the research process.

With many research studies, statistical analyses can be applied in a straightforward manner. For example, when a factorial design is used for an experiment, an analysis of variance can usually be applied to the data of the dependent variable. Some studies may require multiple analyses; for example, several parameters may be estimated in a single survey. Different analyses may be used in the same study. For example, in a survey, if data from two groups are compared, a *t*-test might be used; if classification on another variable produces more groups for the data, a one-way analysis of variance might be applied.

Sometimes the research study yields data that are not amenable to a straightforward statistical analysis, and it is necessary to explore possible analyses that will reveal the information contained in the data. An example of this is data from the time series designs, described in the chapter on quasi-experimental research. There may be more than one analysis done, and the specific analyses may depend on the pattern of results and prior knowledge of possible effects or relationships of variables.

Example 12.6: Analysis of Time Series Design Data

A junior high school science teacher has a ninth-grade science class of 32 students. The class is of heterogenous ability and includes both boys and girls. The teacher is conducting a study on health practices beliefs, or attitudes toward health practices. A 30-item health practices inventory is used, and there are two parallel forms available, so the same form does not have to be used for every measurement. The scoring of responses is such that the greater the score, the more positive the attitude. The items of the inventory focus on beliefs and attitudes, not actual behaviors. (An individual might believe that certain practices are beneficial yet not engage in them.)

The teacher includes a 3-week instructional unit on health and science during the course. The research question can be stated as:

Does the instruction of the health and science unit have an effect on the health practices attitudes of the students?

The design for the study is a single-group time series design. The health practices attitude inventory is administered seven times during the academic year: shortly after the beginning of school, close to the end of school, and five times in between. The measurement occasions are about equally spaced at approximately 6-week intervals. Between the third and fourth measurements, the health and science unit is taught. This is the experimental treatment. Students respond anonymously to the inventory, since the interest is in the pattern of group scores, not individual scores.

The mean scores for each of the seven measurement occasions are computed and the pattern is given in Figure 12.14. The means for the seven Os are:

$$\overline{X}_1 = 45.3, \quad \overline{X}_2 = 46.2, \quad \overline{X}_3 = 46.4, \quad \overline{X}_4 = 57.1, \quad \overline{X}_5 = 61.2,$$
$$\overline{X}_6 = 58.5, \quad \overline{X}_7 = 56.8$$

An inspection of the pattern indicates an increase from O_3 to O_4, a continuing increase but at a slower rate to O_5, and then a tapering off of the mean scores. A one-way analysis of variance[6] is computed using the seven measurement occasions as the

Figure 12.14
Pattern of Results for the Time Series Design Example

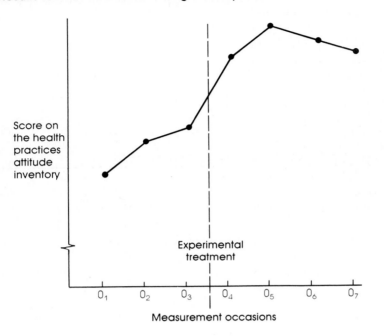

levels of the independent variable for the ANOVA. The *F*-ratio from the ANOVA was statistically significant (α = .05), and a subsequent post hoc test showed the following:

> $\overline{X}_1$, $\overline{X}_2$, $\overline{X}_3$ are not significantly different.
> $\overline{X}_4$, $\overline{X}_5$, $\overline{X}_6$, $\overline{X}_7$ are not significantly different.
> $\overline{X}_1$, $\overline{X}_2$, and $\overline{X}_3$ are significantly different from $\overline{X}_4$, $\overline{X}_5$, $\overline{X}_6$, and $\overline{X}_7$.

Thus, the conclusion is that there is an effect of the instructional unit on the health practices attitudes of the students. An inspection of the pattern of means indicates that the greatest effect is immediate, but there is a continuing effect to the next measurement. Then, for the final two measurements, there is a decline in the means, although not to the preexperimental treatment level.

This result would undoubtedly be of major concern, but other points can also be made about this analysis. The teacher may be interested in other information contained in the data. Consider the following question:

Is there a difference in the mean attitude scores of boys and girls?

Some kind of composite score could be computed for each of the students across the seven measurements. Then the mean for girls and the mean for boys could be determined. Suppose that the results were $\overline{X}_G = 54.8$, $\overline{X}_B = 51.2$. A t-test is computed, and the t-value is statistically significant. Therefore, we could conclude that girls have the higher attitude scores.

When analyzing time series design data, if at all possible, use all of the data in some manner. A t-test for the difference between the mean for O_3 and the mean for O_4 would not be adequate. Such an analysis would omit a good bit of the data and the pattern. If two composite scores were obtained for each student, one preexperimental treatment and the other postexperimental treatment, the overall pattern would be lost. Also, if such a comparison were made, a short-term effect might be lost, since the subsequent decline of the scores might wash it out in the analysis.

Finally, although the analysis procedures suggested here are inferential statistics, there was no random sampling of students for the class. Analyses could have been limited to descriptive statistics—computing means and standard deviations, for example. However, it likely could be argued on a logical basis that the students of the class are representative of some larger populations. If there is no special grouping for the students of this class, they may well be representative of ninth-grade students in the school and possibly of ninth-grade students enrolled in the school over a period of years. Therefore, inferential statistics are often used for such analyses even though a random sample is not used.

The analysis of data from time series designs can be quite complex and is beyond the scope of this book. More extensive analyses are discussed in such sources as McCain and McCleary (1979) and Gottman and Glass (1978).

Using the Computer in Data Analysis

Data analyses can be done by using a hand calculator, especially if it contains special statistical operations. However, most researchers have access to a computer for analyzing data. For many sophisticated analyses, such as factor analyses and multivariate analyses of variance (not discussed in this chapter), a computer is a practical necessity because the complex operations cannot be done by hand. If there are large quantities of data, it is not feasible to do the analysis by hand calculator, regardless of its complexity. Even if an analysis can be done by hand calculator, it is often time saving to use the computer, and the computer enhances accuracy.

Within recent years, microcomputers have come on the scene, such as the IBM Personal Computer and the Apple MacIntosh. Microcomputers are smaller versions of the traditionally large computers found in universities, school systems, and other agencies, but they can perform many of the same functions of data analysis as their larger counterparts. The general procedures for using a computer are the same, regardless of the size, and it is those procedures that are discussed here.

As is true for any tool, the computer must be used properly (and efficiently), and it requires a definite procedure for its use. In the preceding chapter, a sample data file was given, but before the computer can analyze data, it must be told what to do. This is done through a *computer program,* which is a series of explicit instructions for the various operations required by an analysis. Computer programs are called *software,* in contrast to the computer equipment, which is called *hardware.*

To use programs, it is necessary to communicate with the computer. One method of communication is through cards, called *control cards,* which can be used if the data are on data cards. An increasingly more popular approach is through a terminal, which consists of a screen and keyboard similar to that of a typewriter. (The terminal screen was described in Chapter 11.) Commands are typed onto the screen in rows. Microcomputers are similar to terminals in that they have screens and keyboards.

Fortunately, for the behavioral sciences, computer programs are available for commonly used analyses, and even for some that are not so frequently used. If special programming is required, assistance usually can be obtained at a computer center. The remaining tasks in completing an analysis are (1) selecting the appropriate program for the analysis, (2) instructing the computer to use the program (with the data file), and (3) interpreting the results of the analysis.

There are any number of sources of available programs. Microcomputers usually have an entire library of programs available, which may be interchangeable among different brands of microcomputers. Programs typically come in what are called packages of statistical programs. A package contains many programs that have been developed by statisticians. The computer facility or the user then buys the package. The manual that accompanies the package contains detailed descriptions of the programs, necessary commands, and the computer output. *Computer output* is the product of the analysis—large sheets of paper that contain the results in printed form.

Undoubtedly, the three most commonly used statistical packages for behavioral sciences research are:

Statistical Package for the Social Sciences (SPSS[x]), distributed by SPSS, Inc., Suite 3300, North Michigan Avenue, Chicago, IL 60611

Statistical Analysis System (SAS), distributed by SAS Institute Inc., Box 8000, Cary, NC 27511

BMDP Statistical Software, distributed by University of California Press, 2223 Fulton Street, Berkeley, CA 94720

There are manuals and user's guides available for these packages. Because of the changes and advancements made in computers and software, the publications with the packages are being updated almost continuously. Users such as university computer centers usually have the latest versions; at least, they have the versions that fit the programs used by their computer systems.

The tasks in using a computer for data analysis are illustrated in Figure 12.15. To the right are indicated the individuals who do the tasks, with possible sources for assistance. For the most part, the tasks are sequential from top to bottom of the

Figure 12.15
Tasks in Using a Computer for Data Analysis

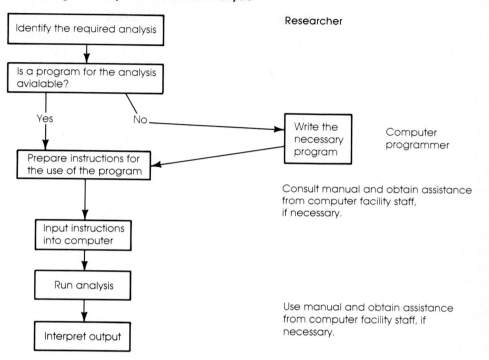

figure. When identifying a program, it may be well to review sample output (usually given in the manual) to make certain the analysis provides the necessary information.

> Data analysis by computer involves a series of sequential steps, using a program available in a statistical package.

Example 12.7: Analysis of Teacher Competency Data

Consider again the data file introduced in Chapter 11—the file consisting of scores on six competency measures for 54 teachers. This is the data file named **FILE: TCHRCOMP DATA.** The research question is:

What are the correlation coeficients among the six competency scores of these teachers?

This question implies descriptive statistics; there is no indication that these teachers were a random sample of some larger population and that inferences are to be made to a population. We will compute the correlation coefficients and also obtain the means and standard deviations of the six scores.

The computer program used for the analysis is for the Pearson product-moment correlation coefficient and is from the SPSS[x] package. It is described in the *SPSS[x] User's Guide* (1983), pages 579–588. To communicate with the computer—that is, inform it of what to do—it is necessary to write a program. For this example, the task consists of typing onto the computer terminal screen the instructions that specify the program from the statistical package the computer is to use, the data file, and so forth. These instructions are given in Figure 12.16. The information contained on each line is also given in the figure. If IBM cards were used, the lines in Figure 12.16 would correspond to control cards.

The analysis is now ready to run. If it were being done through a computer terminal, the command **SPSSX TCHRCOMP** would be typed onto the screen, the ENTER key would be hit, and the analysis would be completed.[7]

When the analysis is completed, the computer will create a file of the results. That file would have the name **TCHRCOMP LISTING.** It would be called up onto the screen and reviewed. Most likely, a printout of it on paper would be desired, which can be obtained by giving the computer the following commands:

ROUTE PRINTER XPRT7
PRINT TCHRCOMP LISTING

The **XPRT7** designates the specific printer to be used—usually the one closest to the computer terminal. Thus, the **XPRT7** here is an example, not a general command.

The computer output containing the results for this analysis is given in Figure 12.17. Actually, the computer output consists of several large sheets. The earlier part of the output contains routine information, including the program file. After the results, there is a page with such information as the data and time of the analysis and the amount of computer time required for the analysis.

To consider the results more conveniently, recall the six competencies:

C-1 Uses a variety of instructional strategies.
C-2 Uses convergent and divergent inquiry strategies.
C-3 Develops and demonstrates problem-solving skills.
C-4 Establishes transitions and sequences in instruction that are varied.
C-5 Modifies instructional activities to accommodate identified learner needs.
C-6 Demonstrates ability to work with individuals, small groups, and large groups.

Figure 12.16
The Analysis Program File for the Teacher Competency Example (SPSS^x)

```
FILE: TCHRCOMP SPSSX     A     UNIVERSITY OF TOLEDO TIME-SHARING SYSTEM


TITLE    TCHRCOMP ANALYSIS
FILE HANDLE TCHRCOMP NAME='TCHRCOMP DATA A'
DATA LIST    FILE=TCHRCOMP RECORDS=1
      /1 ID 1-2 C1 4-5 C2 7-8 C3 10-11 C4 13-14 C5 16-17 C6 19-20
PEARSON CORR C1 TO C6
STATISTICS 1
FINISH
```

Information:

Line 1: File name; programs are also files and since this is an analysis, it must contain SPSSX in the name, which indicates an analysis type file; TCHRCOMP is the descriptive term used earlier.

Line 2: Name given to the analysis.

Line 3: File handle identifies the data file; that name must be the data file name exactly, with DATA as indicating the type of file; A is a necessary notation for the computer.

Lines 4 and 5: Data list indicate how the data are listed; Line 4 shows the file name RECORDS=1 indicates that the data for any individual are contained on one line. Line 5 indicates how the data are coded; the ID number is in columns 1 and 2, score for C1 in columns 4 and 5, etc.

Line 6: Tells the computer to use the program for the Pearson product-moment correlation coefficient, and to correlate the scores for the variables C1 to C6.

Line 7: Statistics 1, tells the computer also to compute the means and standard deviations for the variables.

Line 8: Indicates the program is finished.

The results in Figure 12.17 are quite straightforward. For this particular scoring procedure of the competency data, the scores of a normative group of teachers have been transformed to a distribution with a mean of 50.0 and a standard deviation of 10.0. The means and standard deviations of the six competency scores for this group of 54 teachers are close to these transformed values.

Figure 12.17
Computer Output of Results for the Teacher Competency Example (SPSS^x)

```
15 MAY 85    TCHRCOMP ANALYSIS
10:44:49     THE UNIVERSITY OF TOLEDO          NAS 6650          VM/SP2
```

VARIABLE	CASES	MEAN	STD DEV
C1	54	50.0000	9.9868
C2	54	49.9630	9.9829
C3	54	49.9444	9.9516
C4	54	49.8704	10.0227
C5	54	50.0185	10.0179
C6	54	50.0926	10.0269

- - - P E A R S O N   C O R R E L A T I O N   C O E F F I C I E N T S - - -

	C1	C2	C3	C4	C5	C6
C1	1.0000 (54) P= .	.3058 (54) P= .012	.2954 (54) P= .015	.2422 (54) P= .039	.4720 (54) P= .000	.1877 (54) P= .087
C2	.3058 (54) P= .012	1.0000 (54) P= .	.5865 (54) P= .000	.3961 (54) P= .002	.2466 (54) P= .036	.2326 (54) P= .045
C3	.2954 (54) P= .015	.5865 (54) P= .000	1.0000 (54) P= .	.3340 (54) P= .007	.4003 (54) P= .001	.2033 (54) P= .070
C4	.2422 (54) P= .039	.3961 (54) P= .002	.3340 (54) P= .007	1.0000 (54) P= .	.2336 (54) P= .045	-.1499 (54) P= .140
C5	.4720 (54) P= .000	.2466 (54) P= .036	.4003 (54) P= .001	.2336 (54) P= .045	1.0000 (54) P= .	.3687 (54) P= .003
C6	.1877 (54) P= .087	.2326 (54) P= .045	.2033 (54) P= .070	-.1499 (54) P= .140	.3687 (54) P= .003	1.0000 (54) P= .

(COEFFICIENT / (CASES) / SIGNIFICANCE)   " . " IS PRINTED IF A COEFFICIENT CANNOT BE COMPUTED

The primary focus of interest is on the results of the correlation analysis. The correlation matrix contains three bits of information:

1. the correlation coefficient,
2. the number of scores correlated, and
3. the P-value, which is a level of significance, testing the null hypothesis, that in the population the correlation coefficient is zero.

The final information is of no concern to us in this analysis, since we are interested only in descriptive statistics and not in inferring to a population. The number of scores (cases) correlated here is 54 for all coefficients, since there were no missing data. However, this information can be useful in analyses for which data are missing.

The correlation matrix is a 6×6 square, showing all correlation coefficients between variables in combinations of two. The matrix is symmetrical about the diagonal, and diagonal entries are all 1.00 (the correlation of a variable with itself), so basically there are 15 coefficients of interest, those located above (or below) the diagonal.

The competencies reflect instructional strategies and techniques actually demonstrated in the classroom; they do not deal with activities such as lesson planning or writing test items. Results can be summarized as follows:

1. *All coefficients except one are positive, and the negative coefficient is modest ($-.15$) and the smallest in absolute value of all coefficients.*

2. *Overall, the coefficients are not large; the largest .586, between C-2 and C-3, is the only coefficient above .500. The next largest coefficient, .472, is between C-1 and C-5.*

3. *Overall, C-6 tends to have the lowest coefficients with the other competencies, and it is included in the only negative coefficient (with C-4).*

The conclusions that can be drawn from these results are as follows:

1. *The performance of these 54 teachers is very close to that of the normative group, both in mean scores and in variability of scores.*

2. *Scores on C-6 had the lowest overall coefficients with other scores, except for C-5. Ability to work with groups of differing sizes has little to do with the skills in the other competencies, except for modifying instructional activities to accommodate learner needs.*

3. *When different sized groups are used, there is a tendency to have fewer transitions and sequences in instruction (indicated by the $-.15$ coefficient).*

4. *Using convergent and divergent inquiry strategies goes with problem-solving skills.*

5. *Using a variety of instructional strategies goes with modifying instructional activities.*

6. *Working with different sized groups is close to being independent of using a variety of instructional strategies (evidenced by the .188 coefficient).*

7. *Generally, teachers performing well on one competency have a tendency to do so on others; at least, there is little evidence of inverse relationships.*

These conclusions apply to the performance of these 54 teachers; no use is made of inferential statistics. Any generalizability of these conclusions would have to be argued on a logical basis.

SUMMARY

This chapter has provided an overview of statistical procedures used in the analysis of data. Statistics are often divided into two broad categories: descriptive and inferential. When using descriptive statistics, the characteristics of one or more distributions of scores are computed. In general, descriptive statistics are measures of central tendency, measures of dispersion, and measures of relationship.

In inferential statistics, we attempt to infer from statistics, computed from sample data, to parameters, the measures of the population from which the sample was selected. In general, hypotheses about parameters are tested or parameters are estimated. The chain of reasoning in inferential statistics was identified and discussed in the chapter.

The computer has been around for some time, but within recent years computers have become increasingly accessible, especially with the availability of microcomputers and computer terminals conveniently located for the user. There are many, many programs for statistical analysis available. In this chapter, some of the more commonly used statistical packages were identified and the general process of analyzing data by computer was described. An example of data analysis was also provided.

It was not the intent of this chapter to provide computational procedures or to have the reader perform statistical analyses. Rather, the intent was to provide a rationale for the analysis of data and to review the reasoning of some of the more common analyses. Numerous applied statistics texts are available that include computational procedures for statistical analyses commonly used in educational research. The following is a sampling of such texts:

1. Bartz, A. E. (1981). *Basic statistical concepts in education and the behavioral sciences* (2nd ed.). Minneapolis: Burgess.
2. Bohrnstedt, G. W., & Knoke, K. (1982). *Statistics for social data analysis.* Itasca, IL: Peacock.
3. Clayton, K. N. (1984). *An introduction to statistics for psychology and education.* Columbus, OH: Merrill.
4. Glass, G V., & Hopkins, K. D. (1984). *Statistical methods in education and psychology* (2nd ed.). Englewood Cliffs, NJ: Prentice-Hall.
5. Hinkle, D., Wiersma, W., & Jurs, S. (1979). *Applied statistics for the behavioral sciences.* Boston: Houghton Mifflin.

KEY CONCEPTS

Statistics
Descriptive statistics
Distribution
Frequency distribution
Histogram
Central tendency
Mean
Median
Variability
Standard deviation
Variance
Shape of a distribution
Correlation
Prediction
Criterion variable
Standard error of estimate
Central limit theorem
Standard normal distribution
t-distribution
Analysis of variance (AN-OVA)
F-distribution
Nonparametric analyses

Inferential statistics
Testing hypotheses
Null hypothesis
Estimating parameters
Point estimate
Interval estimate
Sampling distribution
Level of significance
Confidence level
Statistical significance
Type I error
Type II error
Parametric analyses
Parametric assumptions
Chi-square (χ^2) distribution
Contingency table
Correlation analyses
Analysis of covariance
Computers
Computer program
Statistical package
Computer output

EXERCISES

12.1 Discuss the difference between measures of central tendency and measures of varibility. Why are both types of measures necessary in describing a distribution? Present some examples of educational variables that are alike in measures of central tendency but different in variability and some that are alike in dispersion but different in location.

12.2 The end–of–year reading level of approximately 1,000 first-grade students of a city school system is to be estimated. The entire population cannot be tested. Discuss how sampling and inferring from statistics to parameters would be used. Identify the statistic and parameter involved in this situation. Reconstruct the chain of reasoning used to arrive at some conclusion about the reading level of the entire first-grade population.

12.3 Distinguish between a statistic and a parameter in the context of inferential statistics. Discuss the role of the sampling distribution. Describe what we mean by sampling distribution, and give an example of a sampling distribution.

12.4 Suppose that a group of 150 teacher education students has been measured on three measures of scholastic achievement and a measure of performance on a professional knowledge exam. Thus, there are four dependent variables. In connection with what research questions would we do the following:

a. Compute only descriptive statistics for the four dependent variables?
b. Use inferential statistics?
c. Compute correlation coefficients between pairs of the dependent variables?

12.5 The mean science achievement on an objective test of a ninth–grade student population is hypothesized to be 85. A sample of 20 students is randomly selected from the population and given the science test. A t-test is then computed using the sample data, and the t-value is found to be 3.12. Using the .05 level of significance, find the appropriate t-distribution and decide whether or not you would reject the hypothesis. What value of t is necessary to reject the hypothesis at the .05 level?

12.6 A researcher is estimating the mean performance score of a large fifth–grade population on a science achievement test. A large sample of size 400 is selected and tested, and the sample mean found to be 88. A 95% confidence interval is constructed to be 86.5 to 89.5. Suppose that the standard deviation of the population was estimated by the sample standard deviation. What is the appropriate sampling distribution for constructing the interval? Would this sampling distribution change if the sample size had been 25? If so, how? Suppose, with the given mean, that the researcher had constructed a confidence interval of 85.5 to 89.5. Do you think there might have been an error, and, if so, why? If a 90% confidence interval had been constructed, would this interval be shorter or longer than three units?

12.7 A study is being done in which the professional attitudes of four different populations of teachers are being surveyed. Random samples are selected from the populations and measured on an attitude inventory that has interval scale measurement. Thus, means are computed for all samples. An analysis of variance is used to analyze the data. What is the advantage of ANOVA over computing t-tests for the differences between means? What is the null hypothesis being tested? Suppose that we are interested not only in differences in attitudes among the four populations but also in differences between male and female teachers. Could the possibility of such a difference be determined in the same analysis? If so, explain how the ANOVA would be extended.

12.8 Suppose that we have a variable measured on an ordinal scale with five categories. Four independent samples are measured on this variable. The hypothesis is that these four samples were drawn from a common population. A chi-square test is computed and found to be statistically significant at $\alpha = .05$. What is the conclusion about the populations from which the samples were selected? Give the associated probability statement.

12.9 Suppose that in Exercise 12.8 the variable is attitude toward school and that the four samples were students selected from grades 4, 5, 6, and 7. (The data are in a 5 × 4 contingency table.) State the hypothesis of independence. If the χ^2 test is significant at $\alpha = .05$, what is the conclusion? What if the χ^2 test is not statistically significant?

12.10 Define the two possible types of errors in hypothesis testing. Why is there always a possibility of making an error when a decision is made about a hypothesis in inferential statistics?

12.11 Would you expect the correlation coefficients for the following combinations of two variables to be positive or negative, and low, moderate, or high in absolute value?

a. Reading performance of fifth-graders and distance a baseball is thrown.
b. Performance on a mathematics exam and score on an attitude toward school inventory.
c. IQ test score and performance on a geometry exam.
d. Divergent-thinking test score and time required to solve problems in logic.
e. Reflex time score and number of errors on a simulated driving task.

12.12 Briefly review the meaning of a correlation coefficient, and describe how the correlation coefficient can be used as a descriptive statistic and how it can be used in inferential statistics.

12.13 A researcher tests the performance of two random samples of individuals on a task. The performance of each is scored as poor, fair, good, or excellent. A t-test for the difference between means is then computed on the sample data. This result is interpreted as being significant at the .01 level but not at the .05 level. However, it is decided to reject the null hypothesis and conclude that the sample measures are in fact different. The researcher is then concerned about the probability of having made a Type II error. There are several errors in reasoning and procedures in this example. Identify these errors.

12.14 Briefly review the chain of reasoning in hypothesis testing. Consider such points as the meanings of *statistic* and *parameter,* the probability, and the inference to the population.

12.15 If you are affiliated with a university or college—for example, as a graduate student—investigate the computer services for data analysis. Check such factors as the available statistical packages and whether or not computer terminals and microcomputers are available.

NOTES

1. The symbol Σ is the summation operator and indicates to sum what follows, in this case, the deviations. The i on the X_i indicates the individual scores used, in this case, the first through the nth. When no numbers are indicated over the Σ, it indicates that i takes on values 1 through n.

2. The standard deviation of the sampling distribution of the mean is also called the *standard error of the mean*. In general, the term *standard error* is used in inferential statistics to indicate the standard deviation of the sampling distribution of a statistic.

3. This probability statement is not quite technically correct. If there is a 95% confidence level, for example, and if all possible intervals for a given sample size are constructed, 95% of those intervals would span the population mean. In practice, for a specific problem, only one interval is constructed, and that interval either does or does not span the population mean. However, there is 95% confidence that it does span the population mean.

4. Scores from the same individual in repeated measures analyses violate this assumption, but there are ways to deal with the lack of independence in the analyses.

5. Estimates of variance in ANOVA are called *mean squares,* commonly symbolized by MS.

6. In this situation, the parametric assumption of independence of the observations is violated, since the same students are measured seven times. The ANOVA would have to be computed as a repeated measures analysis. It is not necessary to provide the computational details of such an analysis here, since we are focusing on the interpretation of results.

7. If there was an error in the instructions, the analysis would not run, but an error message would appear on the terminal screen, indicating that there was an error and where it was located in the instructions (program file).

REFERENCES

Gottman, J. M., & Glass, G. V. (1978). Analysis of interrupted time-series experiments. In T. R. Kratochwill (Ed)., *Single subject research: Strategies for evaluating change*. New York: Academic Press.

McCain, L. J., & McCleary, R. (1979). The statistical analysis of the simple interrupted time-series quasi-experiment. In T. D. Cook & D. T. Campbell (Eds)., *Quasi-experimentation: Design and analysis issues for field settings* (pp. 233–294). Chicago: Rand McNally.

SPSS, Inc. (1983). *SPSS^x User's Guide* (pp. 579–588). Chicago: SPSS Inc.

13

Writing Research Proposals and Reports

A good bit of information about educational research, both projected and completed, is communicated through the written word. Regardless of how able a methodologist or how knowledgeable, the researcher must also be able to communicate through the written word. Sooner or later, graduate students prepare theses or dissertations, which have been preceded by proposals for the research reported in them. Funding agencies require proposals and reports, and publishing in professional journals is certainly widespread. Thus, the use of the written word in communicating about educational research is extensive.

This chapter discusses two types of written documents: the research proposal, which involves writing about intended research, and the research report, which describes completed research. Although there is a difference of intent, research proposals and reports do have many characteristics in common. Within each there is also variation, especially in length, depending on such factors as the extent of the research, the audience for whom it is being prepared, and, if funded, the requirements of the specific funding agency. This chapter will focus on those characteristics and qualities that make for good proposals and reports.

It is not feasible to include an entire dissertation, journal article, or proposal in this chapter. However, examples of parts of such written accounts will be included. Appendix 1 contains a research proposal prepared as an exercise for a research methods class. Although it contains the necessary components of a proposal, it is relatively brief and should not be considered an adequate proposal for a dissertation, for example. Readers will have to project the description and examples into their own situations when preparing proposals and reports.

Major Sections of the Research Proposal

Preparing a research proposal, as has already been noted, involves writing about a proposed rather than a completed research project. In proposal writing, we discuss what research is contemplated, why it is being contemplated, and how we intend to do it. The sections of the research proposal reflect answers to these assertions. The names of headings and subheadings within the research proposal may differ somewhat for different institutions or agencies. For example, some may require a section entitled "Procedures," others, "Description of Activities," and still others, "Methodology." Sometimes, a "Narrative" section is suggested for which the writer can supply subheadings. However, there is a general format for the content of a research proposal that develops a logical sequence from the statement of the problem in an adequate context and continues through concluding sections, which often provide a justification for the research. (Concluding sections for proposals submitted to funding agencies usually consist of budgets and résumés of the researchers.)

Research proposals discuss what research is intended, how it is intended to be done, and why the research is intended; the sections of the proposal are then directed to these issues.

A general outline for the sections of a research proposal is provided in Figure 13.1. Proposals generally follow this format in order, although in some cases topics may be interchanged. For example, sometimes a major section called "Introduction" is used with such subheadings as "Identification of the Problem" and "Definition of Terms." The significance of the proposed research may be discussed earlier in the proposal. In some instances, a discussion of need for the research is included early in the proposal.

The topics for the major body of the research proposal are contained between the dashed lines in Figure 13.1. Usually, preliminary information is required in the form of a cover page that consists of the title of the proposed research, the names of the investigators, and the institution or agency where it will be done. An abstract may also be required.

The same general criteria apply for all sections of a research proposal. Writing should be concise, with continuity between and within the sections. The description of what is to be done should be comprehensive but not wordy. The sections should be arranged so that the reader can easily follow the train of thought. At this point, comments will be made about the various sections.

Identification of the Problem

Considerable discussion about stating research problems and hypotheses has been presented in an earlier chapter, and those comments will not be repeated here. It is important in a proposal that the problem stand out—that the reader can easily recognize it. Sometimes, obscure and poorly formulated problems are masked in an

Figure 13.1
General Outline for the Sections of a Research Proposal

Cover Page   }
                    Preliminary information as required
Abstract   }
— — — — — — — — —

Identification of the Research Problem   }
    Introduction   }   What research is
    Definition of Terms   }   intended
Review of the Literature   }

Methodology or Procedures   }
    Design   }   How the research will
    Data Collection Procedures   }   be done
    Data Analysis   }
Significance of the Proposed Research   }
                                          }   Why the research is
    Anticipated Outcomes   }   intended
    Relevance to Education   }
— — — — — — — — —

(Other items as required)
    Budget
    Staff Resumes
    Appendices

extended discussion, and a reviewer has difficulty recognizing the problem. If that happens, the remainder of the proposal suffers severely in the review.

The extent of the elaboration on the problem varies somewhat with the magnitude of the intended study. In the research proposal in Appendix 1, the problem is stated very early (second paragraph). It is stated in terms of determining effects. One quite general hypothesis is also presented.

Since research reports as well as proposals require identification of the problem, examples can be selected from the research literature. An example of a concise problem statement is given by Austin and Draper (1984, p. 599):

> The purpose of this investigation was to relate all levels of academic achievement with a more explicit definition of classroom social status.

As any problem statement, this must be presented within a context, and such a context is provided by the authors. They also define the specific sociometric designations that will be used.

In a study for a dissertation dealing with cognitive style and concept learning, Rains (1976) formulated her problem statement as follows:

> . . . to add to the existing information concerning individual success of field-independent and field-dependent students in concept attainment subsequent to initial exposure in a cooperative group. (p. 4)

This statement was followed by two specific research questions:

> *Question 1.* What are the effects of the following variables upon group performance in a concept learning task: (a) homogeneous or heterogeneous grouping with respect to cognitive style, (b) sequence of problem complexity—5-, 4-, 3-, 2-attributes or 2-, 3-, 4-, 5-attributes, (c) instructions—minimal or strategy?
> *Question 2.* Subsequent to initial learning in groups of four, what are the main and interactive effects of the following variables upon individual performance on a concept learning task: (1) cognitive style—field-independent or field-dependent, (b) group structure—homogeneous or heterogeneous quads, (c) sequence of problem complexity in training—5-, 4-, 3-, 2-attributes or 2-, 3-, 4-, 5-attributes, (d) instructions in training—minimal or strategy? (p. 5)

The problem, as identified, is from the dissertation, but it was the same problem as in the dissertation proposal. The problem is well stated, and the questions specifically list the variables to be studied.

As necessary, terms used in describing the research problem should be defined, including any terms that might be ambiguous or broad. Sometimes, operational definitions of variables to be measured are provided in the methodology section, where the measurement is described, rather than in the statement of the problem, especially if operational definitions are somewhat complex.

Review of the Literature

The *review of the literature* provides the background and context for the research problem. Proposals may vary considerably in the length of the review. Dissertation proposals often contain 15 or more double-spaced pages in the review. In any event, it is seldom if ever possible to include every potentially relevant study in the review. Thus, the proposal writer must be selective. The following points are important to remember in preparing the review:

1. Select studies that relate most directly to the problem at hand.
2. Tie together the results of the studies so that their relevance is clear. Do not simply provide a compendium of seemingly unrelated references in paragraph form.
3. When conflicting findings are reported across studies—and this is quite common in educational research—carefully examine the variations in the findings

and possible explanations for them. Ignoring variation and simply averaging effects loses information and fails to recognize the complexity of the problem.

4. Make the case that the research area reviewed is incomplete or requires extension. This establishes the need for research in this area. (Note: This does not make the case that the proposed research is going to meet the need or is of significance.)

5. Although information from the literature must be properly referenced, do not make the review a series of quotations.

6. The review should be organized according to the major points relevant to the problem. Do not force the review into a chronological organization, for example, which may confuse the relevance and continuity among the studies reviewed.

7. Give the reader some indication of the relative importance of results from studies reviewed. Some results have more bearing on the problem than others, and this should be indicated.

8. Provide closure for this section. Do not terminate with comments from the final study reviewed. Provide a summary and pull together the most important points.

One of the marks of a knowledgeable reviewer is the ability to select pertinent information, tie it together to provide an understandable and accurate background for the problem, and demonstrate the continuity between the ideas in the literature and the research problem. The proposal writer should avoid statements implying that information on the problem is very limited or that the review has revealed no information about the problem. The proposal reader will be very suspicious of such statements (and rightly so) and will likely interpret them as a lack of knowledge on the part of the writer rather than as a gap in the literature. The review of literature should reveal that the writer has a good grasp of the area in which research is intended.

> The review of the literature provides the background and context for the research problem. It should establish the need for the research and indicate that the writer is knowledgeable about the area.

Methodology or Procedures

This section of the research proposal provides a detailed description of what is to be done and how it is to be done. Although some proposal guidelines may not require subheadings, in this section headings such as "Design," "Sample," "Data Analysis," and any others that might apply to the specific research problem will not only aid the writer in identifying and describing the various activities but should also help the proposal reader understand the continuity of the activities. One of the most common errors in this section is that the methods and procedures are lacking in detail. The explanation should be complete enough so that the reader has no question about what is anticipated and how it will be accomplished.

The design can be described by a specific name. For example:

> *A pretest-posttest control group design will be used involving four groups, three experimental and one control, with sex and grade level included as independent variables, giving a 4 × 2 × 4 factorial design.*

Many designs have relatively common usage in the research literature, and their descriptive titles can be used. A title can be coined for a design so long as it is descriptive and appropriate.

As applicable, the following project activities, materials, and so forth, should be described in this section in addition to the general research design:

1. Measurement instruments to be used or developed.
2. Individuals participating in the research (subjects).
3. Sample (design and numbers).
4. Experimental procedure if the intended project is an experiment.
5. Data collection procedures.
6. Data analysis (specific analyses to be used).

Each of these topics should be described in detail as it applies to the specific project. If there are potential weaknesses in the design or potential difficulties in doing the research, the writer should describe what will be done to compensate for or eliminate them. For example, there might be the possibility of extraneous variables being confounded with independent variables. Their possible effects should be discussed, and the discussion should indicate how they will be controlled or eliminated. Occasionally, writers are under the misconception that it is sufficient to identify a difficulty without providing a solution. Identifying a potential problem is not the same as solving it, and certainly, indicating that nothing can be done about the problem is no solution.

The matter of sampling is an example of the need for specific detail. The sampling plan must be viewed in terms of the external and internal validity of the research project. When sampling is used, the researcher invariably is attempting to make inferences to a larger population, so care must be taken in selecting the sample so that it represents the population.

In a study involving a sample of high school seniors from a single state, for example, it is not adequate to say that a random sample of seniors will be selected from the high schools of the state; the sampling plan should be described in detail. Assuming an adequate operational definition of a high school senior, the writer should indicate how all members of the population will be identified. What types of information will be available that will include all seniors who fit the definition? Are stratifying variables to be used? If so, what are they, and why are they important? Will it be necessary to sample through an intermediate unit? What will be the replacement procedure if selected units decline to participate?

These types of questions should be carefully answered. For example, if stratified random sampling with proportional allocation is the sampling design, the stratifying variables should be operationally defined, and it should be clear to the reader that students can be identified in terms of stratifying variables from the population information. It would not be adequate to indicate simply that size of district will be a stratifying variable. The definition of the categories for the stratifying variable would have to be given—for example, less than 2,000 students, 2,000–5,000 students, and so on. Information should be provided about the source, probably a state document, on which the size of the district will be based, and it would be well to provide a rationale for the specific categories of the stratifying variable. A complete description of this type will provide the reader with evidence regarding how and why the sample will be selected.

The discussion of the procedures usually follows a somewhat chronological order of how they will be done. This makes it easier for the reader to recognize the continuity of the various procedures. If the intended research is adequately conceptualized by the proposal writers, they should be able to explain what they intend to do. The important thing is to have an appropriate and complete description.

> The *methodology* or procedures section is really the heart of the research proposal. The activities should be described in detail, and the continuity between them should be apparent.

Significance of the Proposed Research

Although empirical results certainly may be important, research is seldom conducted solely for the purpose of generating data. At the least, the proposal writer must indicate the anticipated contribution to the existing knowledge in the area. This contribution in itself is a potential outcome of the research.

Other anticipated outcomes relate to the practical significance of the research. What will the research results mean to the practicing educator? Will the results, regardless of outcome, influence programs or methods? If the research will set the stage for deciding on alternative courses of action for improving education, this can be a significant contribution. What will be improved or changed as the result of the proposed research? How will the results of the study be implemented, and what innovations will come about?

Answers to these questions suggest outcomes that may take different forms. One outcome, for example, might be a product, such as a revised curriculum or a description of how a segment of a curriculum in a specific area might be changed. Another product might be a process for the improvement of learning. A third example of an anticipated outcome would be a program for dealing with disruptive behavior or reducing the number of dropouts. The research in and of itself may not generate a curriculum or program—these would likely have to be developed after the research is completed—but the research provides the basis for such development. It is important to indicate the potential relevance of the research to such outcomes.

The case for the relevance to education is made to some extent when the need for the research is established through the review of the literature. When discussing the significance of the research, it is important to indicate how the anticipated results of this research will tie in to the research results already reported in the literature. The proposal writer should not hesitate to use previously cited or additional references at this point.

The relevance of the research problem to education is pretty well established through the review of the literature and the background for the problem. The case for the results being relevant to education rests on the effects of the anticipated outcomes. If these outcomes have potential benefit or impact, either practically or theoretically, the case can be made. Since this connection exists, the potential relevance to education depends on the likelihood that the anticipated outcomes will be attained.

> The significance of the proposed research can be established on the basis of the anticipated outcomes, which may be in the form of products or processes.

Other Sections of the Research Proposal

The sections of a research proposal described thus far comprise the major body of the proposal, but other sections may be appropriate for specific proposals. Indeed, funding agencies often require certain routine informational sections and, certainly, a budget. Brief comments on these sections are provided here.

Cover Page. The cover page contains introductory information for the proposal: the name of the proposed project, the author of the proposal or principal investigator, and the institution. Some funding agencies have standardized cover pages that may contain additional information, such as a budget total.

Abstract. An abstract is a brief summary statement of the proposal content. At the very least, it contains a statement of the research problem. Abstracts are usually limited to a maximum number of words; seldom do they exceed one page.

Budget. When a proposal is submitted to a funding agency, a budget is required; it is usually placed near the end of the proposal. When a budget is prepared, the proposal writer should use the guidelines of the funding agency to which the proposal will be submitted and those of the institution through which it is being submitted. This should take care of such matters as overhead and benefit rates. Failure to follow guidelines usually results in considerable budget recalculation later and, possibly, unanticipated negotiations. An inappropriate or poorly constructed budget may result in rejection of the proposal.

Research conducted for theses and dissertations usually is not externally funded, so budget preparation is not a concern. A graduate student may be doing research for a dissertation through some larger, externally funded project. However, in such situations a separate budget is seldom developed for the dissertation research.

Staff Résumés. Staff résumés or vitae consist of summaries of the experience, education, publications, and research activities of individuals who will work on the proposed project. Again, résumés are commonly required for externally funded research.

Appendices. If there is considerable supplementary information that may be relevant to the proposal content, it can be placed in an appendix. Appendices contain information that would distract from the continuity of the proposal if it were contained in the main body of the proposal. In a proposal submitted for external funding, an appendix might contain a description of the resources of the researcher's institution, such as the library and computer facilities.

The Evaluation of Proposals

When a graduate student submits a proposal for research (dissertation or other), it is usually reviewed by a professor or a committee of professors. The usual criteria of a relevant problem, evidence of knowledge in the area, appropriate methodology, and good continuity in the proposal apply when a proposal is reviewed. Funding agencies also develop criteria for the evaluation of proposals, and these often appear in guidelines for proposal preparation.

Evaluation criteria of funding agencies are quite general and quite similar across agencies. Except for special criteria, such as the reasonableness of the budget, the evaluation criteria of funding agencies are similar to those for any proposal, including a dissertation proposal. The evaluation focuses primarily on two characteristics: (1) the significance of the proposed research and (2) the quality of the proposed research. The Teaching and Learning Research Grants Program of the National Institute of Education awards 70 out of a possible 100 points to these two characteristics (35 points each).

The following kinds of issues are considered in evaluating proposals relative to the two characteristics:

Significance of the Proposed Research
1. Contribution to basic knowledge relevant to the solution of educational problems
2. Contribution to educational theory

3. Contribution to the development of methodological tools, either for educational practice or research
4. Contribution to the solution of educational problems, either long-range or short-range
5. The potential generalizability of anticipated results
6. The potential of anticipated results to influence the improvement of educational practice

Quality of the Proposed Research
1. The extent to which the writer shows a thorough knowledge of relevant prior research
2. The extent to which prior research is related to the proposed research
3. The comprehensiveness and appropriateness of the research design
4. The appropriateness of the instrumentation and the methodology
5. The appropriateness of the anticipated analyses
6. The likelihood that the proposed research can be completed successfully as described

Funding agencies usually consider the qualifications of the principal investigator and other research project staff, and they may require a statement about facilities and resources available to the researcher. The reasonableness of the budget has already been mentioned. However, this characteristic usually receives few points, because budgets can be negotiated if they do not seem appropriate to fiscal officers of the funding agency.

Implicit criteria are also applied in evaluating any proposal. The writing should be technically correct and neat. The content of the proposal should be well organized, and there should be good continuity from section to section and within sections. Generally accepted formats, including size of margins and spacing, should be followed.

The preparation of a good research proposal is no small task. When submitting a proposal to a funding agency, it is important to follow the proposal preparation guidelines of that agency. Some agencies do not have guidelines; they will accept any standard format. Private foundations and funding programs within large agencies often fund projects for specific purposes or only in certain areas. It is important to be aware of these limitations; there is little point in submitting proposals that do not correspond to agency interest.

When submitting a proposal for dissertation research, it is important to describe as much of the procedural detail as possible. The proposed research should be within the capabilities, resources, and time of the researcher. Thinking things through carefully will avoid difficulties and delays later.

Major Sections of the Research Report

One distinguishing characteristic of the different types of research reports is length. The professional journal article may vary from 5 to 15 pages, but it is seldom longer.

Restrictions of space for individual publications limit the length of journal articles. Dissertations and technical reports submitted to funding agencies are usually longer, commonly around 100 pages and, in some cases, considerably longer. (Sometimes appendices contain substantial amounts of supplementary information that increases the length.) The length of paper prepared for a professional meeting depends on the time allotted for presentation. However, such papers tend to be similar in length to journal articles, and many papers later appear as journal articles.

Even with the different types of research reports, there are some common characteristics in the way they are organized and presented. The sections follow, to some extent, the same sequence as those in a research proposal. However, a research report contains sections dealing with results and conclusions, which are not found in a proposal. In a proposal, there is a great deal of emphasis on how the research will be done. The emphasis for a report shifts to the results and the implications of those results.

> In a *research report* the writer describes completed research. There are discussions of what research was done, how it was done, and the results and conclusions of the research. The significance of the research is also addressed.

The sections of the research report begin with the identification of the problem and continue through the conclusions and implications. The sections have different formats for different types of reports. For dissertations or long reports, they usually take the form of chapters, whereas journal articles and papers commonly contain headings. Figure 13.2 contains the organization for a dissertation and commonly used titles of chapters. The headings within the chapters will vary somewhat, depending on the specific research. In Figure 13.2 general headings are given, which would be used as applicable in a specific dissertation. As an example from a specific dissertation, the table of contents from Bowdouris (1984) is given in Figure 13.3. The research for the dissertation consisted of a survey of science teachers.

The general criteria for preparing a good proposal also apply to writing a good research report. In Chapter 3, Figure 3.15 provided a checklist that can be used for reviewing a research report. It can also be used as a guide to writing a report and making certain that the elements listed are covered adequately. Comments on the major sections of a research report are provided here.

Introduction, Including the Statement of the Problem

The statement of the problem from the Rains (1976) dissertation appeared earlier in this chapter and will not be repeated here. In a dissertation, there is usually a several page buildup to the problem statement, depending, in part, on the complexity of the research problem.

Figure 13.2
The Organization for a Dissertation, with Chapter Titles

Title page

Acknowledgements (as appropriate)

Abstract

Table of contents

List of tables

List of figures

Chapter 1 - Introduction
    Purpose of the study
    |Statement of the research problem (including hypotheses)
    Definition of terms

Chapter 2 - Review of the Literature

    In this chapter the headings will relate specifically to
    the areas reviewed relevant to the problem.

Chapter 3 - Method or Procedure

    Research design

    Description of subjects

    Measuring instruments

    Materials (as necessary)

    Data collection procedures

Chapter 4 - Results

    Results by variables   ⎫
    Results by experiments ⎬ possible organizations for reporting results
    Summary of results   ⎭

Chapter 5 - Conclusions, Recommendations and Implications

    Summary of the study

    Conclusions

    Recommendations for further research

Bibliography

Appendices

Articles in professional journals do not have space for a long buildup to the problem, so the context for the research must be established concisely. This introduction may include the brief review of the literature as well, unless the article deals with historical research or, for some reason, the results of numerous other studies must be brought in. For example, Cunningham and McCown (1984/1985) include the statement of the problem in their introduction as follows:

> The present study investigated the effects of prior knowledge and processing level on the retention of connected discourse. A substantial number of studies (e.g. Anderson and Myrow, 1971; Bower, 1974; Crouse, 1971; Myrow and Anderson, 1972) have demonstrated retroactive interference effects between successively presented passages when test questions consisted of item stems identical or similar for both passages but which required different answers for the two passages. Interference theory predicts response competition and decreased recall and recognition for items of this type, and this is exactly what previous research has shown. None of the above-mentioned studies, however, have attended to the role of prior knowledge or level of processing. (pp. 77–78)

Additional references are given throughout this introduction, which also serves as a literature review.

In a study involving third- and fifth-grade students, Paris, Cross, and Lipson (1984) identified the hypothesis of their research as follows:

> The underlying purpose of this project was to test the hypothesis that by teaching children about the existence, use and value of reading strategies we could improve their reading comprehension. Accordingly, the study provides an experimental test of the relation between metacognition and reading comprehension. (p. 1242)

This statement of the problem comes just prior to a section entitled "Method." There are approximately three pages of background and literature review preceding the hypothesis.

Review of the Literature

In professional journal articles, the literature review often does not have a separate heading; it is incorporated with the introduction and background. Because of space limitations, the writer must make decisions about which references will be included and cited. The pertinent information must then be provided succinctly and tied together to provide a context for the problem.

As indicated in Figure 13.2, an entire chapter is usually reserved for the review of the literature in a dissertation. The headings in chapters are specific to the study. This chapter in the Rains (1976) dissertation had the following headings:

Figure 13.3
Sample Table of Contents from a Dissertation

TABLE OF CONTENTS

		Page
ACKNOWLEDGEMENTS		ii
I.	INTRODUCTION	1
	Statement of the Problem	5
	Significance of the Study	7
	Definition of Terms	9
	Limitations	10
II.	REVIEW OF THE LITERATURE	11
	Local Curriculum Development	11
	External Influences on Curriculum Development	13
	Textbooks and Instructional Materials	15
	State Influences on Curriculum	18
	Educational Standards	20
	College and University Influences	22
	Professional Organizations	22
	Pressure Groups	23
	Foundations	25
	National Commissions and Studies	28
	Federal Government	29
III.	DESIGN OF THE STUDY	36
	Study Objectives and Research Hypotheses	36
	Description of Instrument Used in Study	39
	Procedures	42
	Sample Selection	42
	Collection of Data	44
	Data Analysis	45
	Summary	45

Figure 13.3 (continued)

Source: Bowdouris (1984). Reprinted by permission of the author.

Effects of Grouping
        General Task Performance
        Concept Acquisition
        Transfer from Group Learning to Individual Performance
Studies on Cognitive Style
        General Task Performance
        Concept Attainment
Instructions and Concept Attainment
Concept Complexity
Summary (p. v)

The ideas from the various studies referred to in the review of the literature should relate to each other and to the research problem. A common error is to present ideas from individual studies as little packages within themselves, which makes for a disjointed presentation. A related error is to treat each study in a mechanical way, regardless of relative importance.

The writer should avoid excessive use of quotations. In the context of the research problem, the ideas from several sources usually can be tied together better by the writer's own words than by a series of quotations. The ideas from the review of the literature should be integrated into a logical discussion focusing on the research problem.

The writer is not obligated to discuss information from every source listed in the bibliography. Often, in an article, three or four main points are brought in from an equal number of sources. Additional references may be listed in the bibliography to complement the information from the sources discussed. In the discussion of the review of the literature the writer should demonstrate an adequate knowledge of the problem and the research related to it. An extensive bibliography with almost no discussion is not evidence of an adequate review of literature.

Methods or Procedures

The parts of this section describe how the research was done. How much description is necessary? A good rule to follow is that the description should be detailed enough so that a reader could replicate the study. Descriptions in dissertations tend to be very detailed, because the writer is demonstrating mastery of the methodology as well as the appropriateness of the methods used.

The methods or procedures section of a professional journal article is often two or three pages in length and usually contains subheadings. The following are typical subheadings:

Instruments (or Instrumentation)

Subjects

Data Collection (Experimental Treatment if an experiment)

Materials

Statistical Analysis

Not all of these subheadings would likely be used in the same article.

The following, from Cronnell (1985), is an example of an introductory paragraph for the procedures section of a journal article:

> The study used an extant set of writing samples produced by third- and sixth-grade students as part of an end-of-year assessment in a large school district in the metropolitan Los Angeles area. The third-grade students wrote a story about a drawing of a monkey and an elephant on roller skates at a starting line. The sixth-grade students wrote a letter to convince a friend to watch a favorite television program. (p. 169)

The introductory paragraph is then followed by detailed information about the subjects and the analysis of the writing samples.

The following description of the subjects—the participants in the research study—is from McCormick and Levin (1984, p. 384):

> *Subjects.* Two schools from similar socioeconomic areas in a midwestern university community furnished 220 eighth-grade students (ranging in age from 13 to 15) for the experiment. In all, 11 classrooms were included, with 6 tested according to one question order and 5 according to another (to be discussed shortly). Each of the five instructional conditions (three keyword and two control variations) included 44 subjects.

Descriptions of instrumentation, experimental procedures, and data collection are usually quite straightforward. However, because they tend to be somewhat long—even in journal articles they may be a page or more—one will not be reproduced here. The reader can select almost any article in such journals as the *American Educational Research Journal* and read good examples of descriptions of methods.

The order of presenting the various topics in a methods section is somewhat arbitrary. One logical order is the sequence in which the activities of the topics occurred in conducting the research. It is possible that two or more of the activities were worked on simultaneously. However, the research project usually progresses from the development of the design and selection of the participants through data analysis.

Results

Results are the products of the analysis of the data. Very often, they consist of statistics generated by the analysis, but they may also consist of summary statements synthesized from other documents, as in a historical study, or field notes, as in ethnographic research.

The important concern in writing a results section is to present the results in a clear, well-organized manner. Results can be organized in a number of ways. If several dependent variables are included in the study, the results may be grouped according to dependent variables—for example, grouping achievement measures separate from attitude measures. Sometimes, results are reported in the order of the hypotheses. If several experiments were included in a study, the results could be organized in the order in which the experiments occurred. This is often done in dissertations based on a series of experiments. In ethnographic research, results may consist of a sequential narrative describing what happened. Whatever organization makes the most sense and facilitates reader understanding should be used.

Tables can be used effectively for summarizing results, especially if a report involves a large amount of statistical material. The content of a table should be clear to the reader. This may seem to be an obvious statement, but tables are sometimes confusing and puzzle the reader.

There are some relatively straightforward rules to follow when constructing tables:

1. The title should state specifically what the table contains, including the referent or source of the content.
2. Appropriate subheadings should be included for rows and columns.
3. The number of different types of information a table contains should be limited. For example, means and standard deviations may go together, but correlation coefficients probably would not be included in the same table.
4. Spacing in the table should be such that numbers are clearly separated. Do not crowd.
5. If possible, tables should be limited to a single page. A table that will fit on one page should not be split into two pages.
6. The table should follow the first reference to it as closely as possible.
7. Table formats should be consistent within a report.
8. An excessive number of lines should not be included. Horizontal lines may be used to set off headings, but vertical lines are seldom necessary. The information should not appear caged.

Figure 13.4 contains a sample results table, showing the title and headings. Note that the title does not simply state that the table includes means and standard deviations; it indicates the source of the means and standard deviations.

It should be noted that not all results, including statistical results, appear in tables. If the number of entries is small, say, three or four, it is not necessary to construct a table to report the results. For example, for reporting three means, the writer might insert a sentence such as: "The means of the three experimental groups were 87.3, 84.7, and 95.2, respectively." In the context of the paragraph, it should be clear what "respectively" means.

> Tables can be used effectively for summarizing results, but their content must be adequately labeled and logically organized.

Figure 13.4
Example of Title and Headings for a Table Containing Results

Table 0.0
Means and Standard Deviations of Fifth-Grade Students
on Academic Measures

Measure	Experimental Group 1		Experimental Group 2		Control Group	
	Mean	Standard Deviation	Mean	Standard Deviation	Mean	Standard Deviation
Reading						
Arithmetic						
Spelling						
Science						
Social Studies						

Conclusions, Recommendations, and Implications

The final section of the research report consists of conclusions, recommendations, and implications. Commonly called the "Conclusions" section, it may also go by such names as "Conclusion and Discussion" or "Conclusions and Recommendations." In any event, the term *conclusions* almost invariably appears in the title of the section.

This section usually begins with a brief restatement of the research problem and, possibly, the main points of how the study was done. The conclusions must follow logically from the results and should avoid undesirable repetition of the results section. One common error in dissertations is that the writer is reluctant to draw conclusions and, instead, repeats results and passes them off as conclusions.

> The results of a research study are the products of the data analysis. Conclusions are the inferences and the like that the researcher draws from the results.

The number of conclusions drawn depends in part on the complexity of the results. Supposedly, at least one substantial conclusion can be drawn; otherwise, it would hardly be worth conducting, much less reporting, the research.

This section, in addition to conclusions, should contain a summary and discussion that tie in the conclusions with those of related studies and indicate how the research either supports or refutes conclusions of other writers. Recommendations and implications may also be presented. Almost any study has some limitations, methodological or otherwise, and they should be identified. The results, and possibly the limitations, should generate recommendations for future research in the area. Speculations can be discussed in this section, but they should be clearly distinguished from direct conclusions. Implications should stay within the mainstream of the research study, and tangential areas should be brought in only when their relevance can be described clearly.

Other Sections of the Research Report

As indicated in Figure 13.2, preliminary sections are often found in a research report, and a bibliography and possibly an appendix often follow the conclusions section. The title page usually follows a prescribed format similar to that of the title page of a proposal. Acknowledgments, a table of contents, and any necessary lists are self-explanatory. This leaves the abstract for the preliminary information.

Abstract. The abstract of a research report is similar to that of a research proposal, except that it describes what was done instead of what is contemplated. It contains a brief summary of the results. Again, abstracts can vary in length, depending on the report, but they usually do not exceed one double-spaced typed page.

Many professional journals require abstracts for reports they publish. These abstracts tend to be quite brief. An example of such an abstract, from McCormick and Levin (1984, p. 379), is as follows:

> Seventh- and eighth-grade students were presented fictitious biographies to remember. Keyword students were instructed to use a prose-learning adaptation of the mnemonic keyword method, and control students were left to their own devices. In the initial experiment, each of three variations of the keyword method, differing in terms of the manner in which the mnemonic images were organized, resulted in significantly higher levels of recall than did control instructions. Moreover, the keyword groups could be distinguished from the controls, as well as from one another, on the basis of qualitative differences in their recall patterns. In a subsequent experiment, the basic findings were replicated using both immediate and delayed recognition tests.

A brief overview of what was done is provided. The results are summarized without going into detail.

Bibliography and Reference List. Toward the end of a research report, following the conclusions section, appears the list of references and, possibly, a bibliography.

The American Psychological Association (1983), distinguishes between a reference list and bibliography as follows:

> Note that a reference list cites works that specifically support a particular article. In contrast, a bibliography cites works for background or for further reading. (p. 111)

Professional journals commonly require reference lists, not bibliographies. An extensive report such as a dissertation would require a bibliography.

A bibliographic entry contains a full description of the work, the name of the first author, inverted with last name first, followed by the names of co-authors. Titles of books, monographs, and journals are underlined. There are slight variations in format, as suggested in different editorial style sources. The format given in the *Publication Manual of the American Psychological Association* (1983) has all authors' names inverted with last name first, the year of publication following the author(s) names, and article title with only the first words of the title, subtitles, if any, and proper names capitalized. No quotation marks are placed around article titles. Sample entries for an article and a book are as follows:

> Hughes, D. C., & Keeling, B. (1984, Fall). The use of model essays to reduce content effects in essay scoring. *Journal of Educational Measurement, 21*(3), 277–281.
>
> Light, R. J., & Pillemer, D. B. (1984). *Summing up: The science of reviewing research.* Cambridge, MA: Harvard University Press.

The format used by the American Psychological Association is widely accepted, especially among professional journals in the behavioral sciences.

Entries are placed in the bibliography in alphabetical order, using the last name of the first author. If two or more works by the same author are included, the last name is not repeated in subsequent entries but is substituted for by a long dash, followed by a period. The two or more listings for an author are alphabetized by initial letter of the title, excluding "A," "An," or "The." If entries include publications of which the author is sole author and others co-author, those of sole authorship appear first.

Appendix.   An appendix is included only if it is necessary—for example, when there are materials that do not fit well in the main body of the report. Several types of materials can be placed in an appendix: self-constructed measuring instruments, such as tests or questionnaires; tables of raw scores; or related data. A large volume of related results tends to make the main report cumbersome and difficult reading, and such results can be placed in the appendix. Separate appendices should be used for different types of materials. The appendices appear at the end of the report, following the references or bibliography.

Putting a Report Together

A research report, especially a long one, is seldom conceptualized and written in one sitting. It is usually helpful to work from an outline. Sections often need reworking and rewriting. Generally, revision is a normal part of the task, and the report is usually improved by subsequent revisions, additions, and deletions. Critical reviews (conducted in a positive sense) of initial drafts by knowledgeable colleagues are helpful. Self-criticism or review is also valuable, but it is usually most valuable after the writer has let the report sit for a short time, perhaps a week to 10 days. Explanations may not be so obvious and logical as they seemed to be during the initial writing, and omissions and confusing statements may become more apparent.

There are always several technical considerations when preparing a research report. Correct grammar and spelling and accepted uses of tenses are required. The past tense is used to report research findings, both one's own and those reported by others. For example:

Students in grades five and seven obtained mean scores of 25.3 and 31.6, respectively.

The present tense is used to refer to the presentation of data and well-accepted generalizations; for example, "Table 1 contains the means of all grades, separated by geographic region."

There are acceptable formats for presenting content in a report. Some institutions and associations have their own requirements about such things as margin size, table format, and presentation of graphs and figures. These are technical concerns, and it is simply a matter of knowing the rules and following them. Most institutions will accept any recognized standard format.

There are a number of publications dealing with format and style for preparing reports. The reference desks of most college and university libraries have copies of several such publications. The content of these manuals, guides, or handbooks includes explicit detail about format and style, including how to handle variations of the usual references, and so forth. The following are six excellent publications:

American Psychological Association. (1983). *Publication manual of the American Psychological Association* (3rd ed.). Washington, DC: APA.

Campbell, W. G., Ballou, S. V., & Slade, C. (1982). *Form and style: Theses, reports, term papers* (6th ed.). Boston: Houghton Mifflin.

Gibaldi, J., & Achtert, W. S. (1984). *MLA handbook for writers of research papers* (2nd ed.). New York: Modern Language Association of America.

Manheimer, M. L. (1973). *Style manual: A guide for the preparation of reports and dissertations.* New York: Marcel Dekker.

Mullins, C. J. (1983). *A guide to writing and publishing in the social and behavioral sciences.* Malabar, FL: Krieger.

Turabian, K. L. (1976). *Student's guide for writing college papers* (3rd ed.). Chicago: University of Chicago Press.

SUMMARY

Writing the research report is generally the concluding activity of a research project. With the satisfactory completion of the written report, a well-done piece of research should be a source of satisfaction and pride. But research is a never-ending activity, and the results of one study often lead to new research problems and projects. Conducting research is a valuable learning experience regardless of the level of sophistication of the research procedures. Educational research should be viewed as a continuing activity in which each specific project adds to the store of knowledge or provides solutions to educational problems.

KEY CONCEPTS

Research proposal   *Budget*
Research report   *Staff résumés*
Identification of the problem *Appendix*
Review of the literature   *Conclusions and recom-*
Methodology   *mendations*
Significance of the research   *Bibliography*
Cover page   *Reference list*
Abstract

EXERCISES

13.1 Select a research problem of limited magnitude and write a proposal about doing a research project on the problem. Include in your proposal a statement of the problem, a context for the problem, and a brief (about two double-spaced pages) review of the literature. You may follow the general format of the proposal in Appendix 1. Comment on the anticipated procedures, the analysis that would be used, and the potential significance of the project. Be brief and concise, and pay special attention to the continuity of ideas. Use your mastery of the content of previous chapters to present an adequate and correct methodology for doing the research study. Include a bibliography. This is a writing task of the magnitude of a short term paper.

13.2 Select a research report, probably an article, that deals with an educational topic in your area or one about which you have some knowledge. Read the report through the results (or data analysis) section, but do not read the conclusions. Write a conclusions section of your own. After you have completed your conclusions, compare them to the conclusions of the report.

13.3 Suppose that you were conducting a research study in which the scores of school-age children, grades 3–6 inclusive, on a battery of ten academic and skills areas tests (dependent variables) were analyzed. Within each grade, there was an experimental and a control group, with one-half of the students in each group. Means and standard deviations for each grade, separated by experimental and control groups, were calculated. The analysis also included a series of *t*-tests on the differences between the means of the experimental and control groups within each grade. After this was completed, all scores on the ten tests were correlated in combinations of two. Develop an organization for presenting these results in tables. Provide names and headings for your tables. Number the tests 1 through 10 for convenience.

13.4 Consult a form and style manual such as the *Publication Manual of the American Psychological Association* (3rd ed.) and indicate the editorial style for entries in a reference list for the following:

a. A book that has a corporate author (rather than one or more persons)

b. An English translation of a book

c. An edited book

d. An article or chapter in an edited book

e. An article in a professional journal that has five authors

f. A revised edition of a book

REFERENCES

American Psychological Association. (1983). *Publication manual of the American Psychological Association* (3rd ed.). Washington, DC: APA.

Austin, A. M. B., & Draper, D. C. (1984). The relationship among peer acceptance, social impact, and academic achievement in middle childhood. *American Educational Research Journal, 21*(3), 597–604.

Bowdouris, G. J. (1985). *An assessment of Ohio public school teacher instructional practices and perceptions towards aerospace education as related to the educational services provided to teachers by the NASA Lewis Research Center: A federal government influence on public school curriculum.* Unpublished doctoral dissertation, University of Toledo.

Cronnell, B. (1985). Language influences in the English writing of third- and sixth-grade Mexican-American students. *Journal of Educational Research, 78*(3), 168–173.

Cunningham, D. J., & McCown, R. R. (1984/1985). The retroactive effects of prior knowledge and elaborative processing on prose retention. *Journal of Experimental Education, 53*(2), 77–85.

McCormick, C. B., & Levin, J. B. (1984). A comparison of different prose-learning variations of the mnemonic keyword method. *American Educational Research Journal, 21*(2), 379–398.

Paris, S. G., Cross, D. R., & Lipson, M. Y. (1984). Informal strategies for learning: A program to improve children's reading awareness and comprehension. *Journal of Educational Psychology, 76*(6), 1239–1252.

Rains, M. J. (1976). *The effects of cognitive style, group structure, instructions and training sequence on acquisition and transfer in concept learning.* Unpublished doctoral dissertation, University of Toledo.

Appendix 1:
Sample Research Proposal*

RESEARCH PROPOSAL

The Effects of Parent Participation vs. No Parent
Participation in the Remediation of Speech and
Language Deficient Students

Identification of the Problem

Of recent interest in the fields of special education and speech pathology is the development of parent-implemented remedial programs and parent education. It has become increasingly apparent that professionals must involve parents of exceptional children in developing and implementing remedial programs for their children. Generally, this involvement has two underlying purposes. First, it is necessary for parents of special children to understand the learning problems and disabilities of their children and the need for particular treatment. Second, a number of researchers have found that substantial improvement in children's skills has been noted in programs where parents were teaching their own children.

It is this second purpose that is the major focus of this proposed research study. The research problem is one of determining the effects of parent participation versus no parent participation in the treatment (education) of preschool students who are displaying varying degrees of speech and language deficiency in their development. The research hypothesis is:

The preschool students who receive professional service plus parent intervention will show greater improvements in speech and language proficiency than those receiving professional service only.

*This proposal was written by Ms. Bonita Fumo and is reproduced by permission of the author.

Definition of Terms

Since terms used in special education are often somewhat unique to the area, the terms relevant to this proposed research are defined below.

Parent versus no parent involvement: In the design of this study, parents who volunteer will be trained to implement remedial programs with their children at home. The children of these parents are students who will receive remedial services through the school and in the home. The no-parent group will consist of students whose sole remedial services will be provided by the school.

Preschool students: Students qualifying for this remedial program are between the ages of three and five years.

Home program: This refers to the activities, conducted with students by the parents, designed to reinforce those learning activities presented at school.

Levels of speech-language deficiency: A severe speech and language deficiency refers to that category of students with linguistic skills two years or more below age level. A moderate speech and language deficiency refers to that category of students with linguistic skills that are one to two years delayed. A mild speech and language deficiency refers to that category of students with linguistic skills that are less than one year below age level.

Speech and language deficient students: This term refers to students who have been identified through a diagnostic evaluation as exhibiting speech and/or language proficiency below age level.

Speech-language preschool program: This refers to the preschool special education programs that are similar for all students enrolled in the caseloads of the three speech therapists who will participate in this study.

Language performance age: After computing formal and informal language measures, the therapists will determine an overall functioning level for each child. For instance, the student's chronological age may be four years, but his/her language performance may be around three years of age. The language performance age as compared with the student's chronological age is necessary to determine the degree of language deficiency.

Review of the Literature

A major question regarding the remediation of exceptional children, which is primarily responsible for this research proposal, is the question of "What are the effects of home intervention?" Although parental influences and attitudes toward education are considered very important throughout a child's development, they are of particular importance during the preschool years, when family influence is most intense. For this reason, a remedial program has been designed to include home intervention with parent training, as well as the classroom experience for the student.

The importance of parent-child interaction at this age has been recognized by a number of authors. Resnick, Wang, and Rosner (1977) state that,

> "for young children, the most potent extra-school environment is the family. Therefore, the ultimate effectiveness of a preschool program will depend in part on the extent to which it can successfully involve parents in the education of their children, both within the school and in the home environment" (p. 273).

This is particularly relevant when dealing with exceptional children in programs which are designed for optimal remediation. Lally and Honig (1977) feel that the

> "child can be changed by intervention programs, but that he can also 'change back' when intervention ceases. Therefore, it is essential to make an impact on his permanent environment, his home, and to support parent strategies that will enhance his development long after intervention ceases" (p. 151).

Exceptional children usually require remedial or supportive services for many years, if not throughout their entire academic experiences. If parents are to support and contribute to their child's development, it is important that they possess adequate information regarding retardation, learning deficiencies, speech and language disorders, or whatever special disabilities their child is experiencing. Parents need information regarding the problems and limitations of their child's disability both in general and as it relates to their own child. A related need has been identified by Warfield (1975) as "for self-understanding—to affect a resolution of the emotional stresses and everyday problems involved in rearing a retarded child" (p. 562).

Although a number of authors have supported the notion of early intervention and parent involvement, there has been some question as to whether parents are qualified to train their children, or whether they can acquire those skills necessary to work with their children. Karnes and Zehrbach (1977) investigated this question in three different studies. Two of their studies were designed to determine the effectiveness of parents as teachers, and one examined the effectiveness of older siblings as teachers. In all three studies, the language skills and IQ scores of children in the experimental groups revealed increases significantly higher than those in the control groups who experienced no parental or sibling, educational intervention. These results led Karnes and Zehrbach to conclude "that these projects endorse the provision of home intervention by family members as a viable alternative to the direct delivery of services to the young child" (p. 93).

In seven different infant and preschool programs which were reviewed, the conclusions were quite consistent (Ambron, 1977). Those children enrolled in preschool programs scored significantly higher on IQ measures taken subsequently than those in the control groups. Children in programs also scored higher on other cognitive and language measures, such as the Illinois Test of Psycholinguistic Ability, the Preschool Inventory, and general Piagetian-type tasks. Of the seven programs, four conducted follow-up evaluations. Three of these programs revealed "lasting effects from one to three years after the program ended" (Ambron, 1977, p. 210). These researchers, I. J. Gordon, P. Levenstein, and F. H. Palmer, attributed the success of their programs to their particular approach, that is, parents teaching their own children.

Other research, however, indicates that if parents are to contribute substantially to their child's education, a considerable amount of parent training is necessary. For most parents, understanding, educating, and successfully relating to an exceptional child presents a considerable challenge. Doleys, Cartelli, and Doster (1976) found that mothers of children with learning disabilities perceived their children differently than mothers of nonclinic normal children. Although a higher rate of rewarding behavior was noted on the part of mothers of the learning disabled group, the rewards often followed inappropriate behavior. These results seemed to "emphasize the urgent need for parental counseling and training in how to manage and interact" (p. 46) with their exceptional child.

In summary, it appears that parental support is not only advantageous to school programs, but an important element in the successful remediation of preschool special education students. However, it should not be assumed that parents automatically possess the skills necessary to participate in special education programs. Nevertheless, there is evidence in the literature that seems to indicate that, although parents generally require assistance, they can be successfully trained as educators of their children.

Methods

The experimental design will be a $2 \times 3 \times 3$ factorial design. The independent variables are: (1) treatment; experimental, and control, defined as (exp) parent participation plus direct professional service through the school; (control) professional service through the school only; (2) speech therapist assigned to the case (3 individuals); and (3) level of student deficiency; severe, moderate and mild. The design can be diagrammed as follows.

		Therapist$_1$	Therapist$_2$	Therapist$_3$
Mild	P			
Disability	NP			
Moderate	P			
Disability	NP			

| Severe | P | --- |
| Disability | NP | _____ |

$2 \times 3 \times 3$ Factorial

P = parent involvement
NP = no parent involvement

The dependent variable will be the score on posttest composite language performance as described in the discussion on instrumentation. All students in the experiment will qualify for speech and language remedial services. All students will be preschool level, three to five years of age.

Instrumentation

Each student will be pretested with a battery of formal and informal receptive and expressive language measures. Formal tests will include the <u>Carrow Test of Auditory Comprehension</u>, the <u>Peabody Picture Vocabulary Test</u>, the <u>Carrow Elicited Language Inventory</u>, and the <u>Goldman-Fristoe Test of Articulation</u>. Informal testing will be accomplished through an expressive language sample, which will be analyzed with a language scale that provides normative data.

From the formal and informal measures, a composite language performance age will be determined for each child. The language performance age will be compared with the student's chronological age in order to categorize him/her as mildly, moderately, or severely language deficient.

The therapists will be pretesting their own caseloads and determining a language performance age for every child. Posttesting will be accomplished by having each therapist retest his/her own caseload at the termination of the nine-month school year with the same battery of tests.

Experimental Procedure and Data Collection

In September, 180 preschoolers who have been diagnosed as speech and language disabled will participate in remedial services provided by the three speech therapists. The subjects under study will be those students qualifying for remedial services and assigned to the therapists' caseloads. The participating students will be divided into three groups: mildly deficient, moderately deficient, and severely deficient (as described earlier).

Each student will receive direct remedial service in a school setting; however, the type of therapy approach used in the school may differ across therapists and across levels of deficiency. For example, the direct (or in-school) therapy program will differ for those students who are mildly deficient. Consistency in remedial programs exists in (1) the general characteristics of programs, (2) the amount of time spent in remediation, (3) the type of exceptional child serviced, (4) the option of parent vs. no parent involvement, and (5) the parent training and feedback system.

Since parent vs. no parent participation is of major consideration in this study, the extent and type of parent involvement will now be explained. Parents of those students who are enrolled in the remedial program will be asked to participate in a home program designed to supplement the direct professional service received at school. Since involvement in the home program must be on a voluntary basis, students whose parents elect to participate will make up the experimental group. Those students whose parents do not participate in the home program will function as the control group by receiving the school program only. (Offering no program or a parent home program only is not an option.)

For those parents participating in the home program, a parent-training and feedback system has been devised. Parents will be trained in a workshop situation initially and will be visited in the home by the therapist every 4 to 6 weeks. In addition to the follow-up home visits, parent effectiveness will be monitored periodically with the use of cassette recorders, which are sent home to determine whether or not the parent is following the prescribed remedial procedure.

In the final month of school, posttesting of all students using the same diagnostic measures will be conducted. As with the pretest data, the therapists will determine the language performance age of the students.

Analysis

A three-way analysis of variance will be computed on the posttest scores. Because the numbers in the cells will be unequal, and in fact quite different, considerable adjustment will be required in the analysis. Therefore, within each of the deficiency groups, t-tests for the difference between two means will be computed for the experimental and control group means.

The pretest scores will be used to classify the students on level of deficiency. Pre- and posttest scores can also be used to compute gain scores, and the gain scores analyzed using analysis of variance and t-tests. In all analyses, the interest will focus on the means and their differences, of the various groups. The .05 level of significance will be used for the statistical tests.

Significance of the Proposed Research

The importance of research in this area was alluded to in the early part of the proposal. Parent participation in the education of their children requires considerable effort, not only on the part of the parents, but also of the school personnel responsible for the program. The effects of parent participation may vary with the extent of deficiency experienced by the child. It may be that certain therapists are more effective than others when working in parent programs. Although it is generally believed that parent involvement is beneficial, the various patterns of effects involving the independent variables of this study may well differ. It is important to know the patterns of effects when planning programs (and promoting programs) that include parent participation.

Inferential statistics will be used in the analysis; however, students and parents will not be randomly selected for, or randomly assigned to the program. Such is not an option when dealing with speech and language deficient students. However, there is no reason to believe that this group of students and their parents are atypical. Parent volunteers for participation in this study are not likely to be different from parents elsewhere that would volunteer. So although the study has methodological limitations imposed by the nature of the area in which the research is intended, it should produce usable results with some generalizability.

References

Ambron, S. R. (1977). A review and analysis of infant and parent education programs. In M. C. Day & R. K. Parker (Eds.), The preschool in action (2nd ed.) (pp. 195–215). Boston: Allyn & Bacon.

Doleys, D. M., Cartelli, L. M., & Doster, J. (1976, June/July). Comparison of patterns of mother-child interaction. Journal of Learning Disabilities, 9(6), 371–375.

Karnes, M. B. & Zehrbach, R. R. (1977). Educational intervention at home. In M. C. Day & R. K. Parker (Eds.), The preschool in action (2nd ed.) (pp. 73–94). Boston: Allyn & Bacon.

Lally, J. R. & Honig, A. S. (1977). The family development research program. In M. C. Day and R. K. Parker (Eds.), The preschool in action (2nd ed.) (pp. 149–194). Boston: Allyn & Bacon.

Resnick, L. B., Wang, M. C. & Rosner, J. (1977). Adaptive education for young children: The primary education project. In M. C. Day and R. K. Parker (Eds.) The preschool in action (2nd ed.) (pp. 219–252). Boston: Allyn & Bacon.

Warfield, G. J. (1975, May). Mothers of retarded children review a parent education program. Exceptional Children, 41(8), 559–562.

Appendix 2:
Additional Statistical Procedures
for Data Analysis

Chapter 12 dealt with data analysis and discussed some of the more commonly used and less complex statistical procedures. There are many, many different procedures used for analyzing data in educational research. Many of these procedures are complex, and some of them were computationally impractical until computers became available to do the computations. In this appendix, selected procedures are descriptively defined to give the reader an idea of the conditions under which they apply. There is no attempt to develop computational skill or comprehensive coverage of the procedures. Indeed, entire books have been written on some of the topics singly. The reader who wants to pursue one or more of these topics can do so by consulting appropriate references.

It would be extremely unlikely that an actual analysis using one or more of the procedures described in this appendix would be attempted with a hand calculator. Computer programs are available for the procedures in the statistical packages listed in Chapter 12; the programs are described in the manuals accompanying the packages.

Nested Analysis of Variance

There are many variations of analysis of variance (ANOVA), some of which can become quite complex. In an earlier chapter, factorial designs were discussed; data from these designs are usually analyzed with factorial ANOVAs. Such analyses may include three, four, five, or theoretically any finite number of independent variables. Variations of factorials may include repeated measures analyses and incomplete factorials, in which certain combinations of independent variables may be missing.

Whatever the ANOVA, however, the basic concepts of the analysis are the same; we test hypotheses about means by partitioning variance.

A nested ANOVA is a special case of a factorial ANOVA in which the levels of one independent variable are *contained in,* rather than crossed with, the levels of another independent variable. Crossed independent variables can interact, but an interaction of a nested independent variable and the variable in which it is nested cannot be computed. The effect of the nested independent variable can be tested, but the result must be qualified in that the levels are contained in another independent variable.

Example A2.1

A study is being conducted in a large high school on the effects of two different curriculum materials on performance in geometry. Six teachers agree to participate in the study. Six classes of approximately 25 students each are formed by randomly assigning students to classes, and each teacher teaches only one class using one type of materials. (Preferably, the teachers would be randomly assigned to the materials.) After a one-semester period of instruction, the students are tested on a common examination. The score on this examination is the dependent variable. The independent variables are curriculum materials (two levels) and teacher nested within curriculum materials (three levels within each level of materials).

The design for this research is diagrammed in Figure A2.1. Note that the subscripts for teacher differ for curriculum materials, because each teacher uses only one set of curriculum materials.

The null hypotheses tested by a nested ANOVA for this design are as follows:

Figure A2.1
Diagram of Nested Design in Which the Independent Variable, Teacher, Is Nested in Curriculum Materials

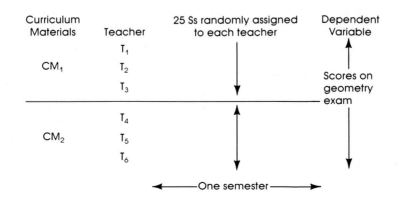

H_0: μ_{CM_1} = μ_{CM_2}—that is, the population means for curriculum materials are equal; and

H_0: μ_{T_1} = μ_{T_2} = μ_{T_3} = μ_{T_4} = μ_{T_5} = μ_{T_6}—that is, the population means for teachers within curriculum materials are equal.

There is no hypothesis for interaction, because the independent variables do not cross.

The hypotheses are tested in the usual manner by setting up F-ratios. If an F-ratio is statistically significant at a specified significance level, we would reject the null hypothesis tested by the F-ratio. Suppose that in the analysis, the F-ratio for testing the null hypothesis for the curriculum materials effect is statistically significant but the F-ratio for testing teacher effect is nonsignificant. We would then conclude that in the population, the curriculum materials do not have equal effects on performance in geometry, but teacher effects are equal within curriculum materials. We could compare the computed means in the geometry exam for CM_1 and CM_2 to determine which curriculum materials are most effective.

The foregoing example included two independent variables. More complex ANOVAs can be developed that include both crossed and nested independent variables. It is also possible to nest one independent variable in another nested variable. These arrangements can be combined with repeated measures. However, ANOVAs should be only as complex as is required by the research study. Interpretation of the results of complicated ANOVAs can become difficult.

Multiple Regression and Correlation

Correlation has numerous uses in educational research; one of the more common uses is prediction—the estimation of one variable from a knowledge of one or more other variables. For example, academic success in college as evidenced by the college grade point average (GPA) has been predicted using high school GPA. The American College Testing Program (1973) consistently found correlation coefficients around .50 between high school GPA and overall college GPA. The greater the correlation between the variables, the predictor variable doing the prediction, and the criteria variable being predicted, the more effective the prediction.

Correlation and prediction involve a related concept called *regression*. If we have two variables X and Y and we study the regression of Y on X, we are asking the question, "How do the Y scores depend on, or go back to (regress), the X scores?" Galton first developed this concept formally in his studies of heredity when he observed that tall men tend to have sons shorter than themselves and short men have sons taller than themselves. He called this tendency a "regression" to the mean of the population. In fact, the symbol r for the correlation coefficient comes from the concept of regression.

In the correlation discussion in Chapter 12, the concept of a scattergram was introduced to show the scores on two variables. Suppose that we have two variables X and Y and we want to predict scores on Y from scores on X. A straight line can be fit to the points of the scattergram. That line has the form:

$$\hat{Y}_i = bX_i + a$$

where $\hat{Y}_i$ = the predicted score on Y for individual i
X_i = individual i's X-score (X is the predictor variable)
b = regression coefficient
a = regression constant

For any given set of data, b and a are constants. The line is fit to the points in the scattergram using the *least squares criterion*. This means that

$$\sum_{i=1}^{n}(Y_i - \hat{Y}_i)^2$$

is a minimum for the specific data, where $(Y_i - \hat{Y}_i)$ is the difference between the observed and predicted scores for the ith individual.

The foregoing equation is the equation of the regression line for Y and X, and it is also the prediction equation. Only one predictor variable is used. Suppose that we had a situation in which it would seem beneficial to use more than one predictor. Such is the case when high school GPA and scores on an aptitude test (such as the American College Testing Program or the Scholastic Aptitude Test) are used in combinations to predict college GPA. When two predictors are used, the prediction equation becomes:

$$\hat{Y} = b_1X_1 + b_2X_2 + a$$

And in general, if k predictors are used:

$$\hat{Y} = b_1X_1 + b_2X_2 + \cdots + b_kX_k + a$$

The X_i's are the predictor variables. In the foregoing equations, the right side is said to be a *linear combination* of the predictor variables. Geometrically, the equations are equations of planes or hyperplanes when there are more than three dimensions; nevertheless, they are fit to the data using the least squares criterion. For any specific set of data, the b_i's and a are constants.

In addition to the prediction equation, we also can obtain the *multiple correlation coefficient*. This is the correlation coefficient between the criterion variable and the linear combination of the predictor variables. The multiple correlation coefficient can take on values from 0 to 1.00, inclusive. The symbol $R_{y\cdot12\ldots k}$ is often used for the coefficient; the subscript indicates that the correlation is between Y, the criterion variable, and the predictors 1 through k. The greater the $R_{y \cdot 12 \ldots k}$, the more effective the prediction will be.

Standard Error of Estimate

Effectiveness of prediction was mentioned earlier without being defined explicitly. To develop the concept of effectiveness of prediction, it is necessary to consider errors in prediction. An error in prediction is a difference between the observed and predicted score for an individual—that is, $Y_i - \hat{Y}_i$. There are as many error scores as original scores, although some may be zero if the predicted and observed scores for an individual are equal. The distribution of error scores has a mean of zero, and its standard deviation is called the *standard error of estimate*. The symbol used for the standard error of estimate is $S_{y \cdot 12 \ldots k}$, and it is determined by

$$S_{y \cdot 12 \ldots k} = S_y \sqrt{1 - R_{y \cdot 12 \ldots k}^2}$$

where S_y is the standard deviation of the observed distribution of criterion scores and $R_{y 12 \ldots k}^2$ is the square of the multiple correlation coefficient.

The smaller the standard error of estimate, the more effective the prediction. By inspecting the formula for $S_{y \cdot 12 \ldots k}$, if $R_{y \cdot 12 \ldots k}$ equals 1.0, the standard error of estimate equals zero. For this to happen, all error scores would be zero and prediction would be exact. When doing prediction studies, we are not concerned about how many scores we predict exactly. We are concerned about reducing $S_{y \cdot 12 \ldots k}$, and to do this, it is important to maximize $R_{y \cdot 12 \ldots k}$.

The square of the multiple correlation coefficient is also called the *coefficient of determination*. $R_{y \cdot 12 \ldots k}^2$ indicates the proportion of the variance in the criterion variable that is associated with or caused by the linear combination of the predictor variables. Thus, multiple correlation can also be used for partitioning variance in the criterion variable into that due to regression (predictor variables) and the residual variance, which is error variance.

Example A2.2

Many studies in the educational research literature involve multiple regression and correlation. An entire study will not be repeated here, but selected information will be given to illustrate the points discussed thus far. In a study of predicting science achievement, Lawson (1983) used multiple regression. The individuals in the study were 96 undergraduate students enrolled in a course entitled "Biological Science for the Elementary Teacher." Five cognitive variables, measured by various tests and inventories, were used as predictors:

Developmental Level (X_1)

Disembedding Ability (X_2)

Mental Capacity (X_3)

Prior Knowledge (X_4)

Beliefs (in special creation or evolution) (X_5)

The criterion variable was Achievement Total Score[1]—the score on a test given at the conclusion of the course.

The prediction equation[2] for Achievement Total Score was:

$$\hat{Y} = 0.67X_1 + 0.10X_2 - 0.45X_3 + 0.22X_4 + 0.43X_5 + 5.88$$

The multiple correlation coefficient between the linear combination of the five predictors and the criterion variable was .563. Thus, the predictors accounted for 31.7% of the variance in the Achievement Total Score. It was concluded that cognitive variables, as defined in the article, do influence science achievement.

The underlying mathematics of multiple regression is complex, and numerous factors must be considered when using multiple regression for prediction. Predictors must be selected, and we generally look for predictors that have relatively low correlations among themselves but high correlations with the criterion variable. We can continue to include variables, but from a practical standpoint there is usually a limit to the number of predictors that can be accommodated. Prediction is seldom enhanced in educational research by including more than five or six predictors. There are procedures for selecting predictors (called *stepwise selection*) so that those variables that contribute most to prediction will be selected in order. When the addition of more predictors will no longer account for a statistically significant portion of the variance, the selection process can be terminated. In this way, the most effective predictors are selected and the prediction equation is limited to predictors that make a contribution.

Discriminant Analysis

Discriminant analysis is closely related conceptually to multiple prediction. However, instead of predicting a numerical score on a criterion variable, we predict group membership. A regression equation is used, which is called the *discriminant function*. The dependent variable or criterion variable is group membership, and if there are only two groups,[3] the dependent variable can simply have values of 1 and 0. The two or more predictor variables are measured on at least interval scales; that is, they are continuous variables. The discriminant function has the same general form as the prediction equation in multiple regression. Sometimes, discriminant functions are given in standardized form, which means that the distributions of the predictor variables have been transformed to distributions with means of 0 and standard deviations of 1.0. In that case, the regression constant is 0.

The discriminant function is developed in a least squares manner so that it maximally discriminates between the members of the two groups. The equation or function predicts the group to which each individual is most likely to belong. If the predicted score is closer to 1 than to 0, the individual is predicted to belong to the group designated 1, and vice versa. The predictor variables are assigned weights so that we have maximum difference between the groups relative to the within-groups variability.

There are two major uses for discriminant analysis in education. One is for classification and diagnosis—that is, predicting group membership and then diagnosing what can be done to enhance membership in the preferred group. Examples of dichotomous groups are pass-fail, successful-unsuccessful, and dropouts-persisters. For example, discriminant analysis could be used to identify (predict) which individuals are most likely to be dropouts in the future. Then some course of action could be implemented to keep those individuals from becoming dropouts.

The second major use is a basic research use—to investigate the relationships between group membership and scores on predictor variables. In this way, discriminant analysis may be helpful in theory development. For example, in a given profession, if successful and unsuccessful practitioners are identified, a study of skills and values possibly related to success (or lack of it) could be studied through discriminant analysis.

Example A2.3

Robyak and Downey (1979) used discriminant analysis to investigate study skills and personality types in underachieving and nonunderachieving university students, primarily freshmen and sophomores. Nine predictor variables were used, although they came from three inventories, as follows:

The Survey of Study Habits and Attitudes, Form C
>   Delay Avoidance (X_1)
>   Work Habits (X_2)
>   Teacher Approval (X_3)
>   Education Acceptance (X_4)

Study Skills Test, Form A—Study Skill Information Section (X_5)

The Myers-Briggs Type Indicator[4]
>   Extraversion/Introversion (X_6)
>   Sensing/Intuition (X_7)
>   Thinking/Feeling (X_8)
>   Judgment/Perception (X_9) (Robyak & Downey, 1979, pp. 307–308, paraphrased)

The group membership predicted was underachieving versus nonunderachieving.
The discriminant function, in standardized form, was:

$$\hat{Y} = .30X_1 - .24X_2 - .31X_3 + .02X_4 + .61X_5 + .63X_6$$
$$+ .33X_7 - .25X_8 - .38X_9 \text{ (from p. 308, Table 1)}$$

The amount of discrimination was statistically significant at the .10 level of significance. An inspection of the discriminant function indicates that high study skill information scores (X_5) and a preference toward introversion (X_6) were the major contributors of the predictor variables. The conclusion of the study was that student characteristics are important considerations when designing instructional approaches to use in study skills programs (p. 308, paraphrased). Of course, this more general conclusion was elaborated on when individual predictors were considered.

Factor Analysis

Factor analysis is a procedure for determining the number and nature of constructs that underlie a set of measures. *Construct* was defined earlier as a trait or an attribute that explains some phenomenon, such as an individual's behavior. In factor analysis, artificial variables, called *factors,* are generated, and these factors represent the constructs. Of course, the factors are obtained from the original variables and must be interpreted in terms of these variables.

Factor analysis is a complex statistical procedure, yet it is done for the purpose of parsimony. It attempts to provide a simpler explanation of the constructs that underlie a set of variables than is provided by keeping the measures intact. In this sense, it is a form of data reduction by grouping variables. Factor analysis is initiated from the correlation matrix of the measures or variables, and variables that are highly correlated are grouped together.

Suppose that we have scores on several tests—say, 15 such scores—for 100 individuals. The question can be asked: "How many different constructs or traits do these 15 tests measure?" There may be two or more tests that measure the same construct, and a single test may measure two or more constructs. The correlation coefficients among the 15 tests can be determined. High correlations between test scores indicate that common constructs are measured. Low or zero correlations indicate the absence of common constructs.

There are a number of ways that factors are extracted from the matrix of correlation coefficients. All are computationally complex and will not be discussed here. If a test measures only one construct, it is said to be *factorially pure.* A *factorially complex* test is one that measures two or more factors. The extent to which a test measures a factor is called a *loading* of the factor, or *factor loading.* In a factor analysis, a factor loading is the correlation coefficient between a test and a factor. Since factors, which are artificial variables generated from the data, must be described and integrated, the factor loadings play an important role in any factor analysis.

Uses of Factor Analysis

The general purpose of factor analysis is to identify the nature and number of constructs (factors) that underlie a set of variables (measures). Factor analysis is often associated with research in measurement, especially in connection with construct-related evidence when establishing validity. Factor analysis is commonly used as exploratory analysis or confirmatory analysis.[5]

When exploratory analyses are used, the intent is to reduce the number of variables to a manageable number for explanatory purposes, the number of factors usually being less than the number of original variables. A set of measures may be factor-analyzed to enhance the explanation of what is measured in a more parsimonious manner. For example, suppose that a group of teachers was observed and measured on 35 teaching competencies. A factor analysis of the competency scores undoubtedly would generate a smaller number of factors, possibly six to eight, that represent the constructs underlying teacher performance.

Confirmatory factor analysis focuses on confirming or refuting the hypothesized constructs measured by a set of variables. It may be used to test a theory. Confirmatory factor analysis is used extensively to establish the construct validity of psychological tests and other measures in the behavioral sciences. Factor analysis of a number of test scores is commonly done, but it can also be used to analyze a single test by factor-analyzing the item scores. For example, we might hypothesize that a 75-item test measures three constructs or traits. A confirmatory factor analysis of the item scores would support or refute this hypothesis.

Example A2.4

Suppose that a battery of 12 tests is given to a group of seniors in a high school. The scores on the 12 tests are factor-analyzed to determine the constructs measured by the test battery. Four factors are generated by the analysis, and the factor loadings (correlations between individual tests and factors) are as given in Table A2.1. How are these factors interpreted?

When interpreting a matrix of factor loadings, we look for the presence of large or small loadings among the tests being analyzed. Sometimes, an arbitrary decision is made that factor loadings of less than .30 in absolute value are ignored. The first factor has substantial factor loadings with all tests and is called a *general* factor. It represents a general ability trait or construct, the kind of trait sometimes called general intelligence or just intelligence.

The second factor can be called the *math ability and skills* factor. Three tests load on this factor—the two math tests and geometric interpretation. The third factor also has three tests loading on it—comprehension, analogies, and vocabulary. Therefore, it can be called the *verbal ability* factor. The final factor has only two tests loading on it—math concepts and geometric interpretation. This can be called the *math reasoning* factor. In summary, the four factors can be labeled as follows:

Table A2.1
Factor Loadings Between Tests and Factors: Hypothetical Data

Test	Factors			
	I	*II*	*III*	*IV*
Comprehension	.85	−.06	.87	−.05
Math concepts	.72	.55	.05	.82
Math computation	.53	.63	−.01	.15
Analogies	.78	−.02	.66	−.01
Vocabulary	.81	−.08	.73	−.01
Number recall	.42	.25	−.06	.08
Picture completion	.61	.05	.33	.12
Picture sequencing	.64	.10	.12	.10
Design (figural)	.52	.15	.08	.22
Geometric interpretation	.48	.45	.02	.66
Block arrangement	.50	.22	.04	.18
Transformations	.55	.11	.06	.14

I General ability
II Math ability and skills
III Verbal ability
IV Math reasoning

The example is quite straightforward and illustrates two types of factors. Factor I is a general factor, and general factors have high loadings with all tests in the analysis. The remaining three factors are group factors—factors that have high loadings with two or more tests but that have at least one near-zero or zero loading. Other possible types of factors (not illustrated in the example) are specific factors and bipolar factors. A *specific factor* has only one test loading on it. A *bipolar factor* has both high positive and high negative loadings but does not necessarily have all tests loading on it. Extraversion-introversion is an example of a trait that would likely appear as a bipolar factor.

Factor analysis is complex, both theoretically and conceptually. Many aspects of factor analysis—such as how to determine the number of factors empirically— are not discussed here. Entire books and monographs have been written on factor analysis; the reader is referred to publications such as Kim and Mueller (1978).

Multivariate Analysis of Variance

Analysis of variance (ANOVA) has been discussed earlier in this appendix and in Chapter 12. ANOVA is an inferential statistics procedure for analyzing the data of a single dependent variable, although more than one independent variable may be included. Such analyses are sometimes called univariate ANOVAs. Multivariate analysis of variance (MANOVA) is an extension of univariate ANOVA to include two or more *dependent* variables in the same analysis. Basically, MANOVA is an inferential statistics procedure; that is, it is used to generalize from samples to populations. In addition, like factor analysis, MANOVA produces descriptive information about the constructs that underlie the dependent variables.

In ANOVA, one or more independent variables are analyzed to determine how they account for variance in the dependent variable. This concept is extended to MANOVA, in that the scores or measures (the data) of groups determined by the levels of one or more independent variables are analyzed for differences. However, by including two or more dependent variables simultaneously, we no longer consider differences between means on a single variable; instead, we consider differences on one or more *canonical variates*. The focus of interest is not only on how the groups defined by the independent variable(s) differ on the canonical variates but also on the nature of the canonical variates.

Canonical variates are artificial variables generated from the data, like factors of factor analysis. They represent constructs, and in addition to knowing that constructs exist, it usually is also desirable to describe them. Since canonical variates are composites of real variables—the dependent variables of the MANOVA—they must ultimately be described in terms of these variables. This is done through *loadings*—correlation coefficients between a canonical variate and the dependent variables. If a loading between the canonical variate and the dependent variable is high and positive, it means that high scores on the dependent variable are associated with high scores on the canonical variate. For example, if a dependent variable consists of the score on an arithmetic computation test and the score correlates highly with a canonical variate, we would infer that the canonical variate represents a construct involving numerical skills. Negative loadings are possible, but the plus or minus sign is used when relating the canonical variate to group scores.

The computation of MANOVA is such that generating canonical variates continues until there is no longer any statistically significant difference between the groups, or until the degrees of freedom (for the independent variable) are exhausted, whichever occurs first. For example, if there are two levels of an independent variable, there is only one degree of freedom, and at most only one canonical variate will appear for the independent variable. The MANOVA will structure this canonical variate so that it accounts for the maximum variance between the groups. The number of canonical variates cannot exceed the number of dependent variables, but usually this number is greater than either the number of statistically significant canonical variates or the degrees of freedom.

The null hypothesis of MANOVA involves groups of means of the dependent variables; specifically, it states that in the population (represented by the sample), these groups of means are equal. A number of statistics can be used to test the null hypothesis; the most commonly used are the Wilks lambda criterion and Hotelling's T^2. If the test is statistically significant for the designated alpha level, we conclude that there is a difference in the groups of means that cannot be attributed to random sampling fluctuation. This means that there is at least one significant canonical variate and that there is some difference among the two or more groups of the independent variable on this canonical variate.

Computer programs for MANOVA commonly position the groups of the independent variable(s) by discriminant scores. Discriminant scores are computed with a discriminant function—a regression equation that represents a composite of the dependent variables. Each group is given a discriminant score on each canonical variate. The discriminant scores position the groups on the canonical variate in a relative sense. The discriminant scores of the groups for an independent variable sum to zero (within rounding errors); therefore, at least one discriminant score must be negative. A high positive discriminant score for a group indicates that this group, relative to the others, scored high on the particular canonical variate. However, at this point the loadings must be considered, since they, too, may be positive or negative. If a dependent variable has a high negative loading, those groups with negative discriminant scores scored high on that dependent variable's contribution to the canonical variate. Thus, discriminant scores are used for interpreting the separations of the groups on the canonical variates, and the loadings are used for tying the results to the dependent variables.

Example A2.5

A study was conducted in a large school system to determine whether seniors in various high school programs differ in their performance on a battery of tests. The battery contained ten tests, comprising a mixture of cognitive area and skills tests and physical performance tests. Scores on these ten tests made up the dependent variables of the study. (See Table A2.2.)

Random samples of 50 seniors each were selected from students enrolled in four high school programs: college prep, general, vocational-trades, and performing

Table A2.2
Correlation Coefficients (Loadings) Between Dependent Variables and Canonical Variates: Hypothetical Data

Dependent Variable	Canonical Variate	
	I	II
English usage	.63	.07
Composition	.58	.02
Literature	.55	−.02
Science	.47	.13
Fine arts	.21	.28
Mathematics	.40	.05
Manipulative skills	−.03	.68
Figural interpretation	.12	.53
Physical dexterity	.05	.42
Spatial perception	.16	.25

arts. The students were administered the battery of tests, and the scores were analyzed using a MANOVA. The results of the MANOVA are given in Tables A2.2 and A2.3.

Two canonical variates were generated by the MANOVA. This was one less than the maximum number possible, since the independent variable had three degrees of freedom. The loadings between dependent variables and canonical variates are given in Table A2.2. The first canonical variate represents a *cognitive knowledge and skills* construct and the second a *physical performance* construct. These are subjective names assigned to the canonical variates, based on the correlation coefficients.

The discriminant scores in Table A2.3 indicate the greatest separation of the four groups on the first canonical variate. The college prep group was positioned high and the vocational-trades group, low. The cognitive knowledge and skills tests load heavily on this canonical variate (see the loadings in Table A2.2); therefore, this group had the highest scores on these tests. Recall that the discriminant scores show relative positioning of the groups. Scores on the dependent variables singly would have to be checked for the absolute scores of the groups.

The second canonical variate had fewer substantial correlations with the dependent variables. In fact, there were only three correlations above .40. The vocational-trades group positioned high on this canonical variate and the college prep group, low. Performance on the manipulative skills test is an important part of this canonical variate, since it had a loading of .68 and many of the other loadings were very modest.

In summary, we can conclude that the performances on these tests by the four samples of seniors were distinguished by two underlying constructs or traits—one, a cognitive knowledge and skills construct, the other, a physical performance construct. College prep tended to position high on the first construct and vocational-trades high on the second construct.

It should be noted that the loadings on canonical variates are conceptually similar to factor loadings in factor analysis. However, there is one important distinction. Canonical variates will appear only to the extent to which there are statistically significant differences between the groups that make up the levels of the independent variable. Conceivably, a MANOVA could have no canonical variates if there were

Table A2.3
Discriminant Scores for Four Groups on Two Canonical Variates: Hypothetical Data

Group	Canonical Variate	
	I	*II*
College prep	1.98	−1.69
General	1.22	−0.50
Vocational-trades	−3.40	1.26
Performing arts	0.20	0.93

no differences among the groups. Factor analysis is often done on the data of a single group, and group differences are not necessary to generate factors.

Analyses such as MANOVA and factor analysis, which synthesize data from two or more dependent variables in a single analysis, are known as *multivariate analyses*. Such analyses typically involve generating one or more artificial variables, such as factors that represent traits or constructs.

SUMMARY

This appendix has described five of the more commonly used complex statistical procedures. Many more procedures of varying complexity are available for data analysis. With the increased availability and sophistication of computers, such analyses are becoming increasingly practical. Since they are conducted on computers, using published programs, computational accuracy is pretty much ensured, so the user's major responsibilities are to understand the application and to interpret the results of the analyses.

NOTES

1. Subtest scores were also used as criterion variables, but they will not be discussed here. The interested reader may consult Lawson (1983).

2. The notation here was changed slightly from that in the article to be consistent with notation introduced in this appendix.

3. Discriminant analysis can involve more than two groups. However, this condition does complicate the analysis, since the number of discriminant functions is one less than the number of groups.

4. For the four subscales of the Myers–Briggs Type Indicator, the higher scores indicate a preference for the characteristic after the slash *(/)*.

5. For a discussion of these uses of factor analysis, see B. Korth, "Exploratory Factor Analysis," and S. A. Mulaik, "Confirmatory Factor Analysis," in D. J. Amick and H. J. Walberg (Eds.), *Introductory Multivariate Analysis for Educational, Psychological and Social Research* (Berkeley, CA: McCutchan, 1975), pp. 113–146 and 170–207.

REFERENCES

American College Testing Program. (1973). *Highlights of the ACT technical report.* Iowa City: American College Testing Program.

Kim, J., & Mueller, C. W. (1978). *Factor analysis: Statistical methods and practical issues.* Beverly Hills, CA: Sage.

Lawson, A. E. (1983). Predicting science achievement: The role of developmental level, disembedding ability, mental capacity, prior knowledge, and beliefs. *Journal of Research in Science Teaching, 20*(2), 117–129.

Robyak, J. E., & Downey, R. G. (1979). A discriminant analysis of the study skills and personality types of underachieving and nonunderachieving study skills students. *Journal of College Student Personnel, 20*(4), 306–309.

Appendix 3: Solutions to Exercises

Note: Solutions are not provided here for exercises (1) that have flexible answers; (2) that direct the reader to some type of extended activity, such as reading a journal article; or (3) that indicate considerable discussion. The purpose of this appendix is to help the reader make the solution of exercises a more profitable learning experience. Answers are brief; not all possible discussion is presented for some exercises.

Chapter 1

1.1 The essential difference between basic and applied research is in the orientation of the research. Applied research is oriented to the solution of a specific, often immediate, problem. Basic research is oriented to the extension of knowledge in the discipline.

1.2 Internal validity involves the extent to which we can interpret the results of a research study. It considers the conditions of the study that make the results interpretable (or uninterpretable). External validity involves the extent of generalizability of the results—the populations, conditions, and so forth, to which the results can be generalized.

1.3 If results cannot be interpreted, they cannot be validly generalized.

1.4 **a.** Internal
  b. Internal
  c. External
  d. Basically, this situation deals with internal validity, because the 12% return makes it impossible to determine voter feeling. External validity is also a major concern, however, since the superintendent undoubtedly wants to generalize to the voter population.
  e. Internal
  f. External

1.5 Reliability means consistency; when applied to research, it is the extent to which research (the methods, conditions, results) are replicable. For (1), there may be inconsistency in the way the four experimenters administer the treatment; for (2), observers may not be consistent when interpreting the teacher behaviors.

1.6 In an experiment, at least one variable is deliberately varied or manipulated by the researcher.

1.7 Historical research focuses on a description and interpretation of past events or facts; ethnographic research focuses on a holistic description of some present phenomenon.

Chapter 2

2.1 The constants are grade level, sex, and school. The independent variable is instructional materials. The teacher is an intervening variable, and the effect of the teacher variable cannot be separated from the effect of instructional materials, since it is implied that each teacher uses only one type of instructional material. The dependent variable is reading achievement.

2.2 Sex of the student is an organismic variable that may also serve as a control variable if the reading scores for boys and girls are separated. School and grade level are likely to be included as control variables. (In essence, they become additional independent variables.) Class and method cannot be separated within schools, so within the schools, class (and also teacher, assuming that each teacher uses only one method) is an intervening variable.

2.3 Hypotheses would be directed to the variables under study. An example is, "The reading achievement of fourth-grade girls is equal to that of fourth-grade boys." This is a nondirectional hypothesis. A directional hypothesis might be, "The reading achievement of fifth-graders is higher than that of fourth-graders." There are other possible hypotheses.

2.4 The research problem may be stated as, "A study of the effects of the amount of lab work on theoretical knowledge of chemistry," or in question form, "Do varying amounts of lab work affect performance in theoretical chemistry?" An example hypothesis: "The greater the amount of lab work, the higher the score on the theoretical portion of the chemistry exam." The independent variable is amount of lab work; the dependent variable is the score on the theoretical portion of the chemistry exam. It may be possible to control for teacher effect and sex of the student. Examples of intervening variables are the scholastic ability of the students and the amount of time spent in individual study.

2.5 a. The type of residential dwelling would be nominal scale. If we were interested in the number of family units, we could go to a ratio scale, but such a quantitative characteristic is not defined when we simply classify according to type.

   b. Calcium deposits could be measured on a ratio scale.

   c. Performance on an essay part of a history test would be measured on an ordinal scale. Considerable objectivity and quantification would have to be defined before such a performance could be measured on an equal-unit scale.

   d. Rating of student teacher performance would be measured on an ordinal scale.

   e. Ratio scale measurement would be involved.

   f. Nominal scale.

   g. Nominal scale, or possibly ordinal if we consider economic resources available to the levels.

2.6 Individualized instruction and scholastic performance require operational definition. Elementary school students would have to be defined in terms of the grade levels (or, possibly, age levels) to be included, which is also an operational definition for the specific study.

2.7 A nondirectional hypothesis is a hypothesis of no difference or no relationship. A directional hypothesis contains the anticipated direction (order) of the results.

Chapter 3

3.2 The major descriptors to use are Instruction, Curriculum, and Education. More specifically, use Mathematics Curriculum (subheadings, Arithmetic Curriculum and Elementary School Math), Curriculum (Mathematics Curriculum and Elementary School Curriculum), Education Programs (International Programs), and Comparative Education (International Education). The foregoing descriptors would be used in combination when referencing in the following ERIC publications: *Educational Documents Index, Resources in Education* (Subject Index), *Current Index to Journals in Education* (Subject Index).

3.3 Descriptors to use are teacher behavior, teacher performance, teacher competency, science, science achievement. To broaden the search, suppose that the results of searching on teacher behavior *and* science achievement produced few references. Then teacher behavior *or* teacher performance *or* teacher competency and science achievement could be used. An example of narrowing the search would be to use high school *and* science achievement. Note the connectors: *and* generally narrows the search; *or* broadens it.

Chapter 4

4.1 One approach would be to do two separate studies—one including boys, the other, girls. This would hold the sex of the student constant. Probably a more effective way to enhance control would be to build sex of the student into the design as an independent variable.

4.2 School might be an independent variable, with however many levels as there are high schools. If there were two or more types of high schools among the schools—for example, vocational and general—type of school could be an independent variable. The region of the city might also serve as an independent variable if there were two or more defined regions. Region would probably closely correspond with socioeconomic level of the school's location. It would not be likely that school, type of school, and region would all serve as independent variables, because any one school would be only one type and would be located in one region. Simply putting school in as an independent variable would likely be the most parsimonious approach to including this variable in the design.

4.3 The ability level of the participants is a likely variable that may have an effect on the dependent variable. The ability level measure could be administered to the participants and then a statistical adjustment made on the basis of ability level score. There may be some difference in the performances of boys and girls or in the manner in which they respond to the motivational techniques. Therefore, the sex of the participant could be included as an independent (control) variable. Assuming that conditions for conducting the experiment are consistent across participants, any variables controlled would be organismic variables.

4.4 The following points should be noted in developing the research design: (1) Since each teacher teaches two classes, each teacher should use both packets, one for each class; in this way, teacher and instructional materials are not confounded. (2) Unless some measure of learning style is available, learning style would likely be controlled by randomization. (3) Sex of the student and teacher could be included as independent variables, although sex of the student could also be controlled through randomization. (4) The available GPA could serve as a measure of ability and could be used as a statistical control.

4.5 When two or more variables are confounded in a research study, their effects cannot be separated.

4.6 There undoubtedly are characteristics unique to each school that are now confounded with the independent variable *instructional method*. The experiment could have been designed so that all five instructional methods are used in each school.

4.7 Subtopics necessary for this study: Selection of the measuring instruments, both pre- and posttests, which would likely be parallel forms of the same test. Reliability checks and revision would be necessary only if a locally constructed test is used. The students would have to be randomly assigned to the two instructional approaches. The pre- and posttesting would be conducted. The data would be assembled by student, grade, and instructional approach.

4.8 Four teachers could be randomly assigned to each of the two instructional methods. Students could be randomly assigned to the two methods. Although it is unlikely that the numbers of boys and girls would be equal, they could be evenly distributed among the four methods (about one-forth of each sex to each method). Sex of the student could then be included as an independent variable.

Chapter 5

5.1 (This exercise is similar to Exercise 1.2.) Internal validity concerns the basic minimum control, and so forth, that is necessary for the results of the experiment to be interpretable. External validity is the extent to which the results of the experiment are generalizable to existing conditions, populations, and the like. Internal validity is often enhanced by increasing control, which may include reducing the number of factors operating in the situation. This tends to jeopardize external validity. The reverse may also occur when the experiment is essentially a replication of the real situation (has high external validity), but so many factors are operating that it is impossible to interpret cause and effect.

5.2 The fact that the teachers can assign students at random within the school gives a measure of control that would be missing if existing classes had to be taken. Existing classes may differ on ability and on other factors related to achievement. Control can be enhanced by building *school* into the design as an independent variable. Since each teacher teaches four classes, one of each size can be assigned per teacher. However, the *teacher* variable would be confounded with the independent variable *school*, since any one teacher would teach in only one school. The *school* variable might have several uncontrolled but relevant variables associated with it, such as extent of lab facilities. These variables are essentially confounded with the *school* variable.

5.4 There are three independent variables with two levels of each; therefore, a 2 × 2 × 2, or 2^3, factorial would be an appropriate factorial design. This factorial design has eight cells, determined by the combinations of levels of the independent variables. However, one-half of the eight cells involve pairs and require two participants. Therefore, one complete replication requires 12 participants, 6 boys and 6 girls. Since there are only 64 boys and it requires 6 boys for a replication, the greatest multiple of 6 we can use is 60. Thus, we would randomly eliminate 36 girls and 4 boys and proceed with 120 participants. Sex is an organismic variable, but we would randomly assign the 60 boys (and girls) to the levels of the independent variables *type of problem* and *group size,* assigning 40 to pairs and 20 to individuals, and 30 to each type of problem. Actually, we would have the eight cells and the frequencies would be 10 and 20, depending on whether the cell includes individuals or pairs. Thus, randomization is built in by assigning participants to cells.

5.5 The primary gain in internal validity is being able to check on an effect of pretesting. A possible interaction between pretesting and experimental treatment can also be checked.

5.6 The pretest-posttest control group design applies. Because the teacher is interested in the amount of algebra learned during the semester, pretesting is necessary. The pretest score may also be used as a statistical control. This experiment would most likely be quite high in external validity, since testing could occur at natural times and the experiment would be carried on in a natural educational setting. The population to which the results are generalized would have to be carefully defined in terms of the students enrolled in advanced algebra classes in this specific type of high school.

5.7 Multiple-treatment interference means that observations taken on the same individual immediately following a specific treatment are affected by prior treatments. When an individual receives more than one treatment, prior treatments may interfere with the effects of subsequent treatments. This is a threat to validity, because it becomes impossible to separate the effects due to specific treatments.

5.8 **a.** No, because the groups have been formed by random assignment.

    b. No, because there is no pretesting of any groups.

    c. (1) There are experimental treatment effects: the four experimental treatments all have differing effects. (2) There are experimental treatment effects: X_1 and X_3 have equal effects; X_2 and X_4 have equal effects (or the same effect), but their effects differ from those of X_1 and X_3. (3) X_1 and X_2 have effects and they are the same. (4) X_4 is the only treatment that has an experimental effect.

5.9 **a.** The researcher can determine the possible effect of X extended in time, along with a comparison group extended in time. Also, a possible diminishing effect of pretesting could be checked.

    b. Compare O_2 and O_9; compare O_4 and O_{10}.

    c. (1) If an experimental effect exists, it is a function of time. There is no long-term experimental effect. No pretesting effect appears in the short-run post-test results of experimental groups. (2) There is an experimental effect that is not affected by the different posttest times of the design; the experimental effect is the same in the short and long run. (3) In the short run, there is no change due to experimental treatment for pretested groups. (4) In the short run, there is no experimental effect, nor is there an effect of pretesting; there is an experimental effect in the long run with the pretested groups.

5.10 a. Gain scores can be analyzed; if necessary, we could also check on subject mortality.

    b. No; an effect of pretesting cannot be checked because there are no nonpre-tested groups with which to make a comparison.

    c. O_3 and O_6 compared with O_9; O_1 with O_3, and O_4 with O_6; O_2 with O_3, and O_5 with O_6.

    d. No, because random assignment was used.

    e. We would conclude that some external factor is causing the control group to change between measurement occasions.

    f. (1) There are experimental effects in the short run, and they are the same for X_1 and X_2. The effects do not persist for the long run. (2) There are experimental effects in the short run that are not the same for X_1 and X_2. (3) There are no experimental effects in the short run. There are experimental effects in the long run, but we cannot tell whether or not X_1 and X_2 effects are the same. We know that $O_2 \neq O_3$ and $O_5 \neq O_6$, but it is possible that $O_3 = O_6$. (4) There are experimental effects in the short run, and the effects are different for X_1 and X_2. There also are effects in the long term, but they do not remain constant between the short and long terms. The long-run effects of X_1 and X_2 are not the same.

Chapter 6

6.1 The primary difficulties that may be introduced when using intact groups are associated with possible lack of equivalence of the groups on factors related to the dependent variable. Such factors may be confounded with experimental treatments, threatening the internal validity of the research.

6.2 There are three sets of laboratory materials, and one set could be designated the traditional or control set, since it is unlikely that a class would do the lab work with no materials. The design can be diagrammed as follows:

$$G_1 - X_1 - O_1$$
$$G_2 - X_2 - O_2$$
$$G_3 \rule{1.5cm}{0.4pt} O_3$$

The pretest-posttest nonequivalent control group design would be applied by administering a pretest at the beginning of the semester. The pretest might cover biology content, but if this study were conducted during the first semester of the school year, it might be a Scholastic Aptitude Test or a science achievement test. The advantages of pretesting are (1) that the preexperiment equivalence of the classes on the pretest can be checked and (2) that pretest scores may be used as a statistical control in the analysis. Internal validity is threatened if the classes are not equivalent, and other variables affecting the dependent variable are confounded with the materials. There is also the possibility that contamination across the classes may occur if students from different classes discuss or share materials. Assuming that the results can be interpreted, they generalize to the biology students in this school taught by this teacher, probably over a period of years if the characteristics of the student body do not change. Generalization to other schools, students, and teachers would have to be argued on a logical basis.

6.3 There is no random assignment of students to the practice treatments. The teacher variable is very apparent and essentially uncontrolled. The assumption is that teachers are most effective with the techniques they prefer. Even if this is true, there is no evidence that different teachers, independent of practice method, are equally effective. With only three schools, it would be difficult to make a case for the assumption that the teachers of each method are a representative sample of fifth-grade teachers, either in general or as a more specific group. There may be other relevant uncontrolled factors within the schools, and since the method is optional to the teacher, there is no reason to assume a balance between schools on such factors. Thus, internal validity is low because of lack of control. External validity is also low because of poor internal validity and questions that might be raised about the representativeness of the teachers. It would be important to have information about the characteristics of the teachers and their similarities across the two practice methods.

6.4 This is an example of a time-series design. A design such as this is susceptible to multiple-treatment interference. In this case, delayed effects may begin appearing on subsequent observations. The pattern of results may be difficult to interpret. The advantage of using such a design is that it can be applied in a natural setting and can provide information on the reading achievement profile of a specific class. A special measurement problem would be attaining equivalent difficulty levels for the various tests given at 2-week intervals. Suppose that there was a marked drop in performance after one period. This would be interpreted as an effect of the method of instruction, when in fact the drop might be due to a more difficult test.

6.5 a. There are short-term effects of the training programs but no long-term effects. In the short term, the effects of the programs are not the same, with X_1 being most effective and X_3, least effective.

b. There are short-term effects that persist for the long term, and the effects are the same for the three training programs.

c. The groups were not equivalent initially, and they retain their relative positions in the short term. We cannot tell if there is a short-term effect. Apparently, there is no long-term effect, and the long term has also eliminated initial differences among the groups.

d. O_3 with O_1 and O_2, O_6 with O_4 and O_5, and O_9 with O_7 and O_8.

e. No, because all groups are pretested. There is no comparison group that was not pretested.

6.6 a. The experimental treatment has a positive effect, an immediate effect, and the effect persists over time.

b. There is a short-term effect of the experimental treatment, which continues for an additional 3 weeks but then disappears.

c. Check G_2 across O_8 to O_{14}. If there are changes in the attitude scores, normal class instruction is having an effect.

6.7 The study would be conducted over an 8-week period, with four observations (O_1 through O_4) taken when no logs were being kept and four observations (O_5 through O_8) taken when logs were kept. If O_5 through O_8 showed improvement in the student's subjects over their performance from O_1 through O_4, the treatment is having an effect. If it were a one-time effect, O_5 would be greater than O_1 through O_4 but consistent with O_6, O_7, and O_8. If there were an accumulative effect, O_5 would be greater than O_1 through O_4, and O_6 would be greater than O_5, O_7 greater than O_6, and O_8 greater than O_7.

6.9 The essential differences are that for (1) we have two or more behaviors, for (2), two or more subjects, and for (3), two or more situations.

Chapter 7

7.1 This is not an experiment, because there is no manipulation of independent variables. This study is ex post facto in nature, since the independent variables have already occurred and a retrospective search for cause-and-effect relationships is implied. Grade level, location of school, and sex of the student are independent variables. The dependent variable is critical thinking test performance.

7.4 Since all schools or guidance offices have telephones, all guidance counselors selected could be contacted by telephone. The advantage of using the telephone over a mailed questionnaire is the direct contact, which might increase response rate and would allow for more flexibility in the questioning, if this is desirable. Using the telephone would essentially shift the study from a questionnaire to an interview. A disadvantage of the telephone survey is that it may interrupt the work of the guidance counselors, and responding by telephone may not allow adequate time for thinking about responses. It would be desirable— almost necessary—to provide prior information and to schedule the telephone call in advance. The additional effort of the telephone survey may not be merited, since the response rate with a mailed questionnaire would probably be quite good for this professional sample.

7.5 It would be well to code the questionnaires so that nonresponse could be identified in terms of state (possibly regions within the states) and level taught. It might also be desirable to code variables such as the size of the school district of the respondent (or nonrespondent).

7.6 The status survey would likely involve a shorter questionnaire than that for the survey in Exercise 7.5, which in itself would tend to enhance the response rate. The nonresponding group would tend to be decreased in size. Respondents would tend to include those who might not respond to the other questionnaires because they dislike responding to items whose results may be used for determining policy.

7.7 The interview has the advantages of (1) allowing for deeper probing of the respondent and possibly pursuing a response, (2) clearing ambiguities, and (3) securing information that would not be forthcoming with a written questionnaire. Also, the problem of nonresponse is reduced and is usually not as great as with a questionnaire. The primary disadvantage of the interview is that it requires considerable resources in terms of time, effort, and personnel. Questionnaires can all be sent at the same time, so that there is no large lapse of time such as may occur between interviews. This could be a disadvantage of the interview if external factors or events associated with time affect responses. A problem with the questionnaire may be securing an adequate response rate. If a great deal of written material is necessary to communicate to the respondent and elicit response, the length of the questionnaire may be a disadvantage. Also, if communication breaks down, there is no opportunity to eliminate ambiguities at the time.

7.8 One advantage of the longitudinal study is the option of studying change occurring in the class as it goes through college. The longitudinal study would take four years or so to complete; the cross-sectional could be done in a much shorter time period, requiring data collection at only one point in time.

7.9 The panel study allows for the opportunity of collecting data from the same group of teachers at different times. In this way, changes over time within specific teachers could be detected. A panel study is always susceptible to the difficulty of keeping the panel intact, and five years is a long period for maintaining a panel. It is also possible that over time the remaining members of the panel are no longer representative of the teacher population. The stability of the teacher population in this school system would impact upon the effectiveness of the panel.

7.10 In the interest of positive school-community relations, it would be well to survey the entire parent population.

Chapter 8

8.2 **a.** Survey
   b. Experiment
   c. Historical
   d. Ex post facto
   e. Historical
   f. Ex post facto, possibly survey
   g. Survey

Chapter 9

9.1 Experimental research involves the direct manipulation of at least one independent variable; ethnographic research focuses on variables as they occur in the natural setting without any intervention by the researcher.

9.2 Perspectives form the cultures, and the cultures collectively make up the organization.

9.3 Triangulation is qualitative cross-validation; it involves comparisons (among sources or data collection procedures, for example) to determine the extent of consistency.

9.5 The concepts of reliability and validity are consistent with their meanings for types of research other than ethnographic research. Reliability is concerned with replicability of research procedures and results. Validity concerns the interpretation of results (internal) and their subsequent generalizability (external).

9.6 Because ethnographic research is so situation- or context-specific, generalizability and, hence, external validity may be limited. Broadening the scope of an ethnographic research study to multiple sites tends to enhance external validity.

Chapter 10

10.1 Since there are 839 population members, three-digit random numbers are necessary. Any numbers selected between 840 and 999 inclusive can be disregarded.

10.2 For stratified sampling, we divide the population into nonoverlapping subpopulations called *strata*. When proportional allocation is used, the sample sizes selected from the strata are proportional to the sizes of the corresponding strata populations.

10.4 In stratified sampling, all strata are represented in the sample, and the random sampling is done within strata according to some allocation. Thus, individuals, not strata, are randomly sampled. In cluster sampling, the clusters are randomly selected from the population of clusters, but if a cluster is selected, all its members are included in the sample.

10.5 The sampling fraction is 450/3,000, which equals 3/20 or .15. Sample sizes for strata 1 through 4, respectively, are 124.5, 99, 72, and 154.5. Since partial units probably cannot be included, the researcher must arbitrarily decide whether to select 125 from stratum 1 or 155 from stratum 4.

10.7 Sixty men and 60 women would be randomly selected from their respective populations. There would be 15 men and 15 women assigned to each of the four levels of the experimental variable. Since selection is random from each population, the first 15 of each sex selected could be assigned to level 1, the second 15 to level 2, and so on.

10.9 If the first 200 adult patients willing to complete the questionnaire comprised the sample, the sample would be biased. It would include only people with some type of health problem. Since only volunteers are included, this sample would not even be representative of the population coming to the clinic. The problem with selecting a sample at the shopping mall is that the population at the mall may not be representative (very likely is not) of the general population. Even if most people in the city shop at the mall at some time or other, at what time would all segments of the general population be there? For example, at 11:00 A.M., many people in the work force would not be shopping.

Chapter 11

11.1 Validity has to do with whether or not a test measures what it is supposed to measure; reliability concerns whether or not it is consistent in measuring whatever it does measure. A test can be reliable but not valid by consistently measuring something it was not designed to measure or by failing to measure what it was designed to measure. An unreliable test cannot be valid, because lack of consistency eliminates the possibility of measuring what it is supposed to measure.

11.4 a. Both researchers have published measuring instruments available, but the one working on achievement would have greater choice. It would likely be easier to find an instrument specifically suited to the needs of the science achievement study.

b. Content-related evidence would be of concern in establishing validity for the measurement of achievement; construct-related evidence would be of most interest for the validity of personality measurement. Evidence for the former would come from a logical analysis; evidence for the latter would most likely be based on information from the test manual, especially if the researcher is attempting to establish the constructs that underlie the junior high personality.

c. Achievement could be measured by a paper-and-pencil test; personality data might be obtained by some type of written group test or might require individual testing.

11.7 A Likert scale is a scale used with individual items; it contains a number of points, usually four or more, with intervals between the points assumed to be equal. The respondents respond to individual items. The semantic differential, on the other hand, contains a series of pairs of bipolar terms (usually adjectives); each pair is located on the end points of a scale (continuum), usually with seven or nine intervals. The respondent is asked to judge the word or phrase (which represents a concept) at the top of the page by checking each of the bipolar scales.

11.8 Consider the following coding scheme, listing the identification information first:

(1) Student identification number: four columns, since there are more than 1,000 students and we can assume that there are fewer than 10,000 in the sample; provide numbers from 0001 to however many students are in the sample.

(2) City school number: two columns; there are 74 schools, and each would be assigned a two-digit number.

(3) Grade level: one column; assign numbers 3 through 8.

(4) Sex: one column; boys assigned 0, girls, 1.

(5) High school district: one column; assign numbers 1 through 9.

(6) Age: three columns; age is to be given in months, and eighth-graders, the oldest students in the study, are typically around 13 or 14 years old, or around 156 to 168 months.

Thus, identification would require 12 columns. The achievement variables would require a minimum of 44 columns, since the ten two-digit variables would require 20 columns and the remaining eight variables would require 24 columns. The actual achievement scores would be recorded. This scheme requires a total of 56 columns for all information, so the information for a single student would fit on a row.

Variations of this coding scheme could be used. For example, if no school has more than 100 students in the sample, the school code could be incorporated into the student number such that the first two columns of the student number indicate the school and the final two columns indicate the student in the school. For example, 1205 would indicate the fifth student in school number 12. This coding would reduce the number of columns required. Since the row is not filled, there is no great concern about reducing the number of columns. If it is desirable to allow three columns for each achievement score, this could be done, and the achievement data would then require 54 columns. In that case, the two-digit scores would have their scores preceded by a zero (or blank); for example, a score of 86 would be recorded as 086.

Chapter 12

12.1 Measures of central tendency are points that locate the distribution on the scale of measurement. Measures of variability are intervals that indicate the dispersion or spread in the distribution. To describe a distribution adequately, we require both types of information, along with information about the shape of the distribution.

12.2 A random sample would be selected and statistics computed from this sample. The sample measures would reflect the population measures within the limits of sampling fluctuation. Hence, the statistics are used to infer to the parameters, again within the bounds of sampling fluctuations. The statistic involved would be the mean reading level of the sample of first-graders measured; the corresponding parameter is the mean reading level of the entire first-grade population. The chain of reasoning follows the implied inference. The population has certain measures, called parameters. The statistics are determined, and from them we reason back to the corresponding parameters and draw conclusions about the parameters. In this situation, conclusions are drawn about the population mean from the observed sample mean.

12.3 A statistic is a measure of a sample, and a parameter is a measure of a population. The sampling distribution is the distribution of the statistic, usually a theoretical distribution. (It is the distribution of all possible values of the statistic for the given sample size.) The sampling distribution provides the theoretical base for how the statistic under study behaves; that is, it identifies the shape, location, and dispersion of the distribution of the statistic of which the researcher has one observation.

12.4 a. If we were interested only in describing the distributions of scores for these 150 students.

    b. If inferences were being made to a larger population of teacher education students and the 150 students consisted of a random sample of this population.

    c. If the relationships between the variables were of interest.

12.5 We would reject the hypothesis because with 19 degrees of freedom and a two-tailed test (no direction is hypothesized), a *t*-value of 2.09 is required for significance at the .05 level.

12.6 The sampling distribution of the mean is used; this would be the *t*-distribution with 399 degrees of freedom *(df)*, but since the *df* are so large, the normal distribution would be used. If sample size were 25, the *t*-distribution with 24 *df* would be used. There would be an error, because the confidence interval is constructed symmetrically about the sample mean; therefore, it must be the midpoint of the interval. The interval would be shorter if it were a 90% confidence interval.

12.7 In this case, the difference between the four sample means could be analyzed simultaneously, rather than analyzing only the difference between two means at a time with a *t*-test. The null hypothesis is that the four population means are equal—H$_0$: $\mu_1 = \mu_2 = \mu_3 = \mu_4$. Differences between male and female teachers could also be analyzed by extending the ANOVA to a two-way ANOVA.

12.8 Since the χ^2-value was significant, the conclusion is that the four samples were not drawn from a common population, or that the population distributions differ with respect to this variable. The probability that the sample distributions would have appeared due to random sampling fluctuation if the population distributions were the same is less than .05.

12.9 Grade level and attitude toward school are independent. If the χ^2 test is significant, we conclude that grade level and attitude toward school are related (not independent) in the student population sampled. If the χ^2 test is not significant, we cannot reject the hypothesis of independence and conclude that grade level and attitude toward school are not related in the population.

12.10 The two types of possible errors are rejecting a true hypothesis and failing to reject a false hypothesis. In inferential statistics, we do not know the values of the parameters about which we are hypothesizing; therefore, there is always the possibility of making an error. Inferences are made to the parameters from the statistics on the basis of probability. Although the probability of making an error may be very small, it is never zero.

12.11 **a.** Around zero or possibly very low positive.

   b. Low to moderate positive.

   c. Moderate to high positive.

   d. Moderate negative, because those individuals scoring high on the divergent-thinking test would take less time to solve the problems.

   e. Moderate negative.

12.13 Errors of reasoning or procedure:

   a. A *t*-test does not apply to data measured on an ordinal scale, and means should not have been computed with ordinal data.

   b. There is confusion on significance; a test that is significant at the .01 level is also significant at the .05 level.

   c. Rejecting the null hypothesis would result in concluding that the population measures, not the sample measures, are different.

   d. Since the null hypothesis is rejected, there is no probability of having made a Type II or beta error. The possibility does exist of having made a Type I or alpha error—that is, rejecting a true hypothesis.

12.14 We want to make some decisions about the population characteristics, which are parameters. We draw a sample and compute characteristics of the sample, which are statistics. The statistics reflect the corresponding parameters within the bounds of random sampling fluctuation. We hypothesize about parameters, and the statistics have a certain probability of appearing by chance if the hypotheses are true. It is not necessary to determine the exact probability, only whether it is less than or greater than the significance level. We infer from the statistics and the results of hypothesis testing to the parameters and thus make decisions about the population.

Chapter 13

13.3 This situation suggests a considerable quantity of results. Since there are ten test scores, four grades, and two groups within each grade, there are 80 means and 80 standard deviations ($10 \times 4 \times 2$). Forty *t*-tests are computed, so there are 40 *t*-values. There are 45 correlation coefficients to report. Thus, to avoid excessively large or complicated tables, the minimum number of tables necessary is four. One way to organize the results would be a table for means, with eight columns for the four grades (experimental and control columns for each grade). The means for a specific test would then be in a row. We would have a similar table for standard deviations; a table of *t*-values containing four columns, one for each grade (it would be well to have this table near the table of means, since the difference between means is being tested); and a table (sometimes called a matrix) of correlation coefficients. The following is an example of a title and headings for the table of means:

Table A
Means for Experimental and Control Groups by Grade and Test

Test	Grade							
	3		4		5		6	
	E	C	E	C	E	C	E	C

Appendix 4: Tables

Table A
Ordinates and Areas of the Normal Curve (in terms of σ units)

$\frac{x}{\sigma}$	Area	Ordi-nate	$\frac{x}{\sigma}$	Area	Ordi-nate	$\frac{x}{\sigma}$	Area	Ordi-nate	$\frac{x}{\sigma}$	Area	Ordi-nate
.00	.0000	.3989	.35	.1368	.3752	.70	.2580	.3123	1.05	.3531	.2299
.01	.0040	.3989	.36	.1406	.3739	.71	.2611	.3101	1.06	.3554	.2275
.02	.0080	.3989	.37	.1443	.3725	.72	.2642	.3079	1.07	.3577	.2251
.03	.0120	.3988	.38	.1480	.3712	.73	.2673	.3056	1.08	.3599	.2227
.04	.0160	.3986	.39	.1517	.3697	.74	.2703	.3034	1.09	.3621	.2203
.05	.0199	.3984	.40	.1554	.3683	.75	.2734	.3011	1.10	.3643	.2179
.06	.0239	.3982	.41	.1591	.3668	.76	.2764	.2989	1.11	.3665	.2155
.07	.0279	.3980	.42	.1628	.3653	.77	.2794	.2966	1.12	.3686	.2131
.08	.0319	.3977	.43	.1664	.3637	.78	.2823	.2943	1.13	.3708	.2107
.09	.0359	.3973	.44	.1700	.3621	.79	.2852	.2920	1.14	.3729	.2083
.10	.0398	.3970	.45	.1736	.3605	.80	.2881	.2897	1.15	.3749	.2059
.11	.0438	.3965	.46	.1772	.3589	.81	.2910	.2874	1.16	.3770	.2036
.12	.0478	.3961	.47	.1808	.3572	.82	.2939	.2850	1.17	.3790	.2012
.13	.0517	.3956	.48	.1844	.3555	.83	.2967	.2827	1.18	.3810	.1989
.14	.0557	.3951	.49	.1879	.3538	.84	.2995	.2803	1.19	.3830	.1965
.15	.0596	.3945	.50	.1915	.3521	.85	.3023	.2780	1.20	.3849	.1942
.16	.0636	.3939	.51	.1950	.3503	.86	.3051	.2756	1.21	.3869	.1919
.17	.0675	.3932	.52	.1985	.3485	.87	.3078	.2732	1.22	.3888	.1895
.18	.0714	.3925	.53	.2019	.3467	.88	.3106	.2709	1.23	.3907	.1872
.19	.0753	.3918	.54	.2054	.3448	.89	.3133	.2685	1.24	.3925	.1849
.20	.0793	.3910	.55	.2088	.3429	.90	.3159	.2661	1.25	.3944	.1826
.21	.0832	.3902	.56	.2123	.3410	.91	.3186	.2637	1.26	.3962	.1804
.22	.0871	.3894	.57	.2157	.3391	.92	.3212	.2613	1.27	.3980	.1781
.23	.0910	.3885	.58	.2190	.3372	.93	.3238	.2589	1.28	.3997	.1758
.24	.0948	.3876	.59	.2224	.3352	.94	.3264	.2565	1.29	.4015	.1736
.25	.0987	.3867	.60	.2257	.3332	.95	.3289	.2541	1.30	.4032	.1714
.26	.1026	.3857	.61	.2291	.3312	.96	.3315	.2516	1.31	.4049	.1691
.27	.1064	.3847	.62	.2324	.3292	.97	.3340	.2492	1.32	.4066	.1669
.28	.1103	.3836	.63	.2357	.3271	.98	.3365	.2468	1.33	.4082	.1647
.29	.1141	.3825	.64	.2389	.3251	.99	.3389	.2444	1.34	.4099	.1626
.30	.1179	.3814	.65	.2422	.3230	1.00	.3413	.2420	1.35	.4115	.1604
.31	.1217	.3802	.66	.2454	.3209	1.01	.3438	.2396	1.36	.4131	.1582
.32	.1255	.3790	.67	.2486	.3187	1.02	.3461	.2371	1.37	.4147	.1561
.33	.1293	.3778	.68	.2517	.3166	1.03	.3485	.2347	1.38	.4162	.1539
.34	.1331	.3765	.69	.2549	.3144	1.04	.3508	.2323	1.39	.4177	.1518

Source: Educational Statistics, by J. E. Wert. Copyright 1938 by McGraw-Hill Book Company. Used by permission of McGraw-Hill Book Company.

Table A (continued)

$\frac{x}{\sigma}$	Area	Ordi-nate	$\frac{x}{\sigma}$	Area	Ordi-nate	$\frac{x}{\sigma}$	Area	Ordi-nate	$\frac{x}{\sigma}$	Area	Ordi-nate
1.40	.4192	.1497	1.80	.4641	.0790	2.20	.4861	.0355	2.60	.4953	.0136
1.41	.4207	.1476	1.81	.4649	.0775	2.21	.4864	.0347	2.61	.4955	.0132
1.42	.4222	.1456	1.82	.4656	.0761	2.22	.4868	.0339	2.62	.4956	.0129
1.43	.4236	.1435	1.83	.4664	.0748	2.23	.4871	.0332	2.63	.4957	.0126
1.44	.4251	.1415	1.84	.4671	.0734	2.24	.4875	.0325	2.64	.4959	.0122
1.45	.4265	.1394	1.85	.4678	.0721	2.25	.4878	.0317	2.65	.4960	.0119
1.46	.4279	.1374	1.86	.4686	.0707	2.26	.4881	.0310	2.66	.4961	.0116
1.47	.4292	.1354	1.87	.4693	.0694	2.27	.4884	.0303	2.67	.4962	.0113
1.48	.4306	.1334	1.88	.4699	.0681	2.28	.4887	.0297	2.68	.4963	.0110
1.49	.4319	.1315	1.89	.4706	.0669	2.29	.4890	.0290	2.69	.4964	.0107
1.50	.4332	.1295	1.90	.4713	.0656	2.30	.4893	.0283	2.70	.4965	.0104
1.51	.4345	.1276	1.91	.4719	.0644	2.31	.4896	.0277	2.71	.4966	.0101
1.52	.4357	.1257	1.92	.4726	.0632	2.32	.4898	.0270	2.72	.4967	.0099
1.53	.4370	.1238	1.93	.4732	.0620	2.33	.4901	.0264	2.73	.4968	.0096
1.54	.4382	.1219	1.94	.4738	.0608	2.34	.4904	.0258	2.74	.4969	.0093
1.55	.4394	.1200	1.95	.4744	.0596	2.35	.4906	.0252	2.75	.4970	.0091
1.56	.4406	.1182	1.96	.4750	.0584	2.36	.4909	.0246	2.76	.4971	.0088
1.57	.4418	.1163	1.97	.4756	.0573	2.37	.4911	.0241	2.77	.4972	.0086
1.58	.4429	.1145	1.98	.4761	.0562	2.38	.4913	.0235	2.78	.4973	.0084
1.59	.4441	.1127	1.99	.4767	.0551	2.39	.4916	.0229	2.79	.4974	.0081
1.60	.4452	.1109	2.00	.4772	.0540	2.40	.4918	.0224	2.80	.4974	.0079
1.61	.4463	.1092	2.01	.4778	.0529	2.41	.4920	.0219	2.81	.4975	.0077
1.62	.4474	.1074	2.02	.4783	.0519	2.42	.4922	.0213	2.82	.4976	.0075
1.63	.4484	.1057	2.03	.4788	.0508	2.43	.4925	.0208	2.83	.4977	.0073
1.64	.4495	.1040	2.04	.4793	.0498	2.44	.4927	.0203	2.84	.4977	.0071
1.65	.4505	.1023	2.05	.4798	.0488	2.45	.4929	.0198	2.85	.4978	.0069
1.66	.4515	.1006	2.06	.4803	.0478	2.46	.4931	.0194	2.86	.4979	.0067
1.67	.4525	.0989	2.07	.4808	.0468	2.47	.4932	.0189	2.87	.4979	.0065
1.68	.4535	.0973	2.08	.4812	.0459	2.48	.4934	.0184	2.88	.4980	.0063
1.69	.4545	.0957	2.09	.4817	.0449	2.49	.4936	.0180	2.89	.4981	.0061
1.70	.4554	.0940	2.10	.4821	.0440	2.50	.4938	.0175	2.90	.4981	.0060
1.71	.4564	.0925	2.11	.4826	.0431	2.51	.4940	.0171	2.91	.4982	.0058
1.72	.4573	.0909	2.12	.4830	.0422	2.52	.4941	.0167	2.92	.4982	.0056
1.73	.4582	.0893	2.13	.4834	.0413	2.53	.4943	.0163	2.93	.4983	.0055
1.74	.4591	.0878	2.14	.4838	.0404	2.54	.4945	.0158	2.94	.4984	.0053
1.75	.4599	.0863	2.15	.4842	.0395	2.55	.4946	.0154	2.95	.4984	.0051
1.76	.4608	.0848	2.16	.4846	.0387	2.56	.4948	.0151	2.96	.4985	.0050
1.77	.4616	.0833	2.17	.4850	.0379	2.57	.4949	.0147	2.97	.4985	.0048
1.78	.4625	.0818	2.18	.4854	.0371	2.58	.4951	.0143	2.98	.4986	.0047
1.79	.4633	.0804	2.19	.4857	.0363	2.59	.4952	.0139	2.99	.4986	.0046
									3.00	.4987	.0044

Table B
Critical Values of *t*

df	Level of significance for one-tailed test					
	.10	.05	.025	.01	.005	.0005
	Level of significance for two-tailed test					
	.20	.10	.05	.02	.01	.001
1	3.078	6.314	12.706	31.821	63.657	636.619
2	1.886	2.920	4.303	6.965	9.925	31.598
3	1.638	2.353	3.182	4.541	5.841	12.941
4	1.533	2.132	2.776	3.747	4.604	8.610
5	1.476	2.015	2.571	3.365	4.032	6.859
6	1.440	1.943	2.447	3.143	3.707	5.959
7	1.415	1.895	2.365	2.998	3.499	5.405
8	1.397	1.860	2.306	2.896	3.355	5.041
9	1.383	1.833	2.262	2.821	3.250	4.781
10	1.372	1.812	2.228	2.764	3.169	4.587
11	1.363	1.796	2.201	2.718	3.106	4.437
12	1.356	1.782	2.179	2.681	3.055	4.318
13	1.350	1.771	2.160	2.650	3.012	4.221
14	1.345	1.761	2.145	2.624	2.977	4.140
15	1.341	1.753	2.131	2.602	2.947	4.073
16	1.337	1.746	2.120	2.583	2.921	4.015
17	1.333	1.740	2.110	2.567	2.898	3.965
18	1.330	1.734	2.101	2.552	2.878	3.922
19	1.328	1.729	2.093	2.539	2.861	3.883
20	1.325	1.725	2.086	2.528	2.845	3.850
21	1.323	1.721	2.080	2.518	2.831	3.819
22	1.321	1.717	2.074	2.508	2.819	3.792
23	1.319	1.714	2.069	2.500	2.807	3.767
24	1.318	1.711	2.064	2.492	2.797	3.745
25	1.316	1.708	2.060	2.485	2.787	3.725
26	1.315	1.706	2.056	2.479	2.779	3.707
27	1.314	1.703	2.052	2.473	2.771	3.690
28	1.313	1.701	2.048	2.467	2.763	3.674
29	1.311	1.699	2.045	2.462	2.756	3.659
30	1.310	1.697	2.042	2.457	2.750	3.646
40	1.303	1.684	2.021	2.423	2.704	3.551
60	1.296	1.671	2.000	2.390	2.660	3.460
120	1.289	1.658	1.980	2.358	2.617	3.373
∞	1.282	1.645	1.960	2.326	2.576	3.291

Source: Abridged from Table III, p. 46 of R. A. Fisher and F. Yates, *Statistical Tables for Biological, Agricultural and Medical Research,* 6th edition, published by Longman Group, Ltd., London, 1974 (previously published by Oliver & Boyd, Ltd., Edinburgh), and reprinted by permission of the authors and publishers.

Table C
Upper Percentage Points of the χ^2 Distribution

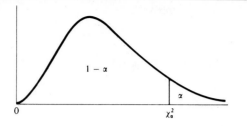

df	.99	.98	.95	.90	.80	.70	.50	.30	.20	.10	.05	.02	.01	.001
1	$.0^3157$	$.0^3628$	.00393	.0158	.0642	.148	.455	1.074	1.642	2.706	3.841	5.412	6.635	10.827
2	.0201	.0404	.103	.211	.446	.713	1.386	2.408	3.219	4.605	5.991	7.824	9.210	13.815
3	.115	.185	.352	.584	1.005	1.424	2.366	3.665	4.642	6.251	7.815	9.837	11.345	16.266
4	.297	.429	.711	1.064	1.649	2.195	3.357	4.878	5.989	7.779	9.488	11.668	13.277	18.467
5	.554	.752	1.145	1.610	2.343	3.000	4.351	6.064	7.289	9.236	11.070	13.388	15.086	20.515
6	.872	1.134	1.635	2.204	3.070	3.828	5.348	7.231	8.558	10.645	12.592	15.033	16.812	22.457
7	1.239	1.564	2.167	2.833	3.822	4.671	6.346	8.383	9.803	12.017	14.067	16.622	18.475	24.322
8	1.646	2.032	2.733	3.490	4.594	5.527	7.344	9.524	11.030	13.362	15.507	18.168	20.090	26.125
9	2.088	2.532	3.325	4.168	5.380	6.393	8.343	10.656	12.242	14.684	16.919	19.679	21.666	27.877
10	2.558	3.059	3.940	4.865	6.179	7.267	9.342	11.781	13.442	15.987	18.307	21.161	23.209	29.588
11	3.053	3.609	4.575	5.578	6.989	8.148	10.341	12.899	14.631	17.275	19.675	22.618	24 725	31.264
12	3.571	4.178	5.226	6.304	7.807	9.034	11.340	14.011	15.812	18.549	21.026	24.054	26.217	32.909
13	4.107	4.765	5.892	7.042	8.634	9.926	12.340	15.119	16.985	19.812	22.362	25.472	27.688	34.528
14	4.660	5.368	6.571	7.790	9.467	10.821	13.339	16.222	18.151	21.064	23.685	26.873	29.141	36.123
15	5.229	5.985	7.261	8.547	10.307	11.721	14.339	17.322	19.311	22.307	24.996	28.259	30.578	37.697
16	5.812	6.614	7.962	9.312	11.152	12.624	15.338	18.418	20.465	23.542	26.296	29.633	32.000	39.252
17	6.408	7.255	8.672	10.085	12.002	13.531	16.338	19.511	21.615	24.769	27.587	30.995	33.409	40.790
18	7.015	7.906	9.390	10.865	12.857	14.440	17.338	20.601	22.760	25.989	28.869	32.346	34.805	42.312
19	7.633	8.567	10.117	11.651	13.716	15.352	18.338	21.689	23.900	27.204	30.144	33.687	36.191	43.820
20	8.260	9.237	10.851	12.443	14.578	16.266	19.337	22.775	25.038	28.412	31.410	35.020	37.566	45.315
21	8.897	9.915	11.591	13.240	15.445	17.182	20.337	23.858	26.171	29.615	32.671	36.343	38.932	46.797
22	9.542	10.600	12.338	14.041	16.314	18.101	21.337	24.939	27.301	30.813	33.924	37.659	40.289	48.268
23	10.196	11.293	13.091	14.848	17.187	19.021	22.337	26.018	28.429	32.007	35.172	38.968	41.638	49.728
24	10.856	11.992	13.848	15.659	18.062	19.943	23.337	27.096	29.553	33.196	36.415	40.270	42.980	51.179
25	11.524	12.697	14.611	16.473	18.940	20.867	24.337	28.172	30.675	34.382	37.652	41.566	44.314	52.620
26	12.198	13.409	15.379	17.292	19.820	21.792	25.336	29.246	31.795	35.563	38.885	42.856	45.642	54.052
27	12.879	14.125	16.151	18.114	20.703	22.719	26.336	30.319	32.912	36.741	40.113	44.140	46.963	55.476
28	13.565	14.847	16.928	18.939	21.588	23.647	27.336	31.391	34.027	37.916	41.337	45.419	43.278	56.893
29	14.256	15.574	17.708	19.768	22.475	24.577	28.336	32.461	35.139	39.087	42.557	46.693	49.588	58.302
30	14.953	16.306	18.493	20.599	23.364	25.508	29.336	33.530	36.250	40.256	43.773	47.962	50.892	59.703

Source: Taken from Table IV, p. 47 of Fisher and Yates: *Statistical Tables for Biological, Agricultural and Medical Research,* published by Longman Group Ltd., London (previously published by Oliver and Boyd, Ltd., Edinburgh), and reprinted by permission of the authors and publishers. For df > 30, the expression $\sqrt{2\chi^2} - \sqrt{2df - 1}$ may be used as a normal deviate with unit variance.

Table D
Upper Percentage Points of the F-distribution

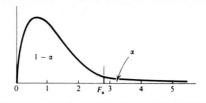

df for denominator	α	df for numerator											
		1	2	3	4	5	6	7	8	9	10	11	12
1	.25	5.83	7.50	8.20	8.58	8.82	8.98	9.10	9.19	9.26	9.32	9.36	9.41
	.10	39.9	49.5	53.6	55.8	57.2	58.2	58.9	59.4	59.9	60.2	60.5	60.7
	.05	161	200	216	225	230	234	237	239	241	242	243	244
2	.25	2.57	3.00	3.15	3.23	3.28	3.31	3.34	3.35	3.37	3.38	3.39	3.39
	.10	8.53	9.00	9.16	9.24	9.29	9.33	9.35	9.37	9.38	9.39	9.40	9.41
	.05	18.5	19.0	19.2	19.2	19.3	19.3	19.4	19.4	19.4	19.4	19.4	19.4
	.01	98.5	99.0	99.2	99.2	99.3	99.3	99.4	99.4	99.4	99.4	99.4	99.4
3	.25	2.02	2.28	2.36	2.39	2.41	2.42	2.43	2.44	2.44	2.44	2.45	2.45
	.10	5.54	5.46	5.39	5.34	5.31	5.28	5.27	5.25	5.24	5.23	5.22	5.22
	.05	10.1	9.55	9.28	9.12	9.01	8.94	8.89	8.85	8.81	8.79	8.76	8.74
	.01	34.1	30.8	29.5	28.7	28.2	27.9	27.7	27.5	27.3	27.2	27.1	27.1
4	.25	1.81	2.00	2.05	2.06	2.07	2.08	2.08	2.08	2.08	2.08	2.08	2.08
	.10	4.54	4.32	4.19	4.11	4.05	4.01	3.98	3.95	3.94	3.92	3.91	3.90
	.05	7.71	6.94	6.59	6.39	6.26	6.16	6.09	6.04	6.00	5.96	5.94	5.91
	.01	21.2	18.0	16.7	16.0	15.5	15.2	15.0	14.8	14.7	14.5	14.4	14.4
5	.25	1.69	1.85	1.88	1.89	1.89	1.89	1.89	1.89	1.89	1.89	1.89	1.89
	.10	4.06	3.78	3.62	3.52	3.45	3.40	3.37	3.34	3.32	3.30	3.28	3.27
	.05	6.61	5.79	5.41	5.19	5.05	4.95	4.88	4.82	4.77	4.74	4.71	4.68
	.01	16.3	13.3	12.1	11.4	11.0	10.7	10.5	10.3	10.2	10.1	9.96	9.89
6	.25	1.62	1.76	1.78	1.79	1.79	1.78	1.78	1.78	1.77	1.77	1.77	1.77
	.10	3.78	3.46	3.29	3.18	3.11	3.05	3.01	2.98	2.96	2.94	2.92	2.90
	.05	5.99	5.14	4.76	4.53	4.39	4.28	4.21	4.15	4.10	4.06	4.03	4.00
	.01	13.7	10.9	9.78	9.15	8.75	8.47	8.26	8.10	7.98	7.87	7.79	7.72
7	.25	1.57	1.70	1.72	1.72	1.71	1.71	1.70	1.70	1.69	1.69	1.69	1.68
	.10	3.59	3.26	3.07	2.96	2.88	2.83	2.78	2.75	2.72	2.70	2.68	2.67
	.05	5.59	4.74	4.35	4.12	3.97	3.87	3.79	3.73	3.68	3.64	3.60	3.57
	.01	12.2	9.55	8.45	7.85	7.46	7.19	6.99	6.84	6.72	6.62	6.54	6.47
8	.25	1.54	1.66	1.67	1.66	1.66	1.65	1.64	1.64	1.63	1.63	1.63	1.62
	.10	3.46	3.11	2.92	2.81	2.73	2.67	2.62	2.59	2.56	2.54	2.52	2.50
	.05	5.32	4.46	4.07	3.84	3.69	3.58	3.50	3.44	3.39	3.35	3.31	3.28
	.01	11.3	8.65	7.59	7.01	6.63	6.37	6.18	6.03	5.91	5.81	5.73	5.67
9	.25	1.51	1.62	1.63	1.63	1.62	1.61	1.60	1.60	1.59	1.59	1.58	1.58
	.10	3.36	3.01	2.81	2.69	2.61	2.55	2.51	2.47	2.44	2.42	2.40	2.38
	.05	5.12	4.26	3.86	3.63	3.48	3.37	3.29	3.23	3.18	3.14	3.10	3.07
	.01	10.6	8.02	6.99	6.42	6.06	5.80	5.61	5.47	5.35	5.26	5.18	5.11

Table D (continued)

				df *for numerator*										df *for de-nomi-nator*
15	20	24	30	40	50	60	100	120	200	500	∞	α	
9.49	9.58	9.63	9.67	9.71	9.74	9.76	9.78	9.80	9.82	9.84	9.85	.25	
61.2	61.7	62.0	62.3	62.5	62.7	62.8	63.0	63.1	63.2	63.3	63.3	.10	1
246	248	249	250	251	252	252	253	253	254	254	254	.05	
3.41	3.43	3.43	3.44	3.45	3.45	3.46	3.47	3.47	3.48	3.48	3.48	.25	
9.42	9.44	9.45	9.46	9.47	9.47	9.47	9.48	9.48	9.49	9.49	9.49	.10	2
19.4	19.4	19.5	19.5	19.5	19.5	19.5	19.5	19.5	19.5	19.5	19.5	.05	
99.4	99.4	99.5	99.5	99.5	99.5	99.5	99.5	99.5	99.5	99.5	99.5	.01	
2.46	2.46	2.46	2.47	2.47	2.47	2.47	2.47	2.47	2.47	2.47	2.47	.25	
5.20	5.18	5.18	5.17	5.16	5.15	5.15	5.14	5.14	5.14	5.14	5.13	.10	3
8.70	8.66	8.64	8.62	8.59	8.58	8.57	8.55	8.55	8.54	8.53	8.53	.05	
26.9	26.7	26.6	26.5	26.4	26.4	26.3	26.2	26.2	26.2	26.1	26.1	.01	
2.08	2.08	2.08	2.08	2.08	2.08	2.08	2.08	2.08	2.08	2.08	2.08	.25	
3.87	3.84	3.83	3.82	3.80	3.80	3.79	3.78	3.78	3.77	3.76	3.76	.10	4
5.86	5.80	5.77	5.75	5.72	5.70	5.69	5.66	5.66	5.65	5.64	5.63	.05	
14.2	14.0	13.9	13.8	13.7	13.7	13.7	13.6	13.6	13.5	13.5	13.5	.01	
1.89	1.88	1.88	1.88	1.88	1.88	1.87	1.87	1.87	1.87	1.87	1.87	.25	
3.24	3.21	3.19	3.17	3.16	3.15	3.14	3.13	3.12	3.12	3.11	3.10	.10	5
4.62	4.56	4.53	4.50	4.46	4.44	4.43	4.41	4.40	4.39	4.37	4.36	.05	
9.72	9.55	9.47	9.38	9.29	9.24	9.20	9.13	9.11	9.08	9.04	9.02	.01	
1.76	1.76	1.75	1.75	1.75	1.75	1.74	1.74	1.74	1.74	1.74	1.74	.25	
2.87	2.84	2.82	2.80	2.78	2.77	2.76	2.75	2.74	2.73	2.73	2.72	.10	6
3.94	3.87	3.84	3.81	3.77	3.75	3.74	3.71	3.70	3.69	3.68	3.67	.05	
7.56	7.40	7.31	7.23	7.14	7.09	7.06	6.99	6.97	6.93	6.90	6.88	.01	
1.68	1.67	1.67	1.66	1.66	1.66	1.65	1.65	1.65	1.65	1.65	1.65	.25	
2.63	2.59	2.58	2.56	2.54	2.52	2.51	2.50	2.49	2.48	2.48	2.47	.10	7
3.51	3.44	3.41	3.38	3.34	3.32	3.30	3.27	3.27	3.25	3.24	3.23	.05	
6.31	6.16	6.07	5.99	5.91	5.86	5.82	5.75	5.74	5.70	5.67	5.65	.01	
1.62	1.61	1.60	1.60	1.59	1.59	1.59	1.58	1.58	1.58	1.58	1.58	.25	
2.46	2.42	2.40	2.38	2.36	2.35	2.34	2.32	2.32	2.31	2.30	2.29	.10	8
3.22	3.15	3.12	3.08	3.04	3.02	3.01	2.97	2.97	2.95	2.94	2.93	.05	
5.52	5.36	5.28	5.20	5.12	5.07	5.03	4.96	4.95	4.91	4.88	4.86	.01	
1.57	1.56	1.56	1.55	1.55	1.54	1.54	1.53	1.53	1.53	1.53	1.53	.25	
2.34	2.30	2.28	2.25	2.23	2.22	2.21	2.19	2.18	2.17	2.17	2.16	.10	9
3.01	2.94	2.90	2.86	2.83	2.80	2.79	2.76	2.75	2.73	2.72	2.71	.05	
4.96	4.81	4.73	4.65	4.57	4.52	4.48	4.42	4.40	4.36	4.33	4.31	.01	

df for denominator	α	df for numerator 1	2	3	4	5	6	7	8	9	10	11	12
10	.25	1.49	1.60	1.60	1.59	1.59	1.58	1.57	1.56	1.56	1.55	1.55	1.54
	.10	3.29	2.92	2.73	2.61	2.52	2.46	2.41	2.38	2.35	2.32	2.30	2.28
	.05	4.96	4.10	3.71	3.48	3.33	3.22	3.14	3.07	3.02	2.98	2.94	2.91
	.01	10.0	7.56	6.55	5.99	5.64	5.39	5.20	5.06	4.94	4.85	4.77	4.71
11	.25	1.47	1.58	1.58	1.57	1.56	1.55	1.54	1.53	1.53	1.52	1.52	1.51
	.10	3.23	2.86	2.66	2.54	2.45	2.39	2.34	2.30	2.27	2.25	2.23	2.21
	.05	4.84	3.98	3.59	3.36	3.20	3.09	3.01	2.95	2.90	2.85	2.82	2.79
	.01	9.65	7.21	6.22	5.67	5.32	5.07	4.89	4.74	4.63	4.54	4.46	4.40
12	.25	1.46	1.56	1.56	1.55	1.54	1.53	1.52	1.51	1.51	1.50	1.50	1.49
	.10	3.18	2.81	2.61	2.48	2.39	2.33	2.28	2.24	2.21	2.19	2.17	2.15
	.05	4.75	3.89	3.49	3.26	3.11	3.00	2.91	2.85	2.80	2.75	2.72	2.69
	.01	9.33	6.93	5.95	5.41	5.06	4.82	4.64	4.50	4.39	4.30	4.22	4.16
13	.25	1.45	1.55	1.55	1.53	1.52	1.51	1.50	1.49	1.49	1.48	1.47	1.47
	.10	3.14	2.76	2.56	2.43	2.35	2.28	2.23	2.20	2.16	2.14	2.12	2.10
	.05	4.67	3.81	3.41	3.18	3.03	2.92	2.83	2.77	2.71	2.67	2.63	2.60
	.01	9.07	6.70	5.74	5.21	4.86	4.62	4.44	4.30	4.19	4.10	4.02	3.96
14	.25	1.44	1.53	1.53	1.52	1.51	1.50	1.49	1.48	1.47	1.46	1.46	1.45
	.10	3.10	2.73	2.52	2.39	2.31	2.24	2.19	2.15	2.12	2.10	2.08	2.05
	.05	4.60	3.74	3.34	3.11	2.96	2.85	2.76	2.70	2.65	2.60	2.57	2.53
	.01	8.86	6.51	5.56	5.04	4.69	4.46	4.28	4.14	4.03	3.94	3.86	3.80
15	.25	1.43	1.52	1.52	1.51	1.49	1.48	1.47	1.46	1.46	1.45	1.44	1.44
	.10	3.07	2.70	2.49	2.36	2.27	2.21	2.16	2.12	2.09	2.06	2.04	2.02
	.05	4.54	3.68	3.29	3.06	2.90	2.79	2.71	2.64	2.59	2.54	2.51	2.48
	.01	8.68	6.36	5.42	4.89	4.56	4.32	4.14	4.00	3.89	3.80	3.73	3.67
16	.25	1.42	1.51	1.51	1.50	1.48	1.47	1.46	1.45	1.44	1.44	1.44	1.43
	.10	3.05	2.67	2.46	2.33	2.24	2.18	2.13	2.09	2.06	2.03	2.01	1.99
	.05	4.49	3.63	3.24	3.01	2.85	2.74	2.66	2.59	2.54	2.49	2.46	2.42
	.01	8.53	6.23	5.29	4.77	4.44	4.20	4.03	3.89	3.78	3.69	3.62	3.55
17	.25	1.42	1.51	1.50	1.49	1.47	1.46	1.45	1.44	1.43	1.43	1.42	1.41
	.10	3.03	2.64	2.44	2.31	2.22	2.15	2.10	2.06	2.03	2.00	1.98	1.96
	.05	4.45	3.59	3.20	2.96	2.81	2.70	2.61	2.55	2.49	2.45	2.41	2.38
	.01	8.40	6.11	5.18	4.67	4.34	4.10	3.93	3.79	3.68	3.59	3.52	3.46
18	.25	1.41	1.50	1.49	1.48	1.46	1.45	1.44	1.43	1.42	1.42	1.41	1.40
	.10	3.01	2.62	2.42	2.29	2.20	2.13	2.08	2.04	2.00	1.98	1.96	1.93
	.05	4.41	3.55	3.16	2.93	2.77	2.66	2.58	2.51	2.46	2.41	2.37	2.34
	.01	8.29	6.01	5.09	4.58	4.25	4.01	3.84	3.71	3.60	3.51	3.43	3.37
19	.25	1.41	1.49	1.49	1.47	1.46	1.44	1.43	1.42	1.41	1.41	1.40	1.40
	.10	2.99	2.61	2.40	2.27	2.18	2.11	2.06	2.02	1.98	1.96	1.94	1.91
	.05	4.38	3.52	3.13	2.90	2.74	2.63	2.54	2.48	2.42	2.38	2.34	2.31
	.01	8.18	5.93	5.01	4.50	4.17	3.94	3.77	3.63	3.52	3.43	3.36	3.30
20	.25	1.40	1.49	1.48	1.46	1.45	1.44	1.43	1.42	1.41	1.40	1.39	1.39
	.10	2.97	2.59	2.38	2.25	2.16	2.09	2.04	2.00	1.96	1.94	1.92	1.89
	.05	4.35	3.49	3.10	2.87	2.71	2.60	2.51	2.45	2.39	2.35	2.31	2.28
	.01	8.10	5.85	4.94	4.43	4.10	3.87	3.70	3.56	3.46	3.37	3.29	3.23

Table D (continued)

					df *for numerator*									df *for de-nomi-nator*
15	20	24	30	40	50	60	100	120	200	500	∞	α	
1.53	1.52	1.52	1.51	1.51	1.50	1.50	1.49	1.49	1.49	1.48	1.48	.25	
2.24	2.20	2.18	2.16	2.13	2.12	2.11	2.09	2.08	2.07	2.06	2.06	.10	10
2.85	2.77	2.74	2.70	2.66	2.64	2.62	2.59	2.58	2.56	2.55	2.54	.05	
4.56	4.41	4.33	4.25	4.17	4.12	4.08	4.01	4.00	3.96	3.93	3.91	.01	
1.50	1.49	1.49	1.48	1.47	1.47	1.47	1.46	1.46	1.46	1.45	1.45	.25	
2.17	2.12	2.10	2.08	2.05	2.04	2.03	2.00	2.00	1.99	1.98	1.97	.10	11
2.72	2.65	2.61	2.57	2.53	2.51	2.49	2.46	2.45	2.43	2.42	2.40	.05	
4.25	4.10	4.02	3.94	3.86	3.81	3.78	3.71	3.69	3.66	3.62	3.60	.01	
1.48	1.47	1.46	1.45	1.45	1.44	1.44	1.43	1.43	1.43	1.42	1.42	.25	
2.10	2.06	2.04	2.01	1.99	1.97	1.96	1.94	1.93	1.92	1.91	1.90	.10	12
2.62	2.54	2.51	2.47	2.43	2.40	2.38	2.35	2.34	2.32	2.31	2.30	.05	
4.01	3.86	3.78	3.70	3.62	3.57	3.54	3.47	3.45	3.41	3.38	3.36	.01	
1.46	1.45	1.44	1.43	1.42	1.42	1.42	1.41	1.41	1.40	1.40	1.40	.25	
2.05	2.01	1.98	1.96	1.93	1.92	1.90	1.88	1.88	1.86	1.85	1.85	.10	13
2.53	2.46	2.42	2.38	2.34	2.31	2.30	2.26	2.25	2.23	2.22	2.21	.05	
3.82	3.66	3.59	3.51	3.43	3.38	3.34	3.27	3.25	3.22	3.19	3.17	.01	
1.44	1.43	1.42	1.41	1.41	1.40	1.40	1.39	1.39	1.39	1.38	1.38	.25	
2.01	1.96	1.94	1.91	1.89	1.87	1.86	1.83	1.83	1.82	1.80	1.80	.10	14
2.46	2.39	2.35	2.31	2.27	2.24	2.22	2.19	2.18	2.16	2.14	2.13	.05	
3.66	3.51	3.43	3.35	3.27	3.22	3.18	3.11	3.09	3.06	3.03	3.00	.01	
1.43	1.41	1.41	1.40	1.39	1.39	1.38	1.38	1.37	1.37	1.36	1.36	.25	
1.97	1.92	1.90	1.87	1.85	1.83	1.82	1.79	1.79	1.77	1.76	1.76	.10	15
2.40	2.33	2.29	2.25	2.20	2.18	2.16	2.12	2.11	2.10	2.08	2.07	.05	
3.52	3.37	3.29	3.21	3.13	3.08	3.05	2.98	2.96	2.92	2.89	2.87	.01	
1.41	1.40	1.39	1.38	1.37	1.37	1.36	1.36	1.35	1.35	1.34	1.34	.25	
1.94	1.89	1.87	1.84	1.81	1.79	1.78	1.76	1.75	1.74	1.73	1.72	.10	16
2.35	2.28	2.24	2.19	2.15	2.12	2.11	2.07	2.06	2.04	2.02	2.01	.05	
3.41	3.26	3.18	3.10	3.02	2.97	2.93	2.86	2.84	2.81	2.78	2.75	.01	
1.40	1.39	1.38	1.37	1.36	1.35	1.35	1.34	1.34	1.34	1.33	1.33	.25	
1.91	1.86	1.84	1.81	1.78	1.76	1.75	1.73	1.72	1.71	1.69	1.69	.10	17
2.31	2.23	2.19	2.15	2.10	2.08	2.06	2.02	2.01	1.99	1.97	1.96	.05	
3.31	3.16	3.08	3.00	2.92	2.87	2.83	2.76	2.75	2.71	2.68	2.65	.01	
1.39	1.38	1.37	1.36	1.35	1.34	1.34	1.33	1.33	1.32	1.32	1.32	.25	
1.89	1.84	1.81	1.78	1.75	1.74	1.72	1.70	1.69	1.68	1.67	1.66	.10	18
2.27	2.19	2.15	2.11	2.06	2.04	2.02	1.98	1.97	1.95	1.93	1.92	.05	
3.23	3.08	3.00	2.92	2.84	2.78	2.75	2.68	2.66	2.62	2.59	2.57	.01	
1.38	1.37	1.36	1.35	1.34	1.33	1.33	1.32	1.32	1.31	1.31	1.30	.25	
1.86	1.81	1.79	1.76	1.73	1.71	1.70	1.67	1.67	1.65	1.64	1.63	.10	19
2.23	2.16	2.11	2.07	2.03	2.00	1.98	1.94	1.93	1.91	1.89	1.88	.05	
3.15	3.00	2.92	2.84	2.76	2.71	2.67	2.60	2.58	2.55	2.51	2.49	.01	
1.37	1.36	1.35	1.34	1.33	1.33	1.32	1.31	1.31	1.30	1.30	1.29	.25	
1.84	1.79	1.77	1.74	1.71	1.69	1.68	1.65	1.64	1.63	1.62	1.61	.10	20
2.20	2.12	2.08	2.04	1.99	1.97	1.95	1.91	1.90	1.88	1.86	1.84	.05	
3.09	2.94	2.86	2.78	2.69	2.64	2.61	2.54	2.52	2.48	2.44	2.42	.01	

Table D (continued)

df for denominator	α	\multicolumn{12}{c}{df for numerator}
		1	2	3	4	5	6	7	8	9	10	11	12
22	.25	1.40	1.48	1.47	1.45	1.44	1.42	1.41	1.40	1.39	1.39	1.38	1.37
	.10	2.95	2.56	2.35	2.22	2.13	2.06	2.01	1.97	1.93	1.90	1.88	1.86
	.05	4.30	3.44	3.05	2.82	2.66	2.55	2.46	2.40	2.34	2.30	2.26	2.23
	.01	7.95	5.72	4.82	4.31	3.99	3.76	3.59	3.45	3.35	3.26	3.18	3.12
24	.25	1.39	1.47	1.46	1.44	1.43	1.41	1.40	1.39	1.38	1.38	1.37	1.36
	.10	2.93	2.54	2.33	2.19	2.10	2.04	1.98	1.94	1.91	1.88	1.85	1.83
	.05	4.26	3.40	3.01	2.78	2.62	2.51	2.42	2.36	2.30	2.25	2.21	2.18
	.01	7.82	5.61	4.72	4.22	3.90	3.67	3.50	3.36	3.26	3.17	3.09	3.03
26	.25	1.38	1.46	1.45	1.44	1.42	1.41	1.39	1.38	1.37	1.37	1.36	1.35
	.10	2.91	2.52	2.31	2.17	2.08	2.01	1.96	1.92	1.88	1.86	1.84	1.81
	.05	4.23	3.37	2.98	2.74	2.59	2.47	2.39	2.32	2.27	2.22	2.18	2.15
	.01	7.72	5.53	4.64	4.14	3.82	3.59	3.42	3.29	3.18	3.09	3.02	2.96
28	.25	1.38	1.46	1.45	1.43	1.41	1.40	1.39	1.38	1.37	1.36	1.35	1.34
	.10	2.89	2.50	2.29	2.16	2.06	2.00	1.94	1.90	1.87	1.84	1.81	1.79
	.05	4.20	3.34	2.95	2.71	2.56	2.45	2.36	2.29	2.24	2.19	2.15	2.12
	.01	7.64	5.45	4.57	4.07	3.75	3.53	3.36	3.23	3.12	3.03	2.96	2.90
30	.25	1.38	1.45	1.44	1.42	1.41	1.39	1.38	1.37	1.36	1.35	1.35	1.34
	.10	2.88	2.49	2.28	2.14	2.05	1.98	1.93	1.88	1.85	1.82	1.79	1.77
	.05	4.17	3.32	2.92	2.69	2.53	2.42	2.33	2.27	2.21	2.16	2.13	2.09
	.01	7.56	5.39	4.51	4.02	3.70	3.47	3.30	3.17	3.07	2.98	2.91	2.84
40	.25	1.36	1.44	1.42	1.40	1.39	1.37	1.36	1.35	1.34	1.33	1.32	1.31
	.10	2.84	2.44	2.23	2.09	2.00	1.93	1.87	1.83	1.79	1.76	1.73	1.71
	.05	4.08	3.23	2.84	2.61	2.45	2.34	2.25	2.18	2.12	2.08	2.04	2.00
	.01	7.31	5.18	4.31	3.83	3.51	3.29	3.12	2.99	2.89	2.80	2.73	2.66
60	.25	1.35	1.42	1.41	1.38	1.37	1.35	1.33	1.32	1.31	1.30	1.29	1.29
	.10	2.79	2.39	2.18	2.04	1.95	1.87	1.82	1.77	1.74	1.71	1.68	1.66
	.05	4.00	3.15	2.76	2.53	2.37	2.25	2.17	2.10	2.04	1.99	1.95	1.92
	.01	7.08	4.98	4.13	3.65	3.34	3.12	2.95	2.82	2.72	2.63	2.56	2.50
120	.25	1.34	1.40	1.39	1.37	1.35	1.33	1.31	1.30	1.29	1.28	1.27	1.26
	.10	2.75	2.35	2.13	1.99	1.90	1.82	1.77	1.72	1.68	1.65	1.62	1.60
	.05	3.92	3.07	2.68	2.45	2.29	2.17	2.09	2.02	1.96	1.91	1.87	1.83
	.01	6.85	4.79	3.95	3.48	3.17	2.96	2.79	2.66	2.56	2.47	2.40	2.34
200	.25	1.33	1.39	1.38	1.36	1.34	1.32	1.31	1.29	1.28	1.27	1.26	1.25
	.10	2.73	2.33	2.11	1.97	1.88	1.80	1.75	1.70	1.66	1.63	1.60	1.57
	.05	3.89	3.04	2.65	2.42	2.26	2.14	2.06	1.98	1.93	1.88	1.84	1.80
	.01	6.76	4.71	3.88	3.41	3.11	2.89	2.73	2.60	2.50	2.41	2.34	2.27
∞	.25	1.32	1.39	1.37	1.35	1.33	1.31	1.29	1.28	1.27	1.25	1.24	1.24
	.10	2.71	2.30	2.08	1.94	1.85	1.77	1.72	1.67	1.63	1.60	1.57	1.55
	.05	3.84	3.00	2.60	2.37	2.21	2.10	2.01	1.94	1.88	1.83	1.79	1.75
	.01	6.63	4.61	3.78	3.32	3.02	2.80	2.64	2.51	2.41	2.32	2.25	2.18

15	20	24	30	40	50	60	100	120	200	500	∞	α	df for denominator
					df for numerator								
1.36	1.34	1.33	1.32	1.31	1.31	1.30	1.30	1.30	1.29	1.29	1.28	.25	
1.81	1.76	1.73	1.70	1.67	1.65	1.64	1.61	1.60	1.59	1.58	1.57	.10	22
2.15	2.07	2.03	1.98	1.94	1.91	1.89	1.85	1.84	1.82	1.80	1.78	.05	
2.98	2.83	2.75	2.67	2.58	2.53	2.50	2.42	2.40	2.36	2.33	2.31	.01	
1.35	1.33	1.32	1.31	1.30	1.29	1.29	1.28	1.28	1.27	1.27	1.26	.25	
1.78	1.73	1.70	1.67	1.64	1.62	1.61	1.58	1.57	1.56	1.54	1.53	.10	24
2.11	2.03	1.98	1.94	1.89	1.86	1.84	1.80	1.79	1.77	1.75	1.73	.05	
2.89	2.74	2.66	2.58	2.49	2.44	2.40	2.33	2.31	2.27	2.24	2.21	.01	
1.34	1.32	1.31	1.30	1.29	1.28	1.28	1.26	1.26	1.26	1.25	1.25	.25	
1.76	1.71	1.68	1.65	1.61	1.59	1.58	1.55	1.54	1.53	1.51	1.50	.10	26
2.07	1.99	1.95	1.90	1.85	1.82	1.80	1.76	1.75	1.73	1.71	1.69	.05	
2.81	2.66	2.58	2.50	2.42	2.36	2.33	2.25	2.23	2.19	2.16	2.13	.01	
1.33	1.31	1.30	1.29	1.28	1.27	1.27	1.26	1.25	1.25	1.24	1.24	.25	
1.74	1.69	1.66	1.63	1.59	1.57	1.56	1.53	1.52	1.50	1.49	1.48	.10	28
2.04	1.96	1.91	1.87	1.82	1.79	1.77	1.73	1.71	1.69	1.67	1.65	.05	
2.75	2.60	2.52	2.44	2.35	2.30	2.26	2.19	2.17	2.13	2.09	2.06	.01	
1.32	1.30	1.29	1.28	1.27	1.26	1.26	1.25	1.24	1.24	1.23	1.23	.25	
1.72	1.67	1.64	1.61	1.57	1.55	1.54	1.51	1.50	1.48	1.47	1.46	.10	30
2.01	1.93	1.89	1.84	1.79	1.76	1.74	1.70	1.68	1.66	1.64	1.62	.05	
2.70	2.55	2.47	2.39	2.30	2.25	2.21	2.13	2.11	2.07	2.03	2.01	.01	
1.30	1.28	1.26	1.25	1.24	1.23	1.22	1.21	1.21	1.20	1.19	1.19	.25	
1.66	1.61	1.57	1.54	1.51	1.48	1.47	1.43	1.42	1.41	1.39	1.38	.10	40
1.92	1.84	1.79	1.74	1.69	1.66	1.64	1.59	1.58	1.55	1.53	1.51	.05	
2.52	2.37	2.29	2.20	2.11	2.06	2.02	1.94	1.92	1.87	1.83	1.80	.01	
1.27	1.25	1.24	1.22	1.21	1.20	1.19	1.17	1.17	1.16	1.15	1.15	.25	
1.60	1.54	1.51	1.48	1.44	1.41	1.40	1.36	1.35	1.33	1.31	1.29	.10	60
1.84	1.75	1.70	1.65	1.59	1.56	1.53	1.48	1.47	1.44	1.41	1.39	.05	
2.35	2.20	2.12	2.03	1.94	1.88	1.84	1.75	1.73	1.68	1.63	1.60	.01	
1.24	1.22	1.21	1.19	1.18	1.17	1.16	1.14	1.13	1.12	1.11	1.10	.25	
1.55	1.48	1.45	1.41	1.37	1.34	1.32	1.27	1.26	1.24	1.21	1.19	.10	120
1.75	1.66	1.61	1.55	1.50	1.46	1.43	1.37	1.35	1.32	1.28	1.25	.05	
2.19	2.03	1.95	1.86	1.76	1.70	1.66	1.56	1.53	1.48	1.42	1.38	.01	
1.23	1.21	1.20	1.18	1.16	1.14	1.12	1.11	1.10	1.09	1.08	1.06	.25	
1.52	1.46	1.42	1.38	1.34	1.31	1.28	1.24	1.22	1.20	1.17	1.14	.10	200
1.72	1.62	1.57	1.52	1.46	1.41	1.39	1.32	1.29	1.26	1.22	1.19	.05	
2.13	1.97	1.89	1.79	1.69	1.63	1.58	1.48	1.44	1.39	1.33	1.28	.01	
1.22	1.19	1.18	1.16	1.14	1.13	1.12	1.09	1.08	1.07	1.04	1.00	.25	
1.49	1.42	1.38	1.34	1.30	1.26	1.24	1.18	1.17	1.13	1.08	1.00	.10	∞
1.67	1.57	1.52	1.46	1.39	1.35	1.32	1.24	1.22	1.17	1.11	1.00	.05	
2.04	1.88	1.79	1.70	1.59	1.52	1.47	1.36	1.32	1.25	1.15	1.00	.01	

Table E
Critical Values of the Correlation Coefficient

	Level of significance for one-tailed test			
	.05	.025	.01	.005
	Level of significance for two-tailed test			
df	.10	.05	.02	.01
1	.988	.997	.9995	.9999
2	.900	.950	.980	.990
3	.805	.878	.934	.959
4	.729	.811	.882	.917
5	.669	.754	.833	.874
6	.622	.707	.789	.834
7	.582	.666	.750	.798
8	.549	.632	.716	.765
9	.521	.602	.685	.735
10	.497	.576	.658	.708
11	.476	.553	.634	.684
12	.458	.532	.612	.661
13	.441	.514	.592	.641
14	.426	.497	.574	.623
15	.412	.482	.558	.606
16	.400	.468	.542	.590
17	.389	.456	.528	.575
18	.378	.444	.516	.561
19	.369	.433	.503	.549
20	.360	.423	.492	.537
21	.352	.413	.482	.526
22	.344	.404	.472	.515
23	.337	.396	.462	.505
24	.330	.388	.453	.496
25	.323	.381	.445	.487
26	.317	.374	.437	.479
27	.311	.367	.430	.471
28	.306	.361	.423	.463
29	.301	.355	.416	.456
30	.296	.349	.409	.449
35	.275	.325	.381	.418
40	.257	.304	.358	.393
45	.243	.288	.338	.372
50	.231	.273	.322	.354
60	.211	.250	.295	.325
70	.195	.232	.274	.303
80	.183	.217	.256	.283
90	.173	.205	.242	.267
100	.164	.195	.230	.254

Source: Abridged from Table VII, p. 63 of Fisher and Yates: *Statistical Tables for Biological, Agricultural and Medical Research,* published by Longman Group Ltd., London (previously published by Oliver and Boyd, Ltd., Edinburgh), and reprinted by permission of the authors and publishers.

Glossary of Research Methods Terms

Analysis of covariance: A method of statistical control through which scores on the dependent variable are adjusted according to scores on a related variable.

Analysis of variance: A statistical technique by which it is possible to partition the variance in a distribution of scores according to separate sources or factors; although variance is partitioned, the statistical test tests for differences between means.

Aptitude: The potential for achievement.

Attitude: A tendency to possess certain feelings toward a specified class of stimuli.

Central limit theorem: A theorem that states that given any population with a mean and finite variance, as sample size increases, the distribution of the sample means approaches a normal distribution, with mean equal to the population mean and variance equal to the population variance divided by sample size.

Cluster sampling: The selection of groups of elements, called clusters, rather than single elements; all elements of a cluster are included in the sample, and the clusters are selected randomly from the larger population of clusters.

Cohort studies: Longitudinal designs (in survey research) in which a specific population is studied over time by taking different random samples at various points in time.

Concurrent-related validity of a test: The extent to which scores on a test match performance scores on one or more criterion measures obtained at about the same time the test is given.

Confidence interval: An interval estimate of a parameter constructed in such a way that the interval has a predetermined probability of spanning the parameter.

Confounded variables: Variables operating in a specific situation such that their effects cannot be separated.

Constant: A characteristic that has the same value for all individuals in a research study.

Construct–related validity of a test: The extent to which a test measures one or more dimensions of a theory or trait.

Content–related validity of a test: The extent to which the content of the test items reflects the academic discipline, behavior, or whatever is under study.

Contextualization (in ethnographic research): The requirement that data be interpreted only in the context of the situation or environment in which they were collected.

Contingency table: The array into which a set of numeration data may be grouped according to two or more classification variables.

Continuous variable: A variable that can take on any value within an interval on the scale of measurement.

Control group (in an experiment): A group of subjects who do not receive any experimental treatment; the group is included for comparison purposes.

Control variable: A variable, other than the independent variable(s) of primary interest, whose effects are determined by the researcher. Control variables are included in designs as independent variables for the purpose of explaining variation.

Correlation: The extent of relationship between two variables.

Correlation coefficient: The measure of the extent of relationship between two variables.

Covariate: The measure used in an analysis of covariance for adjusting the scores of the dependent variable.

Criterion–related validity of a test: The extent to which scores on a test correlate with scores on some external criterion measure.

Cronbach alpha: An internal consistency or reliability coefficient for a test, based on two or more parts of the test but requiring only one test administration.

Cross–sectional studies: Studies in which the data are collected at one point in time from a random sample of a general population that contains two or more subpopulations, with the intention of comparing the data from the subsamples or noting trends across such subsamples.

Data file: The organized array of data and identification information commonly placed in a computer prior to analysis.

Degrees of freedom: The number of ways in which the data are free to vary; the number of observations minus the number of restrictions placed on the data.

Dependent variable: The variable being affected or assumed to be affected by the independent variable.

Directional hypothesis: A hypothesis stated in such a manner that a direction, usually indicated by "greater than" or "less than," is hypothesized for the results.

Distribution: The total observations or a set of data on a variable; when observations are tabulated according to frequency for each possible score, it is a frequency distribution.

Ethnographic research: Research that is intended to provide scientific descriptions of (educational) systems, processes, and phenomena within their specific contexts.

Ethnography: A branch of anthropology that deals with the scientific description of individual cultures.

Experiment (in educational research): A research situation in which one or more independent variables are systematically varied according to a preconceived plan to determine the effects of this variation.

Experimental mortality: The dropping out of subjects participating in an experiment; the failure of certain subjects to continue in the experiment until its conclusion.

Ex post facto research: Research in which the independent variable or variables have already occurred and in which the researcher begins with the observations on a dependent variable, followed by a retrospective study of possible relationships and effects.

Foreshadowed problems (in ethnographic research): Specific research problems, possibly stated in question form, that provide a focus for the research.

Histogram: A graphical representation, consisting of rectangles, of the scores in a distribution; the areas of the rectangles are proportional to the frequencies of the scores.

Historical research: Research directed to the study of a problem in the past, using information from the past.

Hypothesis: A conjecture or proposition about the solution to a problem, the relationship of two or more variables, or the nature of some phenomenon.

Independent variable: A variable that affects (or is assumed to affect) the dependent variable under study and is included in the research design so that its effect can be determined.

Interaction: The effect of one independent variable on another; the lack of the effect of one independent variable remaining constant over the levels of another.

Interval scale: A measurement scale that, in addition to ordering scores, also establishes an equal unit in the scale so that distances between any two scores are of a known magnitude; also called *equal-unit scale*.

Intervening variable: A variable whose existence is inferred but that cannot be manipulated or measured.

Kuder-Richardson methods: Procedures for determining the reliability of a test from a single form and single administration of the test without splitting the test.

Latin square: An $n \times n$ square array that includes different letters or symbols so arranged that each symbol appears once and only once in each row and column.

Level of confidence: The probability associated with a confidence interval; the probability that the interval will span the corresponding parameter. Commonly used confidence levels in educational research are .95 and .99.

Level of significance: A probability associated with the test of a hypothesis using statistical techniques that determines whether or not the hypothesis is rejected. Commonly used significance levels in educational research are .05 and .01. Also called *alpha level*.

Likert scale: A scaling procedure, commonly associated with attitude measurement, that requires a graded response to each item or statement. In scoring, the alternative responses to items are assigned numerical values, and the individual's score is the sum of the numerical values.

Linear relationship: A relationship between two variables such that a straight line can be fitted satisfactorily to the points of the scattergram; the scatter of points will cluster elliptically around a straight line rather than some type of curve.

Longitudinal studies: Studies that involve measuring the same or different individuals two or more times during a period of time (usually of considerable length, such as several months or years)—for example, measuring the mathematics performance of the same students at yearly intervals as they progress from the fourth grade through senior high.

Maturation: Psychological and biological processes operating and causing systematic variation within individuals with the passing of time.

Mean: The sum of the scores in a distribution divided by the number of scores in the distribution.

Measurement: The assignment of numerals to objects or events according to specific rules.

Measures of central tendency: Points in a distribution that locate the distribution on the measurement scale; points within the distribution about which the scores tend to group themselves.

Measures of variability: Measures of a distribution that indicate the amount of dispersion or spread in the distribution.

Median: The point in a distribution below which 50% of the scores lie.

Mode: The point or score of greatest frequency in a distribution.

Moderator variable: A variable that may or may not be controlled but has an effect in the research situation.

Multiple-treatment interference: Carry-over or delayed effects of prior experimental treatments when individuals receive two or more experimental treatments in succession.

Nominal scale: A measurement scale that simply classifies elements into two or more categories, indicating that the elements are different, but not according to order or magnitude.

Normal distribution: A family of bell-shaped, symmetrical distributions whose curve is described mathematically by a general equation; sometimes called the *Laplace-Gaussian normal probability function*.

Norms: Descriptive statistics that summarize the test performance of a reference group of individuals.

Null hypothesis (in inferential statistics): A hypothesis stated such that no difference or no relationship is hypothesized.

Operational definition: A definition expressed in terms of the processes or operations that are going to be used to measure the characteristic under study.

Optimum allocation (in stratified random sampling): Selecting the sample in such a manner that the strata contributions to the sample are proportional to the sizes of strata populations and the strata variances.

Ordinal scale: A measurement scale that classifies and ranks elements or scores.

Organismic variable: A variable that is an existing or natural characteristic of the individuals under study—for example, the sex of the individual.

Panel studies: Longitudinal designs (in survey research) in which the same random sample is measured at different points in time.

Parallel forms of a test: Two (or more) forms of a test that are equivalent in terms of characteristics.

Parameter: A characteristic or measure of a population—for example, the population mean.

Periodicity (in systematic sampling): A periodic characteristic that follows the listing of the elements and the selection interval so that a bias is introduced into the sample.

Personality: In general, the sum total of an individual's mental and emotional characteristics; in the context of psychological testing, personality inventories are usually designed to measure characteristics such as emotional and social adjustment.

Phenomenology: The study of phenomena through observation and description.

Pilot study: A study conducted prior to the major research study that in some way is a small-scale model of the major study; conducted for the purpose of gaining additional information by which the major study can be improved—for example, an exploratory use of the measurement instrument with a small group for the purpose of refining the instrument.

Population: The totality of all elements, subjects, or members that possess a specified set of one or more common characteristics that define it; in inferential statistics, the group to which inferences are drawn.

Prediction: The estimation of scores on one variable from information about one or more other variables.

Predictive-related validity of a test: The extent to which predictions made from the test are confirmed by subsequent data.

Probability sample: A sample selected in such a way that each member of the population has some nonzero probability of being included in the sample.

Proportional allocation (in stratified random sampling): Selecting the sample in a manner such that the sample size is divided among the strata proportional to population sizes of the strata.

Quasi-experimental research: Research involving an experimental variable with intact groups, or at least with groups that have not been formed through random selection or random assignment; single subjects, not randomly selected, may also be involved.

Random (error) variance: The inherent variance in a distribution of scores, which includes variance due to sources such as random sampling (or assignment) and intervening variables.

Random sample: A sample selected in such a way that the selection of one member of the population in no way affects the probability of selection of any other member.

Range: One plus the difference between the two extreme scores of a distribution.

Ratio scale: A measurement scale that, besides containing an equal unit, also establishes an absolute zero in the scale.

Regression (as a threat to experimental validity): A tendency for groups, especially those selected on the basis of extreme scores, to regress toward a more average score on subsequent measurements, regardless of the experimental treatment.

Regression line: The straight line of best fit (usually according to the least squares criterion) for a set of bivariate data.

Reliability coefficient: A measure of the consistency of a test. There are several methods of computing a reliability coefficient, depending on the test and the test situation.

Reliability of measurement: The consistency of the measurement.

Reliability of research—external: The extent to which research is replicable.

Reliability of research—internal: The extent of consistency in the methods, conditions, and results of research.

Response set: The tendency for an individual to respond to items or other stimuli in a consistent manner, regardless of the content or context of the stimuli.

Sample: A subset of the population under study.

Sampling distribution of a statistic: The distribution (usually theoretical) of all possible values of the statistic from all possible samples of a given size selected from the population.

Sampling ratio: The ratio of sample size to population size; also called the *sampling fraction.*

Scattergram: The plot of points determined by the cross-tabulation of a set of bivariate data.

Semantic differential: An attitude measuring technique in which the respondent is asked to judge a word or concept using a set of bipolar adjective scales.

Significant statistic: A statistic whose appearance by chance in the light of the hypothesis is less than the probability designated by the significance level—for example, a significant difference; a difference too large to be attributed to chance (random sampling fluctuation) if the hypothesis is true.

Simple random sample: A sample selected in such a way that all members of the population have an equal probability of selection; in the case of sampling without replacement from a finite population, all possible samples of a given size have the same probability of being selected.

Split–half method: A procedure for determining the reliability of a test by which a single form of the test is divided into comparable halves, the scores on the halves are correlated, and the reliability coefficient is computed by applying a special formula known as the Spearman-Brown step-up formula.

Standard deviation: A measure of variability that is the positive square root of the variance.

Standard error of a statistic: The standard deviation of the sampling distribution of the statistic.

Standard normal distribution: The normal distribution with a mean of 0 and a standard deviation of 1.0.

Standard score: A score given in terms of standard deviation units from the mean of the distribution. A negative score indicates below the mean and a positive score indicates above the mean.

Statistics: In descriptive statistics, measures taken on a distribution; in inferential statistics, measures or characteristics of a sample; in a more general sense, the theory, procedures, and methods by which data are analyzed.

Stratified random sampling: A sampling procedure in which the population is divided into two or more subpopulations, called *strata,* and elements for the sample are then randomly selected from the strata.

Survey research: Research that deals with the incidence, distribution, and relationships of educational, psychological, and sociological variables in nonexperimental settings.

Systematic sampling: A selection procedure in which all sample elements are determined after the selection of the first element, since each element on a selection list is separated from the first element by a multiple of the selection interval.

Test-retest method: A procedure for determining test reliability by correlating the scores of two administrations of the same test to the same individuals.

Trait: A tendency to respond in a certain way to situations.

Trend studies: Longitudinal designs (in survey research) in which a general population is studied over time by taking different random samples at various points in time.

Triangulation (in ethnographic research): Qualitative cross-validation of data using multiple data sources or multiple data collection procedures.

Two-stage sampling: A general term referring to any sampling procedure that requires two steps in the sample selection.

Type I *or* alpha error: In inferential statistics, the error of rejecting a true hypothesis.

Type II *or* beta error: In inferential statistics, the error of failing to reject a false hypothesis.

Unbiased statistic: A statistic computed in such a manner that the mean of its sampling distribution is the parameter that the statistic estimates.

Validity of measurement: The extent to which a measurement instrument measures what it is supposed to measure.

Validity of research—external: The extent and appropriateness of the generalizability of results.

Validity of research—internal: The basic minimum control, measurement, analysis, and procedures necessary to make the results interpretable.

Variable: A characteristic that takes on different values for different individuals.

Variance: A measure of variability that is the average value of the squares of the deviations from the mean of the scores in a distribution.

Name Index

Subject Index